CW01197696

Sinister Yogis

Sinister Yogis

DAVID GORDON WHITE

The University of Chicago Press   Chicago and London

DAVID GORDON WHITE is professor of religious studies at the University of California, Santa Barbara. He is the author of several books, including *The Alchemical Body: Siddha Traditions in Medieval India* and *Kiss of the Yoginī: "Tantric Sex" in Its South Asian Contexts*, both published by the University of Chicago Press.

The University of Chicago Press, Chicago 60637
The University of Chicago Press, Ltd., London
© 2009 by The University of Chicago
All rights reserved. Published 2009
Printed in the United States of America

18 17 16 15 14 13 12 11 10 09   1 2 3 4 5
ISBN-13: 978-0-226-89513-0 (cloth)
ISBN-10: 0-226-89513-0 (cloth)

Library of Congress Cataloging-in-Publication Data

White, David Gordon.
Sinister yogis / David Gordon White.
p. cm.
Includes bibliographical references and index.
ISBN-13: 978-0-226-89513-0 (cloth : alk. paper)
ISBN-10: 0-226-89513-0 (cloth : alk. paper) 1. Yogis—India—History. 2. Yoga. I. Title.
BL2015.Y6W55 2009
294.5'61—dc22

2009004546

♾ The paper used in this publication meets the minimum requirements of the American National Standard for Information Sciences—Permanence of Paper for Printed Library Materials, ANSI Z39.48-1992.

Contents

List of Illustrations vii

Preface ix

Note on Transliteration xvii

Abbreviations xix

1 Tales of Sinister Yogis 1

2 Ceci n'est pas un Yogi 38

3 Embodied Ascent, Meditation, and Yogic Suicide 83

4 The Science of Entering Another Body 122

5 Yogi Gods 167

6 Mughal, Modern, and Postmodern Yogis 198

Notes 255 *Bibliography 303* *Index 337*

Illustrations

Cover Nāth Yogī, wall painting from the *haveli* of Sukhdev Das Ganeriwala

1.1 *Bhairavānand Yogī* chapbook cover 5

1.2 Bherūṃ-jī and seven sisters, women's wedding necklace 11

2.1 Mohenjo-Daro clay seal 420 49

2.2 Śrī, Bharhut railing medallion 50

2.3 Obverse of copper coin of Indo-Scythian King Maues 51

2.4 Sculpture of Artemis of Ephesos, Caesarea, detail of robe 52

2.5 Celtic horned god Cernunnos, detail from inner panel of Gundestrup Cauldron 53

2.6 Seated prince or *bodhisattva* 56

2.7 Obverse of double stater of Kushan emperor Vima Kadphises 57

2.8 Reverse of tetradrachma of Kushan emperor Kaniṣka 58

2.9 Hero Stone (vīragal) portraying apotheosis of a slain hero on a heavenly chariot 66

2.10 Sculpture of Lakulīśa seated on a lotus 80

3.1 Detail of western mural at Lukhang Temple, Tibet 87

3.2 A ray from the sun ignites the pyre of Sarasvatī Satī 119

4.1 Yogī Macchindranāth and his disciples 152

5.1 *Lokapuruṣa* (Cosmic Being) 174

5.2 Cosmic body of a yogi, based on the *Siddhasiddhāntapaddhati* 176

5.3 Kṛṣṇa displays his Universal Form 184

5.4 Four yoga-born sons of Brahmā depicted as yogis 187

6.1 Detail of a lithograph showing an underground crypt 206

6.2 Nāth Yogī tumuli in Kathmandu 207

6.3 Detail of a lithograph showing Indian Fakirs 213

6.4 Nāth Yogī, wall painting from the *haveli* of Sukhdev Das Ganeriwala 221

6.5 A yogi spy in a detail from the illustrated manuscript *Hamzanama* 227

Preface

Like most of the buildings around it, the Trader Joe's supermarket in West Hollywood is a low-slung pastel affair with a parking lot in the back. For a time during the winter and spring of 2007, the parking lot attendant there was an elegant beturbaned Sikh who seemed to be engaged in urgent conversations on his cell phone every time I shopped there. But one day, the Sikh was absent and another person wearing a turban—someone far shorter and chubbier and with an unkempt beard—was standing in the lot. This person walked up to me as I was about to enter the market and said that he could tell by the lines on my forehead that I was a LUCKY MAN. The next thing he told me was that he was a YOGI, a fact that he documented by pulling a black-and-white photograph out of the five-by-seven inch leather satchel he carried in his hand. There in the photo I saw a younger version of the person before me, together with seven or eight possible disciples, sitting around a white-bearded guru in front of what appeared to be a Himalayan backdrop.

"You are so lucky, you are going to become rich three times in September," he told me. He then proceeded to ask me a series of questions involving numbers (my birth date and those of my wife and daughter, etc.), noting my answers on a two-inch square of thin yellow paper. This went on for quite some time, until the paper was nearly covered with the blue ink of his crabbed notations. He then balled the piece of paper up and thrust it into my hand, telling me to hold it in my pocket. As I held it there, he asked me to pick a number between one and ten and tell him the first color that came to mind. Then he told me to take the balled-up piece of paper, which I had never let go of, out of my pocket. And what did I see written on it? NOT the dozens of numbers I had seen on it when he had given it to me to put in my pocket, but ONLY MY TWO FINAL ANSWERS and nothing else! He then asked me to give him some money, which I did, but of course what I gave him wasn't enough, so I said to him that if I got rich in September, I'd come back and give him some more.

To this day, I don't know how he did his trick. But this encounter made me recall a prior meeting with someone who had also called himself a yogi (that person had used the vernacular form, "jogi") and who had also done a trick for me and asked for money when he was done. His name was Bhandarināth, and I wrote about my meeting with him in the final pages of my 1996 book, *The Alchemical Body: Siddha Traditions in Medieval India*. When I look back on that meeting, which took place in Kathmandu in the spring of 1992, I am amazed by the symmetry of these two encounters. Bhandarināth, too, called himself a yogi. Bhandarināth, too, carried a satchel (albeit a larger one, big enough to hold a cobra). And Bhandarināth, too, performed a trick involving sleight of hand—in his case, changing a handful of sand into two small vermilion-coated mineral pellets—before asking for some money. As for me, I stiffed him in the same way I stiffed the Trader Joe's yogi, telling him I'd give him more money later.

But there were things that were different as well. When I met Bhandarināth, I was in my 30s and riding a bicycle, we were in the Himalayas, and Bhandarināth was thin. The Trader Joe's yogi was chubby, he had come to Los Angeles from the Himalayas, and I was driving the sort of sporty motorized conveyance appropriate for persons having midlife crises. In Kathmandu, Bhandarināth and I spoke Hindi; in LA, the Trader Joe's yogi and I spoke English. And the Trader Joe's yogi's trick was a lot better than Bhandarināth's.

This got me thinking. In the photo that the Trader Joe's yogi showed me, he was much thinner and looked to be about fifteen years younger than he did when I met him, and he was in the Himalayas. I had met Bhandarināth fifteen years earlier, in the Himalayas, and even though I was the same person as then, my looks had changed a lot too. So who was this guy from the Trader Joe's parking lot who was calling himself a yogi? In the *Alchemical Body,* I ended the story of my meeting with Bhandarināth by speculating that the Nāth Yogīs on high had perhaps sent him to me to present me with the alchemical elixir (the two mineral pellets). Then I wrote, "Our research continues," followed by three dots, and that was the end of the book. And, in fact, my research has continued in ways I could not have imagined over fifteen years ago.

But what I really would like to know is whether the yogi in the Trader Joe's parking lot was Bhandarināth fifteen years later, or, if not, whether he was part of some cosmic plan in which I too had a minor role to play. I cannot help but think, now that I live in the city that is synonymous with the movie industry, of the David Lynch film *Mulholland Drive*, named for the winding road that runs not more than two miles above the very parking lot where I met the second yogi (or maybe the first yogi, for the second time). That movie—which as far as I can understand it tells two widely divergent stories of the same person who has recently come to Los Angeles—ends with miniaturized versions of all of its characters running as if impelled by the invisible hand that had conjured up all of their life stories. Then there is a gunshot and the screen goes to black.

Both Bhandarināth and the guy I met in the Trader Joe's parking lot called themselves yogis. But what was their yoga? There was no stretching or contorted poses, no deep breathing, no meditation or mantras. They both did tricks for me and then asked me for money.

It had not been my intention to write this book. I was well into a project on the history of South Asian polytheism when I came across a passage from a late portion of India's (and the world's) greatest epic, the *Mahābhārata*, that stopped me cold. Here is what that passage says:

> Yogis who are without restraints [and] endowed with the power of yoga are [so many] masters, who enter into [the bodies of] the Prajāpatis, the sages, the gods, and the great beings. Yama, the raging Terminator (Antaka), and death of terrible prowess: none of these masters the yogi who is possessed of immeasurable splendor . . . A yogi can lay hold of several thousand selves, and having obtained [their] power, he can walk the earth with all of them. He can obtain [for himself] the [realms of the] sense objects. Otherwise, he can undertake terrible austerities, or, again, he can draw those [sense objects] back together [into himself], like the sun [does] its rays of light. Without a doubt, the powerful yogi who is a master of binding [others] is [also] possessed of the absolute power to release [others from those same bonds]."[1]

When I first read that passage, sometime in the winter or spring of 2003, I realized that my research had to continue. I understand now that *The Alchemical Body* was but the first installment of a trilogy, the first -ptych of a triptych. In it, I had traced the likely alchemical origins of many of the concepts, structures, and processes of *haṭha yoga*. However, I remained dissatisfied with it, because I had been unable to find the sources for an underlying assumption of both the medieval alchemical and hathayogic traditions: to wit, that there were "power substances" in the world, which were the homologues of the divine semen and uterine blood of the great god Śiva and his consort, the great goddess (called Durgā, Pārvatī, Devī, etc.), that were capable of transforming matter and energy in inexplicable ways. In the Hindu alchemical context, these power substances manifested as mercury and sulfur; in the hathayogic context, they were human semen and uterine blood. The research I subsequently undertook, to discover the system of knowledge within which the dynamic of these power substances was embedded, resulted in the book that I now realize was the second -ptych of this triptych: *Kiss of the Yoginī: "Tantric Sex" in Its South Asian Contexts*. A history of (mainly) Hindu Tantra, this book pushed the historical parameters of my research back from the tenth- to fifteenth-century time frame of *The Alchemical Body* to an earlier time, the first millennium of the common era.

But *Kiss of the Yoginī,* in its turn, left me with new unanswered questions, not the least of which was why the Tantras used the term "yogi" for practitioners whose goals were supernatural powers, rather than liberation or salvation. The *Mahābhārata* passage quoted above appeared to point to an answer to my question. And so it is that you, the reader, are presented with a book whose project is to go back in time to the (unexpected) origins of yoga in South Asia, origins that can perhaps be dated to the second millennium BCE.

This book differs from every other history of yoga written to date, because it takes as its starting point the practitioner of yoga, the yogi. Whereas the data for the history of yoga remains limited to *analytical* texts (religio-philosophical works like the *Yoga Sūtra*s and *Bhagavad Gītā* with their commentarial literature, the *haṭha yoga* canon, the "Yoga Upaniṣads," etc.), a study of the history of yogis opens the way for an analysis of the extremely rich body of *narrative* accounts. As will be seen, this change of focus entirely transforms the "depth of field" of the historical landscape of yoga, opening new horizons while pushing principal aspects of earlier histories of yoga entirely out of the frame. Philosophical yoga, of which the foundational work remains the 350–450 CE *Yoga Sūtras* attributed to Patañjali, denies the link between yoga and "yoking," in spite of the fact that this is the precise etymological meaning of the Sanskrit term. Viewed through the lens of the narrative approach I take in these pages, that original sense of the term is restored. What is "lost" in the process is, precisely, the principal focus of philosophical or "pātañjala yoga," which far too many modern historians have also abusively termed "rāja yoga" or "classical yoga." That focus is the program of postures, breath control, and meditative introspection that leads to *samādhi,* the state of "com-position" or "pure contemplation" that allows for the disengagement of spirit from matter. In other words, nearly every history of "yoga" written to date has in fact been a history of meditation.[2] Another feature of the historiography of yoga has been the focus on yoga "with modifiers," that is, on yoga as the second part of a compound, as in *bhakti yoga, rāja yoga, haṭha yoga,* or *pātañjala yoga,* to say nothing of yoga for pets and the other inanities that yoga entrepreneurs are continuously inventing. With the yogi as one's focus, it becomes possible to write a history of yoga tout court, because while one never encounters "bhakti-yogis," "rāja-yogis," and so forth in Indic traditions, one does meet many yogis.[3]

Of course, the *Mahābhārata* passage quoted above also provides another explanation for the identities of the yogis I had met fifteen years and worlds apart: they both could have been the same yogi manifesting in two different bodies, who could have been but two among an army of "clones" of one and the same yogi. Or the yogi at Trader Joe's could have been Bhandarināth inside the body of a chubby, bearded man. Or Bhandarināth could have been the yogi at Trader Joe's inside the body of a younger, thinner Hindi-speaking man. The possibilities, which are quite endless, have been explored at length in the fantasy and adventure literature of medieval South Asia, in which the dastardly archvillain of dozens of stories is, precisely, a yogi, a *sinister* yogi who takes over other people's bodies in order to assuage his lust for power. Yogis do not fare better with the authorized scriptures of certain medieval sects: the Vaiṣṇava *Jayākhya Saṃhitā* calls yogis "cruel beings" and classifies them together with evil-doers, the demonic dead (*bhūtas*), and zombies (*vetālas*).[4] Even today, sinister yogis are stock villains in Bollywood film plots, and as soon as one ventures out from the subcontinent's metropolitan areas, yogis are such objects of dread and fear that parents threaten disobedient children with them: "Be good or the yogi will come and take you away." Yogis are bogeymen, control freaks, cannibals, and terror mongers.

Not all yogis are sinister, however, whether inside or outside of texts. While leaving their bodies to yoke themselves to the sun, or to other bodies or selves, in fact constitutes the modus operandi of the yogis of Indic narrative, their motives need not necessarily be nefarious. They can do so for altogether altruistic purposes, for example, to initiate a disciple and thereby prepare them for salvation; this is a principal basis for guru worship in South Asia. They can also take over bodies whose owners have left them (because they have died), a practice that harms no one. Or, by yoking themselves to the sun, they can effect their own apotheosis, dying to this world at a time of their own choosing, a practice tantamount to cheating death (*kāla-vañcana*). These practices are the yoga of yogis, which has little in common with the yoga of philosophers, commentators, and scholars.

Yet, because yogis have belonged to the same world as philosophers, commentators, and scholars, there cannot but be some common ground shared by all of these people. Yoga is a phenomenon of Indic origins, an amalgam of theories and techniques that has drawn on specifically South Asian sources and that has always been grounded in specifically South Asian systems of knowledge and ways of life. The wandering hermit who took over other people's bodies, the vedic chariot warrior who pierced the disk of the sun following his battlefield death, the philosopher who attempted to establish the foundations of true perception and cognition, the contemplative who attempted to see himself in god and god in himself, and the eighteenth-century mercenary who sought to make his fortune from the spoils of war: all of these figures from India's past were in some way engaged in yogic or yogi practice. The task I have set myself in this book has been to discover the broad context within which all of these diverse activities would have been interconnected and made sense.

It has been my good fortune that in the course of writing this book, a number of seminal works on the history of yogis and yoga (as I construe it) were published by outstanding scholars in the field. This book is built on the pillars of their scholarship. Here I'm referring especially to Jim Fitzgerald for his recent publications on the *Mahābhārata*'s Mokṣadharma Parvan; Véronique Bouillier for her many ethnohistorical studies of the Nāth Yogīs, culminating in *Itinérance et vie monastique* (2008); Vijay Pinch for his stunning *Warrior Ascetics and Indian Empires* (2006); Fred Smith for his exhaustive study of possession in South Asia, *The Self Possessed* (2006); and Gerald Larson for his encyclopedic *Yoga: India's Philosophy of Meditation* (2008). Many other scholars and friends have aided me with their advice, as well as material and intellectual support. These include Jason Birch, Christian Bouy, Johannes Bronkhorst, Edwin Bryant, Gudrun Bühnemann, Kendall Busse, François Chenet, Catherine Clémentin-Ojha, Brad Clough, Gérard Colas, Chantal Duhuy, Yves Duroux, Dan Ehnbom, Dominic Goodall, Holly Grether, Caterina Guenzi, Paul Hackett, Donald Harper, John and Susan Huntington, Jaya Kasibhatla, Richard King, Karine Ladrech, Victor Mair, Angelika Malinar, Michael Meister, Daniel Michon, Aman Nath, Patrick Olivelle, William Sax, Peter Schreiner, Martha Selby, Catherine Servan-Schreiber, Ursula Sims-Williams, Bruce Sullivan, Cynthia Talbot, Aaron Ullrey, Somadeva Vasudeva, Francis Wacziarg, Phil Wagoner, and Dominik Wujastyk. I am also grateful to David Brent, my editor here at Chicago, for seeing this book, the fourth of our collaboration, through to its desired conclusion. Catherine, my beautiful muse, moves me in all that I do.

This book's rich iconography would not have been possible without the cooperation of several museum curators, most especially Debra Diamond (Sackler and Freer Galleries, Washington, D.C.), Karni Singh Jasol (Mehrangarh Museum, Jodhpur), Rakesh Tiwari (State Museum, Lucknow), Helga Schütze (National Museum of Denmark), and Jean Collier (University of Virginia Art Museum). I also wish to express my appreciation to the University Seminars at Columbia University for its assistance in the publication of the book's iconography. Material in this work was presented to the University Seminar: South Asia. I was supported in the course of writing this book by the John Simon Guggenheim Foundation; the Council of the Humanities and the Department of Anthropology at Princeton University; the Institut d'Études Avancées (Paris); and David Marshall, Dean of Humanities and Fine Arts in the College of Letters and Science at the University of California, Santa Barbara.

Some passages in this book are revisions of articles or chapters that have previously been published. I am grateful to the editors of these publications for their permission to reproduce those passages here. Portions of chapter 2, part 3, and chapter 4, parts 4 and 6, have appeared in "'Never Have I Seen Such Yogīs, Brother': Yogīs, Warriors, and Sorcerers in Ancient and Medieval India," *Ancient to Modern: Religion, Power, and Community in India*, edited by Ishita Banerjee-Dube and Saurabh Dube (New York: Oxford University Press, 2008), 86–113. Portions of chapter 4, part 2, have appeared in "'Open' and 'Closed' Models of the Human Body in Indian Medical and Yogic Traditions," *Asian Medicine: Tradition and Modernity* (London) 2, no. 1 (Fall 2006): 1–13.

Note on Transliteration

Unless noted otherwise, all transliterations from the Sanskrit follow standard lexicographical usage, with the following exceptions: (1) Toponyms still currently in use are transliterated without diacriticals and modern English-language spellings are applied, when such exist (thus Ganges and not Gaṅgā). (2) Names of authors and editors from the colonial and postcolonial periods are transliterated without diacriticals. (3) The term yogi is used without a macron over the final *i*, except in the case of proper names (Nāth Yogī, Bhairāvanand Yogī, etc.). Similarly, the vernacular form jogī is also used without a macron over the final *i*. (4) The term Nāth is transliterated in its modern Hindi form as opposed to the Sanskritic Nātha. (5) Proper names of historical Nāth Yogīs are transliterated with the -nāth suffix, as opposed to the Sanskritic -nātha. Modern Hindi-Urdu terms are transliterated according to standard lexicographical usage, with the exception of terms found in modern English-language dictionaries, which I reproduce without diacriticals: sadhu, Sufi, Sannyasi, Naga, and fakir.

Abbreviations

AB	*Aitareya Brāhmaṇa*
AH	*Aṣṭāṅgahṛdaya*
AN	*Aṅguttara Nikaya*
ĀP	*Ādi Purāṇa*
ĀpDhSū	*Āpastamba Dharma Sūtra*
APr	*Amaraughaprabodha*
AŚ	*Arthaśāstra*
AV	*Atharva Veda*
AY	*Amanaskayoga*
BA	*Bhagavadajjukīya*
BC	*Buddhacarita*
BhG	*Bhagavad Gītā*
BN	*Bachittar Nāṭak*
BrSū	*Brahma Sūtras of Bādarāyaṇa*
BrSūBh	*Brahma Sūtra Bhāṣya of Śaṅkara*
BṛU	*Bṛhadāraṇyaka Upaniṣad*
ChU	*Chāndogya Upaniṣad*
CS	*Caraka Saṃhitā*
GS	*Gorakṣa Saṃhitā*
GSS	*Gorakṣasiddhāntasaṃgraha*

HC	*Harṣacarita*
HV	*Harivaṃśa*
HYP	*Haṭhayogapradīpikā*
JB	*Jaiminīya Brāhmaṇa*
JS	*Jayākhya Saṃhitā*
JUB	*Jaiminīya Upaniṣad Brāhmaṇa*
KāP	*Kālikā Purāṇa*
KhV	*Khecarī Vidyā*
KM	*Kubjikāmata*
KP	*Kūrma Purāṇa*
KS	*Kaṭhaka Saṃhitā*
KSS	*Kathāsaritsāgara*
KT	*Kiraṇa Tantra*
KU	*Kaṭha Upaniṣad*
LP	*Liṅga Purāṇa*
LT	*Lakṣmī Tantra*
MĀg	*Mṛgendrāgama*
MBh	*Mahābhārata*
MdhP	*Mokṣadharma Parvan of the MBh*
MN	*Majjhima Nikaya*
MP	*Matsya Purāṇa*
MPĀg	*Mataṅgapārameśvarāgama*
MS	*Maitrāyaṇī Saṃhitā*
MSmṛ	*Manu Smṛti*
MU	*Maitri Upaniṣad*
MuU	*Muṇḍaka Upaniṣad*
MVUT	*Mālinīvijayottara Tantra*
NBh	*Nyāyabhūṣaṇam*

NK	*Nyāyakandalī*
NŚ	*Nāṭya Śāstra*
NS	*Nyāya Sūtra*
NT	*Netra Tantra*
NTS	*Niśvāsatattvasaṃhitā*
PADhS	*Padārthadharmasaṃgraha*
PBh	*Pañcārthabhāṣya*
PC	*Pārśvanātha Caritra*
PP	*Padma Purāṇa*
PSū	*Pāśupata Sūtra*
PT	*Pañcatantra*
PU	*Praśna Upaniṣad*
RĀg	*Rauravāgama*
Rām	*Rāmāyaṇa*
RCM	*Rām Carit Mānas*
ṚV	*Ṛg Veda*
ŚB	*Śatapatha Brāhmaṇa*
SB	*Senguehassen Battisi*
SD	*Siṃhāsanadvātriṃśika*
ŚDV	*Śaṅkaradigvijaya*
ŚMC	*Śrī Mastnāth Carit*
ŚMS	*Śaṅkaramandarasaurabha*
ŚP	*Śiva Purāṇa*
SS	*Suśruta Saṃhitā*
SSP	*Siddhasiddhāntapaddhati*
ŚV	*Śaṅkaravijaya*
SvT	*Svacchanda Tantra*
ŚvU	*Śvetāśvatara Upaniṣad*

TĀ *Tantrāloka*

TĀr *Taittirīya Āraṇyaka*

TS *Taittirīya Saṃhitā*

TSB *Tantrasadbhāva*

TU *Taittirīya Upaniṣad*

VāP *Vāyu Purāṇa*

ViṣP *Viṣṇu Purāṇa*

VM *Visuddhimagga*

VP *Vetālapañcaviṃśati*

VS *Vaiśeṣika Sūtra*

VV *Vyomavatī*

YājS *Yājñavalkyasmṛti*

YBh *Yogabhāṣya of Vedavyāsa*

YŚ *Yogaśāstra*

YS *Yoga Sūtras*

YTU *Yogatattva Upaniṣad*

YV *Yoga Vasiṣṭha*

YYāj *Yogayājñavalkya*

ONE

Tales of Sinister Yogis

1. The King Who Wasn't Himself

a. Bhairavānand Yogī

King Maheś of Abhayāpur had seven queens, each one more beautiful than the last. Not far from his palace there lived an oil-presser woman named Muniyāṃ who thought herself to be the fairest woman in the world. Across the Abhayā River from Maheś's capitol was the lodge (*maṭh*) of a yogi named Bhairavānand, a jack-of-all-trades and connoisseur of the magical arts (*jādu vidyā*). Both the king and the yogi were disciples of a teacher named Madhukar. Muniyāṃ and the king's seven wives also sported with Bhairavānand Yogī, who led them in song and dance.

Bhairavānand had a little room built onto the side of his lodge. Beneath its floor he had a pit dug, with spikes in the bottom and a woven leaf mat stretched over the top. One day, the seven queens enticed the city watchman to accompany them to a feast at Bhairavānand Yogī's lodge. They told him to lie down and rest in the little room while the food was being prepared, and when he did, he fell through the mat onto the spikes and died. All of the queens were in love with the yogi, and they took their pleasure with him before returning home that night.

One day, Muniyāṃ announced to the king that the knowledge of women's wiles (*triyā caritra vidyā*)[1] was the sole knowledge worth having. When King Maheś asked Madhukar for instruction in this art, he begged him not to pursue it further, but when the king insisted, he said to him: "If you are to receive instruction, then you must climb up into the city's watchtower and stand guard. Here, I give you this herb. When you place it on your head, you will take on whatever appearance you desire, and when you take it off your head, you will return to your original form." One night, after he had begun to stand guard as Madhukar had told him to do, the king saw Muniyāṃ's husband returning home from a foreign land. Muniyāṃ laid him down on their bed, where he fell sound asleep. Setting about to prepare him a sumptuous meal, she passed near Bhairavānand Yogī's lodge. Seeing her, he flew into a rage, and whipping her across the buttocks exclaimed, "Where have you been all day, and why have you stayed away?" When she explained that her husband had returned from a foreign land, Bhairavānand said, "Well then, if you now belong to him and not to me, why have you come back here? Go back to him!" When Muniyāṃ insisted that she still was his, Bhairavānand told her to prove it by cutting off her husband's head and bringing it to him. She went home directly and did as he said. When Bhairavānand saw her foul deed, he cried, "Murderess! Outcaste woman! Sinner! Begone! How could you, who were not true to your lawful husband, belong to me?" And he drove her away. Regretting what she had done, she returned to her house, placed her husband's head next to his torso, and began to wail loudly. When the townspeople came running and saw her husband with his head cut off and covered in blood, Muniyāṃ told them that a band of robbers had killed him as he was returning home.

From where he stood, King Maheś had secretly seen all that had transpired. At sunrise on the following day, the townspeople came to carry off Muniyāṃ's husband's corpse for burning. Then she said, "I shall burn with my husband and become a *satī*." Seeing her seated on her husband's pyre, King Maheś denounced her, saying that no person versed in women's wiles could become a *satī* after murdering their husband. Muniyāṃ was reduced to ashes on her husband's pyre.

One night from his watchtower the king saw the seven queens preparing all sorts of succulent dishes at Bhairavānand's lodge. The next morning, they called up to him, "Hey watchman! Come down from your tower! Take this plate and come with us!" The disguised king crossed the river with them to the lodge, where they told him to lie down and rest in the little room while the food was being prepared. The queens began to dance together with Bhairavānand, and singing songs in the *gazal* and *dadari* styles, they became drunk with dance and song. Resting back in the little room, King Maheś lifted the mat and saw the pit that had been dug beneath it, and when he peered into the pit, the bones of the dead watchman began to laugh and speak to him: "O king! Have you fallen on the same misfortune as I?" Upon which, the king ran away. As he ran, he heard the seven queens raising the alarm and Bhairavānand shouting, "Don't let him get away!"

The king crossed the river, but saw they were still on his heels. Out of breath, he turned to look back again, and just then a diamond he had had set in his tooth began to twinkle in the moonlight. The queens saw the diamond and said to each other, "What an awful thing! The watchman was the king in disguise!" And so they returned to Bhairavānand and told him all that had happened. Bhairavānand gave them some ash, saying, "Go back home and wait on your king. Anoint his body with unguents and when he has fallen asleep in his bed, blow this ash into his ear. He will turn into a ram! Then beat him on the back with sticks until he dies." They did as he said, and the king, under the blows of their sticks, realized that his life was in danger. The queens had locked all the doors of the palace, but as fate would have it, one window was left open, and the king escaped through it and ran to the house of his guru Madhukar. Scolding him and saying he should never have sought the knowledge of women's wiles, Madhukar said he would turn the king, who was now a ram, into a parrot, so that he could live incognito in another king's realm. So saying, he took a bundle of herbs and thrust it into the ram's wool, and the king, now transformed into a parrot, flew off to the land of King Harewa.

Bhairavānand learned of this and sent the seven queens to Abhayāpur to summon all the kingdom's fowlers, to whom they promised five rupees for every parrot brought to them. As parrots became more and more scarce in the region, the queens increased the bounty to twenty-five rupees per bird. One of these fowlers journeyed into King Harewa's realm and sat down beneath the very tree in which the parrot that was King Maheś was perched. The parrot called out to him, saying, "If you catch me, please don't take me to King Maheś's queens. Instead, take me where I tell you to, and I'll reward you generously." Following the parrot's instructions, the fowler took him to the royal market, where King Harewa's market master asked him his price. The fowler did not answer, but let the parrot name its price—of 100,000 rupees—which the king's man paid to the fowler. The market master brought the parrot to the king, telling him of the bird's reputation for settling intractable disputes.

King Harewa gave the parrot to his daughter Premā, who slept with its cage next to her bed. One night, Premā took the parrot out of its cage and began to stroke its feathers. As she did so, its plumes were replaced by hands, arms, legs, and so on, until in the place of a parrot a man stood before her. The king told her his entire sad story. Thereafter, she transformed him into a parrot by day and her human lover by night.

Word of King Harewa's remarkable parrot eventually reached the seven queens, who decided it had to be their king, because there was no one in the world who was as gifted in settling disputes as he. Putting on the guise of dancing girls, they accompanied Bhairavānand Yogī to King Harewa's court. With Bhairavānand playing the music, they sang songs of Bhairava and Bhairavī as they danced, first for King Harewa and then for the princess. Pleased with their music, they offered gifts to the entire troupe, but when Bhairavānand asked for the parrot, his request was refused. When the yogi insisted, Premā flew into a rage and released the parrot from its cage. The parrot flew up and alighted on an upper balcony, and Bhairavānand, who had transformed himself into a tomcat, pounced on it. Premā threw a bundle of herbs at the parrot, which turned into a dog. The dog fell upon the tomcat and seizing it by the throat, killed it.

Seeing the death of Bhairavānand, the seven queens turned themselves into red birds and flew away to live in the forest, thinking that when they saw their chance, they would kill the king. When King Harewa learned all that had befallen King Maheś, he gave him his daughter's hand in marriage, and so King Maheś began the journey back to his palace, with Premā and her rich dowry in tow. On the way, Premā told him that the seven queens had transformed themselves into red birds of the forest. She said she would catch each of the red birds and throw them to the ground for him to chop up with his sword. She became a tawny falconess, and together they slew the seven queens. They then destroyed the yogi's lodge and filled in the pit beneath the little room, and forever blotted Bhairavānand's name from the face of the earth. The two then returned to King Maheś's palace to rule over the kingdom, and there they lived happily ever after.

Mahadevprasad Singh, the author of *Bhairavānand Yogī*, a twenty-four page Hindi-language chapbook first published some time between 1940 and 1970, introduces this story by calling it a "new tale" (*nayā qissā*), yet also states that "the story of Bhairavānand Yogī is famous throughout the world."[2] Both statements are correct, inasmuch as Singh's is a novel adaptation of a story (in fact of a collection of stories) that is over a thousand years old. But then, so it is with all good stories, which, while they are constantly renewed in the retelling, nonetheless draw on a common treasury of themes, structures, and tropes according to time, place, and the storyteller's craft. In the case of *Bhairavānand Yogī*, a number of standard fixtures of the South Asian fantasy and adventure genre are readily recognizable: talking parrots; a brave, resourceful, and solitary king; a bevy of evil queens; skulls or skeletons that laugh and talk; the power to change bodies; and a sinister yogi.

Figure 1.1 *Bhairavānand Yogī* chapbook cover, ca. 1950.

The most readily identifiable of Singh's literary sources is a body of story that I will call the "Vikrama Cycle." In eleventh-century Kashmir, Sanskrit-language narrative anthologies began to appear in which a legendary king of Ujjain[3] named Vikramāditya or Trivikramasena finds himself pitted against evil ascetics, a talkative vampire or zombie (*vetāla*),[4] and a host of other characters in a series of fantastic adventures. The most famous of these collections are the *Vetālapañcaviṃśati* (VP) or *Twenty-five Vampire Tales*, whose five principal Sanskrit recensions date from between the eleventh and sixteenth centuries,[5] and the *Siṃhāsanadvātriṃśika* (SD) or *Thirty-two Tales of the Throne*, whose four principal Sanskrit recensions date from the thirteenth and fourteenth centuries.[6] Numerous vernacular versions of both, composed in a variety of Indic, Inner Asian, and European languages, have continued to appear over the centuries.[7] Vikrama stories also appear in certain recensions of the *Pañcatantra* (PT),[8] as well as in adaptations by Hindu,[9] Jain, and Muslim authors. The world that these texts recreate is at once that of the golden age of Indian civilization—the first six centuries of the common era; the medieval time of the composition of the texts themselves, a period in which Tantra was at its height throughout much of South Asia; and a world outside of time, an Indian version of the Days of Camelot (with Vikramāditya as King Arthur sans the Knights of the Round Table). However, we must not limit our investigation of the stories of the Vikrama Cycle to the South Asian literary record alone. The building blocks of these tales, if not the plots of the stories themselves, are tropes and structures that were already present in the oral storytelling traditions of South Asia, traditions that have never ceased to simultaneously draw upon and enrich the evolving literary canon.

Singh's *Bhairavānand Yogī* follows the contours of the Vikrama Cycle as attested in a dozen sources, many of which were studied at length by Maurice Bloomfield in an article published in 1917.[10] These include a Sanskrit manuscript of the VP;[11] two Sanskrit anthologies by Jain authors, the 1304 CE *Prabandhacintāmaṇi* (*Wish-fulfilling Gemstone of Narratives*) of Merutuṅga and the fourteenth- to fifteenth-century *Pārśvanātha Caritra* (PC) of Bhāvadevasūri; the *Senguehassen Battisi* (SB), a Persian version of the SD commissioned by the Mughal emperor Akbar in about 1574 CE;[12] several modern Indic-language versions of stories adapted from the two original Sanskrit anthologies;[13] and a number of English-language anthologies from the colonial period.[14]

The most obvious (and recent) of Singh's sources is the twenty-fourth of the SD tales as recorded in the "vulgate" Hindustani version of that anthology,[15] to which he so closely adheres that he has been rightly accused of plagiarism.[16] In this twenty-fourth tale of the throne, however, it is on the orders of "King Vikram," and not a yogi, that the woman after whom Singh's Muniyāṃ is modeled kills her husband, following which she attempts to commit *satī*. Before she dies, she suggests to Vikram that he should spy on his six queens, whom the king observes cuckolding him with a yogi who magically assumes six bodies in order to satisfy all of them simultaneously. After they leave the yogi's lodge, Vikram threatens the yogi, obtains the secret of changing bodies, and kills him. Later, he confronts and kills his six queens. More generally, the theme of the woman who cuckolds her husband with a yogi recurs frequently in the literary subgenre of which *Bhairavānand Yogī* is a twentieth-century example. These are the edifying tales on the wiles of wanton and malicious women known as *trīyā caritr* (Sanskrit: *strī caritra*). A long collection of such tales, called the "Pakhyān Charitra" or the "Chritro Pakhyān," is included in the eighteenth-century Sikh anthology known as the *Dasam Granth*. Seven of the 404 stories in this compendium feature yogis or paramours who disguise themselves as yogis.[17]

b. Parrots, Kings, and Yogis

The episodes in Singh's *qissā* that describe King Maheś's adventures in the body of a parrot may be traced back to Vikrama tales found not in the original Sanskrit versions of the VP or SD, but rather in the two other sources noted above: the Sanskrit-language PC and the Persian-language SB.[18] In the former work, the villain of the story is one of the king's brahmin retainers, whereas in the latter work, it is a yogi who disturbs the tranquility of the royal court. I therefore summarize the latter account here.[19]

In a distant land there lived a certain Jéhabel who traveled the world playing different roles and taking on all sorts of forms to gain his livelihood, which was based on the credulity of the populace: now a sorcerer or a magician, now a diviner, and at other times a charlatan. Most often, he was an itinerant monk or hermit, and he especially played this last role with a perfect hypocrisy. Now, this Jéhabel, having heard of the generosity and wisdom of King *Békermadjiet* [Vikramāditya], set out for *Aotchine* [Ujjain], taking with him a parrot of magnificent plumage. Received by the king, the religious imposter requested a private audience. When the king consented to his proposition and led the *Djogui* [yogi] to a secluded and solitary wing of his palace, the *Djogui* immediately set about closing every window and door, blocking every opening and drawing all the curtains. Following this, he drew from the folds of his garment a dead parrot, which he placed before the king with the words, "I have heard that King *Békermadjiet* is possessed of fourteen arts or talents, of which one is the ability to transport his soul into the body of a dead creature and revive it. I therefore pray that you transfer your soul, for only an instant, into the body of this parrot."

No sooner had the king separated his soul from his body and transferred it into the bird's dead body than did the parrot open its eyes, move its feet, and spread its wings. Seeing this, the *Djogui* swiftly transferred his own soul into the body of the king, and so it was that King *Békermadjiet* found himself transformed into a parrot, whilst the *Djogui* took over the body and appearance of the king. The *Djogui* then attempted to catch the parrot to kill it. The parrot, finding no escape, concentrated his thoughts on the Supreme Being and pleaded for release. There then arose a mighty wind, which threw open all of the windows and openings the *Djogui* had closed, and so the parrot escaped and flew to the immense garden of *Noutkéha*, wherein he perched upon the branch of a *Samboul* [*śālmali*] tree. No sooner had he done so than did thousands of other parrots alight around him to pay him their respects. Formerly a king among men, *Békermadjiet* was now the king of the parrots.

As for the *Djogui* who had infamously betrayed and usurped the body and countenance of the king, he secretly interred the body he had left behind, after anointing it with unguents and perfumes and wrapping it in a lovely shroud. Following this, he returned to the audience hall with no one noticing what had transpired. One day, *Békermadjiet* the parrot returned to the royal palace, where he swooped down on his usurper, who feared he would peck his eyes out. When the parrot had departed, he called together his viziers and told them of a dream he had had in which a parrot had threatened him with death. As a result, he had decided to order that all the hunters in the kingdom be sent out to capture and bring back to him every parrot in the realm, in return for which they would receive one gold piece in payment per bird. The captured birds would be roasted in a great pot and reduced to ashes.

One day, a fowler named *Kalia* went to the garden and spread his nets beneath the very tree on which the parrot king was perched. King *Békermadjiet*, who recognized *Kalia* as a subject to whom he had previously gifted a daily ration of rice, sugar, and gold, flew down into his net. Hearing *Kalia* give voice to his intention of ransoming him for a single gold piece, the parrot *Békermadjiet* spoke to him, promising that if he would spare him, he could fetch a thousand gold pieces for him alone. *Kalia*, considering that a talking parrot was a prize catch, took the bird home with him and fed and cared for him as he did his own children.

In the course of their conversations, *Békermadjiet* informed *Kalia* of the *Djogui*'s perfidy, as well as of his queens' repugnance toward the usurper, whose amorous advances they rejected at every turn. Frustrated, the usurper *Djogui* called upon his viziers to find a maiden suitable for marriage to him. Informed that the daughter of the royal treasurer *Ounian* was endowed with great beauty and talent, the *Djogui* gave orders for the preparation of a great wedding celebration. One day, the bride-to-be left the city to go bathing with her friends. Singing and playing musical instruments along their way, they passed in front of *Kalia*'s house. The parrot so enchanted her with his sayings and songs[20] that the maiden offered the parrot's promised price of a thousand gold pieces to the fowler and took it home with her. Noticing that preparations were being made at *Ounian*'s home for a festive celebration, the parrot asked the reason. Informed by the maiden of the king's plan to marry her four days thence, the parrot burst out laughing, because he had found a way to avenge himself upon the *Djogui*. He instructed the maiden to buy a sickly deer fawn, tie it to her bed, and insist to her new husband on their wedding night that their marriage could not be consummated in the presence of her pet. This she did, and when the frustrated usurper king kicked the fawn to death, the infuriated maiden declared that she would forever refuse his advances until her "poor little brother" was brought back to life. Seeking to placate her, the king entered the body of the dead fawn, and immediately, the king of parrots took back his own body. *Békermadjiet*'s first act was to put the fawn in a safe place, after which he said to the maiden, "It is the scoundrelly *Djogui*'s soul that is now animating the fawn, the soul that had taken over the body and countenance of King *Békermadjiet*. He was nothing but a vile usurper and I am the true king. I inhabited the body of a parrot due to the abominable and traitorous act of this *Djogui*. I have lived this way for twelve years, but now I have at long last recovered possession of my own body."

Following his happy transformation, King *Békermadjiet* and his new wife joyously passed the night in each other's embrace. The following morning, he informed his court and all the grandees of his kingdom of the trials he had suffered at the hands of the villainous *Djogui* and ordered that the word be spread throughout the land. All set out to find the *Djogui*'s corpse, which, when they recovered it, they vowed to bury on the king's road near the gates of the city so that all who passed over it would trample it with their feet. But the king mercifully drew the soul of the *Djogui* out of the fawn, returned it to its own body, and had him escorted from the kingdom to escape the fury of his subjects.

Many of the narrative threads of Singh's *Bhairavānand Yogī* are readily identifiable in this account: the king who is transformed into a parrot and who uses his wits to regain his human body and the throne;[21] the king's possession of occult knowledge; the parrot's ability to name his own price; the cooperative roles of both the fowler and a maiden who is the daughter of a royal functionary; and, of course, a sinister yogi as the villain of the piece.

Many of the narrative themes and tropes from Singh's tale not found in the medieval literary sources reviewed to this point may nonetheless be shown to resonate with a number of Indic religious traditions, as well as oral folk narratives. The use of a bird's body as a temporary residence for the soul—which is itself identified as a bird called the "gander" (*haṃsa*) in many Indic traditions—reappears in Tibetan Buddhist literature, the legacy of the transmission of South Asian Tantra to Tibet from the eighth century onward. An important figure in this history of transmission was Marpa the Translator, the eleventh-century disciple of the great Indian master Naropa (1016–1100), whose "Six Yogas" system included a technique involving the transfer of the soul into another body. This is narrativized in Marpa's early sixteenth-century biography. As Marpa's son Tarma Dode lies dying from a head wound, he follows his father's instructions and temporarily transfers his soul into a pigeon, before taking up permanent residence in the body of a thirteen-year-old brahmin boy, which is about to be cremated.[22] *The Prince Who Became a Cuckoo*, an 1857 Tibetan tale of liberation, tells a story whose plot is closely modeled after those of the PC and the SB.[23]

The seven evil queens who sing, dance, and make love to Bhairavānand Yogi, whom they collude with to murder their husband the king, and who transform themselves into birds of the forest, carry forward the tantric cult of the yoginīs. These dangerous, powerful, and petulant tantric goddesses form a troop led, precisely, by the god named Bhairava, and tantric literature is replete with descriptions of their nocturnal revels together, in which they sing and dance to the pounding beat of drums, gongs, and skull rattles. As shape changers (*kāmarūpinī*), the yoginīs are frequently represented as animal- or bird-headed women, or simply as predatory or carrion-feeding birds or beasts of the forest. The oil-presser woman Muniyāṃ's beheading of her husband to prove her love for Bhairavānand Yogī draws on the same tantric matrix. Yoginīs—who were thought to embody the human women who took part in tantric rites—were also fond of human flesh and severed heads. They shared blood offerings with their leader Bhairava, after the fashion of the Greek Maenads with their leader Dionysios.[24] The association of a group of seven females with a male figure named Bhairava evokes Śākta Hinduism's Seven Mothers (*saptamātṛkā*), whose iconography always links them to a male figure, most often the elephant-headed Gaṇeśa. However, a significant number of local and regional traditions from western India specifically identify Bhairava as the consort (or brother or leader) of a group of seven dire goddesses, all of whom accept blood sacrifices. So, for example, in Rajasthan, the Bayasaab Mātā, seven sisters popularly believed to be responsible for both causing and curing polio and paralysis, are often associated with Bherūṃ-jī (Bhairava) in shrines,[25] sculptural friezes,[26] and women's wedding jewelry.

Figure 1.2 Bherūṃ-jī and seven sisters, women's wedding necklace, Jodhpur, ca. 1990. Private collection.

In the Hindu and Buddhist tantric canon, *yogin* (*yogī* in the nominative singular) is one of a number of terms commonly employed for the male tantric practitioner whose goals were supernatural enjoyments (*siddhis*) rather than salvation (*mokṣa*). The goal of such tantric yogis was, precisely, to become a Bhairava incarnate at the heart of a circle of yoginīs.[27] Human yogis have become objects of worship, as attested in several regional north Indian traditions in which they are venerated and "channeled," in the course of night vigils (*jāgars*), in ways similar to the heroic or honored dead who possess their human spirit mediums.[28] In the Kumaon region of western Uttar Pradesh, in the foothills of the Himalayas, the divinized guru Gorakhnāth and his Nāth Yogī entourage are venerated at the sites of communal village fire pits (*dhūnīs*), where they are said to constitute the court of the royal ascetic King Haru (Harcan, Har Cand, or Hariścandra).[29] This king's name may be the inspiration for Singh's "Harewa."

Singh's Bhairavānand is likely a composite figure. Bhairavānand is the name of the clan deity of the Raikwar Rajputs of the Lucknow region of Uttar Pradesh, who venerate this figure as the deified ghost of a human who was pushed into a well in order to fulfill a prophecy.[30] In this respect, the name of the Singh's villain is itself revealing. One in fact finds a number of figures named Bhairavānand(a) in medieval South Asian literature. Singh's choice of the name very likely comes from the same sources, oral or written, as those that informed an eighteenth-century Newari recension of the SD, which in its twentieth story presents its hero King Bikramādit (i.e., Vikramāditya) in the disguise of a *jogi* (the most common vernacular form of the Sanskrit *yogi*) in order to fathom the wiles of women.

Having asked a queen and her two female companions to guide him across a river "to learn spells," Bikramādit is brought into the presence of an ascetic named Bhairabanand, who lives "beyond the ocean." Bhairabanand offers the disguised king a seat on his couch. Ever watchful, Bikramādit feels beneath it with his foot and finds that it has been placed over a sword-filled pit. When he rushes at Bhairabanand with uplifted sword, the latter sprinkles him with cow-dung ash and transforms him into a dog. Bikramādit is restored to his human form by his guru, who secrets him away to the court of a foreign king, where he marries the royal princess. Bhairabanand learns of this and with murderous intentions comes to the royal capital in the guise of a dancer. Bikramādit's guru transforms him into a coin necklace, which he places on the throat of his queen. The perspicacious Bhairabanand asks for the necklace, which the queen tears off in a rage, at which point Bhairabanand becomes a peacock to swallow the coins. Bikramādit's guru now transforms the king into a cat, which seizes the peacock and kills it.[31]

The *Prabandhacintāmaṇi* presents a terser version of the tale told in the later SB and PC, with one important added detail; in it, Bhairavānanda is the name of a yogi living on the mythic mountain of Sriparvata:[32] "Then, having heard on a certain occasion that all accomplishments are useless in comparison with the art of entering the bodies of other creatures (*parapurapraveśavidyā*), King Vikrama repaired to the Yogī Bhairavānanda and propitiated him for a long time on the mountain of Śrī." The villain of the *Prabandhacintāmaṇi* account is not the yogi, but rather Vikrama's brahmin servant,[33] who has accompanied the king to the mountain, and who insists on receiving instruction together with him. Bhairavānanda, warning the king that he will "again and again regret this request," teaches the art to the pair, which the brahmin abuses by taking over Vikrama's body and the throne when the king has entered into the body of an elephant.[34]

Bhairavānanda is also the name of the hero in a late fourteenth-century play by the same name, written by the Nepali playwright Maṇika.[35] Better known is the tenth- to eleventh-century play *Karpūramañjarī*, written by Rājaśekhara, a court poet to the Pratīhāra and Kalacuri kings of central India. In this drama, Bhairavānanda is the name of a tantric thaumaturge who, through his occult arts, elevates a king to the status of *cakravartin*, a universal conquerer, by magically causing Karpūramañjarī, the eponymous heroine of the story, to miraculously appear in his royal court.[36] That the powers of such figures did not translate directly into respect for them is made clear by a soliloquy placed in the mouth of Bhairavānanda himself:

I don't know mantra from tantra,
Nor meditation or anything about a teacher's grace.
Instead, I drink cheap booze and enjoy some woman.
But I sure am going on to liberation, since I got the Kula path.
What's more,
I took some horny slut and consecrated her my "holy wife."
Sucking up booze and wolfing down red meat,
My "holy alms" are whatever I like to eat,
My bed is but a piece of human skin.
Say, who wouldn't declare this Kaula Religion
Just about the most fun you can have?[37]

A detail concerning the language of Singh's *Bhairavānand Yogī* is worthy of note. While his *qissā* is a prose narrative written in modern Hindi, Singh's tale is spangled with expressions from Bhojpuri, a language widely spoken across much of eastern Uttar Pradesh, as well as the western districts of the neighboring states of Bihar and Jharkhand.[38] One of the songs inserted into the story contains references to the Sufi concept of divine love (*allāh re iśk*) and to *Laila-Majnu*, a Persian story of unrequited love that has often been compared to Shakespeare's *Romeo and Juliet*.[39] The inclusion of such references to Islam and Islamicate literature attests to another cultural context within which Singh lived and wrote. While he was the author of a handful of other tales as well as two original plays and a cycle of *bārah-māsa* songs, Singh's greatest legacy was as a collector of Bhojpuri folktales. Despite his lack of formal training, Singh succeeded in publishing the entire "canon" of Bhojpuri-language legend cycles, word-for-word transcriptions of the complete repertory of songs he had heard sung since his childhood by itinerant yogi minstrels, whose peregrinations always brought them back to the banks of the "Manik Talab" pond of his native village of Nachap, in the Shahbad District of southwestern Bihar.[40] An autodidact culture broker, Singh's composition of *Bhairavānand Yogī* is a watershed of a thousand years of oral and written tradition from across the length and breadth of the north Indian heartland.

The medieval sources of this tradition are eloquently described by Charlotte Vaudeville, who, writing on the subject of the renowned sixteenth-century "yogi romance," the *Padmāvat* of Mallik Muhammad Jāyasī, noted that

> in order to understand Jāyasī's worldview in the *Padmāvat*, one must acknowledge that the religious power that the first Sufis encountered, in the thirteenth and fourteenth centuries, among the deepest strata of the populations living in northwestern India, was neither orthodox brahmanism nor even the Krishnaite current of *bhakti* (which came later). Rather, it was a complex blend of philosophical ideas, religious doctrines, and esoteric practices . . . embedded in a significant body of narrative, gnomic, and lyrical literature which, mainly oral, was for the most part composed and propagated by low-caste musicians and wandering *jogis* . . . [I]n the western part of the country and especially in Punjab and Rajasthan . . . the pastoral and artisan castes seem, in particular, to have remained more or less on the margins of brahmanic society and ideology . . . In these regions, the great bulk of non-oral literature from the high middle ages was the work of "munis" (Jain "ascetics"), "siddhas" (Buddhist "perfected beings"), and "Nāth Yogīs" ("Nāth Panthīs" or "Gorakhnāthīs").[41]

Often, the kings of these legend cycles are identified as Rajputs, the "sons of kings" whose kingdoms extended across much of late medieval, Mughal, and colonial north India.[42] For a period of approximately six hundred years, a constant of Rajput polity was the synergy between the secular power of the Rajputs themselves and the occult power of yogis. As the Rajputs expanded their power and influence eastward out of their original homelands into the Bhojpuri-speaking regions of Uttar Pradesh and Bihar,[43] Garhwal,[44] Nepal,[45] and Kumaon, wonder-working yogis often played the roles of counselors, confidantes, and bards to these princes, often at the expense of brahmins. With the rise of the Rajputs' star, that of a particular group of yogis—the Nāth Yogīs (also known as the Kānphaṭa Yogīs, Gorakhpanthīs, or Nāth Siddhas), a religious order founded by Gorakhnāth in the late twelfth or early thirteenth century[46]—also burned brightly, so much so that by the nineteenth century, the term "yogi" was often construed, by India's British colonizers, to refer specifically to a member of one of the Nath Yogī orders.[47] Therefore, while the deified ancestor Bhairavānand of the Raikwar Rajput tradition mentioned earlier was not himself a yogi, he nonetheless belongs to a pantheon whose hosts include a number of semidivine beings alternately called yogis, nāths, siddhas, or vīrs. The relationship between the Nāth

Yogīs and yogis tout court is a complex one, to which I will return in the final chapter of this book.[48]

c. Laughing Skeletons

A detail from Singh's *Bhairavānand Yogī* not examined to this point is the motif of the laughing skeleton of the murdered city watchman. This too is a recurrent trope in tales from the Vikrama Cycle, as evinced in several narratives. Near the northern rim of the Indian subcontinent, the following tale of a yogi was recounted to Gérard Toffin in 1992 by Joglal Mali, a Navadurgā dancing master from the village of Theco in the Kathmandu Valley.

Once upon a time, a yogi settled in the Nepal Valley. This ascetic had immense powers. He could bless barren women with a son, provided the mother gave him back the child some time after the birth. The yogi would then kill him on the altar of Durgā, his tutelary deity, to whom he made a vow to offer seven human sacrifices. One year, under the reign of Subahal Rāja, the yogi came to the royal palace, begging for food. As the queen was childless, he refused to accept alms from her hands. The queen asked the ascetic to give her a son. The yogi accepted and fulfilled her wish with some magical pills. Some years later, he asked for the child to be returned. The king and the queen postponed the date until the young prince underwent his sacred thread ceremony (*bratabandha*). As soon as the ceremony was completed, the ascetic came back to the royal palace and asked for his due. The parents implored another delay. But when the young prince (*rājakumāra*) reached the age of twelve, the yogi became angry: "Listen, O king, if you don't give me your child as you promised, I will call down curses upon you." Subahal Rāja discussed the matter with his councilors and tried to play a trick on his tormentor: instead of his son, he presented to the yogi a young brahmin boy of the same age.

The yogi then returned to his lodge, his *kuṭī*, located in Siddhapur. While walking, he decided to put the young boy to the test: "Rājakumāra, from here onward, two paths lead to Siddhapur, the main one which is safe and a short-cut with some dangers. Which one do you prefer?" The brahmin chose the first way. The yogi realized that he had been duped. "It is not of the nature of a *kṣatriya* prince to be afraid of danger," he thought. He went back to the palace with the brahmin boy and, with strong menace in his voice, he demanded the real prince. The royal couple was compelled to obey.

To make sure that a new hoax would not be perpetrated, the ascetic successively took the appearance of a tiger and of an elephant. Rājakumāra fought both of them with his bow and arrows. The yogi then felt reassured: his prisoner obviously descended from a royal family. Some time later, they reached a remote hut in a vast forest. The ascetic installed Rājakumāra there and ordered him to cut wood daily, keep an eye on the sacred fire, pluck flowers, and prepare offerings to the divinities.

After some time had passed, he announced to Rājakumāra that the principal festival of his goddess Durgā was to come: "Gather all the necessary ingredients for her cult within the next two days," he said. Durgā was situated not far from there, in a secret temple, which only the yogi could enter. The next day, Rājakumāra followed his master discretely and saw where the key was concealed. In the evening, he entered the goddess's house cautiously and saw an awe-inspiring statue of Durgā on the altar with some spots of blood on it. A strange curtain was fixed on one side. He peeped under it and discovered six human heads hanging from the ceiling. The heads were grimacing at him: "After some days have passed," they said to Rājakumāra, "the yogi will kill you as he has already killed us in front of Durgā. Then, he will behead you. Pretend that you don't know how to worship the goddess properly. The yogi will show you how to do it. So immediately take his sword, cut his head off and sprinkle us with his blood. We will come back to life."

The prince followed this plan and killed the yogi. The six heads were liberated. Strangely, two wonderful young girls, Agni and Jalavatī, emerged from the ears of the dead ascetic. They were so charming that Rājakumāra fell in love and married them. But Durgā flew into a passion: "King, the six corpses that were offered to me are now alive. Is that not so? You have to offer me a human sacrifice every year." The prince bargained: "Venerable goddess, every year will be too hard. I will offer you this sacrifice once every twelve years." The king then established a temple for Durgā in Theco and fixed the details of the cult. Since then, every twelve years, a person disappears in the village during the festival of the Navadurgā.[49]

While ostensibly a foundation myth for a tradition of human sacrifice at the time of the Nine Durgā (*navadurgā*) festival in this part of the Kathmandu Valley, the once upon a time of this story draws freely on the mythic time of other narratives, some of which are found in Hindu scriptures. The most venerable and identifiable of these is a myth—first recorded in the tenth- to eighth-century BCE *Aitareya Brāhmaṇa* (AB) and *Śāṅkhāyana Śrauta Sūtra*, and subsequently retold in the *Mahābhārata* (MBh), *Rāmāyaṇa* (Rām), and several Purāṇas—in which a king, usually named Hariścandra, also childless, pleads with Varuṇa, the vedic god of law and order, to grant him a son. Varuṇa offers the king a son under the same conditions as those of the yogi in the Nepali account: once the child has undergone the appropriate life-cycle rites (*saṃskāras*), he must be returned—that is, sacrificed—to the god who had given him life. A child is born, and the young prince, named Rohita, runs away into the forest before Varuṇa can claim him as his victim. In his wanderings, Rohita meets the god Indra, who, putting on a human form (*puruṣarūpa*),[50] exhorts him to follow the renunciant life. Rohita comes upon a starving brahmin named Ajīgarta, who sells his son Śunaḥśepa to him to serve as his surrogate, and, unlike the yogi in the Nepali account, Varuṇa accepts the prince's brahmin replacement, and in the end mercifully releases Śunaḥśepa from his bonds.[51]

The theme of the yogi as a miraculous provider of sons to barren women is a frequently encountered motif in the hagiography and lore of the legendary founders of the Nāth Yogīs. The best-known narrative incorporating this motif is the story of Gopīcand, which belongs to medieval north Indian oral traditions and has long stood as the most popular song in the repertoire of Nāth Yogī bards.[52] As such, a comparison of the principal themes of this emic Nāth Yogī account with the etic story of Rājakumāra is instructive. Gopīcand's story opens when the young prince learns from his widowed mother Manavatī that he is doomed to die an early death unless he immediately becomes a yogi. As Manavatī tells him, Gopīcand took birth in her barren womb through a boon granted to her by the powerful yogi Jalandharnāth. However, Jalandharnāth's terms are the same as those of the yogi in the Rājakumāra story (it is likely one of its sources): after having reigned as a child-king for twelve years, Gopīcand must now be returned to the yogi who gave him life, or else he will die. Unlike the royal parents of Rājakumāra, Manavatī does not attempt to fool the yogi; but Gopīcand himself, who does not wish to give up his princely life and family ties, does, attempting to kill Jalandarnāth by sealing him inside a well under the dung of seven hundred and fifty horses. Great yogi that he is, Jalandharnāth escapes from the well, and Gopīcand is taken away by Kāl (Death), but Jalandharnāth harrows hell to bring him back to life. However, the young prince's fate is sealed, and he is forced to embrace his fate as a yogi. After a series of fantastic adventures, Jalandharnāth gives Gopīcand an elixir, whereby he becomes immortal.[53]

In the story of Gopīcand as sung by the Nāth Yogīs, renunciation—characterized as "dying to the world" in Indic traditions—ultimately opens the way to eternal life, a far greater good than a princely life that would otherwise have ended in death, the fate of all mortals. Gopīcand does in fact die, only to be resurrected by a yogi who is more powerful than the god of death, and who thereafter grants him the boon of immortality. The story of Rājakumāra does not broach the prospect of what might have happened to its young hero had he not slain his yogi captor and thereby escaped sacrifice to the dire goddess Durgā, but it should be noted that a standard motif of tantric narratives of self-sacrifice to the great goddess is that she immediately restores her victims to life.[54] In both cases, the emic standpoint is that one must die first in order to accede to immortal life. The etic view of yogis, as reflected in the stories we have reviewed to this point, is that their immortality and supernatural powers can only be realized at the expense of others, whose bodies they appropriate in hostile takeovers. However, the testimony of the emic tantric canon is of a different order. Gurus enter into the bodies of young disciples in order to initiate them into a path that leads to immortality and self-deificiation. While it is the case that the initiate is no longer fully "himself" thereafter, because an element of the guru remains permanently inside the body of his initiate, this is nonetheless considered a boon rather than a loss of autonomy, since it ensures his rapid accession to liberation. I will return to this theme in chapter four.[55] As for the social realities of renunciation and yogic inititation, it is the case that poor families in north India have frequently given up their sons to the Nāth Yogīs and other religious orders, simply to survive. Narratives explaining the miraculous birth of sons through the intervention of Nāth Yogīs—who sometimes "reincarnate" themselves through them—would serve, in such cases, as rationalizations for such transactions in which children are, in fact, "sacrificed" into what has been termed the "slave culture" of the yogi orders.[56]

The "laughing skeleton" motif, found in both Singh's *Bhairavānand Yogī* and the Nepali story of Rājakumāra, recurs in other narratives from the Vikrama Cycle. The tenth book of the Persian SB contains a story of King Békermadjiet not found in the Sanskrit versions, but which draws on the same source as the Nepali account:

Békermadjiet found himself in a wild and desolate plain on which the ground was littered with human skulls. Upon seeing him, one of the heads began to grin. The King was filled with amazement and when he had recovered his wits, asked, "Oh lifeless head, what is it that makes you grin?" "I am grinning," the head replied, "because it will only be a few hours before your head will fall here to keep company with our own. A short distance from here lives a genie in the guise of a *Djogui.* He pleasantly greets all who pass by with a frank proposal: that he will show them a curious thing. He tells them to take an iron cauldron full of black peas, put it on a fire, and tell him when it has come to a boil. The genie then has them walk around the cauldron three times, after which he pitches them in, eats them, and throws their head upon the ground." The head then advised the King to ask the demon, at the critical moment, to show him how to do it, and to throw him into the kettle. Then he should ladle out some of the peas and sprinkle them on the heads, by virtue of which four of them, which themselves belonged to genies, would return to life and become his servants. All this happened as predicted. As the *Djogui* began to walk around the cauldron, *Békermadjiet* seized him by the waist, and pitched him into the pot of boiling peas. The *Djogui* cried out horribly, and did all that he could to escape, but in vain: his body, flesh and even his bones were cooked and entirely consumed. The King then revived the owners of the four heads, who swore to him that thenceforward, he had only to think of them for them to come to his aid.[57]

An early twentieth-century English-language anthology from India tells the same story using the "laughing heads" motif also found in the Persian version. Here the prince, named Śaṅkha ("Conch"), held captive by an "evil yogee," discovers a lovely house in the middle of the forest inhabited by

a young damsel fairer than any of her sex whom he had ever seen or formed a conception of before. The girl blushed and the prince stammered. The sweet confusion did not, however, last long, for shortly afterwards, the prince related his adventures, and the lady told him of things that were horrible to hear. "The *yogee*, your guardian," said she, "is a *Tántrik*, that is to say, he propitiates his tutelary goddess, *Káli*, by horrible rites, one of which is sacrifice of human beings at her altar. Hundreds have been slaughtered before this time and you and I shall have to take our turns unless we can contrive our escape or put an end to the monster before the dreadful day comes. The corpses of his victims are all yonder in a pond, and you may see them there." The prince walked down to the spot to have a look at the dead bodies, and very great was his consternation when the severed heads laughed loud and long in his face and the trunks cut capers in the mud. He then returned to the maiden and sat long by her devising how to effect a rescue. Days and months passed away, and every day witnessed the prince and the maiden enjoying hours together in each other's company . . . but now the day arrived on which the prince was to go the way of his predecessors under the guardianship of the ascetic . . . In the evening, the *Tántrik* having finished the *puját* came home to fetch the prince. While following his guide the intended victim heard the roar of laughter that was proceeding from the pond, and arriving at the *ghát* he saw . . . the image of *Káli* . . . The prince paid his devotions to the goddess *standing* and prayed for strength. Scarcely had he finished when the *Tántrik* commanded him to prostrate himself before the altar. Thereupon he said, "I am the son of a king and do not know how to prostrate myself. Show me how to do it." The *Tántrik* complying, laid himself flat upon his breast on the ground. And no sooner had he done so than the prince seized the sacrificial sword, which was beside the altar, and at one stroke severed his head from his body. Just at that instant the trunkless heads in the pond laughed more clamorously than ever, and the maiden of the forest presented herself before the joyful gaze of her lover. To run to the pond with some handfuls of flowers and *bel* leaves from the altar and shower them upon the heads in the mud was for them the work of a minute. And behold! The dead rose from their miry beds and blessed their deliverers in the fullness of their hearts.[58]

In the *Mallinātha Caritra*, a prince named Ratnacandra saves a damsel in distress under similar conditions. While wandering in a forest, he hears her cries and discovers her bound hand and foot, with a skull-bearing yogi with upraised sword about to put her to death. Ratnacandra unsheathes his sword and slays the evil ascetic.[59] Other medieval tales describe the undoing of greedy yogis who change princes into serpents and attempt to sacrifice them, or who withhold jewelry left in their surety in order to realize their perfidious ends.[60] The theme of a prince outwitting a yogi of murderous intentions and of beheading him with his own sword is a standard fixture of Indic fantasy and adventure literature, as has been recorded in several medieval anthologies, the most famous being the frame story of the VP. In the Kashmiri author Somadeva's renowned 1070 CE *Kathāsaritsāgara* (KSS), the "Ocean of Rivers of Story," the frame narrative of this cycle of stories, recounted by a zombie-possessed corpse to the valiant King Trivikramasena, concludes when the king beheads an evil ascetic named Kṣāntaśīla, who had earlier attracted his attention by bearing a fruit-enclosed gem to his court every day for ten years. Following the zombie's instructions, the king asks Kṣāntaśīla to show him how to prostrate himself before an image of the "Master of Spells." When Kṣāntaśīla does so, Trivikramasena uses the ascetic's sword to cut off his head, offering it, together with the heart, to the *vetāla*.[61] While Somadeva's version of the frame narrative calls Kṣāntaśīla a Buddhist mendicant (*bhikṣu*) and, in one place, a *śramaṇa*,[62] Śivadāsa's eleventh- to fourteenth-century Kashmirian recension of the VP calls Kṣāntaśīla both a *digambara* and a yogi.[63] Still later, Jambhaladatta's fourteenth- to sixteenth-century Sanskrit version of the frame story calls Kṣāntaśīla a *kāpālika* ("skull bearer"), but in its conclusion, when Vikramāditya puts him to death, he is termed a yogi.[64] Similarly, an eighteenth- to nineteenth-century Nepali rendering of Kṣemendra's Sanskrit-language VP calls Kṣāntaśīla a *bhikṣuka* at the beginning of the frame narrative, but a yogi at the end.[65] The same is the case in certain Sanskrit-language "Jainistic recensions" of the SD's frame story, which ends with Vikramāditya flinging the evil yogi into the sacrificial fire that had been intended for the king himself. One may detect a pattern here, particularly in the earlier versions of this narrative. When Kṣāntaśīla is first introduced, a neutral term indicating an affiliation with a non-Hindu religious order (i.e., *śramaṇa*, *bhikṣu*, or *digambara*) is employed, whereas when he is unmasked for the villain that he is, he is called a yogi. This use of terminology is reflective, I would argue, of a situation in which independent yogis without allegiance to any particular religious or political institution were perceived as threatening to those very same institutions.[66]

A small group of relatively late Sanskrit recensions of the VP,[67] but especially the 1805 "vulgate" Hindustani edition of the *Baitāl Pachīsī*,[68] offers a sort of "prologue" to the original frame story, in which yogis figure prominently. Here is an abridgement of the *Baitāl Pachīsī* version of the prologue.

There was a city named Dhārānagar,[69] the king of which was Gandarbsen, who had six sons. When this king died, his eldest son, whose name was Śaṅk, became king in his stead. After some days, Bikram [Vikrama], his younger brother, having killed his elder brother, himself became king. He gradually became king of all of India and instituted an era, at which point his mind turned to travel: "I ought to visit those countries whose names I am hearing." Then, having committed the government to the charge of his younger brother Bhartṛhari, he became a jogi and began to travel from country to country. After Bikram had been gone for a time, Bhartṛhari, dissatisfied with the ways of the world, renounced the throne and became a jogi himself, leaving the kingdom without a ruler. When Bikram heard the news, he immediately returned to his own land. In the meantime, a godling (*dev*) sent by Indra had been standing guard over the city. Arriving at the city gates at midnight, Bikram was confronted by the *dev*, who challenged him. Bikram prevailed, but the *dev* requested that before he died, he be permitted to tell Bikram the following story:

"There was in this city a very generous king named Candrabhān. One day when walking in the jungle, he came upon an ascetic (*tapasvī*) suspended with his head downward, inhaling smoke from a fire. The king decreed that anyone who could bring that ascetic to his court would be awarded a bounty of 100,000 rupees. A courtesan declared that she would bring a child sired on her by the ascetic back to the court, and the king took her up on her promise. After some time, she seduced the ascetic, bore a son by him, and brought the child back to the royal court. Learning that he had been duped, the ascetic [now called a jogi] avenged himself by killing both the child and the king."

The *dev* concluded his story to Bikram with the statement: "In short, the history of the matter is that you three men were born in the same city, at the same moment, under the same star. You [Bikram] were born in the house of a king, the second son was born in the house of an oil-presser, and the third, the jogi, in the house of a potter. You have dominion in this kingdom. The oil-presser's son was ruler of the infernal regions. The potter, having performed his penance [of hanging upside down from a tree and inhaling smoke], and having killed the oil-presser, has turned him into a flesh-eater (*piśāc*) of the charnel-ground that he keeps suspended head-downwards from a mimosa tree. He is plotting your destruction." At this point, the *dev* departed and Bikram returned to his court. On the following day, a jogi named Śāntśīl [Kṣāntaśīla] came to the palace, bearing a fruit that was found to contain a precious gemstone.[70]

With this, we are brought back to the familiar territory of the frame narrative of the Sanskrit versions of the VP, which has Vikram depart for the charnel ground to meet his zombified "brother" at the behest of his other "brother," the villainous yogi Śāntśīl. A curious echo to this story is found in the late seventeenth-century *Khulāṣat-ut-Tawārīkh* of the Mughal historian Sujān Rāi Bhandārī, who evokes a legendary "yogi dynasty" that ruled from Delhi between the sixth and ninth centuries. According to this author, the dynasty was founded by a certain "Samandar Pāl Jogī," who slew "Bīr Bikrama" (the "hero Vikrama") to win the throne.[71]

The mention in this prologue of Bhartṛhari deserves further attention. The yogi singers whose songs Mahadevprasad Singh transcribed in the middle of the twentieth century have perennially belonged to a Muslim sect known as "Bhartṛhari Yogis," not for their practice of "yoga," but rather because many of their songs recount the legendary lives of the founders of the Nāth Yogī[72] orders, Bhartṛhari, his nephew Gopīcand, Gopīcand's guru Jalandharnāth, Gorakhnāth, and so on.[73] The songs of these yogi bards draw on a body of oral storytelling traditions concerning yogis and kings, yogis as kingmakers, and sometimes yogis as kings (or more properly speaking, kings as yogis). While their legends are quite distinct from those of the Vikrama Cycle, they converge on a certain number of themes, including that of the king or spy who puts on the garb of a yogi in order to travel incognito through foreign lands, a practice already attested in the circa third-century CE *Harivaṃśa* (HV) and *Arthaśāstra* (AŚ).[74] This is a theme that is found both in Newari- and Persian-language recensions of the SD.[75]

The Bhartṛhari Yogis' songs concerning King Bhartṛhari enshrine the same theme, found in the prologue to the 1805 Hindustani edition of the SD, of a king's renunciation of the throne and embrace of the yogi lifestyle due to world-weariness and disgust with the wiles of women.[76] In this prologue and other late recensions of the Vikrama Cycle, we see the grafting of this theme (which more properly belongs to the "yogi romance" subgenre of Mughal-period north Indian literature) onto the Vikrama Cycle, as Bhartṛhari is made out to be Vikrama's junior king.[77] There is a certain logic here, inasmuch as the legendary Vikrama and Bhartṛhari are both cast as kings of Ujjain in their respective legend cycles. Ujjain,[78] an important cradle of Hindu Tantra, is also closely linked to the origins of the god Bhairava, the fearsome god of the cremation ground located in the precincts of that city's great temple of Śiva-Mahākāla, and the divine prototype of tantric yogis like Bhairavānand.

Like Singh's *Bhairavānand Yogi*, the oral legend of Rājakumāra, recorded by Gérard Toffin in 1992, has also been adapted by a modern author into a published tale. In this case, the Nepali anthologist B. V. Adhikari incorporated the "Rājakumāra" narrative into the first half of his own *Prince Dikpāl*, a tale that he crafted out of both oral and written Newari, Nepali, and Hindi-language sources.[79] Here an added detail found in Adhikari's version is noteworthy: the yogi in the story is called *phusro*, a Nepali term that means "grayish" or "dried out." This likely corresponds to the term *dagdhasiddha* ("burnt-out siddha") used to qualify nefarious ascetics in the medieval Sanskrit-language *Daśakumāracarita* and other sources.[80]

2. Jougee-Eckbar

In the SB version of the Vikrama Cycle, the reader is informed that Vikrama's queens were viscerally repulsed by the yogi who had appropriated the body of their royal consort and so refused his amorous advances. The same language is found in the PC, which relates that the first time the false king entered the royal palace in Vikrama's body, he

> did nothing for those who craved his customary conversation or favors, because he did not know their names, business, or other circumstances . . . When they saw the king in this condition, they wondered: "Has some god or demon in the guise of the king taken possession of the vacant throne? . . . [When the false king was brought before the queen for the first time] the queen arose in confusion . . . [and] when she looked at the king again she fell to the ground as if in a faint . . . On hearing his voice she was greatly pained and thought: "He looks like my beloved, yet afflicts me as an enemy."[81]

In this telling, Vikrama—who has successively inhabited the bodies of an elephant, a parrot (in which he exchanges witticisms with his principal queen Kamalāvatī for a hundred verses, at the end of which she recognizes it to be none other than Vikrama), and a "house-lizard" (*gṛhagodhaka*)—recovers his own body, forgives the man who has betrayed him, and lives happily ever after.[82] Not all such narratives, however, end on this note. The KSS tells the story of a king of Pāṭalīputra named Nanda, a low-caste *śūdra* by birth, whose corpse is revived when a brahmin named Indradatta enters into it after leaving his own body behind. Indradatta is a yogi in everything but name who, at the moment he enters into Nanda's body, is described as *yogasiddhimān*, "possessed of the supernatural power of yoga." Furthermore, once the body of Nanda has been reanimated through Indradatta's appropriation of it, the narrator of the story changes the king's name—presumably for the reader's comprehension—from the original Nanda to Yogananda, "Nanda by Means of Yoga."[83] In this tale, however, a royal minister discerns what has in fact transpired and, in order to keep the king alive, has every corpse in the kingdom incinerated, including the uninhabited body of Indradatta.[84] The brahmin Indradatta, trapped in the *śūdra* body of King (Yoga-)nanda, proves to be a vicious and libidinous tyrant and is eventually put to death through a stratagem devised by the same royal minister who had his corpse burned in the first place.[85] A number of Buddhist sources tell a similar story of a king's dead body being revived when it has been entered, in this case by a dryad (*yakṣa*) named Devagarbha.[86] A detail of this story is worth noting: the king in question is identified as the historical Candragupta (fl. 321—297 BCE), the founder of the Maurya Dynasty.[87]

Another great Indian emperor is said to have undergone a similar transformation. The Mughal emperor Akbar's (fl. 1556–1605) well-known penchant for religious experimentation extended to a period of dalliance with the yogis of his empire, which began in the year 1584. As William Pinch has noted in his remarkable book, *Warrior Ascetics and Indian Empires*, rumors of Akbar's fascination with the yogis reached the ears of the British as well, whence the account that John Marshall of the East India Company recorded in his journals sixty-five years after the emperor's death, under the title of "Jougee-Eckbar."

According to "the Moores" who recounted it for him, during Akbar's reign there was said to have lived a yogi who could fly through the air with the aid of a pellet of quicksilver that he held in his mouth.[88] One day, en route to the shrine of Jagannath in Orissa, this yogi chanced to alight on the terrace of the emperor's harem for a nap. While the yogi slept the pellet of quicksilver slipped from his mouth. Akbar chanced by, sized up the situation, and seized the pellet. When the yogi awoke, he assured the emperor he had not meddled with his women and begged him to return the quicksilver, without which he could not fly. The emperor demurred, demanding instead that the yogi teach him a few tricks. The yogi agreed and offered to put his soul into any living creature. Akbar had a deer brought forth, upon which the yogi demonstrated. Apparently unconvinced, the emperor requested that his own soul be put into the deer. The yogi complied with the request and then brought the emperor back into his own body. Akbar was so frightened by the power of the yogi that he quietly ordered his guards to kill him. The order was duly carried out but afterwards people began noticing a change in the emperor's demeanor.[89]

To quote Marshall, "Immediately after [the execution of the yogi] the King was extreamely altered, and all his life long after lived a retired life, which was for about 10 or 11 yeares, and as to all his disposition hee was perfectly altered, and any that went to him would not have knowne by his discourse or actings that hee was the same man as before. So that the Moores say That when hee ordered the Jougee to be killed, that the Jougee changed soules with the King, so that it was the Kings soule that was gone, and the Jougees soule remained in the King."[90]

The plot of another narrative from the same period also turns on a yogi's power to enter another body, or at least take on another person's appearance.[91] In the first book of his circa 1574 *Rām Carit Mānas* (RCM), the renowned poet-saint Tulsīdās tells the tale of a meeting between a king named Pratāpbhānu and another king who had earlier been deposed by him and who was now living in the forest in the guise of a hermit.[92] When Pratāpbhānu asked him who he was, he cryptically answered that his name was "Beggar" and later that he was "One Body."[93] Seeking his revenge on Pratāpbhānu, the false hermit (*kapaṭ muni*) seized upon a subterfuge that would bring him down. Alone in the forest, Pratāpbhānu confided that his fondest desire was to die of old age, to which the ascetic replied that as a powerful king, he had nothing to fear in that quarter apart from the curse of an angry brahmin. However, he added, through the powers he had gained through "yoking to yoga" (*jog juguti*), asceticism (*tap*), and spells,[94] he was capable of preparing food, which, when eaten by the brahmins of his kingdom, would bring them under the king's power. He then explained the way in which he would enter, unobserved, into the king's palace: "I will never come [to your palace] in this form. Using my wizardry (*māyā*), I'll carry off your royal chaplain and bring him here, and keep him here for an entire year. By the power of my asceticism (*tap bal*), I'll make him look just like me, whilst I take on his appearance to take care of all the arrangements!"[95]

Soon after, the false hermit transported the sleeping Pratāpbhānu back to his palace. Then "he took the king's chaplain and carried him off, and using his wizardry to confuse his mind, placed him inside a mountain cave. Then, constructing a chaplain's body of his own, he went [to the palace] and lay in his [the chaplain's] matchless bed."[96] Now, with the king fully in his clutches, the false hermit could wreak his vengeance. He prepared a meal for the brahmins of the kingdom, mixing in the flesh of animals and—o horror!—the flesh of a brahmin, using his wizardry to mask their flavors. The brahmins sat down to enjoy their meal, but before they began to eat, a heavenly voice warned them of the meal's secret ingredients, upon which they cursed King Pratāpbhānu, whose entire lineage was destroyed. While it is the case that Tulsīdās never calls the villain of this piece a yogi, but rather a false hermit, one can readily recognize him as a yogi through his modus operandi. It is also noteworthy that on two occasions, Tulsīdās refers to him as a "Nāth," a moniker that would have been, in his world, a synonym for yogi.[97]

3. The King and the Corpse:[98] Variations on a Theme

It will be recalled that in the SB, a translation of the SD commissioned by Akbar, a yogi takes over a king's body at the moment when the king has experimentally entered into the body of a fawn. As such, the Jougee-Eckbar story told by "Moores" (i.e., Muslims) to John Marshall in 1670 may have been nothing more than an Akbar-ization of a well-known tale. It also speaks to a piece of yogi lore reported in the AŚ, Kauṭilya's classic work on statecraft: in their roles as spies and agents provocateurs, these arch outsiders could infiltrate royal harems or crime rings through the promise of providing their members with love potions or invisibility salves.[99]

Other kings of South Asian history and legend have been subject to fates similar to Akbar's in Marshall's account. One such king was Mān Singh, who was placed on the throne of Marwar at Jodhpur (Rajasthan) in 1803 through the miraculous intervention of a Nāth Yogī named Āyas Dev Nāth. Six years later, shortly after Āyas Dev Nāth had been put to death through a piece of court intrigue, Mān Singh was reported to have fallen into "a state of mental despondency bordering on insanity," during which time he abandoned his palace and throne to live the life of a yogi, dressed in yogi garb, with hair and beard uncut and unkempt.[100] Dan Gold has offered a sensitive psychological analysis of the king's depression;[101] however, in light of the preceding, it may not be out of place to diagnose the king's insanity as a symptom of yogic possession: following his power-brokering yogi's death, the king was perhaps no longer himself because someone else (Āyas Dev Nāth) was inhabiting his body.

Such is the explicit diagnosis of another king's altered behavior, as described in a number of hagiographies of Śaṅkara (fl. 788–820 CE), the great commentator, Advaita Vedānta philosopher, and apocryphal founder of the Dasnāmi orders,[102] whose philosophical "conquests of the four directions" imitated the royal conquests of the heroes of the MBh and the Vikrama Cycle.[103] While there are over thirty extant hagiographies of Śaṅkara, few have been edited. Of these, three tell the same story of Śaṅkara's takeover of the body of a king named Amaruka: these are the circa fourteenth-century *Śaṅkaradigvijaya* (ŚDV) of Mādhava-Vidyāraṇya,[104] the circa fifteenth-century *Śaṅkaravijaya* (ŚV) of Anantānandagiri,[105] and the circa 1850 *Śaṅkaramandarasaurabha* (ŚMS) of Nīlakaṇṭha.[106] What follows is a synopsis combining material from all three of these versions of the tale.[107]

After he had defeated Maṇḍana Miśra in a debate, Bharatī, the latter's wife, challenged Śaṅkara of her own accord. When she began to question him about the arts of love (*kāmakalā*) and other matters about which he, as a celibate renouncer, was unschooled, he requested that their debate be postponed for several months. He then journeyed with his disciples to a city in which the king, named Amaruka, had died, and employing the "science of entering into the body of another" (*parakāyapraveśavidyā*), he revived the body of the king, which was lying on the funeral pyre. "The yogic power (*yogabalam*) of the teacher, which was joined to his subtle body, entered the body of the king, and that connoisseur of yoga (*yogavit*) guided his breath upward from the toes. Leaving his body via the fontanel, he slowly entered the body of the dead king via the king's fontanel . . ." Then the king stood up, just as he had been before his death.[108] As for Śaṅkara's own body, he entrusted it to the safekeeping of his disciples, who watched over it in a nearby mountain cave. Reanimated by Śaṅkara's presence, the body of King Amaruka rose from its funeral pyre, and within it, Śaṅkara quickly mastered the erotic arts through extended love-play with the principal queen.[109] Meanwhile, his disciples, alarmed that their guru had been waylaid by the sensual life of a king, prepared his abandoned body for cremation. Following this, they came to the royal court in the guise of a dancing troop whose songs of nondualist wisdom awakened Śaṅkara from his stupor. He abandoned the king's body and re-entered his own, which was lying on the already ignited pyre, just in the nick of time.

A number of details from the ŚV and ŚDV versions of this story are worthy of note. In the former, it is said that after he had mastered the arts of love with Amaruka's queen, Śaṅkara went on to "extend his power (*balam*) in every direction, inhabiting lifeless bodies wherever he found them on the earth."[110] This accords with a passage from the MBh on the powers of yogis, which the commentator Śaṅkara quotes on two occasions in his commentary on the *Brahma Sūtras* (BrSūBh). I will return to this passage in chapter four.[111] The ŚDV contains a narrative element that we have already seen in accounts from the Vikrama Cycle as well as the "Jougee-Eckbar" story. Royal ministers, noting a significant change (in this case, for the better) in Amaruka's statecraft, deduce that it is no longer their king at all who is ruling the kingdom, but rather that "someone possessed of mastery (*prāptaiśvarya*), having entered the body of our king, is ruling the earth."[112] They thereafter issue a proclamation that all unburned corpses in the kingdom be destroyed, in order that the new inhabitant of Amaruka's body not return to the body he has left behind.

It is, however, only in the nineteenth-century ŚMS (4.52) that the king's ministers call the unknown usurper of Amaruka's dead body a "great yogi" (*mahāyogī*). The same source is unique among the three versions of this story in its evocation, at the point at which Śaṅkara's disciples disguise themselves as a dancing troop to penetrate their guru's court, of a parallel episode from the life of the Nāth Yogī–turned king, Matsyendranāth. This account, which is found in two seventeenth-century Bengali Nāth Yogī romances, the *Gorakṣa Vijaya* and *Mīn Cetan*, as well as the western India *Yogisampradayāviṣkṛti* (attributed to the late thirteenth-century Jñāneśvara), has the celibate Matsyendranāth entering into the body of a king named Trivikrama—the sole male in a Kingdom of Women (*strīrājya*)—in order to experience the sensual life. In this case, however, Matsyendra becomes totally debauched by Queen Kamalā and her female entourage and completely forgets his original self. Furthermore, Kamalā has discovered his original body and chopped it into pieces, barring his return.[113] His disciple Gorakhnāth, alerted to his guru's quandary, takes on the appearance of a woman, engages himself in a female dancing troop, and enters the court to find his guru in a swoon at death's door. The music begins, and when Gorakh plays the first beat on his two-headed drum, it sings out "Awaken, Matsyendra, Gorakh has come!" Upon hearing the drumbeat,[114] Matsyendra emerges from his stupor and Gorakhnāth spirits him away to safety. Then, with the help of a female dryad (*yakṣiṇī*) who has reconstituted Matsyendranāth's butchered body and placed it atop Mount Kailāś for safekeeping, Gorakhnāth effects the transfer of his guru from the body of the king back into his own.[115] Although most of the picaresque details of Matsyendranāth's misadventures in King Trivikrama's body are not present in the ŚV and ŚDV versions of Śaṅkara's less harrowing foray into King Amaruka's body, Nīlakaṇṭha's evocation of Matsyendranāth's rescue indicates that he was unaware that the yogi prototype of his own ŚMS account was none other than Śaṅkara himself![116] This subterfuge of a group of persons disguising themselves as a dancing troupe to enter into a royal court is another theme adapted by Singh in his *Bhairavānand Yogī*.

Śaṅkara's extant hagiographies, all of which were compiled several centuries after his death, depict his life as a series of victories over proponents of rival doctrines, victories that he won through his debating skill as well as superior displays of supernatural powers. In two of these clashes, his nefarious adversaries are termed yogis and their practice "the magical power of yoga" (*yoga-māyā*) precisely when they attempt to slay the great teacher.[117] If we are to take the narrative ordering and relative length of the accounts of his clashes with his sectarian adversaries as an indication of the relative importance of the latter, then it was the Śaivas who were Śaṅkara's greatest rivals. The names of these sects are listed at the beginning of the fourth chapter of the ŚV: they are the Śaivas, Raudras, Ugras, Bhaṭṭas, Jaṅgamas, and Pāśupatas.[118] Of all of these, it is the last group listed, the Pāśupatas, who were by far the most important Śaiva religious order in the post-Gupta period. Already mentioned in a late portion of the MBh,[119] the Pāśupatas were responsible for the composition or recomposition of several Purāṇas in the centuries that followed.[120] Their institutional presence is widely documented in nearly one hundred medieval inscriptions attesting to lands, monasteries, and temples donated to or administered by the Pāśupatas between the fifth and twelfth centuries CE.[121]

Doctrinally, the Pāśupatas took the yogic god Śiva to be their model, and accordingly, yoga was defined by them as the union or contact of the individual soul with god, by virtue of which the human practitioner partook of the attributes—that is, the eight supernatural powers or "masteries" (*aiśvaryam*)—of the Great Master (Maheśvara).[122] In *all* of the tantric systems that follow—Śaiva, Vaiṣṇava, Śākta, Buddhist, and Jain—this is the reading of yoga that remains operative: yoga is a soteriological system that culminates in union or identity with a supreme being. Accordingly, yogis are persons whose religious vocation is the quest for such a union or identity, including the power to enter into, to permeate, the creator's every creature. Pāśupata yoga is illustrated in a story from the VP concerning a certain Vāmaśiva, a Pāśupata "Lord of Yoga," who, in imitation of Śiva, enters into the body of a youthful brahmin corpse on a cremation ground.[123]

In the . . . cremation ground there lived an old yogi of the Pāśupata sect . . . [who] was like a second Maheśvara[124] . . . A young brahmin had been brought to the cremation ground for burning. When the yogi saw the being that the crowd was mourning, that barely adolescent body, he resolved to enter into it, weary as he was of his own great age. He quickly went to an isolated spot and, shouting with all his might, began to dance with the appropriate gestures and postures. At that moment, the ascetic (*tapasvin*), abandoning his own body out of a desire for youthfulness, thereupon entered into the corpse of the brahmin boy by means of yoga (*yogāt*). At that moment, the young brahmin, revived, arose from the heaped up pyre and began to yawn.[125]

The technique behind Vāmaśiva's takeover of the brahmin boy's body is theorized, in another tale from the KSS, by none other than the mighty titan (*asura*) Maya, who, in this narrative, has risen up out of the ground to offer himself as an ally to a king named Candraprabha. Shortly thereafter, Maya also informs Candraprabha that he (Candraprabha) is none other than his (Maya's) own son, a titan by the name of Sunītha, and that Candraprabha's son, the prince Sūryaprabha, is in fact Candraprabha-Sunītha's younger brother, whose titan name is Sumuṇḍika. In an earlier time, he explains, both of Maya's titan sons had been slain in battle against the gods, but their father had preserved their corpses by anointing them with magic herbs and clarified butter. Now he orders Candraprabha and Sūryaprabha to descend into Pātāla, the subterranean titan realm, to recover their original bodies, through whose power they will be able to defeat all of their enemies.[126] Hearing this, Candraprabha is thrilled, but his minister Siddhārtha is troubled.

"What becomes of the one who has entered into another body, and what happens to the one who has died? What can we hold onto in this confusion? And will he [the king], once he has taken refuge in that other body, not forget us in the same way that a person who has gone to the world beyond [forgets]? Who is he and who are we?" Maya replies: "You must come there [to Pātāla] and see him before your very eyes as he freely enters into that body, by means of the strategem of yoga (*yogayuktitas*). He will not forget you. Listen to the reason why: The person who does not die of his own free will and who is then reborn in another womb remembers nothing. [His past] is concealed from him by his afflictions, death, etc. But the person who, through the strategem of yoga, freely enters into the body of another and penetrates his consciousness (*antaḥkaraṇa*) and his external senses, with his own mind and intellect intact, as if he were going from house to house: such a knower is a Master of Yoga (*yogeśvara*), [who] immediately recalls everything [concerning the person he was in the body that he has left behind]."[127]

The following day, Candraprabha and all of his royal allies go down to the confluence of the Candrabhaga and Irrawady rivers. Following Maya, Candraprabha descends into a fissure in the water (*vivaraṃ toye*), accompanied by Sūryaprabha. After a long road, they come to a wondrous temple. There, Maya tells the king that he will instruct him in the yoga that affords the power of entering into other bodies (*yogam anyadehapraveśadam*) . . . and when he has finished, that king of yogis (*yogīndra*) intones, "This is the supernatural power (*siddhi*)! This knowledge [of entering into other bodies] is [like] a house [inhabited by] autonomy (*svātantryam*), mastery (*aiśvaryam*), minuteness, and the other [supernatural powers]."[128]

Then Maya led him into a second underworld and ushered him and his son and companions into a wondrous abode. Once inside, they all saw the massive body of a man lying, as if asleep, on an enormous bed. He was anointed with powerful herbs and clarified butter, and his altered appearance was terrifying. The daughters of that titan king surrounded the body, their lotus faces downcast. "This is your body, surrounded by your former wives. Enter!" said Maya to Candraprabha. The king, practicing the yoga that had been taught by him, abandoned his own body and entered into the body of the man. The man lying on the bed rose up, as if awakening from sleep, and yawning, slowly opened his eyes. And the cry arose from the rejoicing titan widows: "Thanks be to heaven! Today our lord Sunītha has been revived." But when they saw the fallen lifeless body of Candraprabha, Sūryaprabha and all the others were suddenly crestfallen. But when Candraprabha-Sunītha—who was as if awoken from a sound sleep—saw Maya, he fell at his father's feet and praised him. Embracing him, he [Maya] asked him in front of everyone, "My son! Can you now recall your two lives?" "Yes! I remember!" and he told them what had happened in his birth as Candraprabha and his birth as Sunītha. Calling out to each of them by name, he consoled his queens, Sūryaprabha, and the others, as well as his former titan wives. As a foundation for his dual sovereignty, he had the body in which he had been born consigned to a safe place, [preserving it] in a compound of various potions, saying "Some day it could come in handy."[129]

4. The Yogi and the Courtesan

This type of yoga is explicitly ascribed to Śaiva sources in the *Bhagavadajjukīya* (BA),[130] a seventh-century South Indian farce whose wandering ascetic protagonist, referring to traditions received by Śaiva masters of yoga, observes that "the culmination of yogic practice is the vision of past, present, and future and the attainment of mastery in the form of the eight supernatural powers."[131] The plot of the BA, the "Tale of the Saint-Courtesan," turns on cascading cases of mistaken identity and the practice of yoga, which is defined in the play in a way reminiscent of the Pāśupatas.[132] Pivotal to the plot is an error on the part of a minion of the death god Yama, who has carried off a young courtesan named Vasantasenā instead of another woman by the same name, whose time had truly come. When he provokes Vasantasenā's untimely death through the bite of a venomous snake, her sudden demise is witnessed by an unnamed "wanderer" (*parivrājaka*) and his blockheaded disciple Śāṇḍilya, a dropout from a Buddhist monastery. Seizing upon her death as a pedagogical opportunity, the *parivrājaka*, evoking traditions received by "Maheśvara and the other masters of yoga," decides that he will improve the mind of his young charge and show him that "this is what yoga is all about: I will yoke myself onto the body of this courtesan."[133] Following this, he yogically (*yogena*) enters into the young woman's corpse, at which point his own body becomes lifeless. Enter Vasantasenā's maidservant, mother, and lover (named Rāmilaka), and the plot veers into the realm of screwball comedy.

Rāmilaka, speaking sweet nothings into the ear of his beloved is suddenly rebuffed by the *parivrājaka*'s voice, which tells him to keep his hands off his sari hem. No fool, Rāmilaka justly observes that some other being has introduced itself into Vasantasenā's powerless body.[134] Now Yama's emissary returns to the scene and quickly realizes his error and the confusion it and the *parivrājaka*'s yoga have already caused.

> What is this? This venerable wanderer of a yogi has been having some fun! What am I to do now? I've got it! First I'll put this courtesan's soul into the *parivrājaka*'s body, and then, once I've yoked each to their proper place, my work will be done![135]

However, as soon as Vasantasenā has been revived in the body of the wandering ascetic, she begins immediately to behave like "herself" and to speak through the mouth of the elderly man: "Where, oh where is my Rāmilaka?" "Give me a hug, Rāmilaka!" "I'm getting tipsy from this hooch!" "I'm going to have a little drinky-poo!"[136] Consternation reigns and is compounded by the arrival of a bumbling ayurvedic physician, whose diagnosis is contradicted by the voice of the *parivrājaka*, speaking through the mouth of the courtesan. Yama's emissary returns for a final time and, taking the "courtesan" aside, appeals: "Excellency! Release the body of this low-caste whore!" This the yogi does, and with everyone himself again the farce is at its end.

Two points are to be retained here. The first is that the plot of this play of mistaken identities is driven by yoga. Even before the *parivrājaka* demonstrates the practice of yoga to his disciple Śāṇḍilya, his attempts to instruct the young man (whose mind is truly a blunt instrument) have focused on the nature, practice, and goals of yoga. This is a play about yoga, which is, in terms of practice, nothing other than the yoking of another person's dead body with one's own self (*ātman*). The second is that the appellation of the unnamed protagonist of the play is itself significant. A widely attested aphorism links the *parivrājaka* to another practitioner of "yoga," "These are the two people in this world who pierce the solar disk: the wanderer (*parivrāḍ*) and the *yogayukta* [warrior] who is slain [while] facing [his enemies] on the field of battle."[137] I offer an extended discussion of the compound *yogayukta* in the next chapter. *Paribbājaka*, the Pali cognate of the Sanskrit *parivrāḍ/parivrājaka*, is the term employed in the original Buddhist canon to refer to non-vedic ascetics, and it should be recalled that in the BA, Śāṇḍilya is cast as a former Buddhist monk. One of the earliest *dharmasūtras*, the circa third-century BCE *Āpastamba Dharma Sūtra* (ĀpDhSū), classifies *parivrājakas* together with *vānaprasthins* as renouncers whose goal is liberation from rebirth. However, it condemns the *parivrājaka* style of asceticism as counter to the vedic teachings.[138] This negative assessment is echoed in the Buddhist *Dīgha Nikaya*, in which the Buddha reproaches the *paribbājakas* for their infatuation with asceticism and self-importance.[139]

5. The Yogi Who Came to Dinner

One of the most popular stories in all of south India is that of "The Little Devotee," which comprises a chapter in a twelfth-century Tamil scripture, the *Periya Purāṇam*, and also appears in two Telugu stories from the thirteenth and fifteenth centuries, in medieval sculpture, and in modern-day oral traditions. An Islamic variant also exists, involving a deified fakir named Mānik Pīr.[140] My summary of the story is adapted from George Hart's exquisite 1979 English translation.

In the town of Kaṇapattīccaram there lived a man named Parañcoti whose devoted hospitality toward the servants of Lord Śiva was so great that he came to be known as the Little Devotee (Ciruttoṇṭar). Every day, the Little Devotee would, together with his wife, prepare and offer delicious food to all who came to the temple of his god. Through the grace of the great god, a son named Cīrālan was born to them, and father and mother doted upon him in every way. In time, word of the Little Devotee's service reached Śiva, the Lord who dwells on Mount Kailāś. His heart disposed to grace, the god put on the guise of a Bhairava ascetic, wearing ashes and ornaments of bone on his lovely coral body and carrying the skull of Brahmā and the two-headed *tamaruka* drum in his hands. Acting as if he were insatiably hungry, he came to the home of the Little Devotee. Yet, when the Little Devotee offered to feed him, he said: "It is not possible to feed me. You cannot do it. It is impossible." Still, the Little Devotee insisted, to which the Bhairava ascetic replied that the sole food he would deign to have prepared for him should consist of the perfect body of a human child under the age of five. "It must be a good child in a good family, an only son. The father must cut it as the mother holds it, and both must rejoice in their hearts. Then if they make a curry, I will eat it." The Little Devotee conferred with his wife, and they decided to kill and cook their only son Cīrālan for the mysterious ascetic from the north. The Little Devotee then went to bring his son back home from school. Back at home, he and his wife bathed the child, dressed him in his finest clothes, and took him to a hidden place in their house. The beloved child, thinking, "They are very joyful," laughed happily, and the father cut off the head of his only son with a knife. Leaving the head aside, the Little Devotee's wife butchered the child, took out the marrow after opening the bones, and put everything in the pot; and grinding the spices needed for a curry, she added them, anxious to prepare it quickly. When the meal was ready, the Little Devotee went outside and bade that the Bhairava ascetic come and eat in his home. But when the meal had been served, the ascetic insisted that he be offered the head as well, and so it was made into a separate curry dish for him. When the head had been brought, the ascetic said graciously, "We cannot eat here alone. Invite some servants of the lord who may happen to be nearby." But when the Little Devotee went outside, he found no one, and so the Bhairava ascetic insisted that he share the meal with him. And then, as the Little Devotee was about to eat the flesh of his son, the ascetic stopped him. "You have a faultless son. Summon him." The Little Devotee could not bear it. Saying, "What can we do to make our lord eat here?" he arose and went with his wife to call to their son. By the grace of the Highest One, that unequalled son of faultless beauty came as if he were running home from school. The Little Devotee took his child in his arms and returned, wishing to feed their guest. But the Lord who had become a Bhairava ascetic had disappeared. Distressed, the Little Devotee and his wife came outside and He who had disappeared returned, now together with his wife Pārvatī and his son Skanda, his topknot swaying with the cool white moon—and the divine family raised up the Little Devotee and his family to remain with them forever.[141]

Whereas the devotional aspect of this south Indian narrative has been probed and analyzed in detail by a number of scholars,[142] the person of the ascetic whom the god Śiva impersonates in the story has not. When Śiva decides to visit Ciruttoṇṭar, he "disguises" himself as a *vairavar*, a "Bhairava (ascetic)," which is, as David Shulman has noted, a double mimesis: Śiva posing as a living, human replica of himself in his skull-bearer (*kāpālika*) form.[143] As we will have the occasion to observe in greater detail in chapter five, Śiva's Bhairava disguise is pleonastic on another register. In Hindu and Buddhist Tantra, the divine prototype of the tantric yogi is, precisely, the god Bhairava, or, put another way, the divinity whom the tantric yogi imitates in his *imitatio dei*—and it should be recalled here that the goal of many tantric practitioners is to *become* the god himself—is Bhairava.[144] This play, between the Bhairava persona of the supreme god Śiva on the one hand and that of the tantric yogi on the other, is made explicit in Telugu versions of the Little Devotee narrative. The fourteenth- to fifteenth-century Śrīnātha's poetic compendium of Śaiva myths, the *Haravilāsamu*, opens with the story of the Little Devotee.[145] In Śrīnātha's Telugu-language retelling, while father and son are in complete agreement concerning Śiva's cooking program, the Little Devotee's wife, Tiruveṅganāñci, receives a visit from the goddess Pārvatī herself who tests her, saying:

"People everywhere, in all the lanes and alleys, are saying that you're about to kill your son for the sake of some evil yogi (*durnirvāṇi*). You know these yogis—they'll do anything for the sake of gaining powers . . . It isn't right to kill a child. If a person puts even a tiny bit of sacred ash on his body, he gets crazy as a pumpkin." But Tiruveṅganāñci pays her no heed. "There is no difference between Śiva and the Śiva yogi.[146]

When the child is at last brought home from school, and his parents remind him that his body will be cooked in order to feed "a certain Bhairava yogi who follows the Pāśupata vow," he replies, "I am happy to become food for that false yogi, that Śiva."[147] These medieval south Indian stories—which, it must be noted, are to be counted among the most popular narrative expressions of Hindu devotion and family values of their time—take as given the assumption that wandering Śaiva ascetics, called Bhairavas or yogis, were inclined to eat children.

Who were these cannibalistic yogis? Mere stock villains of medieval South India, or something more? In his account of his travels through Asia and Africa during the second quarter of the fourteenth century, Ibn Baṭṭūṭa describes the predations of a "Joki" (yogi) in the north Indian town of Parwan:[148]

In the surroundings of the city there are many voracious animals. One of its inhabitants related to me that a lion used to break into the city in the night although the gates were closed and that he used to molest the people, so much that he killed many . . . [O]ne night the lion broke into [a] house and carried away a boy from his bed . . . Curiously enough, some one told me that he who did so was not the lion but a man of the magician class called "Joki" who assumed the form of a lion . . . Some of the Jokis are such that as soon as they look at a man the latter instantly falls dead. The common people say that in such a case—of a man being killed by a mere look—if his chest were cut open one could see no heart which, they say, is eaten up. Such is, for the most part, the practice with women, and the woman who acts in this manner is called a "hyena" (*kaftār*).[149]

The literal meaning of the term *kaftār* is "a hyena that digs up and devours dead bodies." This would therefore appear to be a description of a *yoginī* (*jognī* in many north Indian vernaculars), one of the predatory witches and shape-changers who are the female counterparts of the dire yogis described in this passage, as well as in Singh's *Bhairavānand Yogī*.

The eighteenth-century "Chritro Pakhyān" tells a similar story, which combines themes from the adventures of King Békermadjiet, as told in the *SB*.

An ascetic yogi used to live in a thick jungle and he was known in the world as Chetak Nāth. He took one person every day from the village to eat and, due to this, everybody dreaded him. There also lived a queen by the name of Katach Kumārī whose fame had spread all over. She was the prettiest [woman] in the world; she could recite the Vedas and the Shastras. Her husband also feared the yogi [who] took away one person every day. One day the Rānī [Queen] asked, "Listen, my Rāja, you are as sacred to me as my soul. Why should we not take some steps to kill the yogi and save our lives as well? Then the Rānī [carried out her plan] like this: She put on precious attire, collected plenty of sacrificial material and at midnight traveled to the yogi. First of all, she served him dainty dishes and then gave him lots of wine to drink. Then she said, "I have come to exchange thought[s] with you. The way you eat men, please disclose it to me. And then, after that . . . you may make love." When the yogi heard this, he . . . rejoiced. "I [have] never had such an opportunity in my life, neither [on] earth nor in the heavens." He abruptly stood up and wrapped the Rānī around him . . . The cauldron [in which the yogi prepared his victims] was ready [nearby], and he went around [it]. The Rānī followed him and then suddenly pushed him in and he was burnt alive. She saved herself and [scorched] the yogi, and through this trick she saved the Rāja's subject[s].[150]

In this chapter, we have surveyed a body of literature spanning more than a millennium, from the seventh-century BA to Singh's mid-twentieth-century *qissā*. What can we learn from these narratives? In a seminal 1924 article written on the subject of "false ascetics and nuns in Hindu fiction," Maurice Bloomfield reduced the sinister yogis of the Vikrama Cycle to stock characters within a medieval literary trope. Fred Smith has taken much the same position in his recent encyclopedic monograph on possession, when he argues with reference to the account of Śaṅkara and King Amaruka that

this kind of yogic possession . . . is part of a tradition of yoga and a tradition of textuality. If it was ever more than a hagiographical instantiation of yogic lore, it was doubtless employed sparingly . . . nor was it embraced in any popular or festival context. Thus, it is perhaps little more than a textual and narrative oddity, albeit one with a background

> of intertextuality and a foundation in the popular spiritual imagination . . . What could be normative in literature—for example, possession, asceticism, or starvation—was surely extreme or radical in the world.[151]

While there can be no doubt that the south Asian yogi does indeed stand as the Indic homologue of the villainous evil wizard of Western fairy tales, and that his behavior often borders on the inhuman or the monstrous in these narratives, I would suggest that these were not mere literary fixtures. But this is beside the main point that I—and I believe these stories—wish to make, which concerns the nature of the yogi's practice. In the great majority of these stories, characters are identified as yogis precisely when they undertake to enter into or take over the bodies of other creatures. If this is the sine qua non of a yogi's practice, and if the term yogi is, grammatically, a possessive form of "yoga," then what has been the meaning of the term "yoga" for all of these centuries? Put another way, why is it that not a single yogi in these narratives is ever seen assuming a yogic posture (*āsana*); controlling his breath, senses, and mind; engaging in meditation (*dhyāna*); or realizing transcendent states of consciousness (*samādhi*)—all of the practices of what has been deemed "classical yoga"? If these be yogis, then what is yoga?

TWO

Ceci n'est pas un Yogi

1. Yoga and Viyoga

Surveying the history of both Indian and Western interpretations of yoga, one is struck by the absence of reflection on the cognitive dissonance that appears to be operative when the primary sense of the term yoga itself—which means "union," "joining," "junction"—is interpreted to mean its opposite, *viyoga*, which means "separation," "disunion," "disjunction."[1] The prime sources for this reading are not far to seek; they are the 200–400 CE *Bhagavad Gītā* (BhG) of the MBh and commentaries on the 350–450 CE *Yoga Sūtras* (YS), the "Aphorisms on Yoga" attributed to Patañjali.[2] Among the multiple accounts of yoga presented in these two works, those that have received the greatest attention, that have been most championed by later commentators and scholars, are those that privilege a disengagement of the senses, mind, and intellect from the outside world in favor of concentration on the transcendent person within, be it named *puruṣa, brahman,* or Kṛṣṇa. Yet, as we saw in the previous chapter, accounts of yogis, presumptive agents of yoga, *never* portray their practice as introversive or introspective—but rather always as extrovert, if not predatory.

In chapter three, I will reconstruct the vicissitudes in the history of ideas that transformed what were the most ancient forms of yogic practice, as described in vedic, epic and medieval narrative, into the principles promulgated in the philosophical corpus today identified as "classical yoga." The present chapter will be devoted to deconstructing a number of the modernist assumptions that have undergirded the great majority of colonial and postcolonial accounts of the history of yoga, assumptions that have cast aside a massive body of yoga theory and practice found not only in medieval narratives of sinister yogis but also in the foundational texts of "classical yoga" themselves. The reef upon which many of these modernist constructions have stranded themselves is the notion that the BhG and YS were capstone works, literary culminations of an unbroken and unchanging tradition of yogic theory and practice extending back to, if not beyond, the Vedas of the second millennium BCE. In fact, these are works that were compiled toward the end of a five-hundred-year period in which a new synthesis of theory and practice, sometimes referred to as "yoga," was very much in vogue throughout South Asia. In this respect, these were capstone works, but only for the relatively limited time frame of the centuries around the beginning of the common era. The semantic fields of terms like *dhyāna, dhāraṇā, nirodha, samādhi,* and *yoga* were very much in flux throughout this period, a period in which the newly minted doctrines of Sāṃkhya, Buddhism, and the new Hindu theism were being combined in new and creative ways, as evidenced in these seminal works themselves. Prior to these two texts, the rare theoretical treatments of yoga per se that had appeared in a very limited number of Upaniṣads and the circa 450–350 BCE ĀpDhSū were sketchy at best.[3] This is not to say that there had been no preexisting bodies of practice known as "yoga" prior to the earliest upanishadic discussions found in the third to first century BCE *Kaṭha Upaniṣad* (KU) or the later *Śvetāśvatara Upaniṣad* (ŚvU) and *Maitri Upaniṣad* (MU).[4] There were, and it is precisely these bodies of practice that I will excavate in this and the following two chapters.

These ancient practices bore only a limited resemblance to the variety of yogas theorized in the BhG and YS. In fact, the most salient area of overlap between prior traditions of yoga practice and the yoga of these two texts falls under the heading of *vibhūti,* a term I will translate throughout this book as "omni-presencing" (from the Latin *omni* plus *praes-ens,* "being in the forefront in every [being]"). *Vibhūti* is the title of the third book (*pada*) of the YS, which, devoted to the supernatural powers of yogis (including the power to enter into other people's bodies), has historically been the least studied portion of the YS, in spite of the fact that it comprises over one fourth of the entire work. In the BhG, *vibhūti yoga* is the term employed to describe the yoga that the god Kṛṣṇa practices (as opposed to the yoga he preaches) when he reveals his universal form (*viśvarūpa*), thereby showing that his supreme person (*puruṣottama*) is simultaneously the one in the many (individual *puruṣa*s or *ātman*s) and the many in the one.

In distinction to the *vibhūti yoga* that he displays visually, the yoga that Kṛṣṇa teaches orally is similar in many respects to that taught in books one, two, and four of the YS, with a heavy emphasis on meditation as the prime means for a gnoseological realization of an individual's intrinsic freedom from suffering existence. Of course, the BhG was, before all else, the manifesto of an emergent sectarian theism, which argued for the superiority of the path of devotion to a personal god over the inferior paths of action and knowledge. The term in this text that is so often translated as "path" is *yoga*, and it is the case, as we will see in this and later chapters, that the centuries immediately preceding the compilation of the BhG (and the YS) were pivotal times for the formulation of the practice- and knowledge-based soteriologies respectively known as yoga and Sāṃkhya in Hinduism[5] and *samatha* ("concentration-tranquility") and *vipassanā* ("insight-wisdom") in Buddhism.[6] The five centuries preceding the composition of the BhG and the YS were witness to a veritable explosion of scriptural references, particularly within the MBh itself, to a novel but still inchoate collection of speculations on "yoga" as a path to salvation. Part of the BhG's project, then, was to respond to this new soteriology, which it did in no small part by qualifying the term with prefixes, such as *bhakti*, *jñāna*, *karma*, *saṃnyāsa*, and—most significantly for its royal audience—*aiśvara*, the yoga of royal mastery.[7] Here I would argue that the BhG's compilers were, in their famous typology of the "three yogas" (which was, in fact, shorthand for a multitude of yogas), arguing for the superiority of the path of devotion (*bhakti yoga*) over and against not only these specific paths or lifestyles but also the practice of yoga tout court, which was so in vogue at the time, particularly among the warrior aristocracy.[8] By employing the term *yoga* to mean "way" or "path" or "method," the Bhāgavata sectarians were seeking to dilute the preexisting specificities of the term by so expanding its semantic field as to allow *yoga* to mean quite nearly anything, including its opposite, *viyoga*. The most striking example of this strategy is found in the BhG's sixth chapter, in which Kṛṣṇa reveals to Arjuna that

> the yogi is to yoke himself at all times . . . so that the workings of mind and senses are under control . . . let him sit "yoked" (*yukta*), his thought on me, his intention focused on me . . . He is called "yoked" when his restrained mind has come to rest upon his self alone and he is without craving for any [external] object . . . When thought ceases, curbed by the practice of yoga,[9] when he looks upon himself and is contented with himself . . . then he knows that this is the separation (*viyoga*) of his bond with sorrow, which is called "yoga."[10]

Another strategy employed in the BhG for reorienting its listeners—epitomized by the listener in the text, the warrior prince Arjuna himself—away from yoga and toward devotion to Kṛṣṇa was to seek a middle ground between Sāṃkhya, identified as the path of knowledge, and yoga itself. That compromise path, identified as the sole effective means to salvation, was termed *dhyāna*, that is, meditation on Kṛṣṇa as *brahman* or *puruṣottama*, the transcendent self or person.[11]

In many respects, the hermeneutical strategy of the YS and its principal commentators was also to elide yoga practice with meditation, albeit for different reasons than those dear to the Bhāgavata compilers of the BhG. In the case of the YS, it has been a commentarial convention since the time of the 350–450 CE *Yogabhāṣya* of Vedavyāsa (YBh) to maintain that the term "yoga" denotes the culminating meditative state of *samādhi* ("pure contemplation," "com-position"[12]) rather than physical yoking or union. This reading was canonized, as it were, by the great tenth- to eleventh-century commentator Vācaspatimiśra. Noting the fact that the renowned grammarian Pāṇini had proposed two separate etymologies for the verb root *yuj*—the one meaning "to yoke" and the other "to contemplate" (sam-ā-*dhā, from which the term *samādhi* is generated)—Vācaspatimiśra opted for the latter.[13] A number of later commentators took the next logical step, arguing that the meditative separation (*viyoga*) of the mind-stuff (*citta*) or intellect (*buddhi*) from materiality (*prakṛti*) was the goal of the practice of yoga.[14]

It is useful to compare these data with second- to fourth-century CE Jain uses of the term yoga, which meant "activity," "connection," or "juncture." The Jain path of liberation (*mokṣamārga*) required that yoga yield to its opposite, *ayoga(tā)*, through meditation and other techniques. In this early context, the term yoga was not applied to a program of practice leading to liberation, but rather used to signify an impediment to liberation. In the eighth century, however, the Jain philosopher Haribhadra would synthesize *pātañjala* and Jain yoga theory, identifying yoga as a means to liberation while declaring that "the highest form of yoga among all yogis is thus without yoga (*ayoga*). It is characterized by total abandonment since it connects [a yogi] with liberation."[15] To be sure, these readings of the term yoga—as its opposite—are to some extent appropriate for yoga philosophy, for which the disengagement of the mind and intellect from sensory stimuli is the sole effective means to true cognition and ultimate freedom. However, as the preceding chapter's narrative accounts of yogis make clear, it is inadequate, if not erroneous, for an understanding of yoga of any other sort. In spite of this, because the YS's principal commentators were first and foremost philosophers rather than practitioners of yoga, it has been samkhyan interpretations—in which "dry," contemplative inquiry has been privileged over "wet," yogic experience—that have prevailed over the centuries. Until the middle of the twentieth century, nearly all Western scholarship on yoga—which greatly privileged *pātañjala yoga* (i.e., based on Patañjali) philosophy over all other instantiations of yoga in the ancient, medieval, and modern worlds—also denied the link between yoga and "yoking" or "union," opting instead for the "pure contemplation" of the commentators.[16] The latter half of this chapter will trace the scriptural history of the yoga of "yoking," which is, after all, the etymologically correct meaning of the term and the meaning that has been operative in nonphilosophical Hindu sources since the time of the Vedas. As for the relationship between *pātañjala-yoga* philosophy and yoga without modifiers, the identity, even the continuity, of the two is challenged by the earliest commentarial traditions themselves, none of which clearly employed the term "yoga" to refer to Patañjali's philosophy. Prior to Śaṅkara's early ninth-century BrSūBh, no commentator had ever made such an assertion. Nor did Vedavyāsa consider his to be a commentary on a book of yoga philosophy. Rather, he called his *bhāṣya* "Patañjali's authoritative book on yoga, expository of sāṃkhya [philosophy]."[17]

It has been the equation of yoga with meditation or contemplation that has been most responsible for the skewed interpretations that have dominated the historiography of yoga for much of the past one hundred years. My point here is that the recent history of interpretations of the YS and BhG, carried out for the most part by historians of philosophy, has abusively identified accounts of meditation (*jhāna, dhyāna*)—from the earlier Hindu, Buddhist, and Jain textual record—as accounts of yoga, while generally ignoring accounts of yoga in which the term yoga itself or some other derivate of the verb *yuj, "to yoke," was employed, and of which there were many, in the ancient Hindu scriptures in particular. Furthermore, in so doing, historians have largely passed over the YS's third section, neglecting the very set of aphorisms that carry forward the earlier "yoking" paradigm and constitute the most salient link between the earliest sources and the yoga of the Tantras and sinister yogi narratives of the medieval period.[18]

It is this yoga of yoking that constitutes, I believe, the "pure" yoga practice that has been the grail of so many historians since De la Vallée Poussin coined the term "le Yoga pur"[19] over seventy years ago to designate the yoga that was already present when the Buddha began to theorize the Four Noble Truths and Patañjali the refinement of perception. De la Vallée Poussin's occasion for speculating on the existence of a "pure" yoga practice is a teaching from the *Aṅguttara Nikaya* (AN), the "Gradual Sayings," in which the Buddha speaks of "experimentalists" (*jhāyins*) and "speculatives" (*dhammayogas*) who condemn each other's practice as inauthentic. While the Buddha argues that the two modes of practice are complementary to the realization of *nirvāṇa*, many commentators and scholars have noted that they appear to be incompatible, in much the same way as the cultivation of *siddhis* and the *samādhi*-oriented practices promulgated in the YS. Now, the term *jhāyin* is the Pali cognate of the Sanskrit terms *dhyāyin* and *dhyānin*, both of which mean "meditator," from the root *dhyā (or *dhyai). In this AN passage, *jhāyins* are described as those monks who "live having touched the deathless sphere (*amatā dhātu*) with the body," as opposed to the *dhammayogas* who "see ultimate truth by entering into it with their wisdom (*paññā*)."[20]

As De la Vallée Poussin and others have noted, this seemingly insuperable cleavage between two supposedly complementary paths to the same goal is also found in Hindu scriptures and philosophical works. The Hindu cognates to the *jhāyins* and *dhammayogas* of the AN are the *yogas* and *sāṃkhyas*, as they are so often called in the *Mokṣadharma Parvan* (MdhP) section of the twelfth book of the MBh,[21] the same portion of the epic that contains the greatest concentration of narrative accounts of yoga practice.[22] In this portion of the didactic epic, the proponents of the practice of yoga and the teachings of Sāṃkhya philosophy are referred to as *yogas* (or *yogīs*) and *sāṃkhyas*, respectively. This same problematic, of yoga and Sāṃkhya as two complementary, yet in many respects incommensurable soteriological systems, lies at the core of the YS and YBh on the one hand and the BhG on the other. In the latter case, as in the case of the ŚvU, the sole "classical" Upaniṣad to combine the two terms into a *dvandva* compound,[23] the solution to this conundrum is to state that both paths lead to god, who releases from all bonds.

Given, then, that the *jhāyins* ("meditators") of the AN were the Buddhist homologues of the Hindu *yogas* ("proponents, practitioners of yoga") of the MdhP, the following question arises: is the historian authorized to assume an identity between "meditation" (the *jhāna* of the *jhāyins*) and "yoga" (the yoga of the *yogas* or yogis)? This has, in fact, been a fundamental assumption of virtually every historian of yoga, an assumption that I must challenge here. I do so for three reasons. First, these historical reconstructions place inordinate emphasis on the YS and its commentaries, a philosophical canon of considerable importance, but nonetheless not the sole yoga philosophy, and by no means the sole account of yoga in the treasury of Indic literature. Second, following

Vedavyāsa and Vācaspatimiśra's casuistic etymologization of the term "yoga" as *samādhi,* the many YS aphorisms not related to *samādhi* have been largely overlooked, making for incomplete and skewed assessments of the full scope of the yoga tradition.

Finally, even if one allows that Buddhist uses of "meditation" terminology align with Hindu uses of "yoga" terminology—as the experiential counterpart to the speculative inquiry of the Buddhist *dhammayogas* or of the Hindu proponents of Sāṃkhya—this does not authorize a reification of the content of the two operative terms. In other words, in the centuries around the beginning of the common era, the semantic fields of the terms *jhāna*/*dhyāna* and *yoga* were not the same as in the medieval, colonial, or postcolonial periods. As I will argue in chapter three, there is a clear overlap between the most ancient uses of the verb *dhyā and one of the most important components of early yoga theory, as found in certain classical Upaniṣads, Nyāya-Vaiśeṣika philosophy, and the YS tradition. As Jan Gonda has noted, *dhyā is a normal variant of the root form *dhī, whose semantic field covers the concepts of knowledge, vision, and luminosity: one truly knows what one sees in light-filled visions.[24] The yogic parallel to *dhyāna* so construed is the concept of yoga as the prime means to clear and unmediated perception, with the Nyāya-Vaiśeṣika category of "yogi perception" (*yogi-pratyakṣa*) constituting the most incontrovertible of the "true cognitions" (*pramāṇas*).[25] The YS and YBh are in general agreement with Nyāya-Vaiśeṣika positions on this issue, as evidenced in their discussions of the powers realized through a yogi's direct perception.[26]

For the sake of argument, let us assume for a moment that early Buddhist *jhāna* was the equivalent of early Hindu yoga. It nonetheless remains the case that the semantic field of neither of these terms is exhausted by this one area in which they overlap. On the one hand, the semantic range of the terms *jhāna*/*dhyāna* and *yoga* became greatly expanded, in several directions, in later Buddhism, Hinduism, and Jainism. On the other, an enhanced power of visual perception was by no means the sole mark of the ancient Hindu yoga practitioner. In the Vedas, yoga was first and foremost identified with the yoking of draft animals to wheeled conveyances and most particularly to the harnessing of warhorses to war chariots. Here the primary etymological sense of the term yoga is brought to the fore, as the cognate of the English verb "yoke." As I will show in this and later chapters, the yoga of yoking and the yoga of clear and luminous vision coalesced, from the time of the Vedas onward, into a unified body of practice in which yoga involved yoking oneself to other beings from a distance—by means of one's enhanced power of vision—either in order to control them or in order to merge one's consciousness with theirs.

When those other beings were divine, even the absolute itself, this sort of yoking was cast as a journey of the mind across space, to the highest reaches of transcendent being. Over time, this dynamic of visionary ascent was incorporated into nearly every Indic gnoseological system.

Here Stuart Sarbacker's typology—of the "numinous" and "cessative" modes or goals of Hindu, Buddhist, and Jain systems of yoga and meditation—proves to be extremely helpful.[27] "Cessative" refers directly to the concept of *nirodha*, already mentioned, in YS 1.2 ("Yoga is the cessation [*nirodha*] of the changing states of mind"), as well as to allied concepts in Buddhist and Jain meditative traditions. The great bulk of Hindu and Buddhist commentarial literature and, accordingly, of modern-day scholarship on yoga has focused on the cessative aspect of these traditions, that is, on the suppression of the mind and senses as a means to ending one's this-worldly existence, and with it, suffering. However, the "numinous" mode of this-worldly self-deification—which comprises the "attainments" (*samāpattis*) of Buddhist and patañjalian traditions, as well as the "supernatural enjoyments" (*ṛddhis*, *siddhis*) or "omnipresencings" (*vibhūtis*) of Buddhist, Jain, and Hindu traditions, and the practice of visionary ascent and the enhanced powers of perception common to all three—corresponds neatly to the practices of figures often identified, from the earliest times, as yoga practitioners.[28] As was noted over a hundred years ago by Emile Sénart, the supernatural powers of perception and action characteristic of the Buddha, so emphasized in the Nikaya literature, were of the same order.[29] What I propose to do in this book, then, is to write a history of yoga and its practitioners in its expansive, "numinous" mode—De la Vallée Poussin's "Yoga pur"—which, unlike the contractive, "cessative" mode, has been termed "yoga" (as opposed to "meditation") from the time of the Vedas down to the present day. This will therefore be a book that is more attentive to descriptive "yogi practice"—what people called yogis did and do—than prescriptive "yoga practice."

2. *Rāja Yoga* and *Haṭha Yoga*

More than any South Asian commentator or Western scholar, the thinker who has cast the longest shadow on modern appreciations (both popular and scholarly) of yoga and yogis was Swami Vivekananda who, while indisputably a giant of neo-Vedānta reform, was a dilettante on the subject of yoga. This did not prevent him, however, from writing an extensive commentary on the YS, the "essence" of which he identified—following none other than the theosophist Helena Petrova Blavatsky—as the "classical yoga" of India, called *rāja yoga.*[30] The term *rāja yoga,* which Vivekananda contrasted with the "inferior" physical practice of *haṭha yoga,* is nowhere to be found in either the YS or its principal commentaries, nor is it found in the fourteenth-century *Sarvadarśanasaṃgraha* of Mādhava. A brief genealogy of the term is therefore in order. The term *rāja yoga* appears nowhere prior to the advent of *haṭha yoga,* whose doctrines and practices were first promulgated in the writings of Gorakṣanātha (Gorakhnāth), the founder of the Nāth Yogīs. In fact, nearly every feature of the yoga that has become a New Age cultural phenomenon of global proportions has its origins in *haṭha yoga,* a complex system of postures and breath control. In order to distinguish this novel yoga system from the preexisting yogas of the YS, BhG, and other traditions, authors began to employ the term *haṭha yoga,* the "yoga of violent exertion," to distinguish it from all that was not *haṭha,* which was termed *rāja yoga.* The literal sense of the term *rāja yoga* is, of course, the "yoga of kings," a point to which I will return. The *Amanaskayoga* (AY), an eleventh- to twelfth-century text attributed to Gorakhnāth,[31] entitles its first chapter "Rāja Yoga," but uses the term in ways that are at variance with the teachings of the YS.[32] In one verse (2.32), the AY identifies "*rāja yoga* that is free of mental constructions" as the necessary precondition for bodily perfection. While this reading could be construed in a patañjalian mode, it bears noting that this mention of *rāja yoga* appears at the end of a list of practices that includes the sexual technique later known as *vajrolī mudrā,* or "urethral suction," by means of which a male draws his shed semen together with his partner's sexual discharge back from her vulva into his own body. An allied definition of *rāja yoga* as the union of female discharge (*rajas*) and semen in the central channel is found in passages from the fifteenth-century *Yogabīja* and the *Yogaśikhopaniṣad.*[33] Clearly, the *rāja yoga* referenced in these works is not the "classical yoga" that Vivekananda had in mind.

Haṭha yoga and *rāja yoga* are first paired together in a smattering of medieval works—the eighth- to thirteenth-century *Aparokṣānubhūti* spuriously attributed to Śaṅkara,[34] the eleventh- to fifteenth-century *Yogatattva Upaniṣad* (YTU),[35] and the fifteenth-century *Haṭhayogapradīpikā* (HYP) of Svātmarāman. The *Amaraughaprabodha* (APr), a text from which the HYP borrows extensively,[36] contains what may be the earliest explicit identification of *rāja yoga* with doctrines found in the YS: its characterization of *rāja yoga* as "free from the changing states of mind," is a likely paraphrase of YS 1.2.[37] The APr continues by contrasting *rāja yoga* and *haṭha yoga,* stating that both are dual bodies of practice, with *rāja yoga* comprising "herbs and that which is related to the self," and *haṭha yoga* comprising breath and seed.[38] The eleventh-century Buddhist *Kālacakra Tantra* mentions *haṭha yoga* as a means for bringing the breaths into the central channel.[39] The HYP may be the earliest text to subordinate *haṭha yoga* to *rāja yoga*, even if it is essentially devoted to describing hathayogic practice.[40] A definitive statement is found in Vijñānabhikṣu's sixteenth-century *Yogasārasaṃgraha*: "We do not enter into the details of postures, because our subject matter is Raja-Yoga. For a full treatment of all forms of postures and the purification of the veins and arteries we refer the reader to works on Hatha-Yoga [wherein] postures have been described."[41]

Vivekananda's influence has had a trickle-down effect on yoga scholarship, which has adopted his convention to not only identify the content of the YS as "classical yoga" but also to studiously ignore, as Vivekananda did, those portions of the text (as well as an abundance of data concerning other yogas that have persisted in South Asia for well over two thousand years) that fall outside of the modern-day sensus communis.[42] This picture has been further clouded by the publication of "scholarly" accounts of yoga by nonscholars. Ernest Wood, whose 1959 Penguin volume entitled *Yoga* was widely considered to be a balanced work of scholarship, was himself a Theosophist who slavishly followed Vivekananda's flawed analysis, calling the YS "this *rāja-yoga* manual."[43] Scholars who have taken this interpretive path are to be faulted for tautological reasoning that argues that the past resembles the present because the present resembles the past. I propose to go back to the past to examine its data on "yoga," and in the process to demonstrate that the present of yoga in no way resembles the past, or at least the past privileged by modernist proponents of a perennial "classical yoga" or "science of yoga" (*yoga-vidyā*). More specifically, it is an archaeology of the yogi, the agent or practitioner of yoga, that I present in these pages. In this, my analysis will more closely follow the writings of another twentieth-century Indian pioneer of modern yoga, Yogananda, whose *Autobiography of a Yogi* presents the yogis of India as a group far more interested in supernatural powers and self-externalization than in the quietistic, meditative realization of the divine within.

Let it be noted here that, as certain of the sources reviewed in the previous chapter have already made clear, not all yogis of narrative have been "sinister" yogis. Here the three modalities of the biosciences' concept of symbiosis ("living together") may serve as a useful heuristic. When one organism attaches itself to another for the benefit of both, as in the case of yogic initiation,[44] that is the form of symbiosis known as *mutualism*. When the same occurs to the benefit of the "yoking" organism, but with no benefit or harm done to the "yoked" (i.e., the host)—as in the case of Śaṅkara's takeover of the dead body of King Amaruka—this is *commensalism*. When, however, the same occurs to the sole benefit of the "yoking" organism, and at the expense (if not the death) of the host, this is *parasitism*. Here we are in the familiar territory of the sinister yogis of the Vikrama Cycle and other medieval narratives, in which the range of possibilities of yogis who practice the "numinous" mode of yoga are cast in an entirely negative light, not unlike the "evil wizards" or "mad scientists" of Western literary and cinematic traditions.

3. Assuming the Lotus Position

Anyone seeking to reconstruct the history of yoga and yogis must resist the temptation of projecting modernist constructions of this body of practice and its practitioners onto the past. Few are the scholars who have succeeded, as the history of interpretations of an image from the ancient past reveals. Here I am referring specifically to the modernist assumption that, in addition to the cultivation of meditative states, a complex program of bodily postures combined with breath control has been the perennial hallmark of yogic practice. The most ancient piece of evidence garnered in support of this assumption is clay seal number 420 (fig. 2.1)[45] from the Indus River Valley archaeological site of Mohenjo-Daro, a site whose artifacts are dated to the latter portion of the third millennium BCE.

In his authoritative archaeological survey of the Mohenjo-Daro site written in 1931, Sir John Marshall confidently identified the figure on this seal as

> a male god, who is recognizable at once as a prototype of the historical Śiva . . . The God, who is three-faced, is seated on a low Indian throne in a typical attitude of *Yoga*, with legs bent double beneath him, heel to heel, and toes turned downwards. His arms are outstretched, his hands, with thumbs to front, resting on his knees . . . The lower limbs are bare and the phallus (*ūrdhvameḍhra*) seemingly exposed, but it is possible that what appears to be the phallus is in reality the end of the waistband . . . [T]he attributes of the deity are peculiarly distinctive. In the first place, he is three-faced (*trimukha*) . . . The second feature of this pre-Āryan god that links him with the historical Śiva is his peculiar Yogī-like posture . . . Śiva is pre-eminently the prince of Yogīs—the typical ascetic and self-mortifier, whence his names *Mahātapaḥ, Mahāyogī*. Primarily, the purpose of yoga was the attainment of union (*yoga*) with the god by mental discipline and concentration; but it was also the means of acquiring miraculous

Figure 2.1 Mohenjo-Daro clay seal no. 420. Courtesy John and Susan Huntington Archives.

powers, and hence in the course of time the yogī came to be regarded as a magician, miracle-monger, and charlatan.[46]

While many scholars have taken issue with Marshall's identification of the image on this seal with the *five*-headed male Hindu god Śiva, few, with the exception of Jean Filliozat,[47] have ever challenged his assumption that this humanoid figure is seated in a yogic pose and is, by extension, a yogi.[48] This assumption is open to question. First of all, is the cross-legged pose of this enthroned figure necessarily a yogic posture? If such were the case, a number of figures from different parts of the ancient world would also have to be qualified as yogis (or their female counterparts, *yoginīs*). These would include two other figures from Mohenjo-Daro, of equal antiquity as the figure on seal 420.[49] Other images, from the Indus Valley

Figure 2.2 Śrī, Bharhut railing medallion, first century BCE. Courtesy of John and Susan Huntington Archives.

site of Harappa, show figures in identical postures, often enthroned and sometimes in stylized buildings, which some scholars have identified as shrines.[50] Following the watershed of the Indus Valley seals, no South Asian images of figures in "yogic postures" appear for the next two thousand years, until a circa first century BCE bas relief of the goddess Śrī, from the Buddhist Bharhut site in central India (fig. 2.2).

Here Śrī is seated on a lotus and flanked by elephants in a configuration later associated with the iconography of the goddess of prosperity, Gaja-Lakṣmī.[51] Identified with royal sovereignty, Śrī is closely associated with the lotus flower in an account from the MBh, an epic dating from the same period as the Bharhut railing medallion in figure 2.2. In it, Śrī, who is said to "dwell in the lotus,"[52] is identified with Draupadī, the queen of the five Pāṇḍava brothers, mighty heroes in a line of epic kings.[53] This configuration carries forward into the medieval and colonial periods, in which a king's *śakti* is considered to reside in the seat of his throne.

From the same century as the Śrī medallion from Bharhut, two bronze coins were issued by the Indo-Scythian kings Maues (ca. 90–60 BCE) and Azes (ca. 57–10 BCE), each representing the respective king seated in cross-legged posture upon a cushion. These coins, which bear both Greek and Kharoshti inscriptions,[54] date from the period in which the Śakas, the Indo-Scythians, were extending their realms southward and eastward from their central Asian homeland. It was under Maues, the most powerful of the Śaka kings, that Indo-Scythian armies penetrated the South Asian subcontinent, taking Gandhara and its most important city Taxila in 90 BCE.

Figure 2.3 Obverse of copper coin of Indo-Scythian King Maues (ca. 90–60 BCE) showing king seated in cross-legged posture. Courtesy the British Museum, 1860, 1226.63. © The Trustees of the British Museum.

Figure 2.4 Sculpture of Artemis of Ephesos, Caesarea, detail of robe, ca. first through second century CE. Photo © The Israel Museum, Jerusalem. With permission from the Israel Antiquities Authority.

Well to the west, in Anatolia—which was linked with both South and Central Asia by the Silk Road—the first two centuries of the common era saw a profusion of sculptural and numismatic representations of the famous Artemis of Ephesos type, images that in addition to her famous bodices comprised of offerings of bull testicles (often mistaken to be multiple breasts) also feature robes (called *ependytes*[55]) on which are figured bulls, bees, flowers, and figures in cross-legged postures uncannily similar to those of the figures on the Indus Valley seals. These seated figures are not found on all representations of Artemis of Ephesos. In many cases, they are replaced by "winged Nike" figures, whose lower limbs simply disappear.

Still further to the west, but from the same period as the Śrī medallion from Bharhut, the archeological record yields images of another cross-legged figure identified as the Celtic horned god Cernunnos. The most famous of these is figured on an inner panel of the first-century BCE Gundestrup Cauldron, an artifact that, while it was unearthed in far northwestern Denmark in the late nineteenth century, is thought by many scholars to have been manufactured in Thrace, near the Black Sea coast of the southeastern Balkan Peninsula. All other images of Cernunnos hail from France or Italy, the earliest extant image being from Val Camonica, in the Italian Alps.[56] Cernunnos is generally represented in a cross-legged posture; however, the posture is not unique to this god in the West. Other male deities, from second-century BCE Provence and Narbonne, in France, are also represented in cross-legged pose.[57] There is general agreement that much of Cernunnos's iconography was likely inspired by ancient Near Eastern prototypes, and it should be recalled that

Figure 2.5 Celtic horned god Cernunnos, detail from inner panel of Gundestrup Cauldron, ca. first century BCE. Courtesy Kit Weiss, National Museum of Denmark.

in New Testament times, the homeland of the Celts was Anatolia, where they were called the Galatians by the apostle Paul.[58] The coins and large rodent figured in this image also reproduce the iconography of the South Asian deity Kubera, with his moneybag and mongoose.

Returning to South Asia, where nearly every early stone sculpture that has survived down to the present day is Buddhist or Jain, a number of seated Buddhist and Jain figures are shown in what would today be called a "full lotus" posture. These include the earliest of all anthropomorphic representations of Buddha Śākyamuni from the Kushan-era Mathura school, dated to the first to second centuries CE, in which the Buddha is seated upon a dias with eyes wide open and his right arm upraised[59] and a coeval Jain votive medallion, also from Mathura, depicting a Jīna, probably the *tīrthaṃkara* Mahāvīra, seated in cross-legged posture upon a dias with an open flower behind him.[60] From the first century CE onward, one begins to encounter sculpted images, from the Vindhyas to the Swat Valley—precisely the range of the Kushan realm whose dual capitals were located in Puruṣapura (Peshawar) and Mathura—in which the Buddha or the bodhisattva Maitreya is seated in "full lotus posture" with eyes half closed and hands held slightly clasped on his lap.[61]

Here I will leave aside these intriguing iconographic parallels—between figures who are sometimes horned, sometimes enthroned, and sometimes surrounded by or covered with images of animals—to concentrate on the ubiquitous iconographic detail of their cross-legged posture. Is it a yogic posture?[62] If so, then what is one to make of the fact that following its representation on the Indus Valley seals it does not "resurface" for nearly 2,000 years, and that when it does so, it appears at nearly the same time in four geographically distant regions, that is, at Bharhut in central India, in Indo-Scythian Transoxiania, in Anatolia and Thrace, and in France and Italy?[63] If it is correct to assume that the posture of the figure represented on Marshall's seal 420 is a yogic posture, then is that figure a yogi? What is a yogi?

If we hope to make some sense of this iconographic record in its South Asian contexts, then we must seek to confront image with text. We may begin with the Buddhist and Jain images, which, apart from that of the lotus goddess Śrī, are the earliest representations of figures seated in what may be interpreted as the "yogic" lotus position. There is, in fact, a textual record from the Buddhist canon that discusses what may have been the yoga of the period of these sculptures. This record, which has been documented and studied in detail by Johannes Bronkhorst, is enlightening on a number of points. The *Majjhima Nikaya* (MN), the "Middle-length Sayings," are among the earliest scriptures of the Buddhist canon and are considered to have been a part of the Buddha's original teachings to the monks of his fledgling community. A set of teachings in that corpus, dating from no later than the third century BCE, refers disparagingly to a non-Buddhist, probably Jain, method of cultivating the mind called "meditation" (*jhāna*).[64]

This technique involved, among other things, extreme fasting, stopping the breath entirely, and closing the teeth while pressing the tongue against the palate. According to the text, the practice only gave the Buddha headaches, copious sweating, roaring in the ears, great pain, and mental distraction.[65] Against this entirely unsatisfactory set of techniques, the Buddha proposed his own method, which he called the Four Jhānas,[66] precisely the nonascetic, non-self-mortifying path he took to realize enlightenment: this, I would argue, is the state pictured in the many sculptural representations of the Buddha seated in cross-legged posture with half-closed eyes.

It should be noted here that at no point is the term yoga mentioned in the Buddha's teachings, either with reference to the Jain techniques that the Buddha disparages or to the practice that leads him effortlessly toward enlightenment. The operative term is, in both cases, *jhāna*. In fact, prior to the second-century CE Aśvaghoṣa—who employs the term yoga to denote concentration, the limited consumption of food, and breath control—no Buddhist source employs the term yoga in any but the nonspecific sense of "application" or "practice."[67] This is a not insignificant detail that should be borne in mind as one reconstructs the prehistory of the yoga of the YS, BhG, and other texts from the same period: if the term "yoga" is not employed to refer to a technique or theoretical corpus, then that technique or theory ought not to be construed as yogic. In other words, even if later texts, like the YS, use the term "yoga" to describe meditative techniques, one cannot to assume that *jhāna* (or its Sanskrit equivalent *dhyāna*) ever signified "yoga" in these earlier or coeval traditions.

One of the techniques that the Buddha criticizes in the MN closely resembles a description found in a later Hindu source. The sixth book of the MU, most of which is datable to the third century of the common era, states that through the fixing of the mind (*dhāraṇā*), effected by "pressing the tip of the tongue against the palate and suppressing speech, mind, and breath, one sees *brahman* through insight."[68] This description also appears to anticipate that of a technique known as the *khecarī mudrā*, which appears in *haṭha yoga* texts several hundred years later.[69] The MU's sixth book also contains what is likely the earliest mention of a six-fold yoga,[70] whose components it lists as: *prāṇāyāma* (which likely means complete stoppage of the breath in this context),[71] *pratyāhāra* (withdrawing the

Figure 2.6 Seated prince or *bodhisattva*, Afghanistan or Swat Valley, ca. first century CE or later. Private collection.

senses), *dhyānam* (meditation), *dhāraṇā* (fixing the mind), *tarka* (contemplative inquiry),[72] and *samādhi* (concentration). Five of these components are found in Patañjali's formulation of eight-limbed (*aṣṭāṅga*) yoga in the coeval YS. Markedly absent from the MU's list is *āsana*, "seated posture." How does this impact the identification of figures seated in cross-legged poses as yogis?

I would argue that in the centuries around the beginning of the common era, the cross-legged "lotus position" was a mark of royal sovereignty: royal gods or goddesses, their priests, and kings sat enthroned in this posture atop a dias, lotus, or cushion. When Buddhas and Jīnas began to be represented anthropomorphically in Kushan-era sculpture and coinage, their cross-legged posture was originally an indication of their royal sovereignty, rather than of any meditative or yogic practice. This hypothesis is supported by a sculpted image from Swat, dated to the first century CE or later, which has been identified as "either a prince or a bodhisattva." As the art historian Joe Cribb has noted, "while crossed legs and folded hands, postures associated with the practice of meditation, are characteristic of Buddha and Bodhisattva images, and thus suggest that the figure with its bejeweled body is a Bodhisattva, a notable precedent for these postures within a secular context exists in the image of the seated king on the Maues coin" (shown above, fig. 2.3).[73] A similar interpretation has been made regarding a sixth- to eighth-century painted wooden panel excuted in the Sino-Iranian style,[74] found at the Inner Asian site of Dandan-Oilik near Khotan, in which a bodhisattva "was changed from an Indian princeling to a Persian shah . . . forc[ing] his stiff Persian dress into the yoga pose . . . hold[ing] a fragile lotus in one of his

Figure 2.7 Obverse of double stater of Kushan emperor Vima Kadphises, ca. 80–100 CE. Courtesy the British Museum, 1867, 1218.10. © The Trustees of the British Museum.

Figure 2.8 Reverse of tetradrachma of Kushan emperor Kaniṣka portraying "Buddha Maitreya," ca. 128–152 CE. Courtesy the British Museum 2000, 0509.1. © The Trustees of the British Museum.

four hands." In fact, there is nothing Indian about this panel at all. As was the case with the first-century image in figure 2.6, the stylistic source of this cross-legged posture in later depictions of bodhisattvas is to be traced to representations of Iranian kings rather than Indic saviors. Throughout the Kushano-Sasanian cultural region, fifth- to eighth-century enthroned bodhisattva images are depicted with crowns closely resembling those worn by Sasanian kings of Persia.[75]

Here I would suggest that the term "lotus posture" or "position" (*padmāsana*) derives not from the pose itself, which in no way resembles a lotus flower, but rather from a throne or seat (*āsana*) representing a lotus (*padma*). Such is the case in Hindu Tantra, in which the primary sense of the term *āsana* is, precisely, the "throne of a deity."[76] Such a throne, which is altogether appropriate for the royal goddess Śrī—the divine embodiment of royal sovereignty who dwells in the lotus—would also be so for the Buddha, whose royal identification, like that of Christ the King in the Christian West, is so emphasized in early iconographic and textual traditions.

An early and datable window on this transfer of the seated posture, from an emblem of royal sovereignty to one of buddha-hood, appears when one contrasts three Kushan coins that were minted less than a century apart. The obverse of a copper coin minted in Taxila in circa 50 CE under the reign of the first Kushan monarch Kujula Kadphises (ca. 30–80 CE) depicts the king himself seated in lotus posture.[77] So too, a coin of Kujula's successor Vima Kadphises (ca. 80—100 CE), portrays that king seated in the same cross-legged pose upon a cloud or "rocky prominence," with flames of fire rising from his shoulders (fig. 2.7).[78] However, the inscription on the reverse of a copper tetradrachma minted during the reign of the great emperor Kaniṣka (ca. 128–152 CE), which depicts a cross-legged figure seated on a low benchlike throne, identifies this figure *not* as the king himself—as had been the case on the coins of Kujula and Vima Kadphises, as well as the earlier Śaka ruler Maues—but rather as Metrago Boudo, "Buddha Maitreya" (fig. 2.8).[79]

4. Yoga and Chariots

Recall here that in his identification of the cross-legged figure of Mohenjo-Daro seal 420 as a proto-Śiva, Marshall noted that Śiva is known in Hindu traditions as the "Prince of Yogis," a *mahāyogī* ("great yogi") and a *mahātapaḥ* ("great ascetic"). It should be noted from the outset that the early textual record, from Hindu, Buddhist, and Jain sources, does not authorize an identification—which most historians have blithely assumed—between yoga and asceticism or heat-producing austerities (*tapas*),[80] breath control or stoppage of the breath (*prāṇāyāma*), self-mortification, and meditation (*dhyāna*). The terms denote different procedures with different or overlapping goals, the meanings of the terms vary from source to source, and evidence—for knowing whether or to what extent they were practiced in combination with one another—is conflicting at best. Of equal significance is the fact that the epithet *mahāyogin* is nowhere applied to the god Śiva (or any other god or human, for that matter) prior to the circa 200 BCE—400 CE MBh. Of course, one sees very little of Śiva at all prior to the great epic, and nowhere is his so-called forerunner Rudra characterized as a yogi in earlier Hindu sources.

If we are to understand what connection there was, if any, between seal 420 and early Hindu understandings of the practice of yoga, then we would do well to look at the textual record from the time of the composition of the Hindu epics, which bear witness to a veritable explosion in the uses of the term yoga and its derivates. However, in order to understand the earliest epic uses of the term, we must first attempt to recover the vedic contexts out of which they emerged. Prior to the epic period, the referents of the verb *yuj and its derivates were generally restricted to two sorts of activity: the yoking of a wheeled conveyance to a draft animal and, by extension, the linkage between a visionary thinker's mind or consciousness to some transcendent object. In both cases, the person who did the yoking was enabled to journey outward or upward from wherever he found himself. No doubt for this reason, the verb *yuj appears in tandem with the verb *kram in many of these contexts. While the literal meaning of *kram is to "step" (as in the English in*crem*ent), "stride," or "march," such is not an accurate use of the term in the contexts in which it is associated with the verb *yuj, since one does not walk once one has hitched up his chariot. In such cases, "advance," "charge," "rush," and even "mount an assault" are more accurate translations of the term. We should nevertheless bear in mind the fact that, in the ritual context in which liturgies containing the terms *yuj and *kram would have been pronounced, charging outward or upward on a chariot in the real world would often have translated into stepping forward or northward within the limits of the sacrificial ground.

The link between these early uses of yoga terminology as found in the vedic literature and those found in the epic period is best captured in the aphorism introduced near the end of the last chapter: "These are the two people in this world who pierce the solar disk: the wanderer (*parivrāḍ*) and the *yogayukta* [warrior] who is slain [while] facing [his enemies] on the field of battle."[81] Not an obscure aphorism, this, given the fact that it is found in a wide variety of sources, ranging from the first- to sixth-century CE PT (1.345), to certain noncritical recensions of the MBh[82] and a tenth-century Nyāya-Vaiśeṣika philosophical commentary.[83] The same dynamic is pictured on medieval hero stones in Karnataka and narrativized in the *Pṛthvirāj Raso*, a twelfth- to fifteenth-century Rajput epic rife with evocations of dying warriors going to the solar disk (*rabi maṇḍal*).[84] Piercing the solar disk also becomes a prerogative of the yogi who, according to the fourteenth-century *Khecarī Vidyā* (KhV), pierces the sun in the heavens to become absorbed in Śiva.[85] A variant reading, from the fourth- to sixth-century *Yājñavalkyasmṛti* (YājS), makes the yogi the model for the warrior. "Those who, for the sake of [protecting the] land, are slain by faultless weapons without turning tail [on their enemies]: they go to heaven, after the fashion of the yogis."[86]

What is the meaning of the term *yogayukta* as a modifier of a warrior, and what is significant about piercing the disk of the sun? In fact, the path to the vedic afterlife involved nothing less than traveling to or through the sun on a ritually constructed chariot. According to the ideology of vedic sacrifice, every time he sacrificed, the patron of the sacrifice (*yajamāna*)—who was, prototypically, a *kṣatriya*—journeyed to the world of the gods on either a boat or a chariot[87] that was the sacrifice itself. This notion has its origins in the *Ṛg Veda* (ṚV), according to which it is only by virtue of his yogas, his yoked celestial chariots, that Agni, the fire of sacrifice, is himself able to move from the fire altar here on earth to the world of heaven.[88] Thus, with reference to the soma sacrifice, which extended over a period of several days, the *Śatapatha Brāhmaṇa* (ŚB) states:

> Every day he [the *yajamāna*] stretches out the sacrifice and every day he completes it. Every day he yokes (*yuṅkte*) it for [the purpose of taking] the path to the heavenly world, and therefore every day he goes to the heavenly world. That is why one should yoke (*yuñjyād*) [the sacrifice] every day and why one should release [it] every day.[89]

This daily program is termed the "difficult ascent" in the Brāhmaṇas, which divide it into two movements: ascent and descent. Ascent lifts the *yajamāna* up to the heavenly world, but because he wishes to remain in this world until his time to die has come, the counter-movement of descent is of equal necessity. At the culmination of this ascent, which is realized when the sacrificial liturgy is recited from beginning to its end without pause, the *yajamāna* stands on the sun in the heavenly world; at the end of his descent, he returns to solid ground in this world.[90] This rite is given a highly evocative name in the ŚB, which, as we will see, reprises the language of the apotheosis of the chariot warrior: it is called the "Viṣṇu Steps" (*viṣṇukramāḥ*).[91]

> So he steps (*kramate*) [taking] the Viṣṇu steps. The person who sacrifices satisfies the gods . . . [and] having satisfied the gods, he comes to take his place among them. Having taken his place among them, he steps toward (*prakrāmati*) them . . . He thus rises up to those [higher] worlds and establishes himself there. He should now step (*krameta*) back here from up there . . . He thereby conquers heaven . . . midspace . . . and his enemies.[92]

In his daily ascent to heaven on the chariot of sacrifice, it is the *yajamāna*'s "initiation body" that makes the journey, a body that has been generated through the rite of *dīkṣā*. As for his mundane body, it is left under the protection of the same priestly officiant (*ṛtvij*) whose recitiations guide his initiation body up to the higher worlds and back.[93] Already in the last chapter, we saw the importance, for the yogi, of leaving his mortal shell in safe hands while taking on other bodies; here we see that the concept of humans transferring the self between bodies was already present in the vedic tradition.

In a certain respect, one may say that what the *yajamāna* experiences in his daily journey to heaven is a temporary victory over death, prior to a return to the world of mortals. Over the longer term, however, his daily rise also enables him to gradually prepare a permanent place for himself in heaven, for the moment when his allotted time on earth will come to an end.[94] When that time comes, and he dies, it is the chariot of his final sacrifice—the cremation of his mortal remains—that will carry him to the world of heaven. This rise to heaven does not, however, constitute an apotheosis, that is, the transformation of a human being into a god. Rather, the *yajamāna*'s daily chariot journeys to heaven and back have only ensured him a place in the kingdom of Yama, the lord of the dead.[95]

Already, in the time of the Brāhmaṇas, a distinction had been made between the worlds of the deceased human ancestors and the worlds of the undying gods, with the former identified with the kingdom of Yama.[96] As for the worlds of the gods, the Āditya deities were vigilant in blocking the advance of any human who would attempt to force his way onto the path leading to their world. Of course, the Āditya par excellence is the sun, and it is the sun that blocks humans from acceding to these immortal worlds.

> The one that burns [up in the sky] is simply death. Because he is death, the creatures that are below him die, while those that are above him are the gods, which is why they are immortal. If he should desire to take away a person's life breath when he rises, that person dies, and [as for] the person who goes to that other world without having escaped from the sun that is death . . . [the sun] causes him to die over and over again in this world.[97]

In the light of these vedic soteriological constructs, the attractiveness of piercing the disk of the sun, the telos of the persons identified in the aphorism quoted above becomes clear. What, then, of the compound *yogayukta*, and what is its relationship to the "wanderer" or the battlefield hero evoked in the aphorism? The meaning of *yukta* is clear enough: as the past passive participle of *yuj, it either means "yoked" in the literal sense, or, in a more figurative sense, "prepared" or "ready." As for *yoga*, its primary sense, as found in the Vedas, is best rendered by the French "attelage," a term whose semantic fields cover both the act of yoking, hitching, or harnessing; the conveyance (chariot) so hitched; and the draft animals (horses).[98] The English "rig" is the nearest approximation I can find to this. As such, the compound may be either read literally as "hitched to his rig" or "ready to hitch up" and understood in the metaphorical sense of being prepared to take the final journey, from life into a glorious afterlife beyond the disk of the sun, in the luminous realm of the immortals.

The vedic *yajamāna*, who shuttled daily to the sun by yoking his chariot of sacrifice, was not alone in undertaking journeys of this sort. As Louis Renou and Boris Oguibénine have noted, the most common rigvedic meaning of the verb *yuj in its middle conjugation (*yuje*, etc.) was "to yoke one's self to a chariot" and, by extension, "to prepare for battle."[99] Early on, however, the term also came to be applied, with increasing frequency, to the practice of vedic priests who yoked their minds to poetic inspiration in order to con*jug*ate their inspired words to both the world of the sacrifice—within which they operated as ritual specialists—and to the world of heaven, to which they and their clients aspired. Here by yoking their minds (*mano-yuj*), they sought to establish enigmatic links (*brahmo-yuj*) between phenomena of different orders of being: microcosm and macrocosm, ritual world and mythic world, human and divine. Giving voice to such correlative links (*vaco-yuj*) was a means for reducing the distance that separated these phenomena and for moving across that gap. In this way, the vedic poets were able to link their own poetic flights of fancy to the yokings of their warrior patrons, whose yoga also involved "departures" and "journeys" to distant places.[100] A striking image of such poetic journeys is found in a verse from a late rigvedic hymn, in which the poets describe themselves as "hitched up" (*yukta*) and standing on their chariot shafts as they depart on a reconnaissance mission around the world's confines.[101]

These poetic yokings of thought to word—visionary expeditions to the furthest reaches of the imaginable universe—were undertaken by vedic priests in a sacrificial context. Without leaving the sacrificial ground, the priest sought to yoke his mind to inspired language in order to "win" the sacrifice and its rewards, with the cow he received as his honorarium (*dakṣiṇā*) corresponding to the spoils of the victorious cattle-raiding warrior. This type of comparison by the vedic officiants between their agonistic sacrifices and the sorts of combat reserved for warrior elites is a common one: vedic liturgies are rife with references to poetic victories in metaphorical chariot races and dice play, the two principal means for winning the wealth of others, apart from cattle raiding and warfare itself.[102] The combative, or at least competitive, aspect of the vedic poet's endeavor is underscored in another rigvedic passage, in which the singer of a hymn likens himself to the horse that pulls the chariot.

> Like a horse, I who know have yoked myself (*ayuji*) to the [chariot] shaft with my own will. I pull on that [shaft] which moves powerfully forward, ensuring the favors [of the gods]. I do not wish for it to be loosed, nor for it to go backward. May it, which knows the path, and which goes ahead, guide me in a straight line!"[103]

In the same way, the sacrificial offering itself, which is offered on the sacrificial ground, is said to be "yoked like two well-yoked horses" (*suyujā yujānáḥ*) in order that it may travel across rivers and oceans to reach the gods in their distant abode.[104] In all of these usages, yoking allows one to journey across vast expanses, even while remaining grounded in a particular time and place. As we will see in the next chapter, something similar to this visionary yoga of the vedic poets resurfaces over a millennium later, in the form of the mystic ascent detailed in the deity-based meditation programs of the late classical Upaniṣads, MBh, Purāṇas, Āgamas, and Tantras, as well as Mahāyāna Buddhist sources.

Before the term yoga came to be yoked to chariots of poetic thought, however, its earliest referent was the yoking of horses to war chariots in preparation for battle. In this regard, Geldner translates the term *yoga* in ṚV 4.24.4 as "Kriegsfahrt,"[105] while the verb *yuj, employed without modifiers, often signified battle: "The jealous [enemies] . . . have yoked themselves (*yuyujré*) against us." [106] In this regard, it is apposite to note that one of the English-language cognates of the Sanskrit "yoga" is the word "joust."[107]

These readings carry over into the upanishadic literature. A passage from the circa fifth-century BCE *Bṛhadāraṇyaka Upaniṣad* (BṛU) unambiguously refers to the yoked team that pulls a chariot as a "yoga,"[108] while the coeval *Chāndogya Upaniṣad* (ChU) states that the "breath is yoked (*yukta*) to this body in the same way that a draft animal (*prayogya*) is yoked to a conveyance."[109] This last reading belongs to the same tradition as a renowned passage from the third- to first-century BCE KU, which, as Plato does, likens the relationship between intellect and body to that between a charioteer and his chariot. The senses are the horses and the reins the mind (which is controlled, in later yoga systems, by controlling the breaths), such that the charioteer who controls his horses "reaches a plane from which he is not born again."[110]

An analysis of the late vedic usages of the terms *yoga*, *kṣema*, and especially the compound *yoga-kṣema* will bring us back to the relationship between the seated posture and the practice of yoga and aid us in linking ancient ideology to premodern practice. Already in the ṚV, *yoga* and *kṣema* are antonyms, signifying "war" and "peace."[111] In a comprehensive analysis of the uses of these terms in the later vedic literature, Hanns Oertel identifies six passages, from the *Maitrāyaṇī Saṃhitā* (MS),[112] *Taittirīya Saṃhitā* (TS), *Kaṭhaka Saṃhitā* (KS), ŚB, AB, and *Jaiminīya Brāhmaṇa* (JB), in which the terms *yoga* and *kṣema* always stand in opposition to one another, with *yoga* paralleling "expressions of moving [and] yoking up, while *kṣema* is parallel to expressions of standing still, repose at home, unyoking."[113] Thus the MS statement:

On one day he sallies forth (*prakrāmati*), on the next day he stands worshipping; he thus establishes life at home ["repose"] connected with life on the road ["yoking"] (*yoga-kṣema*) for the creatures; therefore some creatures are fond of wandering (*yāyāvara*), others are stay-at-homes; in that, having sallied forth he stands worshipping, therefore he who is fond of wandering comes to the stay-at-home (for support); therefore the stay-at-home is the food for him who is fond of wandering.[114]

When the vedic chariot warrior charged out from his encampment and into battle, he did so on a chariot that was hitched up (*yukta*), with straps and harnesses, to a team of warhorses. In the aphorism discussed earlier, *yogayukta* warriors are said to pierce through the disk of the sun in a battlefield apotheosis.

In the light of the data presented to this point, I would suggest that this language is disclosive of an archaic ritual ideology according to which a dying warrior physically or symbolically lashed himself to his chariot in order that his body-chariot with its luminous soul-charioteer could charge up to, or even mount an assault on, the disk of the sun. Alternatively, the *yoga*, the "rig" that the warrior was hitched to, was not his own but rather a celestial chariot sent down from above to raise him up to heaven. It is this latter scenario that is represented on hundreds of hero stones spread across the subcontinent. In these triptychs, the death of the warrior is represented on the lowest register, his rise to heaven in the arms of heavenly maidens (and more rarely, as in fig. 2.11, on a chariot) on the middle, and his heavenly sojourn above.[115] Such a chariot-borne journey is described in the Rām's account of the apotheosis of the warriors of the monkey army (all of whom were gods incarnate) allied with Rāma, which are portrayed as entering the disk of the sun, with all those who had drowned themselves in the Sarayu River mounting onto

Figure 2.9 Hero Stone (vīragal) portraying apotheosis of a slain hero on a heavenly chariot. Śiva Amṛteśvara temple, Amritapura, Tamil Nadu. Courtesy of Karine Ladrech.

heaven-bound aerial cars (*vimānas*) upon shedding their human bodies in its waters.[116]

In such a context, the rays of the sun themselves would have been viewed as so many luminous reins, yoked to which the *yogayukta* warrior was able to launch himself upward into and through its orb. In fact, the most commonly used term for solar "ray" in Hindu sources is *raśmi*, a term whose primary meaning, as attested in the ṚV, was "rein" or "cord" before its semantic field was expanded in later literature to refer to the effulgent rays or reins of the solar chariot.[117] Both meanings are present in a passage from the first maṇḍala of the ṚV, which identifies the sun's seven rays with the god's daughters: "[The sun] yoked (*áyukta*) the seven resplendent daughters of the solar chariot. He departs by means of these [daughters] who yoke themselves (*sváyuktibhiḥ*)."[118] In summary, we can see that the sun-piercing apotheosis of the chariot warrior was modeled on the daily rise to heaven of the *yajamāna* mounted on the chariot of his sacrifice. However, unlike the conventional sacrificer, who did not make the supreme (and sole "true") sacrifice of offering up his own body as his sacrificial oblation, the chariot warrior who willed his death on the battlefield was empowered to charge upward *through* the barrier of the sun to take his place among the gods.

5. The "Yogic" Apotheosis of Warriors in the *Mahābhārata*

In the MBh, the compound *yogayukta* most often appears in narratives in which dying warriors prepare themselves for the final journey to the world of the gods.[119] As was the case in the vedic literature, the compound is often found together with forms of the verb *kram. As we know, *yajamānas* journeyed to the sun, either on a boat or a chariot that was the sacrifice itself; we also know that the sacrificial "passage" through which they were enabled to reach the heavenly world was termed a *saṃkramaṇa*.[120] Given the fact that the *yajamāna* par excellence was a member of the warrior aristocracy, a chariot warrior, the chariot would have been the most obvious vehicle for his journey to the sun, which, like him, moved across the sky on a horse-drawn chariot. Through his battlefield death, the chariot warrior mounted an assault on the otherwise impenetrable solar disk and forced his way into the world of the immortals on the other side.[121]

As Peter Schreiner has noted, the word "yoga" appears nearly nine hundred times in the MBh, an exponential increase over its occurrence in all earlier scriptural canons. Of these mentions of the term, over three hundred are found in the didactic teachings of the MdhP section of its twelfth book, and over one hundred in the BhG alone.[122] While far less studied than the BhG, the MdhP—which are the teachings of Bhīṣma, who holds forth from his bed of arrows for hundreds of chapters prior to his own self-willed yogic death—is a richer repository of early yoga speculation than the BhG, or, for that matter, the YS or the early Upaniṣads.[123] Generally speaking, didactic or doctrinal discussions of yoga, such as they are found in the MdhP and BhG, are ambiguous on the subject of just what yoga (or Sāṃkhya, the term with which it is often paired) meant in this period. Both present a multiplicity of meanings for a term that was in *statu nascendi* and the object of a conflict of interpretations,[124] a situation also reflected in the YS.

When, however, one looks at *narrative* descriptions of the practice of yoga in the great epic, one finds a remarkable uniformity, with the practitioner of yoga either entering into the disk of the sun or penetrating the body of another being. There exists a total of fourteen such narratives in the epic involving human practitioners. Of these, five concern chariot warriors (Bhīṣma,[125] Kṛṣṇa,[126] Yudhiṣṭhira,[127] Bhūriśravas, and Droṇa) who, termed *yogayukta*, are described as going to the sun or the highest path. One concerns a chariot warrior who has refused to fight (Balarāma): while he is *yogayukta*, a great serpent emerges from his mouth and swims out to sea.[128] Three concern hermits (Śuka,[129] Jaigīṣavya,[130] and an unnamed brahmin[131]) whose journeys take them across the heavens and, in the case of Śuka and the unnamed brahmin, to the sun itself. The five other narratives, found in some of the youngest portions of the epic, involve hermits (Bharadvāja, Vipula, Sulabhā, Vidura, and Kāvya Uśanas), some of whom are termed yogis, whose practice bears the closest resemblance to the modus operandi of the "sinister yogis" of chapter one. Like the *yogayukta* chariot warriors who pierce the otherwise impermeable barrier of the sun, these epic yogis penetrate the otherwise impermeable barrier of other people's bodies, and in both cases, the media through which these penetrations occur are solar rays. Chapter four will be devoted to a discussion of this last set of epic narratives and to the metaphysics and theories of perception and knowledge that undergird them.

Five of the six epic narratives that involve *yogayukta* chariot warriors depict "dying as a yogic event,"[132] by means of which a hero wills his luminous self or lifebody to rise up out of his recumbent, if not comatose, physical body. The earliest of these narratives, found in the epic's Droṇa Parvan, concern the chariot warriors Bhūriśravas and Droṇa, who, at their moment of self-willed death, are called *yogayukta*. In the light of what has preceded, we may see that this use of terminology to denote the death of a chariot warrior is a deliberate vedic archaism employed by epic compilers who never tired of asserting that death in battle was the *kṣatriya*'s privileged path to the highest heaven.[133]

When Bhūriśravas's right arm was severed by Arjuna's sword, and he knew that he was unable to fight on,

> he sat down on the battlefield [in preparation for] departing from life (*prāya*),[134] spreading a bed of arrows with his left hand. Desiring to go to the world of *brahman*, he thereupon offered his vital breaths into [his] breaths. He composed his eye on the sun with his mind placid, in internal acquiescence. Contemplating his great final rest (*mahopaniṣad*), that silent one (*muni*) became hitched to his rig (*yogayukto'bhavat*)."[135]

Upon hearing the announcement of the death of his son, Droṇa, "who was ready to hitch up . . . put down his weapon on the battlefield and sat on his chariot's driving box."[136] Here as well, the sun is evoked in a number of ways. But of greater moment here is the language employed to describe Droṇa's ascension to the heavens, which is evocative of that found—as we will see in the next chapter—in the Upaniṣads.

> Mounting that rig (*yogam āsthāya*), that great ascetic who had become a luminous being (*jyotirbhūta*), that teacher, charged toward (*ākrāmat*) heaven, to which advance is difficult (*durākramam*) even by the good and the true. And when he was gone [toward heaven], the impression arose that two suns had seemingly [merged] into a single point, and the sky was filled with luminaries. Then, that scion of Bharadvāja[137] entered into the moon, which was shining like the sun, and in a twinkling, his light disappeared . . . With Droṇa now gone to the World of Brahman . . . five humans saw that great-souled one who was hitched to his rig going to the highest path (*paramāṃ gatim*).[138]

These and the other narratives of this type depict the apotheosis of the chariot warrior as an ascent, usually via the rays or reins (*raśmi*) of the sun, to the "highest path" (*paramāṃ gatim*), the world of the absolute *brahman*, the place of the immortal gods. This dynamic was part and parcel of a new soteriology that had already emerged in the classical Upaniṣads.

The respective apotheoses of the other epic chariot warriors do not occur on the battlefield itself for the simple reason that in this epic of battle, in which the survival of the victors and their allies was a narrative requirement, the final curtain could not fall for these characters until after the war's aftermath. The accounts of their "yogic" apotheoses are found in the epic's latest strata. In the epic's seventeenth "Book of the Great Departure," the Pāṇḍava brothers and Draupadī, who are "ready to hitch up their rigs"[139] and whose "practice is yoga,"[140] are shown trudging upward to their deaths and, presumably, bodily apotheosis. They at last come into the view of the Himalaya and, beholding an "ocean of sand" (very likely the stars of heaven[141]), are described as "striding over" (*atikramantas*).[142] However, when Draupadī falls dead while still on the path, the text informs us that she is one whose "rig had fallen" (*bhraṣṭayogā*), as if to say that the rig that was supposed to draw her upward to the higher worlds had slipped away, leaving her dead in the snow.[143] In the end, only the *yogayukta* Yudhiṣṭhira, the most righteous of the group, reaches heaven in embodied form.

The case of Kṛṣṇa's death in the MBh is a peculiar one, inasmuch as he is simultaneously a "human" ally of the Pāṇḍavas, a warrior of the Vṛṣṇi clan, and the supreme person and revealer of the BhG. As such, his demise triggers the reunion of his individual self with his universal self. This is the likely explanation for the use of the term *saṃkramaṇa* ("transference"[144]) in the account of his apotheosis.

> That mighty one reflected on the destruction of the Andhakas and Vṛṣṇis, and of the demise of the house of Kuru. He thought that the time for transference (*saṃkramaṇa*) [had come]. Thereupon, he forced together his senses, speech, and mind; and Kṛṣṇa, whose senses, speech, and mind were [thus] forced together (*saṃniruddha*), reached the "great rig" (*mahāyoga*) and lay down. At that time, a terrible hunter [named] Jara ("Old Age") passed nearby, seeking to slay a deer. He saw Keśava [Kṛṣṇa] lying there, hitched to his rig (*yogayukta*). Assuming him to be a deer, Jara the hunter shot him in the sole of the foot with an arrow, and then swiftly drew near, intending to lay hold of him. The hunter then saw a man with many arms and clad in yellow, hitched to his rig.[145]

Jara then sees Kṛṣṇa going upward (*gacchannūrdhvam*) into the sky, passing through ever more exalted realms, until "that teacher of yoga (*yogācārya*), filling the heavens with his splendor, arrived at his own place."[146]

When Bhīṣma was "hitched to his rig (*yogayukta*), his soul rose up into the sky like a great meteor. It then entered into space (*ākāśa*) and disappeared in a twinkling." The luminous rise of Bhīṣma's soul was witnessed by an illustrious body of onlookers: the foremost members of the royal Vāsudeva line, all of the hermits, and Vyāsa himself.[147] As we have noted, similar language is found in the account of Droṇa's apotheosis, which was witnessed by "five humans." Likewise, a king named Bṛhadratha (whose own apotheosis is described in the MU) refers to other kings who rose to heaven "before the unblinking gaze" of their entire families.[148] As we will see in chapter four, eyewitness perception by persons of authority and distinction is the highest form of valid cognition, without which the authenticity of wonders such as this would be open to question. While none of these epic narratives identify the chariot warriors who trigger their apotheosis in this way as yogis, one finds such an identification being made in later texts. The *Bhāgavata Purāṇa* (BhP) calls the royal seer (*rājarṣi*) Parikṣit, the grandson of Arjuna himself, a *mahāyogī* precisely at the moment when he makes the decision to give up his life. Composing his self in the transcendent self with the self (*ātmanyātmanamātmanā*), suppressing his breath and remaining still as a tree, he sits down on the shore of the Ganges, facing east.[149]

6. The "Yogic" Apotheosis of Hermits

Bhūriśravas, Droṇa, Yudhiṣṭhira, Kṛṣṇa, and Bhīṣma are chariot warriors whose apotheoses takes them beyond the sun to the highest path. Three other epic narratives describe non-warriors who rise to the heavens and, in two cases, enter into the sun. Like the other epic narratives of hermits practicing yoga,[150] these three accounts are found in some of the youngest portions of the MBh.

While he is not explicitly termed a *parivrāj* or *parivrajaka*, the epic Śuka is very much a wanderer, and his story graphically illustrates the dynamic of yoking oneself to the sun.[151] Because his name means "parrot," and because he is said to have mastered the practice of yoga, Śuka is more inclined to fly from place to place than to wander on foot, and although he is exhorted to "take a human path," he traverses the sky "on foot."[152]

> [Śuka], the righteous hermit, went to Mithila, able to advance on foot, via the sky, across the earth with its oceans, [by] striding over (*atikramya*) mountains and crossing rivers and lakes . . . Advancing over the continent of Bhārata step by step (*krameṇa*) . . . he traveled that road like a bird moving in the sky.[153]

Shortly thereafter, all talk of walking is abandoned as the *yogayukta* Śuka, who is shining like the sun, races across the firmament.[154] In this, he resembles Arjuna, who, when he journeyed to the distant north to win the weapons of the gods from Indra, is described as advancing (*parākramanta*) "with Indra's own rig" (*aindrena yogena*) and, "hitched to his rig" (*yogayukta*), as charging over (*atikramya*) the Himalaya.[155] Śuka's many wanderings, which have been nothing other than a quest for final release (*mokṣa*), near their end when he comes to the hermitage of his father,

Vyāsa, who schools him on the cosmology of mystic ascent. I will return to this cosmology in the next chapter; here, however, I will turn, as this story does, to the place of visual perception in solar apotheosis. Telling him that his divine eye (*divyam cakṣus*) has now arisen, Vyāsa explains to Śuka that he is now capable of seeing "the self with the self" and of taking the path of the seven winds that leads to Viṣṇu.[156] Śuka then resolves upon the practice of yoga that will ensure his definitive liberation:

"Without hitching up (*yoga*), the highest path cannot be reached . . . Therefore, mounting [my] rig (*yogam samāsthāya*) and abandoning my mortal shell, I will become the wind and enter into the effulgent mass of the sun"[157] . . . He who knew the practice of hitching up that ensures advancing (*kramayogavit*) gradually fixed his self in his limbs, [working] upward from his foot . . . Mounting his rig once again for the purpose of reaching the path to liberation, he who had become a great master of yogis (*mahāyogīśvara*) charged up over (*ati-krāmad*) the atmosphere[158] . . . His body below and his face above, he was carried by his eyes . . . Facing eastward, he who was gazing at the sun silently travelled [there][159] . . . Abiding in the *brahman*, he blazed like a smokeless fire.[160]

When Śuka's eyes lock into the sun's rays, they draw him into its disk, wherein he finds liberation. A similar reading of his apotheosis is found in the *Vāyu Purāṇa* (VāP)—perhaps the earliest of all the Purāṇas[161] and, therefore, more or less coeval with this late epic narrative—where it is said that Śuka, the great hermit, yogi, and ascetic, entered into a state of no return and, abiding in the rays of the sun (*ādityakiraṇopetam*), was fully liberated.[162]

Similar themes are found in the epic account of Jaigīṣavya, a Buddhist mendicant (*bhikṣuka*) and hermit (*muni*) whose display of "yogic" powers inspires a brahmin householder named Asita Devala to renounce his this-worldly ways for the practice of liberation (*mokṣadharma*). Seated in a hermitage located at the Sārasvata-tīrtha, Asita Devala beholds the great ascetic (*mahātapā*) Jaigīṣavya "hitched to his rig" and possessed of supernatural powers.[163] He sees him traveling across the sky, where he is revered by the siddhas, before continuing on to a series of higher realms, including the world of the ancestors (called Somaloka), the world of cattle, as well as the places (*sthāna*) of the Rudras, the Vāsus, and Bṛhaspati. He also beholds the hermit performing various vedic rituals (including the *agniṣṭoma*, *cāturmāsya*, *vājapeya*, and *rājasūya*), in concert with the divine siddhas, to the approbation of the gods. Then, Jaigīṣavya, who is "mounted on his rig" (*yogamāstham*), disappears from view but soon returns, like a bird (*pataṅgavat*), to Asita Devala's hermitage. Asita Devala renounces his householder practice in favor of the practice of liberation and obtains the supreme *siddhi* and the "transcendent rig" (*param yogam*).[164]

The final narrative of the MdhP comprises a description—made by a serpent that has been pulling the solar chariot across the sky to a *yogayukta* brahmin named Dharmāraṇya[165]—of an unnamed brahmin hermit who, remaining faithful to the "gleaning way of life" (*unchāvṛtti*), has entered into the sun in a luminous apotheosis. While the unnamed hermit is not himself termed *yogayukta* here,[166] much of the terminology of solar apotheosis is present. "A second sun, a second luminary, was seen from every quarter . . . as he [the brahmin gleaner] advanced through the sky as if flying, his face turned toward the sun . . . and crossing the sky he entered into the disk of the sun. Immediately, his brilliance became one [with that of the sun] and he became solar (*adityatāṃ gatam*)." The description ends with the brahmin gleaner "charging up to heaven" (*divamākramya*) like an "unsurpassed sun" (*sūrya ivāparaḥ*).[167]

7. Hitching Up

As we have seen, the image of the dying warrior who is "hitched to his rig," or "ready to hitch up" in order to advance upward to the highest path, formed the basis for the earliest yoga paradigm, which privileged a dynamic of outward movement and conquest. Only later, in the period of the latest strata of the epics and of the "classical" Upaniṣads (i.e., the third to fourth centuries CE) would the goal of yogic practice be transferred to a place hidden within the body's deepest recesses, and the seven solar winds internalized into the inner breaths. Yet, even after this inward turn has taken place, the yoga of the chariot warrior persists in the language of later visionary practice. A passage from the MdhP—which describes the rise of a person's soul or lifebody (*jīva*) through the metaphysical categories up to and beyond the unmanifest (*avyaktam*)—is remarkable for its use of the discourse of chariot warfare. This appears to be an account of a meditative program adopted by a person seeking to voluntarily end his life, or who, seeing that his life is near its end, wishes to accelerate his rise to the highest path. While this passage is clearly an expansion on the KU's comparison of the mind-body complex to a charioteer mounted on a heaven-bound chariot, its use of the verb *kram merits discussion here.

After stating that yoking to a single object "with this rig" (*etena yogena*) enables the seeker of knowledge to pass beyond even the absolute,[168] the narrator Vyāsa spins out an extended metaphor, comparing different elements of one's practice—one's yoga—to a war chariot (here called a *ratha*): humility is the chariot's bumper (*varūtha*), out-breath the axle (*akṣa*), in-breath the yoke (*yuga*), seeing and touching the yoke's shoulder pieces, wisdom the nave of the wheel (*nābhi*), and so on. With these homologies in place, the upward advance of this chariot of "yogic" practice is described:

> The celestial chariot that shines in the world of *brahman*, auspicious and pure, is hitched to the [practitioner's] lifebody (*jīvayukta*). Meditation (*dhyāna*) is its range of movement as it follows the wheel-track of [the] abandonment [of life] (*tyāgavartmānuga*). Here I will proclaim the rapid method for a person whose mind is set on going to the imperishable (*akṣayam*), [and] who is hastening in his desire to yoke his chariot. The person who, with speech restrained, obtains for himself (*pratipadyate*) the seven objects of contemplation (*dhāraṇās*) in their totality and as many of the other "fore-objects" of contemplation (*pradhāraṇās*) as there are in the rear and on the flanks [of his chariot[169]], [and] who, "stride by stride," (*kramaśas*), attains mastery (*aiśvaryam*) [over the earth element and the other six objects of his contemplation, also attains] "stride by stride," mastery over the unmanifest (*avyaktam*). And likewise, these "broad strides" (*vikramāḥ*) are his when he yokes [his mind] by means of hitching up [this metaphorical rig].[170]

In his 1901 analysis of this passage, George Washburn Hopkins linked the "strange use of term *vikramāḥ* for stages in his [the would-be yogi's] progress" to the term yoga, which, as he noted "in camp parlance, is hitching up or harnessing up."[171] Once again, both terms draw on the vocabulary of ancient Indian chariot warfare, whence the attention in this passage to the many elements of the chariot's gear. These stages, or "broad strides," are identified in the text as the practitioner's mastery (*aiśvaryam*) over each of the seven *dhāraṇās*, a term that Hopkins translates both as "intentnesses" and "objects of contemplation."[172] *Dhāraṇā* would, of course, take on the more or less fixed meaning, attested in the later YS, of "concentration" (literally, the "holding" of the mind). Furthermore, as I will discuss in chapter four, Nyāya-Vaiśeṣika theories of perception, which were also emerging in this period, privileged the idea that to reach or obtain (*pratipadyate*) the objects of one's contemplation was tantamount to a sort of mastery over them. However, like so much of the terminology related to yoga in the centuries around the beginning of the common era, its meaning was not yet fixed. It should be noted that prior to the extended application of the term *dhāraṇā* to the mechanics of perception and cognition, it also had a specific meaning related to the hitching of horse-drawn conveyances. So, for example, when the verb *dhṛ (from which *dhāraṇā* is generated) takes an object that means "reins" or "harnesses," the meaning is "to draw the reins tight."[173]

Chapter 228 of the MdhP continues by correlating the mastery over each of the seven objects of contemplation—earth, water, air, fire, ether, ego, and intellect[174]—to specific supernatural attainments (*siddhis*) realized by the practitioner who is "yoked to his rig" (*yogayukta*), attainments that he "sees in himself."[175] Mastery over the earth affords the power of "emission," to emit creatures from one's body, after the fashion of Prajāpati, and so on.[176] Employing language redolent of the apotheosis of the epic warrior, the chapter concludes: "[T]hese are the means by which they [who practice this] are liberated through yoga. He who advances beyond (*atikrānta*) yoga-mastery (*yogaiśvaryam*) advances beyond [these worlds and] is liberated."[177] As we saw in the last chapter, "mastery" (*aiśvaryam*) is the term employed by the Pāśupatas to signify the supernatural attainments that were so many proofs of the practitioner's identity with Śiva;[178] and it is perhaps no coincidence that the Pāśupatas are mentioned, for the first time in any Indic scripture, nine chapters later (MBh 12.337.59, 62). However, the absence of references to Śiva in this passage render a Pāśupata link problematic.

8. Yogic Cyclicality

Recently, Thomas Oberlies and Theodore Proferes have, in their reconstruction of the seminomadic existence of the vedic peoples, characterized the *yoga-kṣema* distinction as one that is obtained between periods of mobilization and settlement, or between wartime and peacetime. Proferes summarizes:

> The process of the alternating unification and dispersal of the clans has been connected to the settlement pattern of the vedic groups . . . During periods of fixed habitation, the clans tended their cattle and sheep and practiced small-scale land cultivation. What characterized this period and made its way of life possible was the possession of land resources adequate for the subsistence of the settlement in conjunction with the absence of external threats posed by competing groups. In contrast, during periods of mobilization the clans sought to secure resources from opposing groups through warfare. The causes of these martial phases are to be sought in the economic conditions of the early vedic period. In order to feed their cattle and to permit cultivation, the various settlements required land in the rich river valleys where water was abundant. As such land was limited, conflict between the competing groups was inevitable . . . In [some] cases, the mobilization may have taken the form

of raids to plunder cattle, women, or grain; it may even have been a periodic affair based upon the time of year. In such cases the warriors would have returned after the raiding season to their original place of habitation . . . The difference between the two phases of fixed habitation and mobilization was the difference between peace time and war time.[179]

In his 1988 article "Householder and Wanderer," Jan Heesterman saw in the vedic opposition between *yoga* and *kṣema* further evidence to support his theory of a "pre-classical" alternation between the raiding parties (*yoga*) of the *yāyāvara* and the stasis (*kṣema*) of the householder (*śālīna*) who had set up his sacrificial fires.[180] He concluded his article by describing the shift that occurred when "pre-classical" sacrifice was domesticated into "classical" vedic ritual.

At the beginning, before the rise of the śrauta ritual proper, stands the imposing figure of the aggressive yāyāvara warrior setting out on his chariot to risk his all in sacrificial contests but hoping to eventually return with the goods of life that his prowess has won him. When the ultimately self-defeating cycle of violence was broken and its alternating phases of trekking and settling collapsed, the yāyāvara and his opposite, the śālīna, were fused into the single āhitāgni, the householder who sets up the sacred fires and thereby gains the transcendent world of the śrauta sacrifice . . . [T]his leads right into the renunciatory mode of life . . . So at the end of the road, and bringing its bifurcated paths together again, the yāyāvara emerges once more but now converted into the ultra-mundane ascetic wanderer. His yoga is no longer the yoking of his animals when he sets out on his trek. It has become the even more strenuous discipline for the no less precarious inner journey into the depths of the transcendent.[181]

One may detect, in Upaniṣads as early as the *Taittirīya* (TU), a text belonging to the same Black Yajurvedic lineage as the TB, that the inward turn described by Heestermann had already begun: the TU's esoteric reading of *yoga-kṣema* is "in-breath and out-breath" (*prāṇāpāna*).[182] Similar developments were taking place in several coeval Buddhist scriptures, which interpreted *yogakkhema* (the Pali form of *yogakṣema*) as "the attainment of perfect peace from the four attachments," a necessary precondition for realizing *nibbana*, if not tantamount to *nibbana* itself.[183] The KU and BhG read this compound as "acquisition and peaceful possession,"[184] an interpretation seconded by later commentators on the vedic uses of the term.[185] These later readings, of what was a problematic compound in the vedic literature,[186] are indications that the original sense of *yogayukta* as being "hitched to one's rig" was already on the wane on the eve of the advent of the common era. For this reason, it is more appropriate to translate the compound *yogayukta* as "yoked to the practice of yoga" than as "hitched to his rig" in post-fourth-century texts.

For reasons that will become apparent, I hesitate to follow Heesterman in calling the "precarious inner journey into the depths of the transcendent" as the yoga—or, at least, the only yoga of this period. I say this, not only on the basis of the use of the term in the epic narratives and in aphoristic references to the "yogic" apotheosis of warriors and wanderers, but also because the *yoga-kṣema* alternation appears to have persisted in south Asia, in everything but name, well into the colonial period. Here I am speaking of the cyclical dynamic of what Dirk Kolff has termed the military labor market in Mughal-era Hindustan and, specifically, the "oldest layer of Rajputhood as an open status group of warrior-ascetics in search of patronage and marriage."[187] Kolff takes as his starting point the *bārahmāsa* genre of vernacular north Indian literature, in which village women pine for their absent husbands who are employed as *naukar*s, merchants, or mercenaries in the service of a distant lord. This period of service—during which a present or future husband abandons his home and kin for an extended period of time—was viewed as a form of renunciation, which transformed the man into a yogi.[188] This was not, however, a yoga of postures and meditative states, but rather a yoga of combat, performed in the garb of a yogi, which ended either in the *naukar*'s death or in his return to home and hearth, loaded down with the booty and plunder necessary to ensure the economic survival of his household. As Kolff has suggested, this is a pattern that can be historically documented back to the time of Aśoka.[189]

I will return to specific accounts of such "warrior ascetics" in the final chapter of this book. Here, however, I wish to juxtapose the dynamic of the two moments of this cycle to the vedic *yoga-kṣema* polarity. In much of the popular literature on the subject, renunciant soldiering either followed an annual cycle—of eight months of military service followed by the four months of the rainy season, when the weather made warfare and trade virtually impossible—or it constituted a period in the male life cycle, theoretically twelve years in length, followed by a permanent return to home and hearth. Kolff describes this dynamic in the following terms:

> [T]he crucial point of difference with brahmanical theory was that these Rajputs and the numerous semi-tribal clans that took to the rajputising model were not inspired by the ideal of renunciation as an other-worldly, transcendent aim worth pursuing for its own sake. For them ascetic sacrifice was the necessary complement of the politics of settlement and family life . . . Of foremost importance, therefore, for those who left home as

> *naukar*, or service men, was not the irrevocable renunciation of primordial ties, but the hope of earning the ability to ascetically fight one's way back home. The crucial age below which to achieve this is forty . . . At that age at the latest he hopes to return to his farm, there to fulfill and consummate his life as a householder and family man.[190]

The original vedic meaning of the term *yoga-kṣema* (as well as the cyclical nature of "pre-classical" vedic sacrifice as theorized by Heesterman) has been preserved, I would argue, in the early Rajput ideology undergirding the *bārahmāsa* songs and heroic ballads of thirteenth- to nineteenth-century north India. From the moment that he sallied forth to undertake a period of raiding, trading, and warfare as (or in the service of) a Rajput lord, the warrior was a yogi, practicing yoga in the late vedic and epic sense of the term. However, if all went well, a life of sedentary peace and prosperity (*kṣema*) awaited him at the end of his long road.

9. Conclusion

This semantic shift in the use of the term "yoga"—from its original sense of a chariot warrior's hitching up his rig and engaging with enemies, fortresses, or gods and other beings in this world or in heaven (the predicate objects of his advances: pra-*kram, ā-*kram, ut-*kram, ati-*kram)—to its opposite, disengagement from the world, provides a historical explanation for the dissonance, evoked at the beginning of this chapter, between the etymology of *yoga* and its commentarial description as *viyoga*. A consideration of the original usage of the compound *yoga-kṣema*, found in a passage from the circa eighth- to fourth-century BCE TB,[191] is particularly illustrative: "In the accomplishment of *yoga-kṣema, yoga* is the yoking [of the harness straps]; *kṣema* is the sitting posture."[192] In other words, in this very early context, yoga was in no respect identified with sitting. So too, the YājS (2.3.51), in its review of the activities of the ascetic who is fasting unto death, lists "sitting" and "practicing yoga" as separate activities: "[T]he day he should spend [standing] on the tip of his toes, or standing, sitting, or walking about, or again by practicing yoga (*yogābhyāsena*)."[193] The same is the case in the MBh, as Hopkins observed in his groundbreaking study of yoga in the epics:

> "Posture" is a chief concern of the Yogin, but to the [epic hermit] this technicality is unknown. Through the whole of the earlier epic I believe there is but one case even suggesting the Yogin [*sic*] "posture," whereas the tales are many which show that the [hermits] either stood, or hung themselves upside down.[194]

So it is that several of the earliest uses of the term yoga do not define it in terms of the posture of sitting, in the light of which Marshall's identification of the seated figure of Mohenjo-Daro seal 420 as a proto-yogi is highly questionable.

As a relatively late portion of the MBh, the BhG synthesizes much of the earlier yogic lore contained in the epic in a comprehensive, albeit not always consistent, way. Accordingly, it takes two positions on the seated posture, admonishing the yogi to focus his mind while sitting on a seat (*āsanam*) in its sixth chapter, but unfavorably comparing the imperfect discipline of the mind while one is sitting to *karma yoga*, the "discipline of action," in its third chapter.[195] Of course, *āsana* is listed as the third limb of the eight-limbed yogic practice of the YS (2.29), which also briefly evoke it in three other aphorisms (2.46–48). These, however, give no detail on what "sitting posture" is intended by the term. It is only Vedavyāsa who, in his commentary on verse 46, provides the specific names of eleven *āsana*s, many of which persist down to the present time: *padmāsana*, *vīrāsana*, *bhadrāsana*, and so on. The first of these, *padmāsana*, appears to have by now become a posture, as opposed to the royal seat or cushion, for which the term *siṃhāsana*, "lion throne" (or *vajrāsana*, the Buddha's "diamond throne" at the base of the Bodhi Tree[196]), becomes increasingly applied in the centuries that follow.

Iconographic evidence for this development may also be adduced from the sculptural record. In the fourth century CE, the earliest extant sculptural representations appear of Lakulīśa, the legendary founder of the Pāśupata order whose yogic animation, by Śiva, will be described in chapter five. In his earliest sculptures, Lakulīśa is represented as a standing figure, iconographically similar to representations of Śiva's minions (*gaṇa*s) in the Kushan period.[197] Lakulīśa is termed a yogi in many textual accounts,[198] and following the fifth to sixth century he is often portrayed seated upon a lotus in what might be identified as a yogic posture or with a yoga-band (*yoga-paṭṭa*) wrapped around his knees.[199] The earliest textual references to this cloth band date from the same period.[200] These data allow us to place the earliest incontrovertible references to the yoga of postures in this time frame, in the middle of the first millennium of the common era. In contrast, a number of Chinese sources from an earlier date discuss yogic theory, breathing techniques, and postures in everything but name. The earliest of these, the fourth-century BCE Taoist *Nei-yeh* ("Inner Training"), declares,

> If people can be aligned and tranquil,
> Their skin will be ample and smooth,

Figure 2.10 Sculpture of Lakulīśa seated on a lotus, Mathura, ca. sixth century. Courtesy of State Museum, Lucknow.

Their ears will be acute and clear,
Their muscles will be supple and their bones will be strong.
Then they will be able to hold up the Great Circle [of the heavens]
And tread firmly over the Great Square [of the earth] . . .
For all to practice the Way
You must coil, you must contract,
You must uncoil, you must expand,
You must be firm, you must be regular [in this practice] . . .
When you enlarge your mind and let go of it,
When you relax your vital breath and expand it,
When your body is calm and unmoving . . .
And you can maintain the One and discard the myriad disturbances.
Relaxed and unwound, yet acutely sensitive,
In solitude you delight in your own person
This is called "revolving the vital breath."[201]

More arresting still is a chart of Taoist "therapeutic exercises" excavated from Mawangdui tomb 3, a 168 BCE burial site in Hunan province, which features colored line drawings of a wide variety of calisthenics, some of which resemble yoga postures. Dating from the same century is the *Yinshu*, a medical manuscript devoted to techniques for "nurturing life" (*yangsheng*) through breathing techniques, exercise, sexual intercourse, and dietetics. One of these techniques, called "pulling *yin*," is described in the following terms: "Sit squarely and spread both thighs. Place the left hand on the ground and reach up with the right hand. Bend the waist, extend the lower abdomen forward, and use force to pull the buttocks."[202] Several hundred years prior to these Chinese theories and techniques, Greek "pneumatic physiology" appears to anticipate Indian *kuṇḍalinī* practices.[203] I am not arguing here Taoist macrobiotic hygiene or Greek pneumatics were sources of the Indian yogic postures or techniques of breath control. Rather, my point is that it is inappropriate to project later yoga traditions backward upon early images of persons seated in novel poses or to ancient references to regulating the breaths.

Without an accompanying "label" or coeval text to provide context for it, it is therefore abusive to identify the figure on Mohenjo-Daro seal 420 as a yogi. It is something of a historical irony that in current parlance, the emic term employed by wandering ascetics for a false ascetic or charlatan is "420 Yogi" (in Hindi, *cār sau bīs jogī*). Many times in my meetings with Nāths, Nagas, and other members of the itinerant (and formerly military) religious orders, I have heard this term used derisively for persons who wore the garb of the yogi in order to enjoy the food and shelter offered to holy men by charitable organizations at various pilgrimage sites. In this contemporary usage, the figure 420 is said to refer to the article in the colonial and contemporary Indian Penal Code that defines "cheating and dishonestly inducing delivery of property" as a punishable offense.[204] In the light of the preceding, the same modifier may be applied to the image on Mohenjo-Daro seal 420 that was identified by Marshall as a "proto-Śiva." Rather than representing a proto-Śiva or a proto-yogi, it stands as a monument to a flawed classification system: a proto-yogic impersonator, a proto-*cār sau bīs jogī*.

THREE

Embodied Ascent, Meditation, & Yogic Suicide

In the last chapter, I argued that an archaic warrior soteriology was narrativized in epic accounts of dying heroes who, "hitched to their rigs," charged up from the field of battle to pierce the orb of the sun and attain the world of the immortal gods. In the present chapter, I will trace the ways in which this paradigm was transferred onto another set of actors, who, through their esoteric knowledge of the true nature of the self as well as of powerful spells (the mantra OṂ or AUṂ in particular), were empowered to reach the same transcendent abode or state of being, now called the world of *brahman* (*brahmaloka*). During the course of the first half of the first millennium of the common era, these actors—whose knowledge-based soteriology especially carried forward the legacy of the yoga of the vedic poets—developed novel meditative techniques as a means for projecting their mental apparatus into higher worlds or states of consciousness while still alive. However, even as the old paradigm of "going" was yielding to one of "knowing,"[1] the language of yoga was retained in a fossilized form, with early puranic soteriologies postulating that throngs of still-embodied beings—called "yogis," "great yogis" (*mahāyogīs*), "masters" (*īśvaras*), or "great masters" (*maheśvaras*)—inhabited a sort of antechamber to the highest realm of fully liberated beings, whose total fusion with the absolute entailed their disembodiment and loss of individuality. In the Hindu context, this marked the beginning of the cleavage between the goals of *jīvanmukti*, "liberation while living," and *videhamukti*, "disembodied liberation." Parallel developments are found in Buddhist sources from the same period, evidence for an ongoing conversation among the exponents of these rival traditions.

1. Embodied Ascent and Liberation in the Early Upaniṣads

The early Upaniṣads[2] offer an entirely novel insight, repeated in a hundred different ways throughout the history of this corpus, that there is an absolute ground of all being—called *brahman* (the power of expansion), *puruṣa* (the transcendent person, a reference to the renowned Rigvedic cosmogonic "Hymn of the Man"), or *mahān ātmā* (the "self-magnifying self")[3]—that is the source of all existence and the final goal of all creatures seeking liberation from the flow of rebirths (*saṃsāra*). According to this new insight, which was the hallmark of the nondual mysticism of the upanishadic corpus, this absolute ground is simultaneously the universal *container* of all that exists and that which is *contained* in all that has life, in the form of a luminous thumb-sized "person" (*puruṣa*) ensconced in the heart. These representations of the absolute give rise to two different and incompatible soteriologies, the one immanentist and the other gradualist. Much of the content of the later Upaniṣads—as well as epic, puranic, agamic, and tantric discussions of the paths to the liberation of the soul—are so many attempts to bring these two early soteriologies into conformity with one another.

The two soteriologies are found in early portions of the BṛU, as well as in the final chapters of the ChU's book seven and the opening chapters of book eight of the same work. The immanentist model is grounded in doctrine of the imperishable and expansive nature of the *brahman*—a term whose primary meaning is, precisely, "expansion" (from the root *bṛh, "expand")—and its identity with the transcendent self, or "itself," *ātman*. So, an opening chapter of the BṛU states:

> Thus it is said: "People think that they will become everything (*sarvam*) through knowledge of the *brahman*. What was it that the *brahman* knew that made it become everything?" At first, this [world] was only *brahman*, and it knew only itself (*ātman*): "I am *brahman*." As a result, it became everything. Among the gods, whoever recognized this, he alone became everything. So it was among the seers, and so it was among humans. When he perceived this, the seer Vāmadeva intoned: "I was Manu, and I was the sun." This is true here and now. The one who knows "I am *brahman*" in this way becomes this everything (*idaṃ sarvaṃ bhavati*).[4]

Similar statements are found in other early Upaniṣads, including the following passage from the final chapters of the ChU's seventh book, which are presented as a teaching by Sanatkumāra, a figure who becomes identified in later literature as one of the immortal mind- or yoga-born sons of Brahmā-Prajāpati who dwells eternally on the highest path:[5]

The self (*ātman*), indeed, is below; the self is above; the self is in the west; the self is in the east; the self is in the south; and the self is in the north. The self is, precisely, this everything . . . When he is seeing this to be so, when he is thinking it, when he is knowing it . . . he becomes capable of moving at will in all of the worlds . . . When he is seeing this to be so, when he is thinking it, when he is knowing it . . . then this whole world, precisely, [arises] from the self.[6]

This immanentist approach becomes complicated in the book that follows, the ChU's book eight, which speculates on the postmortem fate of those who are described in book seven as knowing the self. The book begins with a similar reflection that one should seek to know the infinitesimal *brahman* that, while its lotus house is ensconced within its citadel (*pur*) within the heart, is simultaneously massive in size: "The space that is within the heart is as big as *this* space [i.e., the space of this whole world] . . . everything is placed together inside it." This is all well and good, but what happens, the text continues, to the self, this all-encompassing whole, when the body dies? The answer is that although bodies die and pass away, that which is within the citadel of *brahman* neither grows old nor dies. Thus, those who have come to know the self (*ātman*) in life are enabled to move at will in all worlds after death.[7]

It is here that complications arise, as the author of these speculations seeks to link the minuscule *brahman* of the heart to the self-magnifying self (*mahān ātmā*) that is coterminus with the entire universe and, specifically, with the worlds to which "those who know" travel after death.[8] The problem is the following: how can a virtually liberated being—that is, one who knows the entire universe to be coterminus with his own transcendent person or self-magnifying self—ever possibly be external to "himself" when he rises up to the highest path after death? In other words, how can a virtually liberated being—let us call him a "buddha," or a "yogi," since the texts of this period were starting to employ these terms—simultaneously rise up out of himself and yet know that there is nothing outside of himself?

It is here that the authors of this Upaniṣad appear to have adopted the dynamics of the yoga of the vedic poets and of the warrior who becomes hitched to his rig, when they identify the links between this world and the highest path as solar rays that creep into the subtle channels of the human body:

> The channels (*nāḍīs*) of the heart are made of a fine essence that is tawny, white, blue, yellow and red. Verily, the sun on high is tawny, it is white, it is blue, it is yellow, it is red. Like a road between two villages goes from one to the other, so too the solar rays go to two worlds, this world below and the world above . . . Now, when someone has become enfeebled, people who have come sit around him and say "Do you know me? Do you know me?" For so long as he has not advanced upward out of this body, he knows them. But when he is departing from this body, then he advances upward (*utkrāmati*) along these very rays (*raśmibhiḥ*). Verily, he speaks the word "OṂ" [and] he rises up. As soon as he casts his mind there, he goes to the sun. That is truly the door of the world (*lokadvāram*), an entrance for those who know, but a barrier for those who do not know.[9] On that subject, this verse: "There are a hundred and one channels of the heart. One of these passes up to the crown of the head. Going by that one, one goes to immortality. The others, advancing upward (*utkramaṇe*), advance upward in all directions."[10]

As we will see in this and the next chapter, this link, between the solar rays and egress into a transcendent plane, becomes an episteme of Indic soteriologies, as evinced in figure 3.1, a Tibetan Buddhist rendering of the attainment of enlightenment in the intermediate state (*bardo*) between death and rebirth. On this theme, the first- to third-century CE *Praśna Upaniṣad* (PU) explains that the sun gathers together the life breaths (*prāṇān*) of all living creatures into its rays (*raśmiṣu*) as it moves across the sky. The man who meditates on the highest person (*paraṃ puruṣam*) through the syllable OṂ at the end of his life[11] is absorbed into the sun's rays and, delivered there from evil, is raised up to the world of *brahman*. There, he beholds the highest person, abiding in the citadel (*puriśayam*) high above the throng of living creatures.[12] Like the ChU, the PU is not merely describing the postmortem fate of all living beings, which is to be gathered back into the sun that gave them life. Rather, it is making a distinction between the fates of "those who know" and those who do not, in which knowledge comprises a familiarity with the one channel (from among more than a hundred) that leads to immortality and acquaintance with the mantra OṂ. For those who do not know, the sun is a barrier, and their mortality is terminal, irreversible. For those who know, however, the sun becomes a door to immortality, with the mantra OṂ the secret key that opens that door.

Figure 3.1 Enlightenment in the intermediate state between death and rebirth. Detail from western mural, Lukhang Temple, Lhasa, Tibet, ca. 1700. Courtesy Thomas Laird.

As we saw in the last chapter, this division flows from the cosmology of death and immortality described in the Brāhmaṇas, according to which the sun is a barrier to the world of the immortal gods.[13] Immortality, then, becomes a matter of knowing how to raise oneself beyond the sun. The sixth and final chapter of the KU, a teaching that calls itself "the knowledge taught by Death" (here, the death god Yama) and the "entire yoga canon,"[14] provides the aspiring immortal's key to the solar door. This it does by first explaining the relationship between the visible world and the invisible realities beyond, through an early enumeration of the categories of samkhyan metaphysics, an enumeration that would form the basis for the cosmology of the BhG as well as the later structure and dynamic of puranic cosmogony as explicated in the Vaiṣṇava Purāṇas:[15]

> The mind is higher than the senses, the pure essence (*sattva*) higher than the mind. Above the pure essence is the self-magnifying self (*mahān ātmā*); higher than the self-magnifying self is the unmanifest (*avyaktam*). Transcending the unmanifest is the person (*puruṣa*), who is all-pervading and without attributes. Knowing him, a creature is released [from rebirth] and reaches immortality . . . Those who know this become immortal.[16]

A few verses later, the KU quotes ChU 8.6.6, which it then glosses:

> There is a thumb-sized man (*puruṣa*) within the self who is eternally ensconced in the hearts of living creatures. One should, with one's intelligence, strip him out of one's body like the [inner] reed from [a stalk of] sedge grass.[17] One should know it as the shining, immortal one.[18]

Śaṅkara, who cites these verses from KU's sixth chapter repeatedly in his BrSūBh, interprets them to mean that *all* souls are released, through knowledge, after death.[19] This is likely due to his nondualist stance: since there is no real difference between what are apparently multiple selves and the universal self, then the falling away of the body, mind, and senses is the sole necessary condition for their primordial and virtual identity to be realized. In Śaṅkara's defense, there also exist upanishadic passages that describe the rise of the soul after death as automatic, regardless of knowledge, will, or condition. An early example is BṛU 5.10, which simply states:

> When a person (*puruṣa*) goes forth from this world, he comes to the wind. It opens [a space] for him like the hole in a chariot wheel. He advances (*ākramate*) upward through it. He comes to the sun. It opens [a space] for him like the hole in a *lambara* drum. He

advances upward through it. He comes to the moon. It opens [a space] for him like the hole in a *dundubhi* drum. He advances upward through it. He comes to a world without sorrow or snow. He lives in it for years without end.

2. Journeys into Inner and Outer Space according to the *Maitri Upaniṣad*

The later Upaniṣads, and the MU in particular, expand on the speculations found in the ChU and KU, repeatedly linking these earlier texts' discussions of the rise of the soul, via the rays of the sun, to the practice of yoga. In a text-critical study published in 1962, J. A. van Buitenen convincingly divided the extant MU into three principal divisions: (1) an "original" Upaniṣad—belonging to the Black Yajurveda and dating from about the same period as the TU, that is, the fourth to third centuries BCE—which he calls the *Maitrāyaṇīya*;[20] (2) a later text, entitled the *Maitreyi* or *Maitreya* or *Maitrāyaṇī Upaniṣad*, which was grafted onto the former by an unknown hand or hands;[21] and (3) interpolations and additions made to this composite by one or more editors.[22] As Van Buitenen argued, it is due to this text's composite nature that "it is neither a 'principal' or 'classical,' nor yet entirely a 'minor' [U]paniṣad, but falls somewhere between these uncertain and arbitrary categories."[23] Nearly all of the portions of the sixth book of the MU that will concern us here belong to one of the latest strata of the text, which I would date, on the basis of its language and content, to about the third century of the common era. In this, I do not part ways with certain scholars who consider portions of the MU to be late "tantric" additions. Their assessment applies to a small portion of this book,[24] as well as to much if not all of book seven, which, for example, roundly condemns those who vainly wear the yellowish red robes of the Buddhist orders; the wide earrings that were the mark of several Śaiva orders, including the Nāth Yogīs (*kaṣāyakuṇḍalinaḥ*); or who are skull bearers (*kāpāliṇaḥ*). However, the bulk of MU 6 is coeval with the other major early syntheses of yoga theory (the YS as well as the BhG and MdhP) and, as such, constitutes an important bridge between epic narrative and early vedic and upanishadic speculation on the one hand, and puranic and tantric cosmology and soteriology on the other. Of crucial interest for the historian of yoga is the narrative account that frames the book's final nine chapters, within which is embedded an extended and sometimes bewildering theoretical discussion of yogic theory and practice.

No Upaniṣad contains as much data on yoga as this single book of the MU, which also has the distinction of containing the sole mention of the person of the yogi in the entire "classical" upanishadic corpus (6.10),[25] identifying him as a renouncer (*sannyāsin*) and "one who sacrifices for himself (or who sacrifices to the supreme self)" (*ātmayājin*). The same passage goes on to identify the yogi as one who does not touch the sense objects, that is, as one who withdraws his senses from contact with their objects; similar statements are found in the coeval BhG and YS. One should not, however, conclude from such statements that the compilers of these texts intended that yogis were to eschew all contact with the outside world. Rather, they meant that the yogi's intellect or consciousness was capable of apprehending the sense objects directly, without refraction through the sense organs. We will return to this important issue in the next chapter.

MU 6.18 contains the earliest upanishadic account of "six-limbed yoga," followed by the description of a practice that resembles the hathayogic technique of *khecarī mudrā* (6.20)[26] and a listing of the sounds heard within the heart (6.22), not unlike that found in the fifteenth-century HYP.[27] MU 6.21 contains the sole mention (in the "classical" Upaniṣads) of the *suṣumṇā* as the subtle channel that leads to immortality, along which, "through the conjunction of breath, the syllable OṂ, and the mind, one may advance upward (*utkramet*)." Seven chapters later, the same channel, here unnamed, is described as "transpiercing the solar orb, [and] advanc[ing] beyond (*atikramya*) [the sun] to the World of Brahman (*brahmaloka*). They [the dead] go by it to the highest path (*parāṃ gatim*)."[28]

However, the book's twenty-eighth chapter identifies the goal of yogic practice as egress into the space of the *brahman* that is located, not at the summit of the universe, but rather in the innermost recesses of the heart (understood as the core of one's being, rather than as a specific organ), that all-important inner space of earlier upanishadic traditions.[29] How are we to interpret this apparent contradiction concerning the yogi's final goal? Part of the answer to this question may be adduced by recalling a similar alternation found in the KU, an earlier Upaniṣad of the Black Yajurveda, whose sixth book links yoga to both the attainment of the *puruṣa* situated on the highest path and the stripping out of the thumb-sized *puruṣa* of the heart from the body.[30] As we will see, the MU's final books revisit this dynamic of the two *puruṣas*, but in greater detail.

It should also be noted that the KU's two-verse enumeration of the categories of samkhyan metaphysics appears, in fact, in two different places in this Upaniṣad and, therefore, in two different contexts. Unlike book six of the KU, cited above, the verses in question, when they appear in the KU's third book, do so immediately following its homologization of the intellect-body complex to a charioteer in his chariot, without reference to yoga. However, in the third book, the rise through the samkhyan categories is introduced by the statement "the man who has knowledge as his charioteer and mind as his reins obtains the highest path, [that is,] Viṣṇu's highest plane (*tadviṣṇoḥ paramaṃ padam*)," which is further identified with the highest path of the transcendent person, the *puruṣa*.[31]

This, the KU's bilocation of the *puruṣa*, is in fact made into the pivotal issue of the entire MU by the redactors responsible for appending this Upaniṣad's sixth book to the preexisting *Maitreyi* or *Maitreya* or *Maitrāyaṇī Upaniṣad*. This they do by returning, in the midst of the book's discussion of yoga, to the frame story of the entire work, about which some background is necessary. This is a dialogue involving a king named Bṛhadratha who, in the fullness of age, has placed his son on the throne and departed for the forest. There he meets a sage named Śākāyanya, to whom he pours out his heart, decrying the evanescence of existence even as he evokes the apotheosis of great kings who "abandoning their worldly sovereignty, departed from this world to enter into that world before the unblinking gaze of their entire families."[32] He then implores Śākāyanya to teach him how he may become a knower of the self (*ātmavit*), saying repeatedly, "You are our path."[33] Pleased with him, the sage predicts that he will "quickly become a knower of the self who has done what he had to do (*kṛtakṛtya*), renowned by the name of Marut ('He Who Shines')."[34] Asked by Bṛhadratha what he means by "self," Śākāyanya replies (MU 2.2) that "the one who, by stopping the breath (*ucchvāsa-viṣṭambhanena*), has advanced upward (*ūrdhvam utkrānta*) and who . . . dispels the darkness: that is the self . . . That is the immortal, the fearless: that is *brahman*." Chapters 29 and 30 of the MU's sixth book are nothing less than an account of the fulfillment of Śākāyanya's prediction and the narrative climax of the entire Upaniṣad.

After he had spoken in this wise, Śākāyanya, who was inside his heart, bowing to him, said, "By this knowledge of *brahman* the sons of Prajāpati arose onto the path of *brahman*." [At this point, the text continues with a series of aphorisms on the practice of yoga, culminating with a mention of the highest path. Then the text repeats itself.] After he had said this, Śākāyanya, who was inside his heart, bowing to him, said, "Marut, who has duly performed his service and who has done what he had to do (*kṛtakṛtya*), has betaken himself to the northern path. One cannot arrive there by [taking] a high road. This is the path to *brahman* in this world. Piercing the solar door, one proceeds upward."

Śākāyanya concludes his discourse with a paraphrase of ChU 8.6.6, here calling the multicolored channels of the heart "rays," of which one leads up to the world of *brahman* (*brahmaloka*). This narrative closes the frame story in a number of ways. First, the repetition of the expression "he who has done what he had to do" indicates that Bṛhadratha has in fact fulfilled the requirements necessary for attaining knowledge of the self. Second, by now naming him "He Who Shines," Śākāyanya confirms that his disciple has been transformed from a renouncer king named Bṛhadratha into a luminous being. As such, Bṛhadratha, who has advanced upward (*ūrdhvam utkrānta*) through the stoppage of the breath, has in fact become the *brahman*-self that "dispels the darkness."[35]

Here a word on breath control—long considered to have been an essential part of archaic yogic practice—is in order. One of the mystical insights of the Upaniṣads was that mind and breath were linked: in order to halt fluctuations in the mind, the upanishadic thinkers reasoned, it was necessary to control the breaths. In this regard, TU 3.10.2, which is several centuries earlier than MU 6.29, reads the compound *yoga-kṣema* as "in-breath and out-breath." However, as is the case with this MU passage, the bulk of early references to breath control actually refer to the complete cessation of the breath, or to forcing the breaths up out of the body entirely. This is the case in the *dharmasūtra* literature—in which the term *prāṇāyāma* first appears—and it resurfaces in several later sectarian sources, which will be discussed below. As for the BhG, it enjoins both the regulation (5.27) and the stoppage (4.29) of the breaths; a similar alternation is found in YS 2.49–53. As we will see in chapter six, rather than the regulation of the breaths that is the hallmark of hathayogic *prāṇāyāma*, it has been their complete stoppage that has characterized yogi practice.[36]

Finally, Śākāyanya's direct discourse in this passage parallels the rise of the brahmin sons of Brahmā-Prajāpati to the highest path with Bṛhadratha-Marut's own apotheosis.[37] Behind the dense intertextual references found in this passage stands the sun itself, one of whose rays leads upward to the worlds of the gods (i.e., to a place beyond the solar disk), while the others filter down into the world of existence, where the unliberated wander from rebirth to rebirth. Unlike the later Śaṅkara, the redactors of MU 6 viewed "advancing upward" as a willful yogic act, undertaken before one's natural death, for the attainment of release and immortality.[38] So too did the author of the YS (3.39), which states, "From mastery of the upward breath (*udāna*) . . . [the power of] progressing aloft [out of the body] (*utkrānti*)."

In the light of Van Buitenen's demonstration that the MU as we know it is the work of several hands, there can be no question that Śākāyanya's entire monologue—between the editor's reinsertion of his person (which had not been mentioned since the frame narrative at MU 2.3[39]) at MU 6.29 to the penultimate chapter of the text's sixth book—is a late, in this case, third-century CE interpolation. For what we see in the final chapter of the book (6.38) is a nearly verbatim reprising of the language of MU 6.28, with both passages pointedly referring to "the casing (*kośa*) of *brahman* with its four layers of net." What is intriguing about the editor's cut-and-paste operation is that the spatial referents of the *brahman*, enclosed in its casing of nets, appear to be situated at opposite ends of the microcosm-macrocosm continuum, the one infinitesimal (6.28) and the other infinite (6.38). Apart from the KU, the probable source of this ambiguity (or redundancy) is the ChU, which, as we have noted, appears to have inspired the MU's redactors on several points. The ChU, commenting on a famous passage from ṚV 10.90.3, proclaims,

[c]oncerning that which is [called] "brahman," it is indeed this space here, that is [the space] outside of a person (*puruṣa*). Now, this space that is outside of a person is indeed the space that is inside of a person. This space that is inside of a person is indeed the space that is inside the heart. It is a plenitude that has not turned outward (*apravartin*) . . . Far above this world, the celestial glow—that shines on the back of the cosmos [and] the back of everything [in the cosmos], in the highest of the highest worlds—is this very glow that is inside a person . . . This self of mine inside the heart is indeed smaller than a grain of rice, a barleycorn, a mustard-seed, a millet-grain, or even a kernel of millet. This self of mine inside the heart is greater than the earth, greater than midspace, greater than the celestial realm, greater than these worlds.[40]

The solution that the final chapters of the MU sixth book propose, in their expansion on this ChU passage, establishes (or is reflective of) the paradigm for the metaphysical categories and models of visionary ascent that recur across every one of the major sectarian traditions of later "classical" Hinduism. It therefore behooves us to consider these chapters in some detail. The text of MU 6.28 immediately precedes the return to Śākāyanya's direct discourse, which introduces the following chapter ("after Śākāyanya had said this . . . he said . . ."). In it, we find a dramatic account of the yogic practitioner's storming of the abode of *brahman* in the space within the heart, perhaps the earliest witness to what would become a perennial theme of later yoga literature.[41] In spite of the fact that the metaphors are mixed, the passage is a powerful one, opening with an aphorism from an unnamed source: "Someone has said: 'The supreme abode, which is bliss, is a casing whose contours are the space within the heart.'"[42] To gain access to this inner abode, the practitioner, advancing beyond (*atikramya*) the elements and the sense objects, must first strike down the gatekeeper of the "door of *brahman*" with an extended utterance of the mantra OṂ. Then, reaching the far shore of the space within the heart,

> he enters the abode of *brahman* slowly, like a miner searching for the mother lode makes his way into a pit. Then, following his guru's instructions, he should remove the casing of the brahman, which is comprised of four layers of net (*caturjālaṃ brahmakośaṃ*). By doing this, he who has become pristine, purified, empty, pacified, breathless, selfless, eternal (*ananta*), undecaying (*akṣaya*), steadfast (*sthira*), constant, unborn, and autonomous stands in his own glory (*sve mahimni tiṣṭhati*).[43] And as a result of this, he sees [the *brahman*], which is itself standing in its own glory, and views the cycle of existence (*saṃsāracakra*) as a wheel that has been rolled back (*āvṛtta*). It has been said of the embodied [individual] who has constantly [remained] "hitched up" for six months [and] who is [thereby] released, [that] his eternal, transcendent, mysterious properly aligned rig rolls forward (*samyagyogaḥ pravartate*)."[44]

This passage unambiguously describes a journey into inner space, at which point the now pristine consciousness realizes an identity with the absolute within. The language of yoking with which this passage closes recalls the epic narratives of the apotheosis of chariot warriors, who "yoked to their rigs" or "ready to hitch up" are released from rebirth.[45] It also refers to the cycle of the year, with its six months during which the length of the solar day is "rolled back" until the winter solstice, at which point it "rolls outward" for the following six months. This knowledge was critical to the epic Bhīṣma, who prolonged his life for three months until the sun's solstitial turn northward, at which point "hitched to his rig, he was released from [his bed of] arrows."[46] As we have seen, however, the apotheosis of figures like Bhīṣma culminates at the summit of the universe, at the opposite, infinite end of the spectrum.

Immediately following this passage, the editor introduces the awkward transition, "after Śākāyanya had said this," before launching into its account of Bṛhadratha's apotheosis and transformation into Marut, "He who Shines." Eight chapters of additional teachings on yoga follow, at which point the interpolated passage abruptly ends, and the reader is returned, at 6.38, to "the casing of the *brahman*, which is comprised of four layers of net," but in an entirely different context. It is highly probable that these two iterations of the same passage were originally juxtaposed (as they are in KU 6.7–17), with the change of context—from the infinitesimal recesses of the space or cave within the heart to the infinite reaches of the highest heaven—serving as a pedagogical tool for demonstrating the two simultaneous modes of being of both the absolute and of individuals who have realized identity with the absolute, modes of being that would be contradictory for any other sort of being. The MU 6.38 passage reads:

> Then, he pierces the casing of the brahman, which is comprised of four layers of net. That is, having pierced the highest heaven, which here precisely means the spheres of the sun, moon, the empyrean, and pure being, he who has been purified beholds the one known as Viṣṇu—the abode [and] the ground of all beings (*dhāma sarvāparam*)[47]—who, situated within pure being (*sattvāntarastha*), immutable, immortal, infallible (*acyuta*) [and] fixed (*dhruva*)[48] [is] autonomous consciousness, conjoined with omniscience and versimilitude, standing in his own glory.

MU 6.38 concludes by reverting to the infinitesimal once more, repeating key terms from the previous passage to indicate the simultaneity of this dynamic on both registers.

> Here, they declare: Situated in the midst of the sun is the moon, and in the midst of the moon, the empyrean. Situated in the midst of the empyrean is pure being and standing in the midst of pure being is the Infallible One (*acyuta*). When one meditates on him who is more minute than an atom, [one sees] his body [as having] the size of the thumb or a span (*aṅguṣṭha-prādeśa-mātram*), and one realizes transcendence. On this subject, people say: "The one whose body is the size of a thumb or a span, ablaze with light; the one who is two-, indeed, three-fold;[49] the one who is praised as the *brahman*; the god who is great: he has entered the realms, he has entered into living creatures."[50]

This, the final verse of the MU's sixth book, resolves the ambiguities of the preceding chapters. The *brahman*, now identified with both the transcendent *puruṣa* and Viṣṇu, is simultaneously the smallest of the small and the greatest of the great, both the subatomic spark at the heart of every living creature and the luminous, all-encompassing absolute.[51] The practitioner who penetrates the heart of being with his "eternal, transcendent, mysterious aligned rig" is understood to be simultaneously rising through the spheres to the transcendent abode of the Infallible One, also a name or epithet applied to Viṣṇu. As we will see, this is the starting point for later speculations in all three of the theistic traditions of "classical" Hinduism, each of which dresses up the diminutive *brahman* or *puruṣa* of the heart, as well as the transcendent, all-encompassing *brahman* or *puruṣa*, in its own sectarian guise. In many respects, it also appears to be a continuation of the yoga of the vedic poets, whose visionary expeditions to the confines of the universe allowed them to link microcosm to macrocosm and word to world. When, in MU 6.29–30, it is a dying king who departs on this journey of no return, his departure is homologized with that of the "sons of Prajāpati," who were brahmins like the epic Śuka. In this light, one might see in Śākāyanya's homologization of these two apotheoses a restatement of the aphorism, discussed in the previous chapter, concerning the battlefield warrior and the *parivrājaka* who pierce the orb of the sun.[52]

Lastly, we should note a subtle shift in the verbs used in this passage, a shift that carries over into later sectarian traditions. Whereas in MU 6.27 the practitioner is described as "entering" into and "moving" through the space in the heart, wherein he "stands" and "views" the entire wheel of transmigration—panoptically, as it were—in MU 6.38, he first "pierces" and "sees" before a new form of activity is introduced: he *meditates* on the infinitesimal absolute and thereby gains transcendence. This conceptual shift, from journeying to the place of the absolute in an embodied state to meditating on the same without making the journey, marks a parting of the ways in the history of yogic soteriology. Put another way, it marks the victory (within authorized scriptural traditions) of the yoga of the vedic seers over the yoga of the chariot warrior. Hereafter, knowing supplants going as the prime vehicle to salvation. As Bronkhorst astutely observes with reference to this shift:

> A consequence of the fact that practice leads to liberation only in combination with the knowledge of the immovable nature of the soul is that practice no longer has to be predominantly of a bodily nature. Where practice is expected to bring about this knowledge, the mental part is bound to gain prominence. This means that now meditation can become the main means of liberation.[53]

This is not to say that a variety of derivative forms of the root *dhyā are not found prior to this late upanishadic usage. The ChU contains a paean to *dhyāna*; however, its use of the term is entirely obscure.[54] In all other early texts, from the Vedas down through the early Upaniṣads, *dhyā and its derivates have a less specific semantic range, ranging from "vision" to "inspiration" to "thinking" to "contemplation."[55] *Dhyāna* is referred to in three other late Upaniṣads, one of which, already quoted (PU 5.5), stipulates meditation at the time of death on the "highest person"in order to ensure a transcendent postmortem state.[56] The BhG paraphrases this upanishadic injunction, substituting Kṛṣṇa for the "highest person" (*paramam puruṣam*), which is perfectly acceptable given the god's appellation as *puruṣottama*, the "supreme person." The same passage from the BhG also employs language similar to that found in MU 6.28, when it evokes the yogi who is constantly "yoked" (*yukta*).[57] Here Kṛṣṇa teaches that

the person who, uttering OṂ, the monosyllabic [equivalent of] *brahman* [while] remembering me (*mām anusmaran*) as he abandons his body [and] departs (*paryāti*) [life]: he goes to the highest path.[58] I am easily reached by the yogi who is constantly yoked, [and] whose mind is never elsewhere.[59]

This BhG passage diverges from PU 5.1–5 in its substitution of the verb anu-*smṛ ("remember, recollect") for *dhyā ("meditate"). This is a significant development, reflective of a trend that first appeared, shortly before the beginning of the common era, in Mahāyāna Buddhist meditation manuals from Kashmir and Inner Asia. (Although, as Charles Malamoud reminds us, one did not see the gods in the Vedas, rather, one remembered them, evoking them mentally to gain an inner vision of them.[60]) In these Buddhist sources, *anusmṛti* specifically referred to the "iconographic visualization" of a divinized Buddha.[61] This practice may have had its Buddhist origins in the Sarvāstivādin or Mahāyāna technique first attested in a circa first-century BCE work whose title describes the practice: the *Pratyutpannabuddha-saṃmukhāvasthita-samādhi Sūtra* is the "Teaching on Pure Contemplation of a Likeness of a Buddha by One Who is Facing It."[62]

Buddhānusmṛti and *devānusmṛti* were, in fact, adaptations of such earlier Buddhist techniques of mindfulness as *maraṇasati*, the contemplation of death, and *asubhabhāvanā*, "meditation on (the) foulness (of decaying corpses)," which involved the long-term observation of a decomposing dead body.[63] With *anusmṛti*, however, the technique has changed, as its very name indicates. More than simple "remembrance" or "recollection" (which are rendered by *smṛti*, without the prefix), *anusmṛti* is "remembrance subsequent to," "remembrance in accordance with," or "methodical remembrance." Here the core of the practice was to so concentrate one's vision on an image of a Buddha or a deity as to be able to subsequently and methodically envision the same image without the need for the meditation support. I would argue, in fact, that this technique employs the same sort of "eidetic imaging" as does the *kasiṇa* meditation described in Buddhaghoṣa's fifth-century *Visuddhimagga* (VM).

This consists of taking a specific material object—in the case of the earth *kasiṇa* [object of meditation] a clay disc, in the case of the blue *kasiṇa* blue flowers, and so forth—and sitting about eight feet from it on a small chair. The meditator then concentrates on the meditation object until an eidetic image of it can be recalled at will whether or not the external object is present. Briefly, this is a means by which external stimuli can be interiorized, a psychotropic technique by means of which all mental activity can be brought to a single point and concentrated there—in the case of the earth *kasiṇa* upon a clay disc.[64]

This technique, when applied to images of deities,[65] would be especially effective under conditions of controlled lighting, conditions easily met in caves using oil lamps. After contemplating such an illumined image, it would suffice to close one's eyes, after turning away from the light, to perceive a sharp, brilliant eidetic image of the deity behind one's eyes and "inside" of oneself, that is, to directly experience one's own Buddha nature "subsequent to" or "in accordance with" the original image. Repeated methodically, this technique of *anusmṛti* would eventually lead to the ability to conjure the image without the need for the meditation support.[66] Inner Asia, where this technique appears to have originated, is known for a number of caves featuring "numinous" Buddha images. Recently, Nobuyoshi Yamabe has argued that cave paintings from this region constitute illustrations of—and thus an invaluable "practical background" for—Buddhist meditation texts from this period.[67] The walls of a fifth- to seventh-century Buddhist cave shrine at Simsim, in Chinese Turkestan, for example, are painted with representations of the world of humans on its lower walls, with fabulous mountains above these and the firmament with its supernatural powers at the summit of the vault. The Buddha image inside the cave, half enclosed by the stone into which it is cut, is surrounded by a great, flaming halo, a sunburst of light.[68] This is, in fact, one of the earliest Buddhist representations of the "cosmological Buddha," the Buddhist homologue of the emergent Hindu Kṛṣṇa. These Buddhist cave paintings from Central Asia date from the same period as the earliest sculptural representations, from central India and Nepal, of the Vaiṛṇava supreme being in his universal form.[69]

Meditation on (or the mental reconstruction of) an anthropomorphic image of a deity, rather than the MU's more properly cosmological meditation on an attributeless absolute (albeit, who is, at the end of book six, identified with Viṣṇu), has remained a perennial fixture of every theistic worship program in South Asia.[70] In fact, a number of accounts of five- or six-limbed yoga include *smaraṇa* ("recollecting") or *anusmṛti* as their fifth member. In the case of the Buddhist *Guhyasamājatantra* and the *Kālacakra Tantra*, *anusmṛti* replaces *tarka*, "contemplative enquiry," as the fifth member of the MU's six-limbed yoga system.[71]

Remembrance is an especially powerful concept when one recalls that, according to Nyāya-Vaiśeṣika philosophy, all memories are exact transpositions of the past onto the present: if one is but capable of remembering, the content of that memory of the past is wholly actualized in the present and is therefore as true and real as other valid cognitions, such as eyewitness perception, and so on.[72] On the one hand, this axiom explains the importance of a yogi's ability to recall and thereby free himself from the karmic residues of his past lives and his former births, a power evoked in Hindu lawbooks like the *Manu Smṛti* (MSmṛ) and YājS, as well as the YS, YBh, MBh, and KSS.[73] On the other, it valorizes these techniques of meditation and visualization as the prime means for identification or union with the godhead, transcendence, and liberation. However, it should be noted that these are elite forms of practice, reserved for highly trained religious specialists, most of whom would have been either brahmins or Buddhist or Jain monks. With this, we may speak of a sort of "division of labor" among yogic seekers of liberation, with the meditative practitioners hailing from the clerical intelligentsia and the glory-bound battlefield heroes from the warrior class. As for the "sinister yogis" whose stories were recounted in chapter one, their yoga of taking over other people's bodies was a form of possession, which was and remains the principal religious idiom for the masses,[74] the great underclass. Of course, the "sinister yogis" of narrative hail from every stratum of society, including not only the priestly and warrior castes, but also those of the potter and the oil-presser. Whatever the case, "vernacular" Indic traditions of bodily possession and the like are a part of the religious life of everyone, including the exclusivist elites who condemn them.[75]

3. Visionary Ascent in the *Bhāgavata Purāṇa*

Referring to the techniques of *anusmṛti* just described, as illustrated by exemplary narratives from Mahāyāna sources as well as the BhG,[76] Stephen Beyer has characterized the first centuries of the common era as a time of visionary theism.[77] This is supported by a broad sampling of Hindu works in which renouncers—termed *kavis* ("wizards"), *siddhas* ("perfected beings"), yogis, *yogeśvaras* ("Masters of Yoga"), *yatis* ("itinerant ascetics"), *munis* ("hermits"), or *sādhakas* ("practitioners")—are enjoined to undertake a vision quest into inner and outer space, in search of the immanent yet transcendent god. Already in the final chapters of MU 6, a nascent Vaiṣṇava theology was emerging, which was echoed or carried forward in the BhG and MdhP as well as the Purāṇas, traditions to which we will return in chapter five.

Theistic adaptations of upanishadic cosmology appear in the three principal sectarian forms of Hindu theism, as well as in Hīnayāna and Mahāyāna Buddhism. In this and the next section of this chapter, I will focus on Vaiṣnava and Śaiva adaptations of the upanishadic model, leaving aside those attested in Śākta[78] and Buddhist[79] sources. In the three Hindu traditions, the same alternations—between a personalized absolute in its infinite and infinitesimal modes of being and between the acts of traversing space, seeing, and meditating on the part of the practitioner—remain operative. Common to all are the transformation of the impersonal absolute into a personal deity; the transformation of adjectival descriptors of the upanishadic absolute into hypostases or alternate names of god, or into spheres of divine activity that double as metaphysical categories; and the expansion of the nascent upanishadic system of the higher spheres into the multiple superimposed worlds of the puranic, agamic, and tantric cosmologies. As we will also see, these later sources introduce a new dichotomy in the goal of practice. From the third or fourth centuries of the common era forward—the period of MU 6, the MdhP, the BhG, and the YS—there is a parting of the ways in both the techniques and the goals of practice. On the one hand, there is the practice of yoga, which leads to supernatural enjoyments and visionary "embodied" travel to the highest worlds, followed by a deferred final liberation at the end of a cosmic eon; on the other, there is meditation on the absolute, which leads directly to release from suffering existence and a disembodied identity with godhead. The former carries forward the traditions of the yogic apotheosis of the chariot warrior, while the latter, which is clearly on the ascendant, is an adaptation of the visionary yoga of the vedic poets. Or, to employ terminology that was emerging in this period, the former describes *jīvanmukti*, liberation in life, while the latter describes *videhamukti*, disembodied liberation. The two-tiered soteriology presented in these sources, of immediate versus deferred liberation, has a cosmological correlate not only in these sources but also in Sāṃkhya philosophy, which, in its discussions of the *kaivalyapadam* ("state, plane of isolation"), reproduces—if it is not the source of it—the same dichotomy. I will return to this philosophical development later in this chapter.

The BhG is, in many respects a pivotal work, time and again identifying yoga—meditation in a devotional mode having Kṛṣṇa, the supreme person (*puruṣottama*), as its sole object—as the optimal path to salvation. At the same time, this text bears eloquent witness to the fact that the meaning of yoga was still highly fluid in this period, applying the term over a hundred times to a range of theories and practices encompassing posture,[80] breath control,[81] subtle body mapping,[82] and apotheosis (*utkrānti*).[83] The expression *yogayukta* appears seven times in the BhG,[84] but in an altered context that drains it of the specific meanings found in epic narratives of dying warriors or in philosophical accounts of enhanced powers of perception, in the light of which it is inappropriate to translate its use of the compound as "hitched to his rig."[85] So, for example, when Kṛṣṇa maintains that practitioners of both yoga and Sāṃkhya "reach the same place" and see the same things, he states that "yoked to the path (*yogayukta*), a sage quickly goes to the absolute (*brahman*)."[86] Furthermore, the practitioner of yoga so described is without agency or autonomy, given the fact that Kṛṣṇa alone is the sole truly autonomous agent in the universe.[87] In such a context, "the one who is yoked" (*yuktaḥ*) becomes reduced to a simple devotee who has renounced the fruits of his acts or who has found peace by turning inward.[88]

A later Vaiṣṇava source, whose soteriological treatment of yoga clearly flows from that found in MU 6, is the *Bhāgavata Purāṇa* (BhP), the second chapter of whose second book is entitled "Description of Him Who Appears as the Person" (*puruṣasaṃsthāvarṇanam*).[89] A guide for the virtuoso meditator to realize identity with the absolute,[90] this chapter reappropriates the language of KU 6.16–17 and MU 6.38 when it states that some people are able to meditatively recall "the man who is a span in size (*prādeśamātram puruṣam*), residing in the space of the heart within the body."[91] Here the absolute is explicitly portrayed as both a homunculus and a cosmic man possessed of all the attributes of the supreme being Viṣṇu:

> They recall (*smaranti*) him as four-armed, and holding the lotus, the disk, the conch, and the mace. His face is smiling, his wide eyes are like lotuses, and his clothing is as yellow as the filaments of the *kadamba* flower. His golden bracelets are richly bejeweled, and his diadem and earrings shimmer with sparkling gemstones . . . His feet, which are like lotus shoots, are [meditatively] placed, by a Master of Yoga (*yogeśvara*), on the calyx of the fully opened lotus of his heart.[92]

Meditation upon each member and aspect of this minute god within, upward "from his feet to his smile," gradually purifies the mind of the practitioner, preparing him to transcend his own body and the phenomenal world. Successively incorporating his breaths into his mind, mind into intellect, intellect into the conscious principle (*kṣetrajña*), the conscious principle into the individual self, and the individual self into the universal self, the practitioner becomes capable of contemplating Viṣṇu's highest plane (*paraṃ padaṃ vaiṣṇavam*).[93] Now the text enjoins the hermit to practice breath control, such that, by closing the nine bodily orifices and immobilizing his breath for twenty-four minutes in the space between the eyebrows, he may split open the fontanel and leave his body behind to accede to the highest (*param*), also identified as Viṣṇu.

This meditative ascent is presented as the first of two alternatives, the second being the practitioner's enjoyment with mind and senses intact of a heavenly paradise prior to a deferred eternal union with Viṣṇu at the end of a cosmic eon.[94] This is the most enduring legacy in the Hindu theistic traditions of the apotheosis of the *yogayukta* warrior. A bridge between these two soteriologies may be elicited from a long cosmological passage found in the third book of the MBh that speaks of the supreme abode of Viṣṇu-Nārāyaṇa, which is located beyond the "seat of *brahman*."

> Wandering ascetics (*yatis*) go there by virtue of their devotion to Hari, yoked (*yukta*) to optimal ascetic practice, and transformed by their holy deeds. These great-souled ones who have been perfected by their yoga (*yogasiddhas*), and who are bereft of darkness or delusion, go there and never return to this world. This is the fixed (*dhruvam*), undecaying (*akṣayam*), imperishable (*avyayam*) place of the master (*īśvarasya*).[95]

Throughout the Purāṇas, one finds multiple references to a realm reserved for Masters of Yoga (*yogeśvaras*) at the summit of the universe, and it is in its description of the "path of the Masters of Yoga" that the BhP bears the closest resemblance to this epic passage as well as MU 6.38 and ChU 3.12.7–8.[96] As the text indicates, this path (*gati*) is, like the absolute itself, simultaneously located inside and outside the world system.

> It is said that the path of the Masters of Yoga, whose selves are [contained] in their breaths, is [both] inside and outside of the triple-world. They do not reach this path by acts alone. They partake [of it] through *vidyā* ("occult knowledge, magical spells"), *tapas* ("asceticism"), yoga, and pure contemplation (*samādhi*).[97]

Now, the text describes the upward trajectory of the Master of Yoga. His soul, reduced to the size of an atom, rises, via "the luminous *suṣumṇā* channel that is the path of *brahman*" through the higher spheres—of the empyrean and the constellation of the crocodile (the tip of whose tail is Dhruva, the Pole Star, which this text terms the "navel of the universe")—to the world of the one who dwells on high (*pārameṣṭhyam*), where the Lords of the Siddhas are wont to reside, and which endures for a period of a life of Brahmā (*dvaiparārdhyam*).[98] However, before he reaches this exalted station, the practitioner effects a transformative journey through the seven sheaths (*kośas*) that enclose the cosmic egg—the cosmological instantiations of the samkhyan categories of the five gross and subtle elements with their corresponding sense activities, the mind, ego, and intellect (here called *vijñāna*)—before ending in the total cessation of the activities of the three *guṇas* (in *prakṛti*, "materiality," the highest of the samkhyan categories, below *puruṣa*).[99] There the Master of Yoga will remain to the end of time, whereupon his self will reach the supreme self and thereby accede to the highest realm, the realm of Viṣṇu Bhagavān, from which he will never return.[100]

Here BhP 2.2 is—like MU 6.38 with its language of the casings (*kośas*) of net that enclose the *brahman*—able to describe, in a theistic mode, the simultaneously infinite and infinitesimal ground of being with which the individual self identifies through both inward meditation and an embodied journey outward beyond the confines of the universe. Orthodox Vaiṣṇava theology represents the same relationship, of the absolute as both container and contained, in analogous terms. According to the Śrīvaiṣṇava doctrine of the four *vyūhas* ("bodily arrays"), it is the supreme deity Vāsudeva who impregnates his own central womb and gestates the fetus that will develop into the Egg of Brahman (*brahmāṇḍa*) within which all creatures exist and move.[101] The outermost Vāsudeva *vyūha* is thus at once "the body at whose center we exist, [and] the body at the center of our own consciousness."[102] As Dennis Hudson explains,

> In the case of humans, the mapping places the gross body on the outside with the subtle body and soul enclosed by it and the *vyūha* Vāsudeva controlling from the center as the Self of all selves . . . In the case of God, however, the organization of the three bodies is reversed . . . A difference between God and humans, then, is this: As a microcosm, the human is a conscious soul looking outward through its encompassing subtle body and, by means of that subtle body, through its encompassing gross human body. The Bhagavān, by contrast as the macrocosm, is pure being and consciousness looking "inward" to the subtle body that he encloses and by means of that subtle body, "into" the gross body enclosed within his subtle body. God, one might say, gazes inward at his own center.[103]

This divine mode of being, as both the container and the contained, is one that is shared by human actors who are explicitly termed yogis in MBh 12.289. This also becomes the modus operandi of the tantric practitioner, who divinizes his body so as to become the deity looking inside to envision the universe as self. We will return to this matter in chapter five.

As one moves forward through the scriptural history of Vaiṣṇava theism, one sees the transformation of a certain number of the attributes of the *brahman* or *puruṣa* into hypostases or names of the supreme god Viṣṇu. These include Acyuta ("Infallible"), Ananta ("Eternal"), and Dhruva,[104] which is employed both as an adjective ("fixed") and as a noun to refer to the Pole Star as the sole fixed star in the universe. It is for this reason that BhP 2.2.25 calls the constellation in which this star is located the "navel of the universe," while other sources speak of Dhruva as the tether to which are strung the "wind ropes" that hold the planets and other heavenly bodies in their orbits.[105] Viṣṇu is therefore Dhruva in two respects: he is the unmoved mover of all that exists in a universe in flux (*saṃsāra*), and he is located at the immobile zenith of the manifest world. Viṣṇu's exalted station is acknowledged, albeit in an apophatic way, in a seventh-century poem in praise of the sun god, whose cult rivaled that of Viṣṇu and Śiva in many parts of the Indian subcontinent between the sixth and eighth centuries. In his *Sūryaśataka*, Mayūra, a poet in the court of King Harṣavardhana, praises the sun as the heavenly being whose glory surpasses even Viṣṇu's celestial plane (*viṣṇu-pada*) and whose subtle and invisible nature is known to yogis alone.[106]

4. Visionary Ascent in Early Śaiva Scriptures

While it is the case that the cult of the god who would become identified as Śiva was emerging in the same period as that of the Viṣṇu and that Śiva (under the name of Maheśvara in particular) was already depicted as a god of yoga in the MBh's twelfth and thirteenth books,[107] it is nonetheless true, as Biardeau demonstrated over four decades ago, that the earliest theology of a yogi god was a Vaiṣṇava theology, developed in the BhG, HV, and early Vaiṣṇava Purāṇas.[108] I will return to this important theme in chapter five; here, however, I will concentrate on an early Śaiva appropriation of the Vaiṣṇava paradigms just reviewed, which reiterates the simultaneity of the supreme being Śiva's infinite and infinitesimal modes and which appears to build upon a preexisting Vaiṣṇava foundation in its construction of the upper reaches of its universe.

Given the fact that the twenty-five categories (*tattvas*) of Sāṃkhya philosophy comprise the bedrock of every later metaphysical system in South Asia, it is the specifically "super-samkhyan" categories that lend specificity to the various theistic systems.[109] In the Vaiṣṇava systems that one is able to glimpse *in statu nascendi* in MU 6 and the epics, one is witness to the transformation of various names or attributes of Viṣṇu into elevated metaphysical categories, often doubling as cosmological planes or worlds, as in the case of Dhruva.[110] An explicitly Śaiva metaphysics that was emerging in the same period shows the same pattern, employing names and attributes of Śiva for the transcendent categories/cosmological planes extending beyond the samkhyan *prakṛti*.[111] Some of these are found in a passage from MU 6.8, which lists the names of several gods, identifying them with the *ātman* (in this case a term denoting the supreme self and thus a synonym for *brahman* and *puruṣa*): Īśāna, Śambhu, Bhava, and Rudra.[112] Another late Upaniṣad, the ŚvU, further elaborates on this theme, presenting an early Śaiva sectarian version of the KU's and MU's identification of Viṣṇu with the supreme self. Here the god Rudra, whose epithets include *śiva* (the "Gracious One") and *īśa* (the Lord"), is explicitly identified with the *puruṣa* of ṚV 10.90, as well as with the thumb-sized person within the heart, "hidden in all things and enveloping all."[113] As we will see in chapters four and five, the epic often employs the names Īśvara ("Master"), Maheśvara ("Great Master"), and Mahāyogī to refer to Śiva, particularly in his role as a divine yogi. As we will also have the occasion to observe, the nature of Śiva's yoga, as described in epic, puranic, and tantric sources, differs significantly from that of Viṣṇu, tending more toward the "sinister yogi" end of the spectrum.

As was noted in chapter one, the Pāśupatas were the most important and powerful of the early Śaiva sects, being mentioned in the MdhP itself as well as in a 376 CE inscription.[114] The *pañcārthika* theology of the Pāśupatas posited five (*pañca*) categories (*artha*): *paśu* ("animal victim, individual soul"), *pati* ("god"), *yoga* (the "union between *paśu* and *pati*"), *vidhi* (the "prescribed regimen for *yoga*"), and *duḥkhānta* (the "cessation of suffering").[115] The goal of the Pāśupata practitioner was therefore a sort of "communion," by virtue of which he was empowered to partake of the attributes of Maheśvara,[116] a state of being tantamount to the cessation of rebirth and conditioned existence. This communion was termed "yoga," a reading that Pāśupata theoreticians took pains to distinguish from the *samādhi* of the YBh and later commentaries on the YS.[117] Realizing an identity with Maheśvara, the "Great Master," implied that the practitioner had himself become a master (*īśvara*), possessed of the attribute of "mastery" or "sovereignty" (*aiśvaryam*). As we will see in chapter five, both of these terms are used in a particular technical sense in early prescriptive accounts of yoga, found in MBh 12.289 and many other sources.[118]

The Pāśupatas were not alone, however, in the early landscape of Śaiva asceticism. As Alexis Sanderson has demonstrated in a recent article, the Pāśupatas were one of the two early groups comprising the *atimārga* (the "surpassing path"), the ascetic alternative to the orthodox *mantramārga* ("path of mantra"), which was also known as Śaivasiddhānta or agamic Saivism. *Atimārga* initiates were, like the virtuoso practitioners referenced in BhP 2.2, renouncer ascetics, and among these, all Pāśupata practitioners were, theoretically, brahmin males.[119]

On the basis of data culled from a number of early Śaiva scriptures, Sanderson has excavated the metaphysical system and attendant practices of the second, non-Pāśupata branch of the *atimārga*, a group known variously as the Kapālavratins, Lākulas, or Kālāmukhas.[120] While some of these textual sources are relatively late, the traditions that Sanderson has brought to light through them are substantially older, dating from no later than the sixth, and perhaps from as early as the fourth, century CE. An important source is the circa sixth-century *Svacchanda Tantra* (SvT),[121] which defined the *atimārga* as a system that transcended the gnosis, detachment, and mastery (*aiśvaryam*) that were the hallmarks of the yoga system. So-called because its system surpassed this world, the *atimārga*'s adherents sought to escape the world of rebirth to dwell eternally in Īśvara or Dhruva, the name of the highest path in the Pāśupata and Lākula systems, respectively.[122] The most complete extant exposition of the Lākula doctrine and metaphysics is contained in the *Niśvāsatattvasaṃhitā* (NTS), a fourth- to sixth-century CE text,[123] which has been partially translated by Sanderson.[124] In its discussion of the metaphysics of the two branches of the *atimārga*, the NTS indicates that for the Lākulas, the Pāśupatas' highest realm of Īśvara was transcended by two higher worlds: the worlds of the Rudras named Tejīśa (the "Lord of Splendor") and Dhruvīśa (the "Lord of the Pole Star").[125] These two Rudras were hierarchized as follows: the lower Tejīśa bestowed the "state of yoga" that was the immediate antecedent to final liberation, while the higher Dhruvīśa afforded liberation itself. These two goals correspond to the alternative soteriologies presented in BhP 2.2: the embodied rise to the highest path and deferred liberation of Masters of Yoga, and the meditative path leading to immediate liberation. As in the case of the BhP, it was through meditation that the *atimārga* practitioner could directly transcend this world and accede to the higher worlds and liberation.[126]

The specificity of the Lākula branch is to be found in its soteriology. As another early work, the *Niśvāsamukha* (4.95) states, the practitioner is liberated through the mystic knowledge of the eleven realms from the Avīci hell to Dhruva. This knowledge was communicated through initiation. In Lākula initiation, the preceptor meditated on this cosmic hierarchy (*prakriyā*), thereby purifying it and transforming it into an instrument for liberation. He then initiated his disciple through the descent of Śiva's power, as a result of which the latter was ensured liberation at the time of death. In this respect, the goal of Lākula initiation was identical to that of the *nirvāṇadīkṣā* of the nonascetic Śaivasiddhāntins, and this in counter distinction to Pāśupata initiation, which elevated the initiand to the sphere of Īśvara—wherein he became a "Rudra-Master" (*rudreśa*)—but from which he could *not* attain deferred liberation.[127] Following initiation, and for the remainder of his life, the Lākula ascetic's repeated "visionary ascent through a gnosis-driven yoga up a ladder of principles or worlds" was the means by which his deferred liberation became actualized at the time of death.[128] Even upon liberation, however, the soul of the Lākula ascetic, although omniscient, was not omnipotent, omnipotence and the power to activate the universe being reserved for the supreme Śiva alone. As such, even the liberated Rudra-souls that governed various planes of the cosmic hierarchy were without agency,[129] a situation analogous to that of the Masters of Yoga of the Vaiṣṇava soteriology of BhP 2.2.

Like BhP 2.2, these fourth- to sixth-century Lākula sources charted out a soteriological system in which meditation upon the universal hierarchy, up to the most exalted hypostases of the supreme being, stood as the means to immediate, as opposed to deferred, liberation. This corresponded to the soteriology of MU 6, in which the practitioner realized identity with the absolute upon beholding "Viṣṇu . . . the immutable, immortal, infallible, and fixed (*dhruva*)."[130] This was followed, in MU 6, by a description of meditation upon the same absolute in its infinitesimal mode; in BhP 2.2, the infinitesimal Viṣṇu who is the object of meditation is described prior to its account of the practitioner's visionary ascent. Like these two sources, early Śaiva traditions enjoined a similar meditative program, with analogous results.[131] These archaic *atimārga* traditions are preserved in the description of the "Rudra Vow" (*rudravrata*) recorded in an agamic text, the pre-ninth-century *Mataṅgapārameśvarāgama* (MPĀg).[132]

> [H]e should meditate on [Rudra] . . . visualizing him as a radiant figure the size of one's thumb, shining liking a ball of lightning in the calyx of the lotus of his heart, with each of the parts of his body clearly distinct, five-faced, three-eyed, his crest adorned with the sickle moon. When he has visualized [him in this way] he should immerse himself in him entirely, [thinking] "Without a doubt this is who I am."[133] Meditating [thus] he should wander day and night . . . considering . . . that "the universe is contained in myself" or "I abide in all that moves," conquering his mind through yoga (*yogatas*) . . . If he wanders thus from village to village, then after a year he will overcome all the contrasting extremes that torture the body. After two years he will attain knowledge of the past, present and future. Like fire he can burn whatever he wishes. He

becomes free of all impurity [of mind]. After three years he beholds the Siddhas, and after four years the Gods. After five, O best of men, he beholds without doubt the Rudras [themselves]. After six he sports in their company, with strength and power equal [to theirs], accomplishing whatever he desires, O sage, all by the power of his observance (*caryāvīryabalāt*). Thus he constantly rises from level to level (*padāt padam*) [of the universe], excelling [all others] in the beauty of his form. When [finally] he moves at will within the highest void the lord Sadāśiva bestows on the *sādhaka* his own rank as God (*aiśvaryam*), or else the highest and eternal state beyond God himself (*nirīśvaram*).[134]

In this source, the sequence—of inward meditation on an infinitesimal form of the absolute, here deified as Rudra, followed by an embodied "yogic" ascent that affords access to the higher worlds of the siddhas, gods, Rudras (lower hypostases of the supreme being), and the realm of god himself—is analogous to the rise of the Masters of Yoga, as elaborated in BhP 2.2. And, in fact, Śaiva cosmology knows of eight exalted realms, collectively known as the *yogāṣṭaka*, which are said to be presided over by yogis, but which are situated below the World of Rudra at the summit of the cosmic egg.[135] That this was a ritual whose agent was termed a *sādhaka* is significant. As Helène Brunner has argued, it was likely the *sādhakas*, practitioners whose goal was the attainment of *siddhis* rather than salvation, who introduced "yoga-permeated ritual" into the Āgamas.[136] *Sādhakas* occupy a similar niche in the Vaiṣṇava (Pāñcarātra) *Jayākhya Saṃhitā* (JS), although their relationship to yogis—as well as the means and end of the yogi practice itself—are treated ambiguously in this source.[137]

It should come as no surprise that this two-tiered liberation scheme bears little resemblance to narrative accounts of the battlefield apotheosis of epic warriors yoked to their rigs. In these new theistic systems, the dynamics of yoga have been subordinated to the power of an omnipotent deity (whose mode of being permits him to be omnipresent in both infinite and infinitesimal modes) or to the power of ritual or meditative gnosis. By juxtaposing these soteriological systems, we can see that, from about the third century CE onward, yogic ascent came to be supplanted by meditation in these elite intellectualized contexts. This had the collateral effect of transforming embodied ascent into a visionary ascent of much the same order as that of the vedic poets.

Through the lens of these traditions, we may see that the advent of the new theism, combined with an increased emphasis on the meditative yoga of the vedic poets, effected a semantic shift in the referents of the term "yoga" during the first half of the first millennium of the common era. Yoga became emptied of many of its epic and upanishadic (and most of its vedic) significations, as it came to be increasingly identified with meditation or visualization. A striking witness to this shift may be found in the Āgamas, the scriptures of the orthodox Śaivasiddhānta, which are traditionally divided into four sections (*padas*), of which one is "yoga." To begin, the *yoga-padas* of the principal Āgamas are significantly shorter in length than the other traditional divisions, which are devoted to *jñāna* ("higher knowledge"), *caryā* ("customary behavior, observance"), and *kriyā* ("ritual practice").[138] Second, the *yoga-padas* of the various Āgamas tend to limit their discussions to the state of mind and knowledge required when, during worship, a practitioner is engaged in meditation on Śiva, or on the divine spheres through which he rises in his meditative ascent.[139] Furthermore, as one moves forward in time from the *atimārga* scriptures into the Āgamas, one sees that even in its altered sense of visionary ascent, the practice of yoga has become marginalized. In Alexis Sanderson's words, "[W]hat were once the only ways to liberation after initiation (in the *atimārga*) now survive as full-time disciplines only among what were probably relatively small elites within the community of Śaiva initiates . . . The meditator (*yogī*) as opposed to the master of ritual worship (*karmī*) and the gnostic (*jñānī*) has shifted to the periphery of vision."[140] With this, we see that the yoga of the *yoga-yukta* chariot-warrior became the collateral damage of the triumph of the "yogas" taught by Kṛṣṇa to Arjuna in the BhG. In the new theistic traditions of the Purāṇas in particular, it was subordinated to *bhakti*,[141] while in the Tantras, *karma* and *jñāna* came to prevail. Yet, in all of these later systems, the earlier practice of yoga with its goal of an extended "embodied" sojourn in the higher worlds was retained as a less-desirable alternative to immediate and definitive liberation. This is the implicit message of the BhG, which, by its semantic over-determination of the term of "yoga," diluted the specificity of the term in such a way as to reduce it, together with *karma* and *jñāna*, to simply another inferior path to salvation. This is explicit in the circa ninth-century *Mālinīvijayottara Tantra* (MVUT), which devotes fifteen verses to the superiority of the gnostic over the yogi.[142]

The MVUT also appropriates the term in such a way as to distance it from its earlier referents, by calling its soteriological system "yoga," and thereby reducing the many pre-existing Śaiva catalogs of yogic states and processes to so many "epiphenomena of an apperceptive hierarchy with seven distinct levels of linked perceivers," the highest of which was Śiva.[143] Here yogic ascent was neither concretely embodied, as in the case of epic heroes, nor visionary, as in the vedic and theistic traditions. Rather, the seven levels through which the yogi ascended were homologized with increasingly expanded states of subjectivity. At the summit of the hierarchy, the yogi's selfhood became identical to that of the unique, transcendent subject, Śiva, the observer of observers (the *mantramaheśvaras*, situated at the sixth level) who observed observers (the *mantreśvaras* situated at the fifth level), and so on down to the lowest level of observed observers, who merely observed the objects of their senses. Here simply knowing these seven hierarchized principles or worlds afforded one "the fruits of yoga," that is, the sequenced gnoseological attainment of those worlds.[144] Furthermore, whereas the epic warrior's apotheosis was verifiable through eyewitness observation by credible third parties (e.g., the five persons who were witness to the rise of Droṇa's luminous soul, or the eyewitnesses to apotheosis evoked by Bṛhadratha in MU 1.4[145]), the culmination of the tantric gnostic's rise through levels of perception in the MVUT has become entirely solipsistic: none but himself, now identified with the supreme Śiva-self, is conscious of his (self-) perception from the summit of the universe.

5. Two-tiered Soteriologies and the *Prakṛtilaya*s

In the new soteriological systems of the theistic sects, the embodied ascent of the yogi was relegated to a subordinate position behind meditative worship, devotion, and gnosis. This demotion was effected in two ways. First, the final destination of the Masters of Yoga (*yogeśvaras*) or the "Rudra-Masters" (*rudreśas*) became, in these later cosmologies, a sort of antechamber to the "true" locus of salvation, the heavenly abode of Viṣṇu, Śiva, or the great goddess. While theirs was a transcendent plane it was "less transcendent" than that of the supreme being, a plane that was immediately accessible to those who knew god or who selflessly acted out their love for him. This translated to a two-tiered rendering of the "highest path" of earlier traditions. One finds this in *atimārga* accounts of the sphere of Īśvara, a plane wherein an initiate could become a "Rudra-Master" (*rudreśa*) but from which he could not attain deferred liberation (as opposed to the higher planes wherein identity with Śiva was realized), as well as in the many puranic cosmologies that divided the transcendent realm of the virtually liberated into a lower world of asceticism (*tapoloka*) and a higher world of *brahman* (*brahmaloka*).

There are divisions, analogous to those encountered in the theistic Hindu sources, in a number of Buddhist works from the same period, such as the fourth- to fifth-century VM ("Path of Purification") of Buddhaghoṣa, a scholastic Theravāda account of meditative practice. Works such as this elaborate a two-tiered hierarchy of practice and its goals in their system of the nine *jhānas* (or *dhyānas*), which distinguish between a series of eight attainments (*samāpattis*), of the four *rūpadhātus* ("form realms") and of the four *ārūpyadhātus* ("formless realms"), on the one hand, and the attainment of complete cessation (*nirodha-samāpatti*) on the other.[146] According to this system, the four "form meditations" (*rūpa-dhyānas*) lead to rebirth in the form realm(s), while the four "formless meditations" (*ārūpyadhātus*) lead to the formless realms. Here attainment of the form and formless realms was tantamount to realizing the states of consciousness of the gods inhabiting the highest cosmological planes, while *nirodha-samāpatti* (described in MN 1.296 as a state of catalepsy of seven days' duration) constituted "the cessation of all mental and physical functions, in some cases identified with liberation, but not in a locative or cosmological sense."[147]

Interestingly, one also finds an analogous cleavage in Buddhist appreciations of the types of practice leading to these respective goals, which parallels those encountered in *pātañjala yoga*. Here I am referring once more to Sarbacker's numinous/cessative typology and to the Buddhist debates between the "experientialists" and the "speculatives."[148] In this case, the operative terms are *samatha* ("calming"), the affective or psychosomatic component of practice, and *vipassanā* ("insight"), the intellectual or analytic component of meditation.[149] The former, the *samatha* meditations, give rise to the Buddhist *abhijñās*, the "super-knowledges," which are described in the first-century CE *Vimuttimagga* ("Path of Liberation") in the following terms:

> The meditator thus gradually contemplates until he gains mastery over the manifold transformations. Being one, he becomes many. Being many, he becomes one . . . His body moves without impediment, as though through space . . . He fondles the sun and the moon with his hands. Such are his supernormal powers, so great is his might that he ascends even to the Brahma world.[150]

With *samatha*, one is doing nothing less than "approximating the qualities of a divinity . . . with the yogin ascend[ing] the very divine hierarchy,"[151] in contradistinction to *vipassanā*, which gives rise to the wisdom (*paññā*) that leads to cessation. In the former case, the practitioner accedes to *nibbāna*-in-life (*diṭṭadhammanibbāna*), whereas in the latter, it is *nibbāna* tout court that is the goal.[152] As was the case in the soteriologies of new theistic cults of the Hindus, Buddhist sources from the same period are unanimous in denigrating the techniques and goals of the "experientialists" in favor of those of the "speculatives." Here as well, "going" has been subordinated to "knowing," even when the authors and commentators themselves have difficulty in explaining why such should be the case, or how two incommensurable approaches could possibly have been combined. In the words of Paul Griffiths, "[The] result is an unsatisfactory combination of two radically different kinds of soteriology."[153]

This is precisely the same conundrum as is encountered in the YS, in which the techniques and goals of the affective or psychosomatic component of practice are subordinated to those of the means and ends of Sāṃkhya-inflected intellectual or analytic meditative practice, with the former leading only to the *siddhis* or *vibhūtis*, which most commentators have cast as so many impediments to the ultimate goal of *samādhi*.[154] According to Whicher, the YS admit the supernatural powers, but deny them as ends in themselves.

> Insight into the true nature and form (*svarūpa*) of an object in *samādhi* automatically only leads to the powers (*siddhis*) . . . Patañjali and Vyāsa view yogic power as instrumental to the attainment of *kaivalya*, but also as being without intrinsic value . . . These powers, which can be understood as a natural byproduct of the yogin's meditative practice, are accomplishments only from the point of view of the egoic consciousness . . . The powers are made available or accessed by means of an ascension through the *tattvas* (principles of existence) as enumerated in Sāṃkhya . . . Any clinging to or misappropriation of power means that we reinforce the habit of assuming we are ego-personalities rather than *puruṣa*.[155]

In spite of the devaluation of these powers in scholastic and philosophical works such as these, there could be no doubt that the vedic seers and the Buddha himself were clearly "experientialists" whose supernatural attainments, so championed in the narrative literature, cannot be ignored.[156] These traditions were in conversation with one another, and so one should expect to find a common ground for the two-tiered soteriology that they all appear to share, in spite of its apparent internal contradictions, from about the fourth century CE onward. And so one does, once again in the Sāṃkhya philosophy of the YS and YBh, which if they were not the sources of these parallel soteriological developments were nonetheless philosophical records of them. Here I am referring specifically to YS 1.19, which defines the highest form of *samādhi* as a characteristic feature of the "way of being" (*bhava*) of "the disembodied ones" (*videha*) and of "those whose resting place is in *prakṛti*" (*prakṛtilaya*).[157] Here the *samādhi* in question is *asamprajñāta*, the state of pure concentration that obtains when all mental activities have ceased. In his commentary on this verse, Vedavyāsa interprets *prakṛtilaya* by stating that "those whose resting place is [in] *prakṛti* experience something like the state of liberation (*kaivalyapadam iva*)." As is well known, the term *kai-*

valyapada refers in these contexts to the state of consciousness or cosmological plane enjoyed by the transcendent person, *puruṣa*, when it has become isolated from all self-identification with the world of materiality, which had been generated by *prakṛti* for teleological reasons that need not concern us. But a number of questions remain. In what way can an experience be "something like liberation" without being liberation? In what way does the highest form of *samādhi* fall short of affording liberation? More important for our concerns, what is the cosmological location of the *prakṛtilaya*s?

In her analysis of this term in these primary sources for *pātañjala yoga* and Sāṃkhya philosophy, Angelika Malinar points to Vedavyāsa's *bhāṣya* on YS 3.26, an aphorism that describes the supernatural attainments realized through *saṃyama* on the sun,[158] in which the realm of the *prakṛtilaya*s is defined cosmologically and compared with other cosmic realms (*bhuvanas*) and the yogic accomplishments associated with them. Vedavyāsa concludes his mapping of the cosmic realms up through the world of *brahman* with the statement: "However, the disembodied (*videha*) and those whose resting place is [in] *prakṛti* exist in the plane of liberation; that is, they are not located in within the[se] world[s]." In other words, whereas YBh 1.19 states that the *prakṛtilaya*s enjoy something like the state of liberation (*kaivalyapadam iva*), Vedavyāsa appears to contradict himself in YBh 3.26, in which the same practitioners are said to exist in the plane of liberation (*mokṣapade varttante*). Malinar's elegant solution to this problem is the following:

> Thus, "absorption in nature" [*prakṛtilaya*] implies the following incongruence between spatial and temporal aspects of liberation: It seems that while liberation has been reached on a spatial level, it has not been obtained on a temporal level. Why does this happen? It happens because we are dealing with a realm shared by two eternal principles, [and] not just one. The *kaivalyapada*, the place of liberation, is not the exclusive realm of *puruṣa*. Rather, *puruṣa* and *prakṛti* share the premises, [albeit] in different constellations. Therefore it is possible to be in [the] realm of liberation, but yet find oneself in a state that is only "like liberation."[159]

My reason for including this long discussion of the *prakṛtilaya*s who "experience something like the state of liberation" should be clear. As a class of second-tier liberated beings—that is, beings who, while virtually liberated through their yogic accomplishments, are nonetheless not entirely liberated and who are spatially located beyond the worlds, but who temporally remain within the world of becoming—they are the exact homologues of (1) the Masters of Yoga of the Vaiṣṇava BhP 2.2

who are both inside and outside the world system and whose liberation is deferred until the final dissolution; (2) the liberated yet impotent Rudra-souls in *atimārga* Saivism; and (3) the Buddhist meditators whose eight attainments fall short of the ninth state of "cessation." This two-tiered soteriology, which definitively subordinated the techniques and goals of the earliest forms of yogic practice—to either scholasticist, intellectualized forms of meditation in Buddhism, or to devotionalist forms of visionary ascent in Hindu bhakti and tantra—finds its metaphysical rationale, if not its origin, in Sāṃkhya philosophy. While the means and ends of the yogas of the chariot warrior and the vedic poets survived in the narrative traditions reviewed in preceding chapters, they became marginalized into a sort of soteriological and cosmological cul de sac in the theoretical productions of the Hindu Purāṇas and Tantras, as well as those of Mahāyāna Buddhism and Buddhist Tantra.

6. "Yogic Suicide" in the Tantras

Further evidence for the subordination of the apotheosis of the chariot warrior to other forms of practice may be elicited from a number of Hindu Tantras, which preserve the practice and the terminology of this epic form of yoga in a sort of fossilized form. Here I am speaking of what is most commonly termed "upward advance" (*utkrānti*) in Hindu sources, but translated by certain scholars as "yogic suicide."[160] *Utkrānti* is discussed in several medieval Śaiva works, as well as a handful of Śākta Tantras and one Vaiṣṇava Saṃhitā, as a yogic technique by means of which a tantric practitioner is enabled to forcefully abandon his body at a time of his own choosing.[161] In all of these, the practitioner's self pierces through the internal lotuses, knots, or vital organs (*marmans*) of his yogic body by raising his breaths from its base up to the crown of the head. Bursting out through the cranial vault, he rises to the heavenly plane (*padam*) of the supreme godhead, never to return. In the context, however, of the rich variety of meditative, devotional, and gnoseological practices leading to a more definitive or exalted order of salvation, this practice appears to be redundant.

Links between the *utkrānti* of chariot warriors and that of ascetics are found in a number of Indic sources. An eighth-century Jain work, the *Ādi Purāṇa* (ĀP) of Jinasena, explicitly draws the link between the self-willed death of a warrior and that of an ascetic, in this case a Jain monk. Although it eschews the term *utkrānti* in favor of *prāya* (as was the case in the MBh account of Bhūriśravas), its account of a monk named

Vajranābhi is instructive. Reaching the eleventh of the fourteen stages (*guṇasthānas*) on the Jain path to liberation, and knowing that his end is at hand, he enters into the state of going forth (*prāyopaveśana*), climbs to a mountaintop, and abandons all attachment to food and his body. In its explication of its use of the term *prāya*, the text states that through his decision to fast unto death, he was "going forth" against the enemy troops of evil and sin (*duritārikadambakān*). In the end, he abandoned his breaths and rose up to the plane known as "I am Indra."[162]

In many respects, *utkrānti* does not differ, in these sources, from the forms of visionary ascent described earlier in this chapter. Their uses of the verb *kram also link it to the daily journeys of sacrificers to the sun and to the sun-piercing apotheosis of epic chariot warriors and hermits. Three things have changed, however. First, because these are later sources, the transitions between microcosm and macrocosm have become smoother. In this respect, we may see these texts as bridges between the rough constructs of the Upaniṣads and the highly detailed "cosmologies" of the subtle body system that become a commonplace in later yogic and tantric traditions.[163] So, for example, the MPĀg enjoins meditation on the nesting spheres of the sun, moon, and empyrean within the heart—a feature of the MU's early account of visionary ascent—and then elaborates, evoking the visualization of a crest of flame (*śikhā*) that, like a luminous lotus filament in appearance, rises up from the sphere of the empyrean. This follows the straight path that is the path of yoga (*yoga-mārga*) up to the top of the head.[164] In its discussion of *ātma-saṃkrānti*, the *Rauravāgama* (RĀg) mentions the same three concentric spheres, in addition to evoking the upanishadic "cave of the heart."[165] It then gives an account of uppermost reaches of the Śaiva cosmos, situating these within (?and beyond) the crown of the head. One of these levels is named *lokāloka*, a term known from puranic cosmology, in which it designates the circular wall of mountains dividing the visible world from the region of darkness.[166] The SvT likewise identifies the crown of the head with the shell of the cosmic egg. According to it, the deity Daṇḍapāṇi (the "Staff-Bearer"), who is "possessed of mastery and the power of yoga," uses his staff to open that "path to release that is difficult to cleave."[167] The *Parākhyatantra* offers a more extended account of the divine spheres located within the upper body, from the "lotus of the heart" to a point twelve finger-breadths above the bridge or tip of the nose, stating that "by passing higher and higher [within the body], one attains higher and higher worlds."[168]

Second, in terms of practice, the use of spells (mantras, *vidyās*, *astras*), which were never a significant component of epic or puraṇic theism, plays a prominent role in *utkrānti* as described in the tantric texts.[169] Here destructive spells—such as the "Razor of Night which is Death" employed in the MVUT—are directed by the practitioner against his own body, in order to sever its vital channels and destroy its vital organs.[170] Finally, the goal of the practice is not the same, for whereas meditative or visionary ascent is repeatable, in much the same way as the vedic sacrificer's rise to the world of the sun, "yogic suicide" is not. Thus, whereas in the MU, BhP, and MPĀg, meditative ascent to the higher worlds was a *virtual*, visionary self-projection in which the self remained tethered to the mind-body complex, here, the departure of the practitioner's self from his body, together with his breaths, is *physical*, irreversible, and therefore terminal. In this respect, tantric *utkrānti* closely resembles both the battlefield apotheosis of the chariot warrior and the embodied ascent of the puranic Master of Yoga who leaves his body to enjoy a prolonged sojourn in the higher worlds, prior to the final dissolution.

Two of the most extensive tantric accounts of *utkrānti* are found in Śākta sources, the MVUT and the circa eleventh-century *Kubjikāmata* (KM).[171] The MVUT reads as follows:

> When [the yogi] considers all . . . experience to be repulsive, he relinquishes his own body and proceeds to the state of no return. To effect this one should perform the aforementioned imposition [of mantras], whose luster is equal to the fire [at the end of time] in reverse, [each phoneme] enclosed by the two [mantras] *skṛk* and *chindi*. [Then] after performing the fire-fixation, enkindling all of the vital bonds (*marmans*), one should fill the body with air from the big toe to the top of the head. Then, translocating that [vital energy] one should lead it from the big toe to the cranial aperture. The knower of yoga should [completely] sever all vital bonds with the mantra . . . [The "Razor of the Night which is Death" mantra (*skṛk*) is now presented in coded form] . . . After fifty enunciations [of this mantra] a headache arises.[172] Perceiving this sign one should proceed with the visualization of the Conqueror of Death. Having compressed [the air] there [in the head], one should meditate on the Drop, Resonance, etc. Then, quickly extracting [the air] in that place, he should dismiss it once and for all with the [mantra of the] Night which is Death.[173]

There is not complete agreement in these texts on the yogi's motives for suicide by these means. The MVUT invokes world-weariness, but other sources speak of failing powers, life crisis situations, the desire to choose one's time of death, or a simple sense of closure.[174] Abhinavagupta (fl. 975–1025), the great Kashmiri polymath who was the most important commentator on the MVUT, takes issue with an assumption that appears to underlie these sources' ascription of motives to the yogi who ends his life in this way. Because his was a radically nondualist ontology, Abhinavagupta could not accept the position that a yogi could leave his body and expect to find the omnipresent Śiva somewhere outside of himself. Like Śaṅkara's *brahman*,[175] the sole knowing, experiencing subject was, for Abhinavagupta, Śiva, who perceived the world as himself. In order to reconcile the MVUT's teaching with his own view, Abhinavagupta proposed two readings of this passage, the one yogic and the other gnostic. In the yoga system (which Abhinavagupta considered inferior), the purpose of *utkrānti* was the supernatural enjoyment, in the ether element, of the yogi's transcendent autonomy. Here we would appear to be in the presence, once again, of the alternate goals of meditative ascent as encountered in the BhP and MPĀg: deferred liberation and the enjoyment of *siddhis* in the upper reaches of the universe, or immediate union (or identity) with the absolute. In the gnostic system that he espoused, *utkrānti* became the highest form of initiation, issuing in liberation the realization of one's intrinsic identity with Śiva. It should be noted, however, that this was a fatal initiation, which, with its vital organ-piercing mantras, would have necessarily issued in the initiate's physical death.[176] Given, however, that both of these goals were attainable by simpler means, one cannot help but see Abhinavagupta straining to fit a square dualist peg into a round nondualist hole here. In the words of Somadeva Vasudeva, "[When] Abhinavagupta demotes yogic egress [i.e., *utkrānti*] to a practice for the pleasure-seeker he is successfully completing his task of relegating yoga fully into the (for him irrelevant) domain of Sādhakas intent on Siddhis. But at the same time he is undoing, as it were, the principal achievement of the *Mālinīvijayottara*'s compilers."[177]

Of great interest to the historian of this yogic technique is the fact that when Abhinavagupta invokes a precedent for the practice of *utkrānti*, he refers to Bhīṣma—the MBh hero who yogically prolonged his life for nearly three months after he had been riddled with Arjuna's arrows,[178] thereby permitting him to hold forth for hundreds of chapters on every topic under the sun, including yoga—as one who had died spontaneously, of his own free will.[179] In the last chapter, I listed Bhīṣma as one of the five epic chariot warriors who, "hitched to their rigs," abandoned their bodies to rise up to the highest path. While the epic account of Bhīṣma's self-willed death does not employ the term *utkrānti*, its description of the process is nonetheless illuminating. According to this passage, his breaths, forced together (*prāṇāḥ saṃniruddhā*), split the crown of his head (*bhittvā mūrdhānam*), causing his soul to rise up into the sky like a great meteor.[180] Certain features of the process of Bhīṣma's apotheosis are taken up again a few chapters later, in the epic's general discussion of the process of dying, a discussion that draws heavily on ayurvedic theory.[181]

As one is dying, heat is driven through the body by a powerful wind, which forces together the breaths (*prāṇān ruṇaddhi*) and splits (*bhinatti*) the vital organs (*marmāṇi*).[182] However, another epic passage indicates that liberation, not death, follows on this process when, "at the time of death, one is liberated by forcing the breaths, with the mind alone, into the [channel of the heart called the] mind-conveyor."[183] Still another epic teaching on yoga, pronounced by Sanatsujāta, one of the mind- or yoga-born sons of Brahmā, states that "in the end, the ascetic who lies down and who causes his entire body to burst through his practice of heat-producing austerities . . . stops death."[184]

Perhaps the most celebrated yogic suicide in all of Hindu mythology is that of Satī, who takes her own life to protest her father's snub of her husband Śiva. As is well known, Satī's suicide stands as the mythological model for every faithful wife (*satī*) who ends her life by throwing herself onto her deceased husband's pyre. In Satī's puranic mythology, however, the goddess does not throw herself upon a sacrificial fire or a burning pyre, but rather relinquishes her body through the practice of a form of yoga.[185] According to the two principal Śaiva Purāṇas, she takes or employs the "path of yoga" (*yoga-mārga*) to reduce her body to ashes.[186] In the *Śiva Purāṇa* (ŚP), she is depicted as raising her upward breath (*udāna*) and mind into the navel (*nābhi-cakra*), heart, breast, throat, and space between the eyebrows prior to combusting.[187] The Śākta *Kālikā Purāṇa* (KāP) bypasses the element of fire entirely, to rather portray her suicide in a yogic mode not unlike that found in agamic and tantric portrayals of *utkrānti*. "She made a bursting sound (*sphoṭa*), and yogically (*yogatas*) inverted all of her doors [bodily orifices]. With that expanding burst (*sphoṭena*), her life's breaths split open the tenth door [the fontanel] and exited [her body]."[188] As Catherine Weinberger-Thomas has demonstrated, modern-day depictions of human *satīs*, women who immolate themselves on their husband's funeral pyres, identify a ray of light emanating from the sun (or from the god Śiva or the goddess Śakti in the sun) as the element that ignites the pyres on which they burn.[189]

In fact, the goddess Satī is, as a result of her yogic prowess, reborn as the goddess Pārvatī, and as such, she remains the spouse of Śiva in her reincarnated form. While this is not the prescribed outcome of *utkrānti*, it appears to be a fallback option for human practitioners of yoga as well. Both the BhG and the *Yoga Vasiṣṭha* (YV) state unambiguously that a yogi "whose yoke has fallen" (*yogabhraṣṭa*), that is, who has not achieved transcendence of the human condition in this life, will be reborn "into a family of wise yogis" and thereby be empowered to carry his practice

Figure 3.2 A ray from the sun ignites the pyre of Sarasvatī Satī. Polychrome, western India, ca. 1980.

forward to its completion in a future body.[190] This doctrine, which has persisted down to the present day, is attested in John Marshall's late seventeenth-century notebooks, in which he reports a discussion with "a Sober, Serious Fuckeer (fakir), a Hindoo" (i.e., a yogi):

> Some live 2 or 300 years of age, and when their bodies are therewith decayed, they acquaint their friends that they desire to leave that body and assume another. So without any violence offered to their body, after their prayers said, they sit down and die voluntarily and at what time they please, but before do acquaint their relations at what place they desire to assume a Body, at Agra or Dilly [Delhi], or the like. And then they leave their owld body and go into the belly of a woman, and so it is borne againe.[191]

The use of the term *utkrānti* to designate a special power arising from yogic practice is at least as old as the YS, which in its enumeration of the supernatural enjoyments obtained through practice, states that upward progress is realized when the upward breath (*udāna*) has been mastered. This verse immediately follows this text's aphorism on the power of entering another person's body (*parakāyāveśa*).[192] Of course, we have already seen that a participial form of the verb ut-*kram appears in ChU 8.6 with reference to the rise of the soul or lifebody from the dying body up to the sun at the end of life. However, this foundational passage does not, contra to Śaṅkara's ninth-century commentary, allow that this upward advance is automatic for all who die. In order to reach the sun and pass through its door, the text tells us one must utter the syllable OṂ, "cast one's mind there," and be "one who knows."[193] Here one is tempted to see that the prototype for the agamic and tantric "missile spells" (*astra*[194]) employed for the purpose of *utkrānti* would have been the upanishadic OṂ cast by the mind of the practitioner.[195]

In Śaṅkara's defense, it should be noted that, while the earliest uses of the verbal root ut-*kram and its nominalized form *utkrānti*—attested in the circa tenth-century BCE *Vājasaneyī Saṃhitā*—had the simple sense of "go[ing], step[ping] upward; ascend[ing]," by the time of the circa eighth-century BCE ŚB the term's semantic field had expanded to mean "pass on, die."[196] I would nonetheless argue that the prototype of the *utkrānti* of the Purāṇas, Āgamas, and Tantras was the self-willed battlefield death of the chariot warrior, whose upward charge was termed *ākramaṇa* (in the case of Droṇa), *saṃkramaṇa* (in the case of Kṛṣṇa), or *ati-kramana* (in the case of the five Pāṇḍavas and Draupadī, as well as of Śuka). This last term was employed in MU 6.28 in what was portrayed as an assault on a citadel, the abode of *brahman* in the space of the heart: "advancing beyond (*atikramya*) the elements and the sense objects, one strikes down the gatekeeper of the door of *brahman*." As we will see in the next chapter, a yogi's takeover of another person's body is also styled as a military assault in the *Netra Tantra* (NT), which speaks of his assault (ā-*kram) upon his victim's lifebody, located in his heart.[197]

FOUR

The Science of Entering Another Body

In the previous two chapters, we saw that when the early Hindu scriptures evoked the rise of persons who were dying—whether of natural causes or through one or another type of self-willed death—they often employed the term *raśmi* to denote the reins or rays that conveyed them to their final destination, regardless of whether it was beneath or beyond the disk of the sun. As one moves forward in time, reins are gradually forgotten in favor of rays (for which there exists an abundance of terms in the Sanskrit language, *marīci, kiraṇa, arcis, ketu,* etc.), with these rays being understood as conduits, rather than harnesses, for the rise of the luminous person (*puruṣa*), self (*ātman*), or lifebody (*jīva*) of the dying or departing individual. Both connotations of the term appear to be present in the epic and puranic accounts of Śuka's apotheosis that describe the hermit as being conveyed via the rays of the solar orb or the reins of the solar chariot, which lock into his eyes and draw his lifebody skyward.[1] Similarly, the epic accounts of the apotheoses of Droṇa and Bhīṣma in particular both depict these chariot warriors as luminous entities that are absorbed into the heavenly luminaries even as they retain the language of the yoking of chariots. In this chapter, I will trace the ways in which this Indic metaphysics of rays came to be applied to the diverse yet interconnected fields of aesthetics, epistemology, climatology, medicine, and the yogi's art or science of entering into foreign bodies. As will become apparent in these pages, all living beings are not only connected to the sun through its rays but also have the potential for being linked to all that exists—including one another—through the rays emanating from their incandescent inner selves or persons and outward via their sense organs in every act of perception.

In the Brāhmaṇas and Upaniṣads, the inner selves of individuals are portrayed as tiny points of light, with each linked, at birth and at death, to a ray of the sun. In life, the inner self apprehends the outside world through its contact with the mind, which receives and processes data through its contact with the senses.[2] In the case of visual perception, that sensory data is received through the organ of sight that travels outward along a ray emitted by the microcosmic sun in the eye. In the case of yogis, their special powers of perception enable them to not only perceive other beings but also to penetrate their bodies to the point of entering into direct contact with the inner selves of those beings and taking their place, if they so will. In this context, the phenomenal world with its multitude of creatures is transformed into a network of diminutive suns (embodied selves), linked to one another through their individual rays of perception, all linked to the great sun in the sky through its infinite rays—and with the yogi resembling the sun inasmuch as he is able to penetrate multiple creatures' bodies simultaneously. This worldview finds its expression in analytical accounts of the relationship of the sun to the world and its creatures in speculative passages from the philosophical, epic, ayurvedic, and upanishadic literature; in Buddhist narrative accounts of the relationship of Buddhas to Buddha worlds; and in epic narratives of encounters between the sun god and humans.

1. Light Rays, Life Rays, and Death Rays

a. Indic Theories of Perception

The various Indic philosophical schools admit between one and six sources of knowledge or valid cognition (*pramāṇas*), with *pratyakṣa* ("perception"[3]) being the sole *pramāṇa* upon which all agree.[4] The Nyāya and Vaiśeṣika schools, which are the earliest among these, set the agenda for all that follow. The principal sources for these two schools are their respective root texts, the circa second- to first-century BCE *Vaiśeṣika Sūtra* (VS) attributed to Kaṇāda and the first- to second-century CE *Nyāya Sūtra* (NS) attributed to Gautama;[5] as well as the 450–550 CE

Padārthadharmasaṃgraha (PADhS) of Praśastapāda, the principal commentary on the former work, and a number of its sub-commentaries.[6]

The *pramāṇas* that will concern us here are the first and fourth, as listed in Nyāya and Vaiśeṣika sources. These are *pratyakṣa* on the one hand, and *ārṣa*, the valid cognition or verbal evidence of the *ṛṣis*, the vedic seers, on the other.[7] As the etymology of the former term indicates, the paradigm for all sensual perception is visual or ocular: *pratyakṣa* is that which is present before (*prati*) the eye(s) (*akṣa*).[8] However, the eyes of exceptional beings, conjoined with their inerrancy in interpreting their perceptions, render theirs the supreme and most authentic source of valid cognition. This was the case with the vedic seers, the authority of whose verbal evidence—the inerrant word (or mantras) of the Veda itself—grounded the entire Vaiśeṣika philosophical system, just as it did for the Mīmāṃsakas.[9] In a similar vein, the NS postulates that true knowledge is achieved through a special practice of pure concentration (*samādhi*)[10] or through the practice of yoga,[11] with all other valid cognitions being inferior.[12] As such, the unsupported support for all valid cognition is, in India's two most ancient philosophical systems, the perception-based gnosis of practitioners of yoga, the vedic seers, or the perfected beings (siddhas). Beginning with Praśastapāda, this is termed "yogi (or yogic) perception" (*yogi-pratyakṣa*), a source of valid cognition also admitted by his Buddhist contemporary Dignāga (ca. 480–540 CE).[13] The importance of true or accurate perception as the basis for valid cognition cannot be overestimated here. When the VS introduces the term "yoga," it does so precisely to identify this practice as the prime means for enabling the mind to apprehend the self without the distorting interference of the sense perceptions. When the mind apprehends the self directly, that is, when it truly "knows" in the upanishadic sense of the term, then the embodied self ceases to identify with the world of suffering it otherwise experiences when still receiving sensory data. Once this link is broken, the self no longer experiences pain, a condition that is tantamount to liberation.[14]

I will return to the extraordinary category of yogi perception later in this chapter. Here, however, an examination of the mechanics of ordinary perception as described in early Indic sources is in order. As we will see later in this chapter, it is likely that an important source for (or mirror of) these early philosophical theories of perception was the MBh itself. The solar mysticism of the Upaniṣads and the light metaphysics of Mahāyāna Buddhist philosophy provide additional data for tracing the development of this and allied concepts. Earlier still, the Vedas and Brāhmaṇas contain speculations on the relationship between the eye and the sun, which appear to anticipate the later philosophical formulations.

A common denominator of Mīmāṃsaka, Sāṃkhya, Vedānta, and Nyāya-Vaiśeṣika theories of perception is that the sense organs are *prāpyakāri*; that is, that they receive sensory data (i.e., perceive) when they come into direct contact with their objects.[15] This "projective model" of perception is described by the seventeenth-century Advaita Vedānta commentator Dharmarāja as an outpouring of light (*tejas*), akin to the flowing of water around an object:

> Just as the water of a tank, having come out of an aperture, enters a number of fields through channels assuming like [those] fields a quadrangular or any other form, so also, the internal organ, which is characterized by light, goes out [from the body] through the door [sense organ] of sight, etc., and [after] reaching the location of the object, say a pitcher, is modified in the form of the object like a pitcher.[16]

For the Nyāya-Vaiśeṣika school, this means that while the bodily support of the visual sense faculty is the eyeball or the pupil of the eye, visual perception in fact occurs when the organ of visual perception, emitted from the pupil in the form of a ray of light (*tejas*), comes into direct contact, even con-forms, with its object, from a distance.[17] Whence the *NS*'s terse formulation, "Perception is the consequence of contact between a ray and an object."[18] Why can we not see these rays of perception? As the *Nyāyabhūṣaṇam* (NBh) explains, these rays are invisible to the eye because "the eye itself, having gone to the site of its object via the aperture of the ray is bound together with it, like a lamp [to the light it emits], and its rays, due to their [consequent] invisibility, are not seen [by it]."[19] This core foundational concept of Nyāya philosophy's "direct realism"[20] is reiterated and expanded upon in myriad ways throughout the Nyāya-Vaiśeṣika corpus.

As Richard King has noted, this understanding of perception appears to flow from an insight found in the BṛU (4.3.6), which intimates that the self is an inner light that shines outward (through the eyes) and illuminates the objective world, even in the absence of the external lights of sun, moon, and fire.[21] This insight is amplified in the MU (2.6), which portrays the igneous self that dwells in the heart as punching holes out through its surface in order that its five rays (*raśmi*), that is, the sense organs, may spread outward, enabling that self to grasp ("eat" in the Sanskrit) its sense-objects.[22] This opinion is shared by the medical tradition, which explains vision in terms of the presence of an igneous element within the eye (*ālocako 'gni*), a concept also found among the ancient Greeks.[23]

b. The Sun, the Eye, and Death

In addition to being the source of light in the world—or more likely, *because* it is the source of light in the world—the sun has also figured as a principal deity in Indic and Indo-Iranian pantheons since the time of the Vedas in India and the *Avesta* and its ancillary literature in Persia. Its prominence in the scriptural traditions under study here draws on a substratal (Indo-Iranian) cult of the sun god Mithra from the pre-vedic period, as well as on adstratal influences from Persia, particularly during the first millennium of the common era, beginning with the Kushan reintroduction of the Iranian sun god as Mihira, the Sanskritized form of his Middle Iranian name of Mihr, via the Bactrian Miiro.[24] This was also the period during which the Mesopotamian solar calendar was imported into India, effecting a revolution in Indic astrology, which also translated into the rise of mainly Vaiṣṇava astrologers in the royal courts of the subcontinent, at the expense of both the old vedic sacrifice-based priesthood and the astrologers of the old vedic calendrical system, whose system had been lunar.[25]

Numismatic evidence for the importation of the ancient Iranian solar cult into South Asia is also found in the coinage of the Kushan kings, who transposed the fiery nimbus surrounding the head and shoulders of the ancient Iranian sun god onto numismatic depictions of themselves. Prior to the Kushans, representations of Zeus-Mithra on the reverse of coins issued by the circa 95–70 BCE Indo-Greek (Bactrian) King Hermaeus depicted the god with rays emanating from his head. Later proto-Kushan Yeuzhi imitations of the Hermaeus coins (ca. 70–55 BCE) further exaggerated the size of these rays, or added rays where there had been none, in the case of their imitations of the Heliocles I coins.[26] Then, at the close of the first century CE, the Kushan ruler Vima Takto (ca. 80–100 CE)—the son of the same Kujula Kadphises who had extended Kushan control southward into the Mathura region of the Indian subcontinent—issued a series of coins depicting a diademed male bust with rays emanating from the head on its obverse. Here, however, the coin's legend identified the head as that of the sovereign himself, who called himself the "king of kings, the great savior" and a *devaputra*, a "son of the gods."[27] Finally, a coin of Vima Kadphises (ca. 100–128 CE), portrayed that king—seated in the same cross-legged pose as those found on the Maues, Azes, and

Kujula Kadphises coins discussed in chapter two—with flames of fire rising from his shoulders (fig. 2.7).[28] What we see, then, is a progression in the transposition of symbols figured on the coinage of rulers from Inner Asia, whose realms extended from the eastern borders of the Parthian Empire down into the heart of the subcontinent. Solar rays, emanating from the heads of Persian *gods* on coins from the early first century BCE were transposed to the heads of *kings* some two centuries later, while the seated posture of *kings* as figured on coins from the early to mid-first century BCE was transposed onto figures of the *Buddha* or bodhisattva some two centuries later.

The solar deity of the Vedas was known by several names, which tracked with the sun's position in the sky: at sunrise he was named Sūrya, Savitṛ, and Vivasvat; at noon he was Mithra (the name of the Indo-Iranian sun god); at sunset he was again called Savitṛ; and the "nocturnal sun" was named Varuṇa.[29] In addition to these names, the rays (*gāvo*), or more properly speaking the "spirit" of the sun's rays, were deified as Viṣṇu, the god whose most illustrious feat, as recorded in vedic mythology, involved taking three great strides. These strides further linked the vedic Viṣṇu to the sun, which was referred to as *vikrama* ("wide striding" or "broadly advancing"),[30] a name adopted by many Indian kings, including Vikramāditya ("Wide Striding Sun"), the royal hero of the Vikrama Cycle of medieval yogi mythology. As we will see in the next chapter, the epic and puranic Viṣṇu and Śiva both came to be explicitly portrayed as solar deities in their divine practice of yoga.

Textual sources for the projective model of perception may also be traced back to the vedic period in sources that speculate on the relationship between the eye, the heart, the sun, and the process of dying. Here I will briefly trace the early development of this model, which derives from observations of the sun, whose radiant effulgence was understood to be the cosmic homologue of the eye as organ of visual perception. The locus classicus of this homology is found in the renowned creation hymn of ṚV 10.90, according to whose thirteenth verse the sun arose from the eye of the sacrificed cosmic person, Puruṣa. The ṚV makes the same statement concerning the human eye: when a person dies, his eye goes to the sun (10.16.3). The ṚV also calls the sun an eye in the sky (1.22.20, 1.136.2), the eye of the world (1.50.6), and the foundation for human vision (6.11.5, 9.10.8, 10.158.4).[31]

In a *prāpyakāri* system of perception, the eye is itself a wide-ranging organ, and so one finds it identified with its solar homologue. So, for example, the "eye of the sun," which is evoked in several vedic passages,[32] is related in the later literature to the human eye. In a myth from the BṛU, a series of deities named speech, breath (*prāṇa*), eye, ear, and mind come under assault from the titans (*asuras*). These deities sing the High Chant in sequence, and when "the breath that is in the mouth" (*ayāsya prāṇa*) has its turn, it defeats the demons and then carries these deities beyond "the evil that is death." When the deity named "eye" escapes death, it becomes the sun.[33] According to the same source (3.2.13), the sun is also the final abode of the human eye, following the dissolution of the body after death. The fact that the igneous eye "shines" or is luminous makes such linkages obvious, as attested in a passage from the ChU concerning the *brahman*: "The eye is a quarter, a foot, of *brahman*. With the sun as its light it shines (*bhāti*) and radiates heat (*tapati*)."[34]

As we had the occasion to observe in chapter two, the links between the sun and death are more profound.[35] As the source but also the eater of all food—that is, all creatures—the sun is portrayed, from the earliest times, as a divine being that both gives life and takes it away. In the ancillary literature of the White Yajurveda, these links are explored in metaphysical speculations concerning the relationship between the sun, the eye (or more properly speaking, the "person of the eye" [*cākṣuṣa puruṣa*]), and death. In the circa eighth-century BCE ŚB, we read that

> a person's other half (*mithuna*) is found in the right eye of the sun's face. Its complement is the image one sees in the left eye of the [human] sacrificer . . . That person who is in the solar orb up there, and this person who is in his [i.e., the human sacrificer's] right eye are, in fact, none other than death. His feet are solidly planted on a man's heart. When he withdraws them, and when he leaves there, the man dies.[36]

Although the language of this passage is ambiguous, it clearly indicates that human life is sustained by a luminous bond, extending from the sun on high down through the human eye and into the heart. When that lifeline (or light line) is broken, a man's eyes go dim, and he dies. In the last chapter, we saw an upanishadic development of this concept in the link made, in ChU 8.6, between the channels of the heart and the rays of the sun. This reading is seconded by a passage from the BṛU, a text considered to be an "appendix" to the ŚB, on the advent of death.

> When the self becomes debilitated and has seemingly fallen into a stupor, the breaths converge on it. Taking back with it those luminous elements (*tejomātrāḥ*), it advances down toward (*anvavakrāmati*) the heart. When the person of the eye turns away from this self, it ceases to know forms [i.e., one's eye grows dim] . . . The uppermost region of that self's [space of the] heart begins to glow, and the self emerges (*niṣkrāmati*) with

that glow, either through the eye, the head, or other parts of the body. As it advances upward (*utkrāmanta*), the vital breath follows its upward advance (*anūtkrāmati*); as the breath advances upward, all of the senses [or breaths] follow its upward advance.[37]

Another BṛU passage relates the person of the eye directly to the solar disk. At the divine level, the essence of the immortal *brahman* is the person in the circle (of the sun), while at the human level it is the "person who is in the right eye" who embodies that immortal absolute. At death, when the person of the right eye leaves the body, he rejoins his homologue in the sun, with the conduit for their union being the rays (*raśmi*) of the sun, which merge or morph into the human breaths.

What truth is, the sun is.[38] The person (*puruṣa*) who is in its orb and the person who is in the right eye are supported on one another. That one rests on this one through its rays, and this one rests on that one through its breaths. When one is about to depart, one sees that circle pure [without rays]. The rays do not come to him again.[39]

The ChU and the *Jaiminīya Upaniṣad Brāhmaṇa* (JUB), two Upaniṣads of the *Sāma Veda* that were likely coeval with the BṛU, are particularly rich in homologies of this sort. Two chapters in the JUB draw direct parallels between the sun, the eye, mortality, and immortality on the levels of both body and universe. First, on the universal level, the range of the sun's movement is divided into two parts: the mortal, comprised of the ocean that surrounds the earth, and the immortal, that which lies beyond that sea. In the course of a day, the sun moves from immortality (as it rises from beyond the horizon of sea and sky) to immortality (as it sets beyond the horizon), "advancing toward (*ākramate*) immortality on the back of the wind." Its threefold form, which death cannot reach, is comprised of "the white, the black, and the *puruṣa*." Its white form, identified with fire, is death. Its *puruṣa* form, which is identified with breath and the *brahman*, is immortality.[40] Now the text turns to the sun's human homologue, stating that the eye is threefold in the same way as the sun and repeating verbatim the respective homologizations of its white, black, and *puruṣa* forms.[41] It then continues:

This [the *puruṣa* who is identified with the breath and immortality] is the upward advance (*utkrānti*) of the *brahman*, and its assault (*parākranti*) [is initiated] from there. Here, the [white] ray[42] is what constitutes its advance (*ākrānti*) . . . The one who is in the ray is none other than the *puruṣa*, who is breath . . . immortality . . . and the *brahman* . . . This is the *puruṣa* that is in the eye. The one who is in the sun is the "surpassing *puruṣa*." The one who is in the ray is the "supreme *puruṣa*." These are the three *puruṣas*.

This one that is in the eye is named "con-forming" (*anu-rūpa*), because it follows in the direction of all forms . . . All forms indeed follow after it. The [*puruṣa*] in the sun is the likeness [literally the "counter-form" (*pratirūpa*) of the *puruṣa* in the eye] . . . The [*puruṣa* that is] in the ray is the one that has all forms.[43]

One cannot help but see in this discussion the anticipation of later *prāpyakāri* theories of perception, as well as the inspiration behind Kṛṣṇa's BhG 15.15–19 teaching on the three *puruṣas*: the perishable *puruṣa* that dwells in every creature's heart, the imperishable *puruṣa* that is "seated in the peak" (*kūṭasthā*), and the supreme *puruṣa*, with which Kṛṣṇa identifies himself as the eternal master (*īśvara*) who has penetrated the three worlds.[44] This language may also be linked to the trilocation of the *puruṣa* in BṛU 4.3.9: this world of waking reality (*idam*), the other world (*paralokasthāna*) of deep sleep, and the "place of dreams" (*svapnasthāna*), which corresponds to the atmosphere, in which the luminous *puruṣa*, illuminated by its own light, is able to see into both this world and the world beyond. As we have seen, this threefold typology of regions and states of consciousness is also found in early Buddhism.[45]

In the JUB, however, it is the sun that is described as the supreme being in ways reminiscent of the *Atharva Veda*'s (AV) depiction of Kāla, the thousand-eyed god of time—whose chariot is drawn by seven horses, attached by seven reins or rays (*raśmi*)[46]—in whom the sun burns, the eye sees, and all creatures dwell.[47] What is innovative in the JUB's reading is that each of the sun's seven rays is identified as a type of sense perception, speech, food, breath, and so on. Concerning the sense of sight, the text states that "the [ray] consisting of the eye . . . is the sun . . . Its ray, having become the eye, was placed in all of these creatures. Whosoever sees, sees by virtue of one of its rays."[48]

The JUB's extended reflection on these homologies, between sun, eye, life, and death, concludes with a statement concerning the rays that echoes the ChU 8.6, albeit sans reference to death.

As paths would lead up a mountain . . . the sun's rays go from every direction to the sun. Verily, he who knows this and who begins [his invocation] with OṂ goes to the sun from every direction by means of its rays.[49]

As for the ChU, it locates the person of the eye at the place "where the eye is fixed out in space," homologizing him with the transcendent self (*ātman*), whose "divine eye" (*daivam cakṣus*) allows the mind to see the things it desires in the world of *brahman*. Here as well, it would appear that the upanishadic authors were articulating an early theory of visual perception, which occurs, as we have noted, at the site of its object. As for the "divine eye" mentioned here, its objects are, like the objects of "yogi perception," located in a world that is invisible to nonyogis. Furthermore, according to this passage, the gods who contemplate the transcendent self obtain all of the worlds and all desires.[50] These sorts of connections lay the groundwork for the meditation programs described in the previous chapter, through which the mind's eye travels upward to distant worlds and makes them its own.

c. The Heart in Early Subtle Body Mapping

The early BṛU also sought to link the eye to the heart, which was considered to be a seat of the self, mind, and—from the time of the ṚV itself—the ability to see what is invisible to the physical eye.[51] In BṛU 4.2.2–3, this person of the right eye is called Indha, "the Kindler," while the "form of the person in his left eye is his wife Virāj, 'the Queen.'"[52] These meet in the heart, out of which they travel upward along a channel (*nāḍī*) that is but one of a multitude of such channels. The *hitās*, the subtle channels of the heart, are evoked a number of times in this early Upaniṣad, once in its discussion of deep sleep, which the text contrasts with dream sleep. Whereas in the latter state, "the person made of knowledge" (*vijñānamayaḥ puruṣa*) circulates throughout the entire body, in deep sleep he moves along the seventy-two thousand channels called *hitā*, and through them reaches the heart and then the citadel (*purītat*) of the heart. "Having crept through them he lies down in the citadel."[53] As we will see later in this chapter, the body of a king named Janaka is described as an "empty citadel" (*purāgāram*), after a Buddhist nun named Sulabhā has entered into his body and dwelt for a night in his heart. A passage from the AV etymologizes the term *puruṣa* on this basis: "Neither the eye nor breath abandons the person . . . who knows the *brahman*'s citadel (*púr*), from which *puruṣa* is named."[54] This vedic legacy—of identifying the body or heart that encloses and shelters the inner self, that is, the *ātman* as a "citadel"[55]—is carried forward into the medieval literature of the Tantras, in which "subtle yoga" is described, precisely as an assault on another person's body-citadel.[56]

These passages from the ŚB and early Upaniṣads provide a glimpse into what were some of the earliest of the "subtle" body constructions, which are further elaborated in the later Upaniṣads as well as in the sectarian sources discussed in the last chapter.[57] What is most striking in these early accounts of the subtle body is that it is neither autonomous nor self-contained, but rather one pole in a bipolar system. Grounding the system is the disk of the sun,[58] within which is inscribed a person or an eye that is the replica or simulacrum of the human "person of the eye" or the eye as a whole.[59] These two *puruṣas* are joined by a solar ray that is both a breath channel (or a beam of visual perception) and a rein or yoke between two worlds. This dynamic reproduces those of both the apotheosis of the epic chariot warrior and the yoga of the vedic poets. I would also argue that it forms the conceptual foundation for the oft-repeated expression, found in the Upaniṣads, BhG (as well as elsewhere in the MBh), Rām, and numerous commentaries with regard to the meditating practitioner: "he sees the self in the self (by means of the self)."[60]

At the heart of the mysticism of the early Upaniṣads is the identification of both of the "persons" (*puruṣas*) of the two poles of the system as the one luminous *brahman*, which manifests as the sun whose being extends into every living creature in the form of a ray. This identification can in fact be traced back to the ŚB, which, in its discussion of the Viṣṇu steps, states that "the rays of the one that shines on high are the goodly ones (i.e., the ancestors)." The great fourteenth-century commentator Sāyaṇa expands on this verse: "The deceased fathers (*sukṛtaḥ*) are the rays of the sun, which, like the filaments of the *Nauclea cadamba* flower [a brilliant yellow-to-orange flower with multiple spikes radiating out from a central core] are infinite in their divisions. Those who were *yajamānas* in the past are, precisely, those ray-bodies [*tejaḥśarīrāḥ*] on high."[61] The ninth-century Śaṅkara works from the same conceptual foundation, as evinced in his discussion of the fate of the person who dies at night, when the sun is not shining. Quoting ChU 8.6.6 on the "rays of the heart," Śaṅkara asserts that for so long as the body with which the individual self is associated exists, it is connected to a ray of the sun, arguing that the rays persist even when the sun is invisible, as for example after darkness has fallen on summer nights, when they manifest as residual heat.[62] In so doing, however, he is forced to explain away a teaching from the BhG (8.23), in which Kṛṣṇa reveals—paraphrasing BṛU 6.2.15–16 and ChU 5.10.1–6—that those yogis who depart life in the night, the dark lunar fortnight, or the southern course of the sun must be returned once again to the world of cyclic rebirth. This he does with great casuistic aplomb.[63]

At the human end of this bipolar system, a luminous channel, the most prominent of a vast network of channels, runs down from behind the eye or below the crown of the head into the "cave" or "citadel" of the heart. As we saw in the last chapter, the MU adds a layer of detail to the subtle body system of the earlier Upaniṣads, ensconcing the solar wheel or sphere (*maṇḍala*) within those of the moon, the empyrean, and pure being at *both* ends of the system, both within the space of the heart and at the upper reaches of the universe. This model becomes further elaborated in the Purāṇas and Āgamas, which layer on additional levels, within both the subtle body and the cosmic egg, laying the foundation for the highly elaborate inner cosmologies of the later yogic literature.[64]

d. The Puruṣa as Gnomon

In these metaphysical systems, we find ourselves in the presence of a logic of projection, wherein an entity, most often called "the person" (*puruṣa*) is shown to be simultaneously present in both the sun in the heavens and the luminous eye or space in the heart of the human body. Linking these two *puruṣas* is a ray of light, which, originating from the sun, provokes the death of a man when it is withdrawn. This configuration has its origin in an unexpected source, which may be approached by considering the dimension of the *puruṣa* in the space of the heart, as described in MU 6.38, BhP 2.2.8, and elsewhere: he is a "thumb" or a "span" in size (*aṅguṣṭha-prādeśa-mātram*).[65] In a highly insightful study, Harry Falk has pointed to the frequent references in the vedic literature to Viṣṇu as a span-high post or stick.[66] In the ancient Indian system of measures, a span, the distance between the outstretched thumb and little finger, was the equivalent of twelve finger breadths (*aṅgulis*).[67] These measurements only make sense when one considers the dimensions of ancient Indian sundials, which, according to the earliest mentions of them, comprised a gnomon twelve finger breadths in height, inscribed in a circle twenty-four finger breadths in diameter. This combination of a stick (the gnomon) and string (for tracing the circle) was employed from the time of the Vedas for plotting the movement of heavenly bodies on an earth-based plane.[68]

One use of this sundial was to establish a "true" east-west line, called the *prācī*, in the construction of sacrificial altars. This was found by marking the two points at which the end of the shadow thrown by the gnomon's tip crossed the traced circle, once in the morning and once in the evening. Between these two, the moment at which the shadow of the gnomon was the shortest was the noon point.[69] These three points constituted "Viṣṇu's three strides (*trivikrama*)," in the light of which the most obvious referent of Viṣṇu's vedic mythology is shown to be this device,[70] which served to plot or project the movements of the heavenly sun onto an earthly plane twenty-four finger breadths wide. As a twelve-*aṅgula*-tall gnome, Viṣṇu's three steps across the circle of the sundial track the sun's daily crossing of the entire circle of heaven.[71] Viṣṇu is also styled as a span-sized embryo (*garbha*) in the ŚB,[72] a possible source of the epic and puranic mythology of the *puruṣottama* who appeared before Markaṇḍeya in the form of the infant Kṛṣṇa;[73] as well as of the infant (*śiśu*) situated in the highest heaven in an enigmatic BṛU passage that also brings together the eye, the movement of the sun, and temporal cycles.[74] The Vedas also speak of Viṣṇu's seven strides, with reference to the plotting points of the gnomon's shadow on the circle, in the solstice-to-solstice displacement of the sun in the course of a solar year.[75]

As we noted in the previous chapter, the MU, BhG, and BhP frequently identify Viṣṇu and Kṛṣṇa with the *puruṣa* or *puruṣottama*, with BhP 2.2 entitled "Description of Him Who Appears as the Person." But is he merely a person? Here the AŚ's description of the gnomon is illuminating: "Twelve *aṅgulas* make a span and the height of the gnomon," literally the "shadow-person" (*chāyāpuruṣa*).[76] Here, when Kauṭilya plots the length of shadows cast by the gnomon, he uses the term *pauruṣa*, "relating to the gnomon's length," as a unit of measure.[77]

When the shadow (of the gnomon) is eight *pauruṣas*, one-eighteenth part of the day is past; when six *pauruṣas*, one-fourteenth part (is past); when three *pauruṣas*, one-eighth part; when one *pauruṣa*, one-fourth part; when eight *aṅgulas*, three-tenths part (is past), when four *aṅgulas*, three-eighths part (and) when there is no shadow, it is midday. When the day has turned [i.e., in the afternoon], one should understand the remaining parts [of the day] in like manner.[78]

While the twelve finger breadths of the *chāyāpuruṣa* establish the *pauruṣa* unit of measurement for sundials, it is not the case that all *pauruṣas* are created equal. The *pauruṣa* used for measuring a moat is different from that used for measuring a fire altar. But the householder's measure (*gārhapatya pauruṣa*) is the measure of the man himself: a ninety-six-*aṅgula*-high pole, the equivalent of 1.65 meters, the average height of an adult Indian male,[79] as well as of this author. This measure makes intuitive sense; the height of a man-high (*pauruṣa*) pole is the height of an average man. What of the twelve-*aṅgula*-high gnomon? What makes it a *puruṣa?* What is its relationship to the vedic Viṣṇu as gnomon? A simple answer, that the great god of Hindu theism is none other than the Puruṣa of ṚV 10.90, turns out to be more complex than it first appears.[80] As Falk argues, the opening verse of this hymn may be read as a description of a ten-finger-high post: "The *puruṣa* has a thousand heads, a thousand eyes, a thousand shadows (*sahásrapāt*). While proceeding across the earth [the circle of the sundial] in all directions, he has risen [to the height of] ten finger-breadths [above the plane of the sundial]."[81] In his discussion of this passage, R. Shamasastry notes that ten *aṅgulas* is the length of the shadow cast by the *puruṣa* on the day of the summer solstice.[82] The divergence of two finger breadths between the *puruṣa*'s height in ṚV 10.90 and that found in other sources has been explained by Paul Mus in terms of classical measures of the human head, which need only concern us here inasmuch as it contains an explanation for the tantric term *dvādaśānta*, "end of the twelve," for that point at or beyond the crown of the head where the individual self merges with the transcendent self.[83] For our purposes, the significance of this archaic usage of the term *puruṣa* is that (1) it clearly links a person in this world (the gnomon) to the person in the sun through a ray (the ray that throws the shadow of the gnomon onto the circle of the sundial); (2) it anticipates the *prāpyakāri* model of visual perception, with the man in the sun traveling out from that orb to grasp and illuminate its homologue, the gnomon; (3) it stands at the center of a mesocosm (the circle of the sundial), which is a constructed replica of the circle of the heavens through which the sun passes; and (4) it also stands at the center of a microcosm (the inner space of the heart), which, as the early Upaniṣads state, is as great as the outer space of the cosmos. Here as well, there are three *puruṣas*, the transcendent person in the solar disk, the person in the sundial's circle, and the person in the eye/heart. Furthermore, the plotting of the celestial movements of the sun's yoked chariot to three points (the three "Viṣṇu steps") on the tiny circle of the sundial constitutes another case in which the verb *yuj would have functioned in tandem with the verb *kram.

2. Solar Yokings in Upanishadic, Epic, and Ayurvedic Sources

Projection was not the sole conceptual model employed in these sources to theorize the relationship between the person and the world, and inner and outer space. Among the many early metaphysical explanations for the sun's power to give life and to take life away, the most powerful are those that depict that heavenly body as the thermodynamic motor of the ecosystem through the food cycle. The earliest vedic speculations viewed the sun both as the celestial form of fire and as the source of all fire in both the world (where it resides, *in potentia*, in trees, the waters, etc. and is released when wood burns, water boils, or lightning flashes) and in the human organism (as the inner fires responsible for digestion, the body heat that sustains life, and the light in the human eye). Already in the ṚV, the rays of the sun are said to perform the three functions of dispensing heat, cold, and moisture throughout the three levels of the universe.[84] By the time of the Upaniṣads, these functions have been integrated and expanded into the renowned "five fires doctrine" of the BṛU and ChU, the earliest Indic articulation of the principle of cyclic rebirth, which is itself grounded in the food cycle, whose motor is the interplay between the sun, fire, time, and the production and consumption of food.[85]

The opening chapter of the MU's sixth book identifies two eaters of food: the "person made of gold within the sun" and the person "resting inside, in the heart lotus."[86] In the chapter that follows, both of these persons are identified with "the fire that is spread over the sky, the solar fire called 'Time,' who, unseen, eats all beings as food."[87] In its penultimate chapter, book six links the sun to both the production and the consumption of food in the world via its rays. The same rays are identified as the source of food, which the sun "rains down with its rays," fostering life in creatures.

The "sun of time" is also made out to be the source of food in MU 6.14. Here the text elaborates on the divisions of time, explaining that the year, the baseline measure for the temporal cycles, is in fact divided into two halves, belonging to Agni (fire, the diurnal sun) and Varuṇa (water, the nocturnal sun). These halves are the semesters of the year, between the winter and summer solstices and the summer and winter solstices. Such associations make intuitive sense in South Asia, where the first half of the year, the sun's northern course, is a time of increasing heat, dessication, and mortality; whereas the latter half of the year, its southern course, is a time of increasing coolness, humidity, and fertility.[88]

This dynamic is analyzed with the greatest clarity in the classical literature of Āyurveda, which also dates from the first centuries of the common era and that, moreover, uses derivates of the term "yoga" to denote the links between microcosm and macrocosm. In the introductory chapters of the three principal ayurvedic treatises—the *Caraka Saṃhitā* (CS), the *Suśruta Saṃhitā* (SS), and *Aṣṭāṅgahṛdaya* (AH)[89]—one finds descriptions of the year as a bipolar system in which the relative influences of the sun and moon (here replacing Agni and Varuṇa, fire and water, from MU 6.14) directly generate balances or imbalances of heat, moisture, and wind in the ecosystem, which in turn indirectly provoke discontinuities (*doṣas*), within the bodily microcosm, of the three humors: bile, phlegm, and wind. In these descriptions, the term yoga ("junction" or *saṃyoga*, "conjunction") is employed, together with a variety of prefixes, for particular seasonally determined interactions between the outer world of the ecosystem and the inner world of the human organism.[90] Throughout the ayurvedic year, it is the extreme effects of the sun and moon—and, to a lesser extent, of the wind—on the ecosystem that must be mitigated within the body through special diets, regimens, and behaviors, and it is the task of the physician to effect a "balanced junction" (*samayoga*) when confronted with humoral imbalances provoked by an "over-junction of time" (*kālātiyoga*), an "under-junction" or "non-junction of time" (*kālāyoga*), or a "dys-junction of time" (*kālamithyāyoga*).[91]

In this literature, the impact of the sun and moon on seasonal changes is explained in terms of the "pouring out" (*visarga*) of the moon's cooling moisture, which "swells" (*āpyāyayati*) or moistens (*kledayati*) the ecosystem during the latter half of the year, as opposed to the sun, which desiccates (*śoṣayati*) living organisms as it takes back (*ādatte*) the same during the first half of the year. These semesters are termed "lunar" (*saumya*) and "fiery" (*āgneya*), respectively.[92] The AH describes these relationships in the following terms:

> Now, one should know the northern course [of the sun] by those three [seasons] that begin with the cold season. That [which is known as] "taking back" (*ādānam*) daily takes back the power (*balam*) of men. In this [semester] especially, the solar winds—which, due to the nature of the path [taken by the sun], are exceedingly hot, penetrating, and dry—diminish the lunar [i.e., moist] qualities of the earth. Here, the bitter, the astringent, and the sharp are [the] strong[est] flavors. Thus the [semester of] taking back is fiery. The southern course [comprises] the seasons beginning with the rains and the [the period of] pouring out, and power is what it pours out.[93] At this time, due to its lunar qualities, the moon alone is strong [whereas] the sun is on the wane on the surface of the earth whose [accumulated] heat has subsided through the effect of the cooling clouds, rain, and breezes. Here, the oily, the acidic, salty, and the sweet are [the] strong[est] flavors.[94]

The CS describes this bipolar dynamic in terms of the hydration and dehydration of the ecosystem: the moon, "filling the world with its cool rays, causes it to swell,"[95] while "in the hot season, the sun intensively drinks up (*pepīyate*), [i.e., evaporates], the world's moisture [via its rays]."[96] These rays are not simply comprised of effulgent light but are conduits for the transfer of matter and energy between the heavens, the earth, and the bodies of creatures. This makes perfect sense when one observes a puddle after a monsoon rain: after the sun reemerges from behind the clouds, the water in the puddle is quickly drawn off by the sun, whose rays are so many drinking straws. It is these conduits that make possible, in the words of Francis Zimmermann, "the relationships between a living being and his natural environment, which give rise to a vast metabolism of foods and fluids."[97]

The MBh offers an early mythological presentation of this dynamic. Here when the Pāṇḍava king Yudhiṣṭhira has gone into exile in the forest together with his brothers, his wife, and a sizable community of brahmins and finds himself unable to provide for them, he asks the advice of the sage Dhaumya, who replies with an origin account:

> In the beginning, the emitted beings were greatly afflicted with hunger. Then Savitṛ [the sun], out of compassion, [acted] like their true father. Going to its northern course, and drawing resins of effulgence (*tejorasān*) [of the earth] upward with his rays, the sun, having now returned to his southern course, entered into the earth. When he [the sun] had become the field, the Lord of Plants [i.e., the Moon], condensing the effulgence of heaven (*divastejaḥ*), engendered the plants with water. Sprinkled with the resins of effulgence of the moon, the sun that had gone into the earth was born as the nourishing plants of the six flavors. He [the sun] is the food of living creatures on earth. Yes indeed, solar food is the staff of life of every living being. The sun is the father of all beings. Therefore, take refuge in him![98]

This concept, of the sun's power to give, take, and transform life with its rays is so pervasive in South Asia as to constitute a cultural episteme. At the elite end of the cultural spectrum, the RĀg, in its account of the transformative power of initiation (*dīkṣā*), explains that

> [j]ust as darkness quickly vanishes at sunrise, so too after obtaining initiation one is freed from merit and demerit. Just as the sun illuminates these worlds with its rays, so too god shines with its energies in the mantra sacrifice . . . When [ritually] yoked these [energies] pervade practitioners' bodies, just as the sun with its rays removes impurities from the ground.[99]

A vernacular expression of the same principle is contained in the following song, which opens the performance of the *pāṇḍav līlā*, a dramatization of the MBh epic, in a small sub-Himalayan village in Garhwal:

> O five Pandavas, for nine days and nights
> the rhythm of the season will sound through these hills.
> We have summoned our neighbors, and the faraway city dwellers.
> O singers and listeners, we have summoned the five gods
> to this gleaming stone square.
> I bow to the netherworld, the world, and the heavens,

to this night's moon, to the world of art.
The gods will dance in the square like peacocks.
They will dance their weapons in the square until dawn,
when they will be absorbed by the rays of the sun.[100]

The YV's narrative account of the hermit Vītahavya is also illuminating in this regard.[101] After remaining in a state of *samādhi* for three hundred years, his mind begins to stir in his heart, and he experiences a series of births as a sage on Śiva's Mount Kailāś, a demigod, the god Indra himself, and then as an attendant of the god Śiva for an entire eon. Throughout this entire period, the original body to which his mind had been tethered has remained in its original place on earth, in a cave in the Vindhya mountains. Having at last realized infinite consciousness, he decides to revisit his body. What is interesting here is that Vītahavya's consciousness does not simply reenter his former body, as Śaṅkara had done after living in the body of King Amaruka. Rather, he enters the sun with his subtle body, and the sun in turn projects that subtle body—in the form of a sunbeam (*sūryāṃśukavadākṛti*) called Piṅgala[102]—back into his body on earth. The body is immediately revived. Piṅgala returns to heaven, and Vītahavya goes off to bathe, just as he had done hundreds of years before when he had previously inhabited his body.

Space travel via solar rays also emerges as a theme in an account related by a sub-inspector in the Benares police in the 1930s.

He saw a yogi floating in the air above the Ganges. According to the sub-inspector, this event occurred just as the first rays of the sun fell on the ascetic, who was seated cross-legged on the edge of the holy river. Frozen in that posture, the yogi's body slowly rose and remained suspended in the air for a while.[103]

3. Yogic Penetration in the Sixth Book of the *Maitri Upaniṣad*

In the preceding chapter, I offered a lengthy discussion of yogic ascent as described in the MU's sixth book, a book that in many ways encapsulates a host of perennial themes from the Vedas, Brāhmaṇas, and the earliest Upaniṣads. Rising via the *suṣumnā* channel, this source tells us, one pierces the sun and continues to the world of *brahman*.[104] Yet, as we have seen, the same book identifies union with the *brahman* located in the inner recesses of the heart as the yogi's ultimate goal, appropriating the MU's frame story to correlate the practitioner's journeys into both outer and inner space. As we have seen, that frame story involves a sage named Śākāyanya and a renouncer king named Bṛhadratha. Here I wish to return momentarily to the context in which MU 6.29–30 frames Śākāyanya's direct discourse.

> After he had spoken in this wise, Śākāyanya, *who was within his heart*, bowing to him, said, "By this knowledge of *brahman* the sons of Prajāpati were arisen onto the path of *brahman*" . . . After he had said this, Śākāyanya, *who was within his heart*, bowing to him, said, "Marut, who has duly performed his service and who has done what he had to do (*kṛtakṛtya*), has betaken himself onto the northern path."

What is significant here is that Śākāyanya is portrayed as residing in the heart of his royal disciple while making these pronouncements, which are embedded within two lengthy expositions on the practice of yoga and bodily ascent. Here it is noteworthy that no mention is made of Śākāyanya's ultimate fate. Since his last words are spoken from inside Bṛhadratha-Marut's heart, are we to understand that the guru has passed, together with his disciple, through the solar door to the world of *brahman?* While the text leaves this question unanswered,[105] we can state with assurance that the MU narrative of Śākāyanya and Bṛhadratha-Marut is one that combines the two principal types of yoga narrativized in the MBh, both that of a warrior's apotheosis (experienced by Bhūriśravas, Droṇa, Bhīṣma, Kṛṣṇa, and Yudhiṣṭhira) and a second type of practice, to which I will turn momentarily. As we have seen, the former of the two branches into two derivative practices: the visionary ascent of a meditating practitioner through the cosmic levels, into union with a specific god or goddess in theistic traditions, as well as the tantric technique of "yogic suicide" called *utkrānti*.

As for Śākāyanya's sojourn in Bṛhadratha-Marut's heart, this becomes the model for the dynamic of "co-penetration" (*samāveśa*) in tantric initiation (*dīkṣā*), in which a guru penetrates the body of his disciple via the mouth, eyes, or heart, through the conduits of "rays" or "channels," to transform the latter from within, thereby ensuring his future release from this world. The oft-repeated ChU 8.6.6 verse ("there are a hundred and one channels of the heart") to which Śākāyanya refers at the end of this narrative also identifies a single ray as rising up from the heart to pierce the sun and afford access to that higher world of *brahman*. In many tantric sources, the guru's passage from his own heart into that of his disciple is effected via rays emanating from the bodies of both; in other sources, these rays are said to emanate from the eyes.[106] Apart from this passage from MU 6.29–30, the earliest narrative sources for this dynamic are found in coeval sections of the MBh itself.

4. Yogic Penetration in the *Mahābhārata*

a. Vidura and Sulabhā

In the two previous chapters, my discussion of the epic yoga of the chariot warrior (and of the hermits Śuka, Jaigīṣavya, and the unnamed brahmin "gleaner") was anchored in a set of eight narratives from the MBh. Here I will once again ground my discussion in a set of epic narratives, in this case five narratives in which hermits (Bharadvāja, Vipula, Sulabhā, Vidura, and Kāvya Uśanas) yogically enter into the bodies of other beings, usually humans. These narratives are the most obvious source for the many medieval tales of sinister yogis reviewed in chapter one. Among these, only one narrative, that of Kāvya Uśanas (who it may be argued is a superhuman figure in his role as the *purohita* of the Daityas), calls its protagonist a "yogi" or a "great yogi" (*mahāyogī*).[107] In this myth, Kāvya Uśanas's rival, the god Śiva, is himself called a *mahāyogī*; the same god is also referred to as a Master of Yoga (*yogeśvara*) several times in the epic, including one case in which he generates ten million Rudra-replicas of himself.[108] The god Viṣṇu-Nārāyaṇa and the titan Vṛtra,[109] as well as the hermits Vyāsa[110] and Māṇḍavya,[111] are also termed *mahāyogis* in the great epic, but no narratives describe their practice. The great warrior Bhīṣma is called a *mahāyogī*, but this epithet is not used to describe him at the time of his apotheosis, but rather in the heat of battle.[112] Kṛṣṇa is termed a Master of Yoga in the BhG precisely when he is generating multiple forms of himself in the epiphany of his universal form, an epiphany that is accompanied by multiple references to yoga. I will return to this important narrative in the next chapter.

Also in the great epic, certain gods are depicted as generating "yoga images" (*yoga-mūrtis*), to reveal themselves anthropomorphically before deserving humans, and in some cases to enter into their bodies. This is what the sun god does after doubling himself through yoga (*yogāt kṛtvā dvidhātmānam*) in order to simultaneously shine in the sky and appear before the virgin Kuntī in a human guise. Following this, he enters (*āviveśa*) her as his "yogic self" (*yogātmā*) and "touches her in her navel," thereby impregnating her with the future hero Karṇa.[113] A similar process is hinted at in ChU 1.5.2, in which a hermit named Kauśītaki tells his son, "I only sang the praise of the one [sun], and therefore you are my one [son]. Turn [your mind] toward its [multiple] rays, and yours [i.e., your sons] will be multiple." Here one cannot help but see an echo of these Indic accounts of solar impregnation in the Christian doctrine of the incarnation of the Logos, as promulgated by the church father, Tertullian.

God made this universe by his word and reason and power . . . This Word, we have learnt, was produced (*prolatum*) from God and was generated by being produced, and therefore is called the Son of God, and God, from the unity of substance with God. For God too is spirit. When a ray is projected from the sun it is a portion of the whole sun, but the sun will be in the ray because it is a ray of the sun; the substance is not separated but extended. So from spirit comes spirit, and God from God, as light is kindled from light . . . This ray of God . . . glided down into a virgin, in her womb was fashioned as flesh, was born as man mixed with God. The flesh was built up by the spirit, was nourished, grew up, spoke, taught, worked, and was Christ.[114]

Most of the narratives of human yogis are found in late strata of the MBh, with three appearing in the MdhP and one in the epic's very young thirteenth book. The best-known narrativization of this type of yogi practice involves the Pāṇḍava king Yudhiṣṭhira and his Kaurava uncle Vidura, both of whom are incarnations of the god Dharma. After the final battle has been won, Yudhiṣṭhira withdraws to a hermitage in the vicinity of which he comes upon Vidura alone in the forest. Yudhiṣṭhira announces himself, at which point Vidura

fully fixed his gaze upon the king, having conjoined his gaze with his own. And the wise Vidura, who was fixing his breaths in his breaths and his senses in his senses, verily entered [Yudhiṣṭhira's] limbs with [his own] limbs. Applying his power of yoga (*yogabalam*), Vidura, who was as if incandesecent with fiery splendor, entered into the body of the king. Then the king likewise saw that the body of Vidura, whose eyes were dull and glassy, and which was propped up against a tree, was devoid of consciousness. He then felt himself to be several times stronger than before, and the righteous king of great splendor recalled his entire past; and . . . the practice of yoga (*yogadharma*) as it had been recounted [to him] by Vyāsa.[115]

In this case, the yogic transfer is final: Vidura has left his now dead body behind to permanently cohabit the body of Yudhiṣṭhira. Other epic accounts of less permanent yogic transfers explicitly designate rays as transfer media. So, for example, in a story from the MdhP, a nun (*bhikṣukī*) named Sulabhā has abandoned her former body through yoga (*yogatas*) and assumed the form of a beautiful woman to appear before King Janaka of Mithila.[116] After first entering his body, she instructs him on the nature of liberation.

That connoisseur of yoga entered (*praviveśa*) into the king, having conjoined (*saṃyojya*) his consciousness with [her] consciousness, [his] eyes with [her] eyes, and [his] rays (*raśmīn*) with [her] rays (*raśmibhiḥ*). With the bonds of yoga did she bind him.[117]

I have already discussed the coeval MU narrative of Śākāyanya and Bṛhadratha-Marut, which also features a yogic preceptor instructing his disciple from within the latter's heart. The same language is found in this account of Sulabhā, who enters King Janaka's being with her being (*sattvam sattvena*) to communicate with him telepathically.[118] In the course of their dialogue, Janaka refers to Sulabhā as one who has "entered into my heart" (*praviṣṭhā hṛdayaṃ mama*), while she refers to his body as an "empty citadel" (*purāgāram*) in which she has passed the night.[119] Unlike Bṛhadratha, Janaka is a king who thinks himself liberated while he is not, and so Sulabhā's sojourn in his body does not end in his apotheosis, but rather simply in her announced departure from his body.

Here a brief excursus on the place of King Janaka of Videha is in order. We have already seen Janaka, the builder of Videha's capital city of Mithila,[120] as a king who twice receives two practitioners of yoga—Śuka[121] and Sulabhā—in royal audience. The same Janaka is none other than the great-great grandfather of King Bṛhadratha of the MU, both being descended from the dynastic founder Ikṣvāku.[122] Janaka of Videha is also known to the BṛU as the illustrious king in whose court a teacher named Yājñavalkya led a symposium of philosophers debating karma and rebirth and related issues, including subtle body physiology and the five fires doctrine.[123] An echo of this upanishadic and epic theme is found in the BhP, which describes the kings of Mithila as being "freed from duality, even in their homes," by the grace of these Masters of Yoga" (*yogeśvaras*) who were their preceptors.[124]

In his recent book, Bronkhorst has taken these upanishadic dialogues between Janaka and the teachers of the new esotericism to be significant evidence for the prior existence of a distinctly non-vedic religious system whose homeland would have been the eastern part of the Gangetic plain. According to his theory, the Hindu literature of the third century BCE to the second century CE (i.e., the bulk of the Upaniṣads,[125] the MBh, etc.) is the scriptural record of a fusion between the religion of the Vedas and that of this eastern region, which he terms "greater Magadha."[126] In this context, figures like Janaka, Bṛhadratha, Yājñavalkya, Śuka, Sulabhā, Jaigīṣavya, and Śākāyanya would have been exemplars of the new and creative synthesis that was emerging during that period, precisely the period in which what can only be termed as an explosion of yoga references appeared in texts ranging from the MU to the BhG, as well as the YS, MBh, and HV.

As Bronkhorst has argued most convincingly, doctrines of karma and rebirth,[127] as well as notions of cyclic time, the nature of the self, and a number of distinctive practices,[128] were synthesized with preexisting brahmanic doctrines in this period. The Greater Magadha region was the birthplace of Buddhism, Jainism, and Ajīvikism, in whose scriptures references to these concepts predate any found in Hindu sources. In the light of Bronkhorst's theory, it may be argued that whereas epic narratives of the bodily apotheosis of a dying chariot warrior who was "hitched to his rig" (*yogayukta*) drew on earlier vedic traditions, those of the yoga of hermits, ascetics, and the sorts of people that King Janaka of Videha invited to his court perhaps bore a Greater Magadhan stamp. This is supported by the chronology of the epic narratives, with those of the apotheosis of two chariot warriors (Bhūriśravas and Droṇa) embedded in the relatively early Droṇa Parvan of the Mbh, and those of yogis' appropriations of other persons' bodies being found in the epic's youngest strata.

The non-vedic pedigrees of certain interlocutors of King Janaka are made explicit in the epic. "One hundred masters (*ācāryas*) were continuously residing in his own house. They were expounders of their respective disciplines (*dharmān*), proponents of diverse heresies (*nānapāṣaṇḍavādināḥ*)."[129] Sulabhā is termed a *bhikṣukī*, a moniker generally applied to a Buddhist nun, and the account of her yogic entrance into the body of King Janaka occurs near the end of a cluster of stories and dialogues that feature either the king himself or a figure called a *bhikṣuka* or a *bhikṣukī*, or both. Beginning with the 285th chapter of the epic's twelfth book, King Janaka of Videha (or his son, Karāla Janaka) engages in discussions on the sorts of issues identified by Bronkhorst as first emerging in the BṛU, even if these are most often ranged under the heading of "Sāṃkhya"—or less frequently, of "yoga." Janaka is instructed by a series of sages, including Parāśara (12.285–290), Vasiṣṭha (12.291–305), and Yājñavalkya himself (12.298–306). In the final verses of this last sage's teaching, a list of teachers is given, which includes many of the figures already encountered in these pages, including Jaigīṣavya and "the *bhikṣu* Pañcaśikha."[130] And, in fact, the chapter that follows (12.307) is, precisely, a teaching by Pañcaśikha to Janaka; and chapter 308 the story of the *bhikṣukī* Sulabhā's yogic penetration of King Janaka. This is followed by the extended account of Śuka's apotheosis, which includes, as has been noted, an audience with Janaka.[131]

The figure of Jaigīṣavya is noteworthy here, since his name is found in both Hindu and Buddhist sources. While he does not enter into the body of another being, Jaigīṣavya, who is termed a *bhikṣuka* and described as practicing yoga in MBh 9.49, imparts his teachings to a brahmin householder at a Hindu *tīrtha*.[132] Jaigīṣavya is mentioned in both the second-century CE *Buddhacarita* (BC) of Aśvaghoṣa, as well as in Vedavyāsa's commentary on YS 3.18. In the former source, the future Buddha's teacher Arāḍa names him together with Janaka and the elder Parāśara in what appears to be a direct reference to the traditions found in the MdhP, calling all three "liberated" (*muktā*). In the latter, he is credited with having acquired knowledge of his past births extending over a period of ten eons and finding every birth, including his births as a god, to have been painful compared to the bliss of the state of liberation.[133]

One does, in fact, find a Buddhist discussion of the type of yogi practice undertaken by these epic figures in the VM's instructions for the penetration of other minds.[134] Because, however, this is a fifth-century work, it cannot have been the source of the accounts found in the MBh. In light of this, an alternative thesis—that the non-vedic aspect of the yoga of entering foreign bodies had its origins in some other non-vedic (or pre-vedic) tradition—is worthy of consideration. As it happens, two of the three epic narratives of yogic penetration in which the yogi does *not* pay a visit to King Janaka involve hermits who are identified as Bhārgavas or Bhṛgus. In addition, a dialogue between Janaka and an unnamed Bhārgava seer is recorded in the same MdhP section as those involving figures identified with *bhikṣus* (MBh 12.297), and the account, found at the end of the MdhP, of the solar apotheosis of a brahmin who survives by gleaning, is reported as having been transmitted by Bhṛgu's son Cyavana "while he was dwelling in the house of Janaka."[135] I will return to this hypothesis shortly.

b. Bharadvāja and Pratardana: A Proto-Tantric Initiation?

Returning to the MU account of Bṛhadratha and Śākāyanya, it would appear that this is unique in the literature of the period, inasmuch as it blends the two types of yogic practice found in the epic narratives: the apotheosis of the dying warrior "hitched to his rig" and the yogic penetration of a disciple by a teacher. This latter type of practice is, I would argue, the model for later tantric initiation. Such an initiation appears to be implied in the language of a late epic account of a seer (*ṛṣi*) named Bharadvāja, in whose hermitage Divodāsa, the king of Kāśī, has taken refuge after having lost every man in his family, army, and kingdom to the sons of a rival king named Vītahavya. The seer comforts him, saying, "Today I will perform a sacrifice for the sake of a son, so that you will be able to conquer a thousand sons of Vītahavya." Pratardana, the child who is born out of the sacrifice, immediately grows, at the moment of birth, into a thirteen year old , fully learned in the Veda and the science of archery. Then "fully penetrated through yoga (*yogena . . . samāviṣṭa*) by the wise Bharadvāja, and taking on a splendor (*tejas*) that suffused the entire world, he [Pratardana] fully penetrated (*samāviśat*) [Bharadvāja] in that place. And so, with his armor, bow, and arrow, he blazed like a fire."[136] Not only does the verbal form *sam-ā-viś* figure prominently in the classical terminology of tantric initiation, but the multiple references to light, if not a ray of light (*tejas*), are of a piece with the many explicit solar associations found in these early accounts of yogi practice.[137]

This sort of yogic "co-penetration" (*samāveśa*) between two bodies is altogether commonplace in the Tantras, where it becomes the model for a guru's initiation of his disciple.[138] While there are multiple types of initiation in these sources, all follow a common scenario: after a ritual "fusing of the channels" (*nāḍīsaṃdhāna*), the guru enters the disciple's body, from within which he guides the latter's soul upward along a path that extends across the universe, from earth to Śiva, with that path being identified with the disciple's *suṣumnā*.[139] While it is the case that prescriptive accounts of tantric initiation place their greatest emphasis on the breath channels as the principal conduits, "rays" emanating from the eyes or other bodily orifices are also evoked as transfer media.[140] So, for example, Abhinavagupta, elaborating on the practices of a newly consecrated master (*ācārya*), describes an initiatory mantra that "blazes brightly like a submarine fire and bursts forth from his eye sockets and pores . . . [and] reaches his disciple's heart."[141] A list of "initiation[s] through the eyes, etc." (*cākṣuṣyādi dīkṣā*) is found in several Āgamas, including the RĀg and the *Uttarakāmika*.[142] In the *Īśvara Saṃhitā*, a Pāñcarātra work, a segment of the initiation ritual entails the preceptor placing his hand on the disciple, through which he transfers to the deity's power to the disciple. Here the preceptor is instructed to "visualize all the principal deities as illuminating [his right hand] by their rays of light . . . He should [then] touch [the disciple] with this *acyuta* ["Infallible"] hand," which destroys all sins that were formerly accumulated in thousands of other births.[143] The language of rays is employed, in a less specific sense, in the eleventh-century *Rasārṇavam*, which evokes the "rays of light emanating from the guru's teachings" that confer upon his disciple the secret alchemical doctrines. So too the opening aphorism of the *Kaulasūtra* of Bhaṭṭaśrī Śitikaṇṭha, which identifies the sole guru in the universe as "the uninterrupted transmission of rays (*marīci-saṃkrāmaṇam*) that have come to us through the initiatory lineage (*ovalliḥ*)."[144]

It is in the scriptures of Mahāyāna and tantric Buddhism, however, that rays become the prime media for the transmission of teachings and the transformative process of initiation and yoga.[145] Here we again find ourselves in the Indic and Central Asian Buddhist world, in which visionary theism involves the recollection of luminous Buddhas and bodhisattvas.[146] Particularly vivid accounts of this phenomenon, found in the second-century *Aśokāvadāna, Lotus Sūtra,* and other works, cast bodhisattvas or the Buddha himself, in their roles as teachers of the *dharma*, as beaming their teachings in the form of multicolored rays of light to an infinity of Buddha worlds: I will discuss these in the next chapter. In the same "luminous world of the Mahāyāna Buddhist scriptures,"[147] descriptions of initiations generally portray the initiate or practitioner visualizing rays of light originating from the body of a Buddha or *bodhisattva*. A novel rendering of *buddhānusmṛti* is found in the fifth- to sixth-century "Yoga Treatise from Qïzïl," a manuscript that was critically edited and translated by Dieter Schlingloff under the title of *Ein buddistische Yogalehrbuch* (*A Buddhist Yoga Primer*) in 1964. While this Mahāyāna-influenced Sarvāstivāda work was likely composed in Kashmir,[148] it dates from the same period and was found in the same Chinese Turkestan region as the "numinous" Buddha images from the Simsim caves.[149] In this work, the meditator, who is termed a *yogācāra* ("yoga-practitioner") generates Buddhas from his body—or more properly speaking, his "psychosomatic form" (*āśraya*)—in a display of multicolored rays of light.[150] In one such visualization, the practitioner meditatively projects from his forehead a woman whose body is composed of the cat's-eye gemstone as the first member of an emanatory sequence comprised of oil-filled vessals, diamond thrones, solar disks, and exalted Buddhas. The sequence is then reversed, with the emitted Buddhas entering into solar disks, and so on, before finally reentering the yoga practitioner's forehead. This culminates in the practitioner's consecration (*abhiṣeka*), the culmination of the meditation process, by means of which he becomes what he has visualized.[151] In the end, the yoga practitioner's psychosomatic form becomes radiant with the marks and signs of a "Great Person" (*mahāpuruṣa*), which is tantamount to his becoming a bodhisattva.[152] In other words, the practitioner realizes an identity with the Buddhist supreme person, in what appears to be an anticipation of the supreme goal of the tantric yogi.

This Buddhist variation on the now familiar theme of piercing the sun is but one of many such meditations found in this text. Another such visualization has the yoga practitioner receiving visions of Buddhas emitting light rays, which, mediated by an ethereal female being, strike his fontanel, pass through his body, and reemerge into the world.[153] In a Chinese Pure Land scripture entitled the *Guan Wuliangshou jing* (*Sutra on Contemplating the Buddha of Measureless Life*), an Indian queen named Vaidehī is informed that when she visualizes the Pure Land paradise, "her body will be illuminated by hundreds of colorful rays of light" emanating from the pores of the solar bodhisattva Amitāyus.[154] Tantric Buddhism follows a similar visualization program, with rays appearing both in initiation proper and in the generation stage of meditative practice following initiation. In the "secret initiations" taught in the *Kālacakra Tantra* (KCT), the initiate's visualization of rays of light, emitted from his preceptor's heart, is crucial to his attainment of the *saṃbhogakāya* (the Buddha's body of enjoyment, perceptible only to bodhisattvas).[155] In the generation stage of his practice, the Buddhist tantric yogi generates the body of the Buddha Kālacakra as the sublimated form of the universe and of his own body by visualizing Kālacakra standing on the discs of the sun, moon, and Rāhu and emanating five rays of light. These five rays symbolize the five types of gnosis, the purified aspects of the meditator's psycho-physical aggregates.[156]

c. Vipula and Kāvya Uśanas

Another epic account that portrays the yogic penetration of one being by another, for the benefit of the latter (but without the initiatory overtones), is the story of Vipula, a young hermit who protects his guru's wife Ruci from the advances of the lascivious god Indra during his guru's absence. This story is embedded in an anthology of stories concerning the wiles of wanton and malicious women, evidence for the antiquity of this literary subgenre. Prior to Indra's arrival at the hermitage, Vipula's guru Devaśarma forewarns his young charge of Indra's cunning ability to create or take on a variety of bodies for himself, a power already attested in the ṚV.[157]

Hereupon, Vipula in fact entered Ruci there through yoga, [in order] to protect his preceptor's wife from the multi-formed offerer of one hundred sacrifices [Indra].[158] With [his] two eyes [engaged] in her two eyes, having conjoined [her] rays with his rays, Vipula entered into [her] body like wind into the sky. [With his] mouth precisely in [the place of her] mouth, and [his] sexual organ in [the place of her] sexual organ, he remained motionless [inside of her]. The hermit was gone like a shadow.[159]

Shortly thereafter, when Indra comes to the hermitage, he finds the lovely Ruci seated beside the now inanimate bodily envelope of Vipula, which looks like "a body in a painting." But of course, Vipula is inside of Ruci, whose wanton feminine instinct, when she sees the enchanting beauty of Indra, compels her to offer him her favors. But when she attempts to rise and invite him to her, Vipula,

> that splendiferous (*mahātejā*) descendent of Bhṛgu, observing the bodily expressions of his preceptor's wife, held her back with his yoga . . . and he bound all of her sense organs with the bonds of yoga (*yoga-bandhanaiḥ*) . . . [such that] she was immobilized by his power of yoga (*yoga-bala-mohitā*).[160]

This passage in fact encapsulates, in narrative form, an important theoretical statement found in the MdhP concerning yogi practice, a statement embedded in a long analytical discussion regarding the power of yogis to enter into other people's bodies and to replicate themselves at will.[161] The statement in question reads: "Without a doubt, the powerful (*balastha*) yogi who is a master of binding (*bandhaneśa*) [others] is possessed of the absolute power to release [others from those same bonds]."[162] *Balam*, *īśvara* (and its abstraction, *aiśvaryam*), and *bandhana* are technical terms used with great regularity in texts from this period to describe the person of the yogi and his techniques.[163]

Another late epic narrative involving a yogi's penetration of a foreign body—this time, however, in a hostile or predatory mode—is the account of Kāvya Uśanas who is termed both a yogi and a "great yogi" (*mahāyogī*), as is his divine rival, Śiva.

> Kubera was a powerful king, an overlord of the Dryads and Protectors, the lord of the treasure house of the earth, and likewise mighty. [Kāvya Uśanas], who was a great hermit accomplished in yoga (*yogasiddha*), entered into his [Kubera's] body, and by means of yoga lay siege to that god, the Lord of Plenty, and carried off his riches.[164]

A disconsolate Kubera appeals to Śiva, the Great Master (*maheśvara*), saying, "Now that I have been besieged by the yogic self (*yogātmakena*) of Uśanas, my wealth is gone, and that great ascetic has slipped away on a path of his own yogic making."[165] When Śiva attempts to spear Kāvya Uśanas on his pike, the latter appears on the weapon's tip, at which point the god bends it back on itself and tosses the rival yogi into his mouth. Then, "the mighty Uśanas enter[s] [into] Maheśvara's stomach, and . . . move[s] around there."[166] By virtue of his own great yogic power, Kāvya

Uśanas is able to survive Śiva's fiery energy, but, feeling the heat, he implores the god to release him:

And the *mahāyogī* praised the god, even located where he was. He was desirous of going forth, but was held back by [Śiva's] fiery energy. So . . . the great hermit dwelling in the belly [of Śiva] then repeatedly said "Be gracious to me!" Blocking up all of his bodily orifices, the . . . Great God said to him: "Go to release via [my] penis."[167]

And so Kāvya Uśanas's hostile penetration of Kubera, followed by a yogic sojourn inside the body of the great yogi Śiva, ends with his ejaculation, whence his well-known sobriquet of Śukra, "Semen."[168] As was noted above, both Vipula and Kāvya Uśanas are Bhārgavas, scions of Bhṛgu. Here a passage from the MU's sixth book is worthy of note. Proposing an etymological explanation based on the *gāyatrī mantra* formula *bhargo devasya* ("the radiance of the god [Savitṛ]"),[169] it glosses the term *bhargas* by stating, "The one that is placed in the sun, that is starlike in the eye, is called radiance. It is radiance because of its going (*gati*) via rays of light (*bhābhiḥ*)."[170] The Sanskrit noun *bhargas* is related to the root *bhrāj ("shine, beam"), from which the proper name Bhṛgu and the patronymic Bhārgava are derived.[171] These etymological links likely flow from the close associations of the Bhṛgus and fire, both in the Vedas and the Iranian *Avesta*; they also may further explain the recurring references to radiance, fire, and light in the accounts of yogic penetration by the Bhārgava hermits Vipula and Kāvya Uśanas. Closely linked to the cult of fire, the Bhārgavas are often associated with the Atharvans, a group identified in the *Avesta* as ancient Iranian fire priests.[172] In this context, Jatindra Mohan Chatterji has argued that the "Bhārgava Saṃhitā" referenced in the *Gopatha Brāhmaṇa* and other early sources refers, in fact, to the *Avesta*.[173] According to the *Gopatha*, a very late Brāhmaṇa, the first beings to be created, even prior to the three worlds and the three Vedas, were none other than the sages Bhṛgu and Aṅgiras. Following these, lesser Vedas—including a "Serpent Veda," "Flesh-Eater Veda," and an "Asura Veda"—were created, with the sacrificed body of Aṅgiras replacing that of the Rigvedic Puruṣa as the source of the moon, herbs, and twenty-one types of sacrifice.[174]

The Bhārgavas are, as Robert Goldman has argued, [175] a mythologically problematic lineage. Specialists of the destructive charms and spells of the *Atharva Veda* (AV), they are generally portrayed negatively in the epics as "military brahmins" whose supernatural powers are often linked to violence, sorcery, confusion, and hostility to the gods.[176] The *Taittirīya Āraṇyaka* (TĀr) describes the casting of a curse that involves looking upon one's victim "with the evil eye of the Bhṛgus."[177] Accounts of the Bhārgava Kāvya Uśanas's extraordinary powers (including his power over death), as well as his problematic relationship with the gods, are already attested in the ṚV and AV.[178]

The Old Iranian term *kauui*, the source of Kāvya Uśanas's name, was applied, in the *Avesta*, to an accursed class of priests.[179] As Georges Dumézil has demonstrated, the epic mythology of Kāvya Uśanas and the Iranian myths of Kavi Usan (or Kavi Usaδan) clearly arose from a common Indo-Iranian tradition. Likewise, the epic mythology of two kings with sky-faring chariots, Yayāti and Vasu Uparicara, are strongly inflected by the Iranian mythology of Yima.[180] During the epic period, Indo-Iranian traditions of Bhārgava figures such as these would have been "reimported," together with their shared solar cult, into the Indian subcontinent and the Indic textual record by the Śakas and Kushans. Also with the Bhārgavas, we perhaps find ourselves in the presence of an epic bridge between the vedic "warrior aspect of yoga," as typologized by Renou, Geldner, and others,[181] and the yoga of later tantric yogis.

5. Yogi Perception

A passage from the 289th chapter of the MdhP typologizes the "Bhārgava type" of epic yogi, who is comparable to a celestial luminary that rivals the sun—the greatest yogi of all, with which the *mahāyogī* Śiva is clearly identified in the Kāvya Uśanas myth[182]—in its brilliance and power to "yoke" others into its "orbit" with the irresistible reins of its rays.[183]

> Yogis who are without restraints [and] endowed with the power of yoga (*yogabalānvitāḥ*) are [so many] masters (*īśvarāḥ*), who enter into [the bodies of] the Prajāpatis, the sages, the gods, and the great beings. Yama, the raging Terminator (Antaka), and death of terrible prowess: none of these masters (*īśate*) the yogi who is possessed of immeasurable splendor . . . A yogi can lay hold of several thousand selves,[184] and having obtained [their] power, he can walk the earth with all of them. He can obtain [for himself] the [realms of the] sense objects. Otherwise, he can undertake terrible austerities, or, again, he can draw those [sense objects] back together [into himself], like the sun [does] its rays of light.

The last two verses of this particular passage are quoted in Śaṅkara's BrSūBh—which I follow in reading the term *yoga* as *yogi* and *ātmanām* (selves) as *śarīrāṇi* (bodies). Here Śaṅkara expands on the matter, invoking the simultaneous yoking of several bodies (*yugapad-aneka-śarīra-yoga*)

Figure 4.1 Yogī Macchindranāth and his disciples. Polychrome, western India, ca. 1990.

by yogis possessed of the supernatural powers (*aiśvaryas*) of minuteness (*aṇima*), magnitude (*mahattva*), and so on.[185] As we saw in chapter one, the "yogi" Śaṅkara himself became possessed of just this sort of mastery, "extend[ing] his power (*balam*) in every direction, inhabiting lifeless bodies wherever he found them."[186] Śaṅkara returns to this issue in his commentary on one of the final verses of the BrSū of Bādarāyaṇa (4.4.15), a work that was, in many respects, a response to the philosophical positions of the Vaiśeṣika school.[187] The BrSū aphorism in question states that the entrance (*āveśa*) of a self that has realized final release into several bodies is "like a lamp," whose flame can light the wicks of other lamps. According to the principal commentators on this verse, this aphorism is related to the practice of yoga. The first of these was the mid-seventh-century CE Bhāskara, who stated that whereas a liberated person could assume many constructed bodies, his mind or consciousness alone controlled those bodies.[188] The same language is found, in fact, in Vedavyāsa's commentarial introduction to YS 4.4: "Now, when the yogi constructs (*nirmimīte*) many bodies (*bahūn kāyān*), do they have one mind or many minds?" Vedavyāsa's answer is that the yogi uses his egoity (*asmitā*) to make the multiple minds with which he equips the bodies he has constructed. YS 4.5 continues this line of reasoning, asserting that the one mind responsible for creating both the multiple minds and bodies directs the latters' activities.[189] As we will see at the end of this chapter, these concepts undergird the arguments advanced by a twentieth-century scholar-practitioner in favor of the salvific power of the guru who penetrates his disciple's mind-body complex through initiation.

In his commentary on BrSū 4.4.15, Śaṅkara likened the proliferation of a flame, from a single lamp into several lamps, to the sun with its rays,[190] invoking a passage from ChUp 7.16.2 to argue that a self's occupation of one or another body was not necessarily a serial affair, but could occur in more than one body at the same time.[191] In the same way, a man who has attained knowledge is capable of creating other bodies possessed of minds that would follow the lead of his one mind, which yokes them to its will. This was the same procedure, Śaṅkara concluded, as that of the yogis described in the yoga teachings (*yoga-śāstra*) as yoking multiple bodies.[192] The *Mṛgendrāgama* (MĀg), a foundational scripture of orthodox Śaivasiddhānta dating from Śaṅkara's time, paraphrases this MBh passage, with one important difference: the yogi's power to take hold of other bodies is homologized, in this text, to the sun's rays (*tviṣaḥ*), which penetrate all things.[193]

The two aphorisms that follow BrSū 4.4.15 discuss the nature of the special knowledge available to a person who is liberated. All of the sub-commentaries on Śaṅkara's *bhāṣya* on these verses explain that the all-pervasiveness (*vyāptitva*) of a liberated person allows for that knowledge to spread in any direction, in any place, into the senses and the consciousness (*antaḥkaraṇa*) of embodied beings.[194] Here as well, certain subcommentaries retain the image of a lamp's flame to evoke the ability of persons possessed of special knowledge to enter into many bodies simultaneously.[195]

All of these commentaries presuppose the fundamental concept concerning sense perception, already described, according to which the sense faculties actually travel outward via rays to encounter their objects. The repeated homologization in these sources of the sun in the heavens to the human eye as well as to the luminous self or person in the heart appears to be the same as that which undergirds upanishadic conceptualizations of the process of embodied ascent. More than this, it also makes it conceptually possible for the subtle elements of one being to penetrate another, through either the eyes or the channels of the heart, whence the ChU linking of the upward tending channel of the heart to the rays of the sun and the MU account of Śākāyanya's entrance into the heart of his disciple Bṛhadratha. But we should also note that there is something more than "projective perception" going on in these accounts. The rays of the sun or of the inner self are not only touching or grasping their objects, as in the case of the sense of sight in eyewitness perception (*pratyakṣa*); rather, they are actually penetrating, eating, or possessing their objects. Depending on the dating of these sources (which remains problematic), the upanishadic, ayurvedic, and epic accounts reviewed in this chapter are either foundational to, or the narrative expression of, contemporary or subsequent epistemological axioms found in Nyāya-Vaiśeṣika theories of "yogi perception."

According to the "direct realism" of the Nyāya-Vaiśeṣika theory of perception, the sense organs directly apprehend their sense objects when they come into contact with them, whence the NS 3.1.35 formula, "Perception is the consequence of contact between a ray and an object." This theme is taken up in MU 6.31, which states that the inner self (*ātman*) sends out or restrains the five sense organs, which are identified here as the Marīcis ("Sunbeams"), the daughters of the sun: "So he eats the sense objects with five rays." While this pentad is a likely reconfiguration of the seven radiant daughters of the sun evoked in ṚV,[196] Teun Goudriaan has suggested that these feminine powers, emitted by a unique knowing male subject, may be the forerunners of the all-devouring tantric goddesses (*yoginīs*), who are termed "rays" (*marīcayaḥ*) in the Kubjika

Tantras.[197] Elsewhere, a number of tantric commentators employ the term *cinmarīcayaḥ*, the "rays of the light of consciousness," to designate the sense organs when they are turned outward.[198] Here "eating" is also analogous to the luminous sun's "drinking" or evaporation of fluids in the ecosystem. In the later context of temple worship, "eating" with the eyes becomes the modus operandi of the divine images of gods, who consume the *bhog* offered them through their gaze.[199] Language similar to that of MU 6.31 is found in the coeval MdhP.[200]

Just as the sun on its ascending course emits a circle of rays, and again withdraws the same into itself at the approach of sunset, so too the inner self (*antarātmā*), having entered the body [at birth], penetrates (*āviśya*) the five sensorial objects by means of the rays of the senses and again withdraws [these rays] at the time of one's demise.

By now, this language should appear familiar: the luminous "solar" self, which pours itself out into the world in the form of rays (including rays of perception), is capable, like the sun, of both animating and consuming bodies in the outside world. How do these homologies—if they are not identifications—inform early philosophical explanations of the extraordinary power of yogi perception? Jayantabhaṭṭa, a late ninth-century Kashmirian Nyāya-Vaiśeṣika commentator, resorts to what would appear to be circular reasoning when he defines the term "yogi" as a function of the power of visual perception: "Those whose are possessed of this [surpassing power of vision] in the highest degree are praised as yogis. Their surpassing power of vision [arises from] the fact that their field of vision comprises objects which are subtle, hidden, and remote, as well as [objects] from the past and future."[201]

The classic philosophical account of yogi perception dates from several centuries earlier, appearing in Praśastapāda's commentary on three aphorisms from the VS of Kaṇāda. Those aphorisms close a long discussion begun at VS 8.1.2, to wit, that because they are not substances, the self and mind are imperceptible through the senses. How then can the self and mind (one's own or those of others) be perceived? Kaṇāda answers this question by stating that the "perception of the self [results] from a special conjunction, within the self, between self and mind," expanding on this theme by referring to perception "into other substances" by two types of persons: "those whose internal organ is not composed" and "those whose com-position is complete."[202] In other words, unlike normal perception, which is the result of a fourfold contact (*catuṣṭaya-sannikarṣa*)—between the self, the mind, a sense organ, and an object[203]—the perception of imperceptibles occurs through a "special" (*viśeṣa*) and direct conjunction (*saṃyoga*) between a mind and its object.

In his commentary on these three aphorisms, Praśastapāda explains what it is that makes this contact special, and by way of interpreting the two types of persons alluded to in VS 9.1.13, he introduces the concept of an enhanced level of perception on the part of yogis.

> In the case of those who are different than ourselves, that is, of yogis who are "yoked" (*yogināṃ yuktānām*), it is by virtue of a mind [whose power has been] enhanced through yoga-generated practice (*yogaja-dharma*) that there arises the vision of the true form (*svarūpa*) of their own self as well as [of the selves] of others, the quarters of space, time, atoms, wind, mind . . . Then again, in the case of those [yogis] who are "unyoked" (*viyuktānām*), direct perception into subtle, hidden and distant objects arises through a fourfold contact that has been enhanced through yoga-generated practice.[204]

A later commentary on VS 9.1.11–14 is that of the fifteenth-century Śaṅkaramiśra, who defines the "yoked" (*yukta*) yogi as one whose internal organ (*manas*) remains composed or fixed (*samāhita*). Yogis who have risen higher, who are called "unyoked" (*viyukta*), have minds that need no longer remain composed. In the case of the former, there arises a special conjunction between mind and self (*ātmamanasoḥ saṃyoga*), which derives from the merits accrued through the practice of yoga. By means of this conjunction, yogis gain a vision "of their own self as well as the self of others." As for the latter, they have obtained such supernatural powers of the body (*śarīra-siddhi*) and senses (*indrīya-siddhi*) that they consider the simple fixation of the mind to be insufficient, and thus with the aid of their superhuman powers "they make the whole universe of things, hidden and distant, objects of their perception." A yogi thus empowered is able to perceive imperceptible objects in one of two ways: either his own consciousness (*antaḥkaraṇa*) becomes conjoined with these objects, or his self causes "sterile minds" (*paṇḍamanāṃsi*)—disembodied minds that no longer belong to a self—to be conjoined with these objects.[205]

While Kaṇāda does not divulge his sources in his terse aphorisms, one cannot help but think that portrayals of mythological figures like Saṃjaya, the "narrator in the text" of the entire MBh, would have served as his models. Although blind, Saṃjaya was granted "divine vision" by Vyāsa at the beginning of the epic, empowering him to view not only what was taking place in his proximity but also actions in distant places, the thoughts of other persons, and so on. This he explained to Dhṛtarāṣṭra in the following terms:

Listen . . . to what has been beheld by me with my own eyes (*pratyakṣam*) or through the power of yoga (*yoga-balena*) . . . [Because] I am possessed of divine gnosis (*divyam jñānam*), my faculty of vision is extra-sensory, [including] hearing at a distance and the knowledge of the thought process [or the mind (*citta*)] of others.[206]

Buddhist accounts of a Buddha's "divine eye" or "buddha-eye," with which "he beheld the entire world as if it were in a spotless mirror," or of the "wisdom-eye" or "*dhamma*-eye" of enlightened beings could also have served as Kaṇāda's mythological models,[207] although he more likely had in mind the enhanced powers of vision of the vedic seers, who are the subject of another aphorism, which his many commentators curiously ignore in their discussions of yogi perception. That aphorism states: "Now, [the vision] proper to the vedic seers (*ṛṣis*) and the vision of the *siddhas* [arises] from [their] practices." [208] Kaṇāda's referent here is the panoptical vision of the vedic *ṛṣis*, which enabled them to grasp the entire corpus of vedic mantras, as well as the entire universe, in a single sensory act that afforded them omniscience and immortality. Praśastapāda's reading of this aphorism follows the argumentation of his commentary on VS 9.1.11–13: the seers' and siddhas' "flashes of insight" (*pratibhaṃ jñānam*), intuitive knowledge arising from the direct contact of self with mind, permit them to see things as they truly are. Furthermore, the gnosis arising from their exceptional powers of vision is not different from knowledge generated by direct perception, because their magical practices—of applying a foot cream (*pādalepa*) that enables them to fly through the air, of reducing themselves to the size of a globule (*gulika*) to enter into other people's bodies, and so on—affords them direct perception of what is distant or hidden to normal humans. [209] His and subsequent commentators' emphasis on the infallibility of the seers' immediate cognition of any and all objects flows from the fact that their direct and unmediated vision of the Vedas was and remains the ground for all valid knowledge. With respect to their exemplary powers of vision, the seers and siddhas were the prototypes of the yogis who, likewise, are capable of viewing the entire universe in a single act of perception and of entering into the minute space of the heart or rising up to the cope of heaven to gain an unmediated vision of the absolute. The philosopher Bhartṛhari, a contemporary of Praśastapāda, expands on this concept, maintaining that *pratibhā* not only enables yogis to know the thoughts of others but also empowers demonic Protectors and Flesh-Eaters to become invisible and enter into the bodies of other creatures.[210]

The "vision of the siddhas" (*siddha-darśanam*) is one of the supernatural powers also enumerated in the YS's third book, the "Section on

Omni-presencings" (*vibhūti-pada*): "[From perfect discipline] on the light in the head, the vision of the *siddhas*."[211] The aphorism that follows—"[F]rom flashing insight (*pratibhāt*), [knowledge of] everything"—may be the source of the language of Praśastapāda's circa 450–550 CE commentary.[212] Now, the first of these aphorisms may be read in either of two different ways. The first reading, which was adopted by Vedavyāsa (and that I followed in a recent publication), takes *siddha-darśanam* to signify an act of perception that has the siddhas as its object. Whence Vedavyāsa's gloss: "There is an opening in the cranial vault through which there emanates effulgent light. By concentrating on that light, one obtains a vision of the siddhas who move in the space between heaven and earth."[213] In the context of the (subsequent) homologization of the cranial vault to the upper shell of the cosmic egg, such a statement makes perfect sense. Like the *prakṛtilayas* of the YBh and the "Masters of Yoga" (*yogeśvaras*) of the BhP, the siddhas inhabit a region that is "both inside and outside the triple-world," where, bathed in the light of the transcendent *brahman*, they remain in an embodied form until the end of a cosmic eon. However, in the light of VS 9.2.13 and Praśastapāda's commentary, a reading of *siddha-darśanam* as the "vision proper to the siddhas" becomes a more attractive alternative, and all the more so when combined with YS 3.33, which applies a Vaiśeṣika hermeneutic of "direct realism" to the siddhas' power of perception.

The principles of *ṛṣi* perception as presented in VS 9.2.13 are echoed in another pair of aphorisms from the YS's same *pada* (3.25–26): "By the imposition of light on the mind's activity, knowledge of what is subtle, hidden, or distant; from perfect discipline on the sun, knowledge of the worlds."[214] This latter aphorism becomes the occasion for the commentator Vedavyāsa to enter into an extended description of the worlds of which one has knowledge through concentration on the sun; this constitutes, in fact, the second longest *bhāṣya* in his entire work. Vedavyāsa's account closely approximates the cosmologies of the Purāṇas, detailing the seven worlds (*lokas*) proceeding upward, from the sphere of the earth through *satyaloka* (an alternative name for *brahmaloka*, the world of *brahman*) to the *prakṛtilaya*, and the seven netherworlds that proceed downward from the earth. The disk of the earth receives the greatest attention, with its seven island continents separated by seven roiling oceans of assorted fluids, all surrounding the cosmic axis of Mount Meru at the heart of Rose-Apple Island (*jāmbu-dvīpa*). At the conclusion of his commentary, Vedavyāsa states, "The yogi should make this manifest by practicing *saṃyama*[215] on the door of the sun, and not otherwise. The more he practices, the more visible everything becomes (*yāvad idaṃ sarvaṃ dṛṣṭam*)."[216] Why this concerted attention to the prescriptive geography of the cosmic egg? In the light of the history of this concept, we can see that a yogi's pan-optical vision of the universe is grounded in those supernatural powers that afford him the possibility of viewing the universe from above, from beyond the solar door, as Vedavyāsa's commentary underscores. By Vedavyāsa's time, this overview of the universe could have been understood in two different ways, either as the result of a yogi's embodied apotheosis, or as part of a prescriptive program of cosmological meditation.

Two other aphorisms from the YS's *vibhūti-pada* also assume the *prāpyakāri* model of visual perception: "By *saṃyama* on concepts, knowledge of other minds . . . There being no contact with the light of the eye, disappearance [of the yogi's body]."[217] With all of these elements in place, it is possible to conclude that the conceptual foundation for the yogi's technique of entering into foreign bodies, via rays often emanating from his eyes, was already present, *in statu nascendi*, in these philosophical sources. That is, the conceptual divide—between direct perception of the surface of objects and the perceptual penetration of those surfaces—had already been crossed. Nonetheless—and here we return once more to the tension found in the YS and its commentaries between the *siddhis* and *samādhi*—yogi perception, which connects the interiority of the observer with the interiority of the observed, is not an end in itself, according to yoga philosophy. As Whicher notes, in a yogi's perception, only a mental transformation (*vṛtti*) is generated, toward which the practitioner must develop an attitude of detachment or dispassion.[218]

In his commentary on VS 9.1.13, Praśastapāda identifies yoga-generated practice (*yogaja-dharma*) as the adjunct necessary to normal perception to transform it into yogi perception. An echo of this concept is found in the BhP, which states that "the wise ones behold the entire universe with an eye that has been perfected by yoga."[219] What is it in normal perception that comes to be rectified or enhanced by this practice? The greatest wealth of commentarial speculation on yogi perception by Hindu philosophers[220] is found in two tenth-century subcommentaries on the PADhS—the 991 CE *Nyāyakandalī* (NK) of Śrīdhara, a native of Bengal whose influence extended into western India, and the mid-tenth-century *Vyomavatī* (VV) of Vyomaśiva, a native of south India and protegé of the grandfather of King Bhoja of Malava.[221] As B. K. Matilal has shown, many of these Nyāya-Vaiśeṣika commentators were, from as early as the fifth century, influenced by, if not members of, the Śaiva Pāśupata order and the Māheśvara laity;[222] and so we should not be surprised to find syntheses between Śaiva-inflected myth, theory, and practice appearing in their medieval writings.

The NK explains that in the case of distant objects, for example, "perception . . . is indistinct, [because] the object of the ray going out from the eye—a sense organ whose constituent parts are scattered in the intervening distance—is not reached."[223] By way of explicating this statement, Śrīdhara provides the conceptual bridge between normal perception, yogi perception, and the power of entering into another body.

> [The perception] "of those who are different than ourselves" means "yogi perception" (*yogi-pratyakṣam*) . . . "Yoga" means "com-position."[224] It is of two sorts: conscious (*samprajñāta*) . . . and unconscious (*asamprajñāta*) . . .[225] The latter, which is proper to those desiring liberation (*mumukṣūṇām*), becomes fully ripened in one's final birth . . . But the former [type of] yoga . . . illuminates (*uddyotayati*) the object whose essence [the yogi] is desirous of knowing . . . [But] they [i.e., yogis] cannot have an extrasensory vision of objects until they remove the coverings of impurity (*malam*) [from their minds] . . . The innate (*svabhāvikam*) true form of the self is beheld by yogis . . . When, however, out of a desire to know them, he directs his continuous train of thought toward another [person's] self [or] the quarters of space, time, etc., then he augments [his] disciplined practice to an inconceivable degree . . . and by virtue of that power (*balāt*) his consciousness, exiting his body, is yoked to those of other selves, etc.[226]

As we have seen, the coeval MdhP unproblematically narrativized this process by simply depicting Vidura, Vipula, Sulabhā, and Kāvya Uśanas as yogically entering the bodies of Yudhiṣṭhira, Ruci, Janaka, and Kubera, respectively. What is new in the NK is its attention to the mechanics of these penetrations. Yogi perception arises when one's own self or mind is yoked, via a ray of perception, to another being's self inside that other being's body. This opens the way to a variety of ritual techniques that become commonplace in medieval Hindu religious practice, most especially (1) tantric initiation, through which the guru perpetuates the lineage "from another body into another body" (*pārampara*);[227] (2) *prāṇa-pratiṣṭhā*, the enlivening of worship images through the "installation of breath," a practice that can also involve the locking of the practitioner's eyes into those of the image;[228] and (3) *darśana*, the mutual "beholding" of deity and devotee, in which a channel, created between the eyes of the worship image (*mūrti*) and those of the devotee, effects immediate contact between the transcendent self of the deity and the inner self of the devotee.

In sum, the philosophical axiom that yogis have a special type of perception that enables them to see things as they truly are is predicated on the presupposition, common to virtually *all* of the Indic philosophical schools, that yogis are able to move between, inhabit, and even create multiple bodies. These were the terms employed by Vyomaśiva in his solution to the conundrum that arises when one juxtaposes the teachings of BhG 4.37 with those of *Devībhāgavata Purāṇa* 9.29.69–70. Whereas the former asserted that the fire of knowledge reduces the results of prior actions (the cause of cyclic rebirth) to ashes, the latter (as well as many other sources) maintained that the results of actions are not exhausted even for eons. According to Vyomaśiva, a yogi could, by virtue of his power to take over multiple bodies simultaneously, use his fire of knowledge to burn off his accumulated karma at an accelerated pace.[229] In another context, Vyomaśiva argued that the all-pervasive character of each individual self is the necessary precondition for a yogi's ability to inhabit multiple bodies simultaneously.[230]

Witnesses to the power of yogis to both see and enter into foreign bodies are found across the entire range of Indic literature, both sacred and secular. The MBh speaks of the power of accomplished yogis (*siddhas*) to perceive, with the "eye of knowledge" (*jñānacakṣus*), the lifebody of a recently deceased person as it moves away from its old body, is reborn, and as is made to enter a womb once again.[231] This is echoed in the eleventh-century commentary on the CS authored by Cakrapāṇidatta, who explains that the otherwise invisible passage of a karmically determined self (*ātman*) into the embryo growing inside a woman's womb is apprehended through the "yogi eye" (*yogicakṣus*) of yogis.[232] Powerful beings, including serpents, gods, demons, "brahmins who have drunk soma,"[233] and yogis,[234] are able to kill or control others with their glance. For reasons that should by now be clear, steadying the eyes is one of the foremost prerequisites for a yogi to succeed in his practice. Gāndhārī, mother of the epic Kauravas, deforms Yudhiṣṭhira's fingernails with her angry gaze when her usually blindfolded eyes are briefly exposed.[235] In their discussions of actors "getting inside their roles," commentaries on the *Nāṭya Śāstra* (NŚ) evoke the example of yogis taking over the bodies of other creatures.[236]

6. The Technique of Entering into a Foreign Body

The principal commentarial theories concerning the link between yogi perception and the science of entering into foreign bodies date from the late ninth to the late tenth centuries. However, the actual mechanics of the applied science of this practice had been comprehensively presented prior to these in a Kashmirian Tantra that predated all of these commentaries.[237] Here I am speaking of the early ninth-century NT's discussion of "subtle yoga,"[238] which is, in many respects, a variation on the theme, discussed above, of tantric initiation. However, whereas in initiation the guru's entrance into another body is salutary for his disciple inasmuch as it ensures his salvation, in subtle yoga the takeover is hostile, accruing to the sole benefit of the predatory yogi. This discussion is found in the middle section of the NT's twentieth chapter, which is explicitly devoted to a discussion of the "three yogas"—the transcendent, the subtle, and the gross.[239] The first of these yogas mainly involves the practices of the Yoginīs ("Female Joiners," "Female Yokers,"), who destroy (by eating their bodies) the ontological stain (*malam*) that tethers their victims (*paśus*) to suffering existence. In the same way that initiation (*dīkṣā*) by a guru liberates a disciple, their consumption of their victims' *malam* ensures the latters' future identity or union with Śiva, whence the Yoginīs' name: they yoke or join their victims to Śiva. Gross (*sthūla*) yoga comprises techniques for appeasing and protecting against the Yoginīs and their ilk. Subtle yoga, the text teaches, is practiced by Mothers and Guhyakas in order to draw into themselves, by means of their yogic virility (*yogavīryataḥ*), the life force of their victims.[240] As the text goes on to explain, this same type of yoga may also be undertaken by a human connoisseur of yoga (*yogavid*). Most noteworthy here is what the "subtle yoga" section of this chapter does *not* contain, which is a discussion of the cakras and *nāḍīs* of the subtle body. These are discussed at length in the seventh chapter of the NT, which is introduced by the statement, "Now I will speak further of the highest [form of] subtle meditation (*sūkṣmadhyānam*)."[241] With this, we once again find that a technique—today assumed to lie at the heart of "classical" yogic theory and practice—was called "meditation," rather than "yoga," in an earlier time. The hathayogic practices relative to the cakras and *nāḍīs* are beyond the scope of this book.[242]

Following a brief synopsis, (20.28a-29a), the NT provides detailed instructions for the practice of "subtle yoga":

> Having mounted an assault (*ākramya*), out through the upper or lower entrance [of his subtle body], into that other body's living self (*jīvam*), which is situated in that person's heart, and having attacked its integrity, [the yogi] should go to work on [that self's] equanimity [and then], attaching [himself] to its prime mover [i.e., the ego], he should work on its autonomy. With his own all-pervasive energy (*śakti*), he should smash . . . encapsulate . . . and annihilate that self's energy. Thereupon . . . the connoisseur of

yoga . . . should heat up [the other body's self] with . . . the solar nature of his mind-stuff (*citsūryatvena*). Situated in the other [body's heart], it will melt away [the other self's] rays in the same way as the sun, with its rays [melts away the rays of the moon]. He should then yoke, in the [other body's] heart, all of the action organs, beginning with the organ of speech . . . [and he should yoke] from every side those [organs' associated] elements, [which have become] liquified . . . [And then], having laid hold of the accumulated debris of [the other body's] inner organ (*antaḥkaraṇa*) with his own consciousness, the yogi should then enter [that body with his own self], assaulting (*ākramya*) that body-citadel from every side. He should quickly bring all that has been melted down and captured into his own self's place [i.e., his own body or heart]. At that very moment, he [also] brings the [other body's] living self [into his own heart], through the yokings of seals and spells.[243]

This process—of a yogi's gradual reduction of the sensing, knowing, and action capacities associated with another person's self to a fluid amalgam that he then incorporates into his own self—is explicated by the Kashmiri Kṣemarāja's helpful commentary, which, written in the first half of the eleventh century, is at least fifty years younger than the *Nyāyakandalī*. In it, Kṣemarāja summarizes a lost work entitled the *Tattvārthacintāmaṇi*, a text attributed to Kallaṭabhaṭṭa, a late ninth-century disciple of Vasugupta, the author of the *Spandakārikas*.[244] Here, in a description of "globule practice" (*golakābhyāsa*), Kṣemarāja writes that the yogi can reduce himself to the size of a globule and through breath control enter into the body of another person. After remaining there for a period of one hundred morae, he then mounts an assault on that "city of eight" (*puryaṣṭakam*) with his own city of eight, by means of his breath, whose energy-based power has been projectively augmented."[245] Later in his commentary, Kṣemarāja quotes an unnamed source, on the powers that define a yogi.

[A person] becomes a yogi when his activities result in [control over] the movement of every limb of the person [whose body has been] invaded [by him], whenever [that person] eats, drinks, moves, stands or sleeps. Accordingly, he can make him come to him, cast him off, immobilize him, make him open [his eyes], make him whole, or cause him to attain the most excellent (*viśiṣṭa*) abode."[246]

Finally, referring to the NT's use of the language of solar rays, Kṣemarāja comments, "With the rays that originate from his own enflamed eyes,[247] [the yogi] who is situated there in that other body melts the rays coming from that body's eyes, like the [rays of] the sun [melt] the rays of the moon."[248] Here we see that, even in a situation in which the physical eyes set in his eye sockets are no longer operative, the yogi's eyes—as disembodied sense faculties capable of perceiving and even penetrating other bodies and selves via their rays—continue to function as they would have while still embodied.[249] In this respect, Kṣemarāja's commentary neatly synthesizes all of the partially adumbrated models of yogi perception and penetration found in the epic, upanishadic, ayurvedic, Nyāya-Vaiśeṣika, and tantric sources that precede him.

The NT's complete and nuanced description of this technique for entering into a foreign body, living or dead, is one of many found in medieval sources from the same period, including the mid-tenth-century *Yoga Vasiṣṭha* (YV),[250] the Jain Hemacandra's (1088–1172) *Yogaśāstra* (YŚ) with his *Svopajñavṛtti* autocommentary,[251] the thirteenth-century *Gorakṣa Saṃhitā* (GS),[252] and Lama Jey Tsongkapa's fourteenth-century treatise on the Buddhist Naropa's (1016–1100) six yogas. Whereas Naropa's own instructions for this (as well as the Buddhist homologue of the Hindu practice of *utkrānti*) are terse and elliptical,[253] Tsongkapa's instructions for the sixth of Naropa's six yogas, called the "forceful projection of consciousness into another body," are quite detailed.

> To practice the technique one first acquires a fresh, undisintegrated human corpse of a person who did not die from serious wounds or a debilitating illness . . . One washes the corpse with fresh water, adorns it with beautiful ornaments, and places it in the cross-legged posture on the mandala platform that was constructed earlier . . . Now one visualizes oneself and the corpse as being tantric deities, a mantric syllable HUM in the heart of each. One faces the corpse squarely and breathes out, with the airs passing through the right nostril. The HUM at one's heart exits one's body via the right nostril and enters into the body of the corpse via its left nostril. The forces of subtle energies and mind are brought into play in the process of moving the syllable HUM, and the airs are expelled forcefully. Eventually the corpse will be resuscitated and will begin to breathe. When this happens, one has a beautiful friend offer it appropriate food and tend to it. For half a month it is kept hidden inside; and until this new "residence" becomes steady, one also keeps one's old body hidden inside the hut. Then one can cremate the old body in a tantric fire ritual, have the ashes mixed with clay and pressed into holy images and so forth, in order to show respect to it for the kind service it had rendered to one. One then takes up one's new life in the newly acquired body, and performs great deeds for the benefit of living beings.[254]

This is not a dead tradition. Just as the medieval tales of sinister yogis were adapted by twentieth-century anthologists like the Indian Mahadevprasad Singh and the Nepali B. V. Adhikari, so too have medieval theories of the science of entering a foreign body persisted well into the twentieth (if not the twenty-first) century. The Bengali polymath Gopinath Kaviraj (1887–1976) is to be counted among the last great tantric scholar-practitioners of South Asia. After a brilliant career as a sanskritist and university president at the Government Sanskrit College in Benares, he retired from his academic duties in 1937 to devote his life to personal practice, taking initiation from Swami Visuddhananda, a tantric yogi of Benares who had gained fabulous magical powers under the tutelage of a mysterious Tibetan master. He was also strongly influenced by Anandamayima, whom he met in 1928 and in whose Benares ashram he died. Another influence was the Bengali Shobha Ma, whom he questioned, on the occasion of their first meeting in 1938, on the topic of yogi perception (*yogī brahmajñān*).[255]

In 1964, Kaviraj published a chapter entitled "Parakāyapraveśa," in which he synthesized both his intellectual and experiential knowledge of the power of entering a foreign body.[256] In it, he wrote:

Concentration (*dhāraṇā*) normally implies a bodily support, but for yogis, disembodied (*videha*) concentration is also a requirement. By disembodied concentration, I mean that the mind-stuff (*citta*) located inside the body can be sent outside of the body to some desired place . . . In the same way that the unified rays of the eye leave the eye and, becoming yoked (*yukt*) to the external object to be perceived, become conformed (*pariṇat*) to its form, just so rays emanating from the mind-stuff also act upon their external objects . . . An ordinary person's mind does not leave his body until the time of death; this is not so for the yogi, whose mind-body connection has been loosened through initiation, practice, etc . . . The body contains multiple "mind-bearing" channels (*manovāhā nāḍī*) . . . It is not the case that these inner channels are only inside the body. They also fan out from the body into the entire cosmos (*virāṭ viśva*). By means of this network of channels (*nāḍījāl*) every man is [joined] together with every [other] man. Why is this so? *Because everything is connected to everything else* . . . It is necessary for the yogi to maintain a separation in his field of vision between the body he has entered (and of which he has become the experiencing subject [*bhoktārūp*]), and the channel through which his yoking [of that body] to his own was established . . . This is because he will need that path [of the channel] to leave that body [and return to his own body] . . . Having gained this sort of ability, a yogi becomes empowered to undertake the practice . . . known as enhanced disembodied concentration (*mahā-videha-dhāranā*). It is this that makes entering into another person's body possible. A yogi's "root mind" (*mūl man*) remains in his body while a separate mind voluntarily inhabits another body, and is yoked to that body. But . . . both remain joined by a luminous threadlike substance . . .[257] [Then, discussing the link between the yogic entering of foreign bodies to tantric initiation, Kaviraj continues]. When a yogi's mind that has fully penetrated (*samāviṣṭ*) another body then returns to its own place [i.e., his own body],

> it takes a portion of the mind that it has separated off from the other body, and brings it back with it . . . In addition, a portion of guru's mind is left behind in the body of his disciple, where it remains for a long time, even until disciple's death . . . [Thus] the disciple's mind becomes dependent . . . upon that of his guru . . . At the time of the disciple's death, the [portion of the] guru's mind [that had remained with his disciple] draws out the disciple's mind, and returns it to his [the guru's] own body . . . When his [the disciple's] mind merges with the guru's mind, after having come to the guru's place in the guru's body, he [the disciple] attains a plane of being commensurate with that of the guru . . . Upon arriving at that place, i.e., upon attaining that plane of being within the guru's body, he enters into an unaging and immortal state, and is saved from the world of death . . . The more people's bodies a yogi is able to make his own by entering into foreign bodies, the greater the number [of bodies] will be pervaded by his mind, and the more he will be able to use his own action-energy (*kriyā-śakti*) for the general welfare, in his all-pervasive form.

In many ways, these data speak for themselves. To begin, they explain, in concrete terms, why tantric gurus are venerated as gods: they embody the power of salvation. More importantly, they explode our received notions of the limits of the body. Rather than being unidirectional in its extension beyond its visible physical contours, the body bristles with openings and extensions that are nothing other than the rays of perception that flow out of every sense organ to "touch and take the measure of every being at every level in the hierarchy of transmigrations"[258] and, in the case of the sun, yogis, enlightened Buddhas, and gods, to penetrate those beings and transform them as they please. Lastly, these accounts of the body's extensions buttress McKim Marriott's theories of Indic transactions in substance-code, according to which "pervasive boundary overflows" are the rule in a system in which "dividual" or "divisible" persons are constantly absorbing and diffusing particles of one another's "coded substances."[259] Before it was closed off from the world to ensure the splendid isolation (*kaivalyam*) of spirit from matter, or the vacuum necessary for the "hydraulic" practices of *haṭha yoga*, the yogic body was conceived as an open system, capable of transacting with every other body—inanimate, animate, human, divine, and celestial—in the universe.

FIVE

Yogi Gods

As we saw at the end of the last chapter, a yogi's powers of omniscience entail extensions of his person that radiate far beyond the contours of his physical body, into the furthest reaches of the cosmos. In effect, a yogi's mind-body (or more properly speaking his consciousness-body[1]) complex becomes virtually coterminus with the limits of the universe. In this chapter, we will follow the ways in which the implications of this extension of the person or self came to be applied to the theology, anthropology, cosmology, and soteriology of the Hindu Purāṇas and Tantras, as well as the scriptures of Buddhist Mahāyāna and Tantra. These new developments appear to follow parallel tracks, with the bodies and powers of yogis and gods being magnified in homologous ways in coeval sources.

I have already discussed what I believe to have been the textual point of departure for the linked phenomena of the deification or "cosmi-fication" of Indic yogis and the "yogi-fication" of Indic deities (including *jīna*s and *bodhisattvas*). These are the gnoseological speculations of the early Upaniṣads, according to which the man or god who "knows 'I am *brahman*' in this way . . . becomes this everything (*idaṃ sarvaṃ bhavati*)."[2] In the centuries that follow, this insight was expanded upon in a number of ways. The leitmotiv of the new theism—ushered in through the teachings of the KU and MU,[3] the "Book of the Nārāyaṇa Cult" in the MdhP, and the BhG—was that Viṣṇu or Kṛṣṇa was none other than the *brahman* or the supreme person (*puruṣottama*) and, by implication, coextensive with the universe. Similar identifications between Rudra and the absolute are found in the

ŚvU, which says of the god that his eyes, face, arms, and feet are everywhere before identifying him with that "magnificent person" (*puruṣam mahāntam*).

Everything in this [universe] is filled with the *puruṣa*, beyond or below whom there is nothing, more minute than whom there is nothing, greater than whom there is nothing. He stands in heaven, immobile as a tree.[4]

In like fashion, the universal *brahman* or *puruṣa* or transcendent *ātman* became the model for the yogi-as-universe,[5] a theme narrativized in the epic account of the yogi Śuka, who vows to "enter into all the beings in all the worlds" and about whom it is later said that "he became all the beings."[6] The question—of whether the innovators of the new theism were theorizing their respective deities' omnipotence and omnipresence in terms of powers already attributed to yogis, or whether the theorization of the omnipotence and omnipresence of fully realized yogis was modeled after the attributes of the gods—remains an open one.

1. The Yogi as Cosmos

a. Samkhyan Gnoseology in Mahābhārata 12.290

"This self of mine inside the heart is greater than the earth, greater than midspace, greater than the celestial realm, greater than these worlds."[7] As we have seen, this upanishadic identification—of the individual self with the simultaneously infinite and infinitesimal *brahman* or *puruṣa*—is reprised in theistic terms in the eighth- to ninth-century MPĀg's discussion of the "Rudra Vow." After visualizing a thumb-sized Rudra in the lotus of his heart, the practitioner fully immerses himself in the god, thinking "without a doubt this is who I am," and conquering his mind through yoga (*yogatas*) considers that "the universe is contained in myself . . . I abide in all that moves."[8] The MVUT, a text more or less coeval with the MPĀg, characterizes "the fruits of yoga" as the sequenced gnoseological attainment of seven "worlds" that are nothing other than increasingly expanded states of subjectivity, culminating in the gods-eye view of Śiva himself, who views "that" (*idam*), that is, the universe, as "I" (*aham*), himself.[9]

These passages present the yogi's self-realization, as the universal subject, in a gnoseological mode, according to which what one knows determines what one is. Knowing was not, however, the sole means to realizing this expansive (sense of) self, as the MdhP chapter (MBh 12.289) entitled "Yogavidaḥ" (*An Understanding of Yoga* or *An Understanding of the Yogi*) makes plain. Before I turn to this chapter, a word of background is in order. In a recent study, James Fitzgerald has argued convincingly that the final seventy-five chapters of this epic subparvan (MBh 12.278–353) comprise an anthology of fifteen discrete "texts," which were carefully crafted into a unified work. In his study, Fitzgerald identifies five "text pairs" within this portion of the MdhP. Each of these text pairs juxtaposes elements from the emergent systems of yoga practice and Sāṃkhya philosophy, with MBh 12.289–290, the third in this series of five, having the added feature of "dramatically subordinat[ing] the two paths of yoga and Sāṃkhya to the theology of the divine Lord Nārāyaṇa."[10] MBh 12.289 is also of pivotal importance for reconstructing the history of yoga. As I indicated in my preface, it was my reading of a passage from that chapter that launched this book. As Fitzgerald has noted, there is a distinction between the respective climaxes of these paired chapters. In chapter 289, the yogi enters into all of the creatures of the universe before he *becomes* Nārāyaṇa, whereas in chapter 290, the Sāṃkhya practitioner *goes to* Nārāyaṇa.[11] The reason for the presence of this god at the summit of the universe in both of these narratives is not difficult to understand: they are, as it were, the overture to the *grand finale* of the MdhP, of which the penultimate "text" is the nineteen-chapter-long "Book of the Nārāyaṇa Cult" (MBh 12.321–339).[12]

Before turning to the yoga chapter (289) of this text pair, I first offer an abridged rendering of thirty verses from the Sāṃkhya chapter (290), which describes the meditative ascent of the Sāṃkhya practitioner. I do this for two reasons. First, these verses constitute yet another link in the chain of speculations on human salvation in the context of the relationship between the "two infinities" of the absolute in its infinite and infinitesimal modes of being. Second, when juxtaposed with the "coda" of the yoga chapter,[13] they place in higher relief the difference between the theory and practice of salvation through meditative insight (the samkhyan path) and the means and end of yogi practice. These differences are clearly enunciated in the introduction to chapter 289, which states that "the yogis are those whose proofs are based on perception (*pratyakṣa*), whereas the adherents of Sāṃkhya are those whose settled opinions are grounded in the sacred teachings."[14] In other words, whereas the samkhyan-*cum*-devotee's saving knowledge of the nondifference between individual person and transcendent person of the divine is a gradual process, the yogi is able, like the vedic seers, to penetrate the impenetrable in a single panoptic act of perception.

MBh 12.290.69–75 describes the visionary ascent of the "true practitioner" of Sāṃkhya in the following terms:

By means of gnosis (*jñāna-yogena*), those perfected hermits cross over . . . and having crossed over [beyond the world of] birth—a crossing that is difficult—they enter into the clear sky (*nabhas*). Then . . . the sun carries those true practitioners of Sāṃkhya [upward] with its rays which, penetrating (*āviśya*) them like lotus fibers,[15] convey them toward the [most distant] objects of the senses.[16] There, the conveying wind takes hold of those perfected ascetics . . . Gentle, cool, fragrant, and pleasant to touch is that most excellent of the seven luminous winds (*maruts*[17]), which goes to the shining worlds. It bears them to the higher path of the sky.[18] The sky bears them to the [still] higher path of the firmament (*rajas*), and then the firmament bears them to the [still] higher path of pure being (*sattva*), and pure being bears them to the highest, the Lord Nārāyaṇa; and that lord whose self is innately pure bears them to the supreme Self (*paramātmānam*). Having reached the supreme Self they are immaculate in its abode. They are fit for immortality; they do not return.

The twenty verses that follow comprise a discussion of the trajectory of the Sāṃkhya practitioner's mind, which, detached from the sense organs, advances toward (*ā-kram*)[19] the supreme being whose attributes are then described.

Then, having advanced beyond (*atikramya*) nature (*prakṛti*), he goes to the immutable (*avyayam*) self that is [none other than] the supreme Lord Nārāyaṇa self, which transcends the dualities of nature . . . [As for] the *brahman*, which is undecaying, fixed (*dhruva*), unmanifest, primordial and primeval . . . [and] situated in the peak . . . brahmins who desire it and who are intent on its good qualities call it *brahman*, as do practitioners of yoga who are yoked (*yuktāḥ*), and practitioners of Sāṃkhya whose vision capacity is without limit.[20]

This epic chapter appears to take its inspiration from MU 6.28–38 (or from a source common to both texts), inasmuch as it appropriates and expands upon that late Upaniṣad's nascent Nārāyaṇa theology. Some of the same descriptors of the god, who is identified with the *brahman*, are found in both sources, descriptors that became epithets if not alternate names for Viṣṇu-Nārāyaṇa in later sources: *dhruva*, *ananta*, *acyuta*, and so on The four spheres of MU 6.38, ranging from the solar sphere to the sphere of pure being (*sattva*) are mirrored in the four paths of MBh 12.290, which extend from the path of the sky (in which the sun is the agent of motion) to the path of pure being. Beyond these is the abode called "Viṣṇu" in MU 6.38, which corresponds to "the highest, Lord Nārāyaṇa" in Mbh

12.290.74; however, in the epic text, the god is superseded by an utterly transcendent "Supreme Self" (*paramātman*), in whose abode the liberated remain. Like the BhG (15.17), this epic passage describes the absolute as "situated in the peak," a probable reference to the crown of the head, the point of exit from the body of the channel that is evoked for the first time in ChU 8.6.6 as rising up from the heart.

b. Yogi Practice in Mahābhārata 12.289

Whereas the Sāṃkhya chapter of this text pair reprises the by now familiar upanishadic programs of meditative ascent upward to god, the four-verse "coda" of its yoga chapter offers a novel expansion on the theories of perception and the science of entering foreign bodies introduced in chapter four. According to its colophon, the title of this chapter is "Yogavidaḥ," a compound that would normally translate as "An Understanding of Yoga." However, when one examines the uses of the term "yoga" in much of this chapter (as well as in all but one of the other didactic chapters on yoga found in the MdhP), it becomes clear that the referent of the term is, in fact, the agent of yogic practice, that is, the yogi. Throughout these chapters, the contexts in which the term is found as well as its frequent plural declensions demand such a reading.[21] In the first half of this particular chapter, the term "yoga" is extensively used to denote the yogi, whereas, in its second half, the term *yogī* (in the nominative singular) is employed almost exclusively. This is further evidence, if such be needed, for the fact that the vocabulary of yoga was still far from uniform in the first centuries of the common era. It also points to the likelihood that this chapter combined two separate discourses on yoga, the former more philosophically oriented and the latter more related to practice.[22]

Introducing the text pair as a structured discourse, MBh 12.289 begins with general remarks on the differences between the methods of the two systems. It then goes on to describe the powers of the yogi, asserting that his fiery energy is capable of scorching the world, "like the sun at the end of time," and, as we have seen, that he is able to take on multiple bodies and "walk the earth with all of them."[23] The focus of the verses that follow, in which the term *yogī* is employed in the nominative singular, is the practice of concentration (*dhāraṇā*). Here a reference to the parts of the body in which the yogi is to be "composed" (*samāhita*) appears to anticipate later formulations of the cakras. "In the navel, in the throat, and in the head, in the heart, in the breast, [and] in the two flanks, in [the organs of] seeing, as well as in [the organs of] touching and in [the organs of] smelling: the yogi who, in his great vow, is fully composed in these places, uniformly yokes the self with the self."[24]

The four final verses of this chapter (which comprise its *triṣṭubh*-meter coda) go to the heart of the yogi traditions that have persisted down to the present day, in blatant contradiction with the meditative traditions of "classical yoga."

When his self-magnifying self (*mahān ātmā*) and the magni-ficent (*mahān*) [universe] have fused into one another, a yogi may enter [into] women, men and the assemblies of Gandharvas, the quarters of the sky, the hosts of Yakṣas, the mountains and the dragons, and the clouds together with the forests and all the rivers, and the terrible oceans and all the mountain peaks, and the ancestors and serpents and all the divinities, [and] verily the immaculate overlord of men together with the stars, and the greatly massive firmness [i.e., the earth element], and the whole [circle of] splendor [i.e., the fire element], and [the goddess] Siddhi, the spouse of Varuṇa [i.e., the water element], and supreme Nature [together with] pristine pure being, massive passion and evil darkness (*sattva, rajas, tamas*), and the six high-minded sons of Brahmā and the six-faced one (Karttikeya) and Dharma and Bhava and the boon-granting Viṣṇu, Brahmā the master and . . . indeed That, the magni-ficent highest *brahman*. He is liberated shortly thereafter . . . Surpassing all mortal yogis, [the yogi] whose body is the magni-ficent [universe] and whose self is Nārāyaṇa, acts.[25]

Here the use of the term *mahān ātmā*, which I translated in chapter three as self-magnifying self, is of signal interest. As the nominative singular of the present active participle of *mah, a verb root that from the epic period forward carried the sense of "magnify," *mahān* may be literally translated as "magnifying." Its Indo-European cognates (Greek, Latin, and English, respectively) are *mégas, magnus*, and "much."[26] Combined with *ātman, mahān* can only be read here as the self-magnifying self, in other words, a self whose quality of expansiveness empowers it to become coterminus with the entire magnified or "magni-ficent" universe (*mahān*, or the neuter form *mahat*).[27] As such, its semantic field overlaps that of *brahman*, with which the yogi identifies himself. Derived from the root *bṛh, this term reflects the "magical power of expansion" of an absolute that, even in its infinitesimal form, is virtually massive—like the tiny seed that generates the massive banyan tree, as elucidated in Uddālaka Āruṇi's classical upanishadic teaching to his son Śvetaketu.[28]

As was noted in chapter three, the term *mahān ātmā* was first introduced in the KU as the metaphysical category or essence (*tattva*) situated immediately below the unmanifest (*avyaktam*) and the supreme person (*puruṣa*). This early adumbration of the three highest samkhyan categories is to be juxtaposed with that of the YS, in which the categories of *buddhi* and *prakṛti* immediately precede *puruṣa*. In both the *pātañjala yoga* and classical Sāṃkhya philosophical systems, the *buddhi* (intellect) or its analogue the *mahat* constitutes the ground for all that exists,[29] in the light of which the use in this passage of *mahān* and *mahān ātmā* for the whole of existence and the yogi whose self is coterminus with the whole of existence makes perfect sense. In both soteriologies, the goal of practice is to free the intellect or "the magni-ficent" from the afflictions (*kleśa*s) that skew its perception of its true nature as free and limitless, that is, as the self-magnifying self that "knows 'I am *brahman*' [and thereby] becomes this everything."

It is also the case that this same sequence of the uppermost samkhyan categories undergirds normative Vaiṣṇava accounts of the reabsorption of the emitted cosmos by the *mahāyogī* Viṣṇu, as described in the *Viṣṇu Purāṇa* (ViṣP) and other Vaiṣṇava Purāṇas, as well as late recensions of the HV. As the great god retracts his sense faculties, the universe and all its creatures are absorbed into his supreme person, such that his self-magnifying self finally becomes coextensive with the magni-ficent universe, which is now inside of him, Nārāyaṇa, the Abode of Men.[30] This is the meaning of the term in MBh 12.289.62, and the means by which the final redactor of this chapter transformed what would otherwise have been a straightforward account of a yogi's penetration of every self in the universe—up to the very self of the universe itself[31]—into a Vaiṣṇava manifesto.

Other sources describe the same dynamic, of a yogi's practice culminating in his becoming coextensive with the universe, without the Vaiṣṇava inflection. A particularly rich account is that found in the twelfth-century YŚ of the Jain scholar Hemacandra, who, while he calls his actor a yogi, describes his self-expansion to the confines of the universe as a meditation (*dhyānam*). Here it should be recalled that the Jain universe is frequently represented as a gigantic anthropomorphic being called the *loka-puruṣa*, the "Universal Man."

A yogi who has acquired infinite knowledge and perception and whose longevity remains less than forty-eight minutes should instantaneously perform the third [kind of pure] meditation (*dhyānam*) . . . During the [first] three instants [of this process], the yogi [expands the spatial units of the self (*jīvapradeśa*) outside the gross body. In the first instant, the mass of spatial units of the self reaches the end of the inhabited universe, entering the upper and lower regions in the form of] a column (*daṇḍa*), [which

Figure 5.1 *Lokapuruṣa* (Cosmic Being), 1775–1799. India, Rajasthan, Bikaner. Opaque color on cloth, 34 ½ x 27 inches. Museum purchase, 1995.6.2. Courtesy the University of Virginia Art Museum.

is equal in thickness to his own body. During the second instant, the self reaches the end of the inhabited universe, sideways, in an east-west direction, like] a door (*kapāṭa*). [In the third instant, the self reaches the same by moving sideways in a south-north direction, like] a churning-stick (*manthānaka*). During the fourth moment, the yogi fills up the entire [inhabited] universe [by stretching the self in the form of a churning-stick into the remaining gaps]. Within [the course] of four moments after that, the meditator . . . retrieves [his self] from this act of occupying the [inhabited] universe through the reverse path.[32]

Hemacandra follows his account of this "meditation" with a brief description of two additional acts of "pure meditation," at the end of which the practitioner becomes solid and immutable like "the lord of mountains" (*śaileśī*) and enters into the fourteenth and final stage of liberation, in which he "reaches the apex of the universe—the abode of the liberated beings (*siddhakṣetra*)—in a straight line within a single instant."[33]

Many scholars, myself included, have identified Indic discourse of this type as descriptive of the human "microcosm," a miniaturized replica of the universal "macrocosm."[34] A significant number of medieval hathayogic texts, including the *Siddhasiddhāntapaddhati* (SSP), a twelfth- to sixteenth-century work attributed to Gorakhnāth, represent the body of the yogi as containing all of the elements of the universe within its contours. Figure 5.2 is an illustration of the same, based on the SSP.[35] But does this make the yogi's body a microcosm? This ancient Greek term, which entered into the English language via postclassical Latin and Middle French, of course means "miniature universe."[36] Behind this term lies a number of aphorisms that ground Western religious anthropology: "God created man in his own image," "Man is the measure of all things," and so on. One need not look far to find analogous statements in Indic sources. To cite but one example, the CS (4.4.13) states that "this world is the measure (*sammita*) of man. However much diversity of corporeal forms and substances there is in the world, that much [diversity] there is in man; however much there is in man, that much there is in the world." However, there is no term in the Sanskrit language for microcosm. Monier-Williams's reverse English-Sanskrit dictionary proposes *sūkṣmajagat*, *sūkṣmaloka*, and *sūkṣmasaṃsāra*, but I have yet to find such terminology anywhere else, either in the Sanskrit canon itself or Sanskrit lexicons, including Monier-Williams's own Sanskrit-English dictionary. In the light of the data presented here, I would argue that the yogic body represented in the literature of *haṭha yoga* ought not to be viewed as a cosmos in miniature, but rather as a self-magnifying self that has become fully realized as the "magni-ficent" universe.

The opening verse of the SSP's third chapter says as much: "He who cognizes the mobile and the immobile [universe as existing] inside of his body becomes a yogi possessed of comprehensive knowledge of his body."[37] As we have seen, more than all other types of human being, yogis are able to ascertain things as they truly are, including objects normally invisible to others: the distant quarters of space, past and future

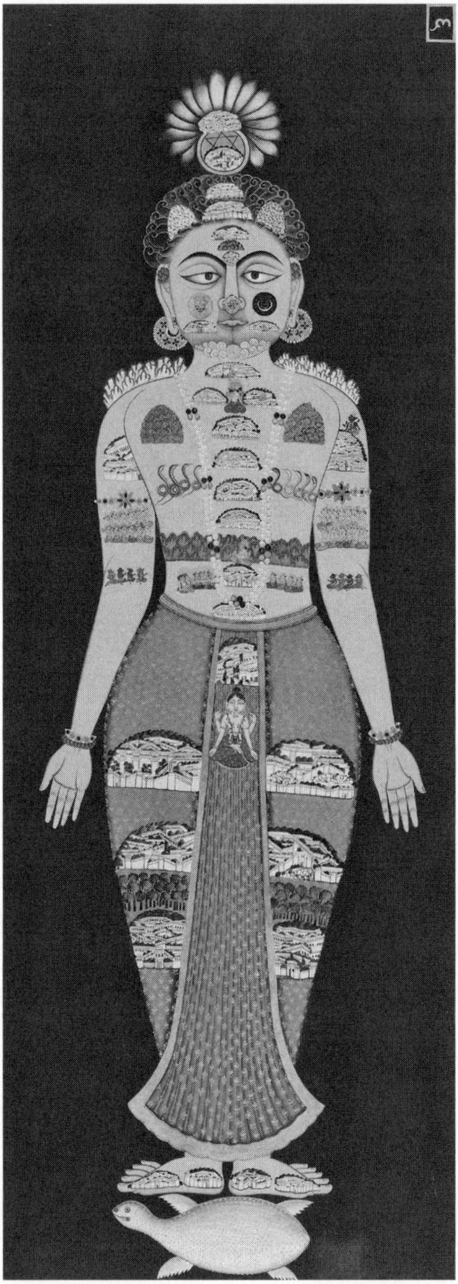

Figure 5.2 Cosmic body of a yogi, based on the Siddhasiddhāntapaddhati. Jodhpur, India, 1824. Courtesy of Mehrangarh Museum Trust, Jodhpur. Acquisitions no. 2378.

time, atoms, wind, the mind, their own souls, the souls of others, and the interior of people's bodies. Therefore, this opening statement constitutes a nonfalsifiable truth claim: this is what the inside of the body—or at least a yogi's body—is really like. It also infers that it is this knowledge, of the identity of the interior of his body with that of the universe, which makes one a yogi. Nowhere, however, does this SSP chapter say that the universe a yogi sees inside has been miniaturized to fit inside the contours of his human body. The SSP's sixth and final chapter, a celebration of the fully realized yogi, here called the *avadhūta-yogi*, expands on this theme:

He who causes the entire [universe] to revolve inside of himself, and who always knows the universe to be himself due to his identity with it, is called an *avadhūta* . . . he is a yogi, a knower, a perfected being, a vow-taker, a master (*īśvara*).[38]

2. Yogic Displays by Gods and Buddhas

a. Nirmāṇakāya

The Buddhist literary record is replete with accounts of Buddhas and bodhisattvas who replicate their bodies, albeit without specific reference to the practice of yoga. Very often, the term used for such a constructed body is *nirmāṇakāya*. According to the *vetulyaka* theory, the transcendental Buddha in the Tuṣita heaven creates such doubles or likenesses of himself for the sake of teaching mankind. He is said to have done so during his stay at Śrāvastī, at which time he expounded the Abhidhamma to his mother Māyā who was in heaven.[39] Tradition has it that, also while in Śrāvastī, the Buddha performed the "miracle of double appearances" before an assembled multitude, in which he put on a display wherein flames and water issued from every part of his body, shooting up as far as Brahmā's heaven and out to the edges of the universe, illuminating the entire cosmos. Thereupon, according to the *Prātihārya Sūtra* (Discourse on the Miracle), the Buddha, seated on a lotus throne, replicated his own body in every direction until he had filled the whole sky, up to the heavens, with Buddhas.[40]

More impressive still are descriptions found in several circa second-century Mahāyāna works of the Buddha's luminous cosmic displays. In the *Aśokāvadāna* (AA), the future great emperor Aśoka is identified as having lived during the time of the historical Buddha in the body of a certain Jaya, the son of a distinguished family living in Rājagṛha. When the Buddha entered Rājagṛha, "the entire city was filled with the radiance of the Lord, his golden rays more resplendent than a thousand suns." Young Jaya offered a handful of dirt into the Buddha's begging bowl, making a vow to become a king as he did so. The Buddha accepted the dirt, and "the seed of merit that was to ripen into Aśoka's kingship was planted."

The Blessed One then displayed his smile. Now, whenever Blessed Buddhas smile, it is usual for rays (*arcis*) of blue, yellow, red, white, scarlet, crystal, and silver-colored light to issue forth from their mouths, some shooting upwards and others going downwards. The rays that travel downwards enter into the various hells . . . Becoming warm they penetrate the cold hells, and becoming cool, they enter the hot ones . . . Then in order to engender their faith, the Blessed One emits for these hell-beings a constructed image (*nirmitam*) of himself that causes them to think . . . And contemplating that constructed image they become serene and full of faith, and casting off the karma yet to be suffered in the hells, they are reborn among the gods or men, where they become vessels of truth. The rays that travel upwards go to the realms of the various gods[41] . . . After roaming throughout the Great Trichilocosm, all of the rays then reenter the Buddha's body. If a Buddha wants to reveal a past action they vanish into him from behind; if he wants to predict a future action they disappear into him from the front. If he wants to predict a rebirth in hell they vanish into the sole of his foot . . . if he wants to predict the kingship of a *balacakravartin* [a powerful world sovereign] they vanish into his left palm . . . if he wants to predict the enlightenment of a disciple they vanish into his mouth; if he wants to predict the enlightenment of a *pratyekabuddha* they vanish into his *ūrṇā* [whorl of hair between the eyebrows]; if he wants to predict the unsurpassed complete enlightenment of a Buddha they vanish into his *uṣṇīṣa* [cranial protuberance]. In the case at hand, the rays circumambulated the Blessed One three times and vanished into his left palm . . . [and the Blessed One said] "because of that meritorious deed . . . that boy will become a king named Aśoka . . . He will be a *cakravartin* who rules over the four continents, and he will distribute my body relics far and wide."[42]

Here the Buddha's display is triggered by a child whose gift has ensured his future birth as a universal sovereign, enabling him to later spread the Buddha's "teaching body," his *dharmakāya*, throughout the world. As we will see below, the Hindu god Kṛṣṇa puts on his most pyrotechnic display of his cosmic body in the presence of another potential universal sovereign, in this case Arjuna. Another account of such a universal manifestation of the Buddha's body is found in Sudhana's vision of the cosmos, as recounted in the second-century CE *Gāṇḍavyūha Sūtra*. This work is expressive of the Avataṃsaka doctrine of the total interpenetration of Buddhahood and the world of existence and the utter "fullness" of all *dharmas*, wherein each and every element of reality holographically contains the entire cosmos within itself.[43] Unlike the future emperor Aśoka, the witness to this cosmic display is the son of a guild-master whose vision of the bodhisattva Samantabhadra places him on the path to becoming a bodhisattva himself.

Then Sudhana, the son of the guild-master, reflecting upon the body of the bodhisattva Samantabhadra, saw in every single pore of that body untold quadrillions of Buddha fields being entirely filled up with Buddhas. And in every single one of those quadrillions of Buddha fields he saw Tathāgatas surrounded by countless assemblies of bodhisattvas. And he saw that all those quadrillions of fields had various bases, various forms, various arrangements, various surrounding mountains, various clouds covering the sky, various Buddhas arising, [and] various proclamations of the Dharma. And just as he was all this in every single pore, so too he saw it in all the pores without exception, in all the major and minor physical marks, in all the major and minor limbs of Samantabhadra's body. In every single one he saw quadrillions of fields, from which issued clouds of Buddha bodies, equal to the number of atoms in all Buddha fields, pervading all of the world systems in the ten directions, bringing beings to the maturity of unsurpassed complete enlightenment. Then Sudhana, the son of the guild-master, guided by the words and instructions of the bodhisattva Samantabhadra, entered into all the world systems within the body of Samantabhadra and brought beings there to maturity . . . In a moment of thought, he entered more Buddha fields . . . in a single pore of the bodhisattva Samantabhadra than the whole series of fields he had entered from the time of his arousing the thought of enlightenment to the time of his audience with Samantabhadra. And as it was for one pore, so it was for all pores. Proceeding, in each moment of thought, through world systems as numerous as the atoms in countless Buddha fields, he still did not arrive at the end . . . And gradually he came to equal the bodhisattva Samantabhadra.[44]

Here these displays of the Buddha and the bodhisattva Samantabhadra rival those of the epic Śiva, who is termed a *yogeśvara* (in MBh 3.80, 126–27) precisely when he generates ten million replicas of himself, and the *yogeśvara* (or *yogayogeśvara*) Kṛṣṇa when he does the same, as well as those of other epic deities who create *yoga-mūrti*s of themselves to simultaneously dwell in heaven and appear before deserving humans. And, in fact, the Buddhist Tantras use the term *yogeśvara* to denote the Buddha himself, while the medieval Jain authors Haribhadra and Hemacandra refer to the *jīna*s as *yoginātha*s.[45] Already in the ṚV, we see the god Indra assuming multiple forms through a creative stratagem (*māyā*)—a term constructed on the same verbal root (*mā) as *nir-mā-ṇa*.[46] These are Hindu gods who "yogically" reduplicate themselves to appear in manifold forms before humans. What of the Buddha's *nirmāṇakāya?* Because Buddhist tradition maintains that such displays are the creations of transcendent beings, it would seem to be inappropriate to classify these multiple self-manifestations as examples of yogi practice.

However, as Kaviraj demonstrated in a seminal article, the concept of *nirmāṇakāya* was common property among all of the ancient philosophical systems of South Asia.[47] More than this, the concept was applied more frequently to yogis than to deities, so much so that one may question whether its conceptual "prototype" was yogic or divine. While *nirmāṇa* was the term employed early on for the numinous power of manifestation realized by *samatha* meditators,[48] the theory of the *nirmāṇakāya* was probably not invented by the Buddhist Aśvaghoṣa with specific reference to the Buddha, but rather in samkhyan circles. Evidence for this may be found in Vedavyāsa's YBh (1.25), wherein the three original founders of Sāṃkhya are brought together, with Pañcaśikha being quoted as stating that Kapila assumed a *nirmāṇa-citta* ("constructed mind") in order to teach the samkhyan system to his disciple (and Pañcaśikha's guru) Āsuri. If Vedavyāsa's attribution and the traditional chronology of the founding Sāṃkhya gurus are both accurate, then Pañcaśikha—who is named as one of Janaka's preceptors in MBh 12.307[49]—predates Aśvaghoṣa.[50]

In any case, a preponderance of references to *nirmāṇa* in the commentarial literature relates the term to the body or bodies that a yogi is able to assume—or, more properly speaking, in these philosophical contexts, to make, construct, or generate—at will. This is the interpretation of Vātsyāyana, who, in his 300–400 CE *Nyāyabhāṣya* commentary on NS 3.2.20, explains how it is possible to have multiple simultaneous cognitions in spite of the fact that the mind is incapable of doing so: "When his superhuman powers have become manifest, the yogi who is a practitioner of transformation constructs (nir-*mā) different bodies with senses intact, and simultaneously perceives [multiple] objects of cognition in them."[51] As was discussed in the previous chapter, similar language is found in YS 4.4–5, and Śaṅkara makes the same argument in his commentary on BrSū 4.4.15.[52] More germane to the present discussion is Śaṅkara's commentary on BrSū 1.3.27, wherein he quotes in full the quintessential epic aphorism on the powers of yogis (MBh 12.289.24–27).[53] It should be noted that in verse 26 of this passage, the verb that is used is *kuryāt,* of which the primary meaning is "make," rather than "lay hold of." Therefore, whereas the verse in question, when applied to human yogis, is best rendered as "a yogi can *lay hold of* several thousand selves, and having obtained [their] power, he can walk the earth with all of them," it is more appropriate to read it as "a yogi can *make* several thousand selves" when it is applied to gods and Buddhas.

While the vast majority of narrative accounts of human yogis show them appropriating other already existing bodies to replicate themselves, gods and Buddhas simply generate additional forms of themselves. The Buddhist VM identifies the power to become manifold as one of the principle supernatural powers (*iddhis*) realized by persons who have become *arhants*. When the *bhikkhu* who has mastered the four *jhānas*, the four roads to power (*iddhi-pādas*), and so on, and who is "normally one . . . resolves with knowledge, 'Let me be many,' he becomes many," that is a hundred, a thousand, or a hundred thousand replicas of himself. While the verb nir-*mā is not employed in this passage, the process of mental creation or construction is clearly signified. Here, the example of a figure named Cūḷapanthaka (the "Lesser Path-taker") is given. Although his elder brother Mahāpanthaka had effortlessly become an arhant in a short time, Cūḷapanthaka showed himself to be so inept in his practice that he was expelled from his monastery. However, the blessed Jīvaka felt compassion for the defrocked monk and through his skill in means caused him to instantaneously "command the nine supramundane states attended by the four discriminations and the six kinds of direct knowledge." The next day, a man sent by Jīvaka beheld Cūḷapanthaka who had "multiplied himself up to a thousand [sitting] in the pleasant mango wood."[54]

Returning to Śaṅkara's use of MBh 12.289.24–27 in his commentary on BrSu 1.3.27, what is most fascinating is the fact that he takes the yogi's power to put on multiple bodies to be his paradigm for supporting this *sūtra*'s contention that the gods are capable of assuming more than one body.

This passage [from MBh 12.289] demonstrates the simultaneous yoking of different bodies on the part of yogis who are possessed of the supernatural powers (*aiśvaryams*) of minuteness and so on. What, then, should we say concerning the gods, in whom such perfections are innate? It is therefore possible that, due to his acquisition of multiple bodies, a deity may distribute his self, by means of [his] multiple forms, and so go to several sacrifices simultaneously in an embodied form.[55]

Rāmakaṇṭha follows a similar line of reasoning in his commentary on *Kiraṇa Tantra* (KT) 3.19, in which he argues that

just as a yogi, through his power of yoga, can inhabit and abandon a wall or such [an inanimate thing], even though it is not a body, in order to bestow grace on transmigrating souls . . . in the same way the Lord (Īśvara) too can, for the sake of bestowing grace, inhabit and abandon a form of His on which it is possible to meditate . . . just as He can [enter and abandon] an external image.[56]

In other words, for the purposes of these commentators' argument, the powers and practices of yogis are prototypes for the powers and practices of the gods!

b. Kṛṣṇa's Yoga of Omnipresencing in the Bhagavad Gītā

When, according to the Purāṇas, the *mahāyogī* Viṣṇu-Nārāyaṇa reemits all of the elements and creatures of the universe from his universal body at the end of a cosmic night, he yogically enters into every one of their bodies, in the form of the person (*puruṣa*) ensconced in their hearts, and thereby becomes the omnipresent one in the many. This same principle is echoed in a medieval Vaiṣṇava treatise from Kashmir, the *Saṃvitprakāśa*, according to which the world is created, sustained, and destroyed by Viṣṇu, who, in doing so, forms himself into the universe (his outer form), before reverting to his own inner, intrinsic, undifferentiated nature when the universe is destroyed.[57] However, the earliest Vaiṣṇava identifications of the supreme being as a yogi are not to be found in these cosmogonic accounts. That distinction falls to the BhG, which in its dramatic climax casts Kṛṣṇa as a Master of Yoga (*yogeśvara*) when he reveals his body to be coextensive with the entire universe and all its creatures. Here, the god's yoga is modeled after that of the human yogi, with Kṛṣṇa putting on a luminous display of the multiple bodies or forms of himself. Indeed, the MBh says as much: "People who are called *tāmasa*s [i.e., who are of an ignorant, deluded nature] confuse Vāsudeva with a yogi who, being a self-magnified self, has entered a human body."[58] However, Kṛṣṇa's yoga differs from that of human yogis inasmuch as he is never portrayed as taking over already existing bodies in order to become multiple. This is because he is the supreme being and source of all creation and thereby already present in and consubstantial with every created being.

In the BhG, it is when the hero Arjuna calls Kṛṣṇa a Master of Yoga and asks him to show him his "yoga of omni-presencing" (*vibhūti yoga*) that Kṛṣṇa offers him a vision of his self-magnifying self, which is not only a body that is as great as the universe (*viśvarūpa*) but also a body that contains, and is holographically present in or as, every creature in the universe. Kṛṣṇa's theophany immediately follows chapters four to eleven, the chapters containing the highest density of references to yoga in the text—in the course of which Kṛṣṇa defines the yogi in precisely the sorts of terms found in MBh 12.289.58–62—and then goes on to define himself as the yogi whose body contains all other yogis.

The person whose self is *yoga-yukta*[59] sees himself in all creatures and all creatures in himself. His vision is the same, wherever [he looks]. When he sees me in everything and everything in me, I am not lost to him, nor is he lost to me. The yogi who partakes of me, present as I am in all creatures, becomes one with me. Likewise, wherever he moves, he moves inside of me.[60]

These chapters close with Arjuna's request that he be permitted to see the divine yogi in his true form: "If you think I shall be able to look upon it, O Master of Yoga (*yogeśvara*), display to me your imperishable person."[61] And as he begins his display, Kṛṣṇa intones, "behold my hundreds and thousands of bodies (*rūpāṇi*) . . . behold the entire universe with standing and moving creatures centered here in this body of mine . . . I give you divine sight (*divyaṃ . . . cakṣuḥ*): behold my masterful yoga (*yogam aiśvaram*)!"[62] While Kṛṣṇa terms this his "masterful yoga" in chapter eleven, this is not the same terminology the god employed in the preceding chapter, in which he prepared Arjuna to view his universal form. In chapter ten, it is a yoga of self-replication, of the proliferation of his supreme self into the many selves that populate the universe, that Kṛṣṇa evokes. Here the specific term used is *vibhūti yoga*, the "yoga of omnipresencing,"[63] and there are no fewer than eight occurrences of *vibhūti* in this, the sole chapter in the BhG in which the word appears. "He who truly knows my *vibhūti yoga* is himself yoked to unshakable yoga," says Kṛṣṇa.[64] Later in the chapter, Arjuna queries him:

"You can fully tell me of the divine omni-presencings of yourself (*ātma-vibhūtayaḥ*), by means of which you permeate and dwell in these worlds . . . How am I to know you, who are a yogi? . . . In which modes of being? Tell me more about your *vibhūti-yoga*!"[65] [To which Kṛṣṇa replies,] "I will relate to you my divine omni-presencings . . . there is no end to my expansiveness. I am the self (*ātmā*) that dwells in all beings." [Then, after naming dozens upon dozens of beings and abstractions, ranging from gods to crocodiles to the game of dice, he concludes,] "There is no end to my divine omnipresencings. Each and every being that instantiates power, sovereignty or strength . . . is arisen from a particle of my radiant light."[66]

The display that follows, of the "masterful yoga" of the great Master of Yoga (*mahāyogeśvara*), is a veritable light show. Saṃjaya, the narrator, describes it in solar terms. "If the light of a thousand suns were to rise

Figure 5.3 Kṛṣṇa displays his Universal Form. Polychrome, ca. 1975.

simultaneously in the sky, such would be the light of that expansive self."[67] Arjuna's reaction highlight's the god's manifestation as the self-magnifying self. "All of the space that extends between heaven and earth, all horizons are filled by you alone . . . you who are brushing the sky."[68] However, as in the case with the effulgent vedic god Kāla, the embodiment of time and death who stands in the disk of the sun, all that arises from Kṛṣṇa is also consumed by him, in the end time, as food. Arjuna cries out in terror, "I see you with your mouth a fiery inferno, burning this world with its flames . . . I see throngs of gods entering into you[69] . . . Swallowing everything, you lick these worlds on all sides with your flaming mouths, filling the entire universe with fire."[70] This, the destructive side of the divine as yogi, is also recognized by the *Rām*, whose sole mention of a *mahāyogī* is placed in the mouth of Mandodarī, the widow of Rāvaṇa, who surmises that the sole being who could have slain her husband was the "great yogi . . . who, greater than the magnificent (*mahataḥ paramo mahān*), the supreme author of darkness . . . is Viṣṇu."[71]

Clearly, it is Kṛṣṇa's power to simultaneously embody himself in multiple bodies that makes him a *yogeśvara* here.[72] Through his yoga, Kṛṣṇa shows his imperishable self to be comprised of hundreds and thousands of bodies, with countless eyes and mouths and aspects, and in this respect, he epitomizes the yogi of Mbh 12.289.26, who is able to lay hold of—or make—multiple bodies and walk the earth with all of them. This language, of divine multiplicity and manifoldness, is far more prevalent in the BhG than are allusions to the uniqueness of god's divine personality,[73] yet another indication that Kṛṣṇa's *yogeśvara* epithet was modeled after the mode of being of the epic yogi and, therefore, meant to be taken in a literal sense. It also provides a glimpse into the choice of terminology in naming the third *pada* of the YS, devoted to supernatural powers, the *vibhūti-pada*, the section on a yogi's omni-presencings. An additional witness is the canon of the Nyāya-Vaiśeṣika school, according to which the material form that a god takes on for the express purpose of teaching the creatures of the worlds he has created is called his *vibhūti*.[74]

c. Kṛṣṇa and Viṣṇu as Masters of Yoga in the Purāṇas

In later Krishnaite mythology, this yoga of omni-presencing is brought to the fore in new and novel ways. When Kṛṣṇa reduplicates himself in his extramarital idylls with the *gopīs*, the cowherding maidens of Vṛndāvana, his storytellers employ the same language as that found in the BhG. So it is that in the BhP's account of Kṛṣṇa's *rās līlā*—in which he dances divinely with each and every one of the *gopīs* simultaneously—the god is referred to, pointedly, as a Master of Yoga.[75] The redactors of this narrative introduce the *rās līlā* dance proper with a rich metaphor that ingeniously divulges yet another facet of the god's yogic omnipresence, one that we have already had the occasion to observe. In its textual rendering of the tableau of the seated Kṛṣṇa at the heart of a circle of adoring *gopīs*, the text reminds the reader that this is the same being as the master (*īśvara*) who is seated in the heart of every (human) Master of Yoga (*yogeśvara*)—yet another way of speaking of the relationship between the multiple *puruṣa*s and the one *puruṣottama*.[76] Another BhP tradition maintains that Kṛṣṇa is the householder husband of 16,000 wives. So it is that when Nārada investigates the lifestyle of this Master of Yoga who, as he has learned, simultaneously dwells in the houses of each of those wives, the nosey sage finds the god omnipresencing as he plays dice with his wife in one house, cavorts with his children in another, and so on.[77]

In fact, the BhP is a watershed for references to Kṛṣṇa as a Master of Yoga, with the term being applied to the god in over twenty contexts, ranging from his role as creator of the universe to his theft of the *gopī*s' clothes and his wrestling match with Cāṇūra.[78] The same text refers to a number of other beings as *yogeśvara*s, including the archfiend Arjuna Kartavīrya, a royal "bull among the kṣatriyas,"[79] a long list of sages,[80] as well as the sons of Brahmā-Prajāpati.[81] This last group, of the four or seven eternally youthful sons of the vedic demiurge,[82] becomes commonplace in Hindu cosmology. Called divine yogis or Masters of Yoga, they are the perennial inhabitants of the uppermost reaches of the cosmos, a region already assigned to them in MU 6.29 ("by this knowledge of *brahman* the sons of Prajāpati were arisen onto the path of *brahman*").[83] One of these, named Sanatsujāta, narrates a long MBh passage on the practice and accomplishments of yoga, which is in every respect a prelude to the BhG's presentation of Kṛṣṇa as the god of yogis and yoga.[84] Identifying the *brahman* as the primeval Bhagavān, Sanatsujāta repeatedly evokes the yogis' vision, from on high, of a supreme being situated at the luminous summit of the universe as well as within their hearts.[85] As we saw in chapter three, this localization of throngs of Masters of Yoga in the world of *brahman* (*brahmaloka*) or elsewhere in the highest heavens becomes a standard fixture of puranic cosmology.[86] The tenth book of the BhP, which contains by far the greatest number of references to divine and human Masters of Yoga in that entire scripture, attempts to establish a hierarchy of such masters by repeatedly referring to Kṛṣṇa as the *yogeśvareśvara*, the "Master of the Masters of Yoga."

Also in the BhP, Kṛṣṇa is called the Lord of the Masters of Yoga (*yogeśvarādhīśvara*) with specific reference to his role as the creator god.[87] As was mentioned in chapter three, this becomes a staple of puranic cosmogonic accounts, in which Viṣṇu-Nārāyaṇa is portrayed as a god whose yoga generates the cosmic cycles. This mythology, which was analyzed in depth by Madeleine Biardeau in the late 1960s, is grounded in the upanishadic teaching of "the entire yoga canon" in KU 3.9–11 and 6.7–9, passages that contain the earliest enumerations of the samkhyan hierarchy of the *tattva*s, culminating in "Viṣṇu's highest plane."[88] As

Figure 5.4 Four yoga-born sons of Brahmā depicted as yogis. South junction wall of Lakṣmaṇa temple, Khajuraho, ca. 954 CE. Photo by David Gordon White.

Biardeau argues, this return or reintegration of the lower *tattvas* into their higher sources is reversed, in puranic cosmogonies, when the yogi god Viṣṇu-Nārāyaṇa emits the universe to initiate a new eon (*kalpa*) of cosmic manifestation.[89] Here, as the VāP describes it, "the Master of Yoga makes and transforms [the] bodies [of creatures], which appear through his play (*svalīlayā*) in their many various shapes, activities, names and forms."[90] Then, at the end of an eon, the yogi god's resorption of the manifest universe follows the reintegrative sequence found in the KU. In other words, Viṣṇu-Nārāyaṇa practices yoga when, precisely, he is drawing all of the mass, energy, *karma*, and mind-body constituents of all of the beings of the universe into himself, that is, practicing the "subtle yoga" of the NT on a universal scale. He is named Nārāyaṇa, the "abode of men" for this selfsame reason, since it is within his yogic body that all creatures (including human yogis) dwell, until such time as the god ceases to practice yoga, whereupon they are reemitted and a new cycle begins. This, too, aligns with the KU's definition of yoga as "appearance and disappearance."[91] It should be noted that when Viṣṇu-Nārāyaṇa reemits the universe, the yogis and other realized beings who inhabited the upper two levels of the cosmic egg (*tapoloka* and *brahmaloka*) are *not* emitted from the god's cosmic body: they remain within, in eternal identity with the supreme person. Their transcendence of the cycle of rebirths is thus definitive, extending into a new *kalpa*.

The vedic Viṣṇu's solar associations also figure prominently here, as his emission (*sṛṣṭi*) and resorption (*pralaya*) of the universe are often explicitly linked to the sun's influence on the ecocosm. In its account of the *pralaya*, the *Matsya Purāṇa* (MP) relates that "becoming a yogi though the manifestations of his seven forms, Nārāyaṇa dries up the oceans with his fiery rays. Then, drinking up every sea, river, and well . . . and taking back all of the mountains' waters with his rays . . . that supreme person (*puruṣottama*) takes back (*ādatte*) the urine, blood, and every other fluid found in living creatures."[92] In a similar vein, in the eleventh- to fifteenth-century cosmogonic account known as the "Manifestation of the Lotus," a group of Siddhas informs Viṣṇu that "you were born as an Āditya, inasmuch as you eat the entire universe, burning it, as it were, with your rays."[93]

d. Śiva as a "Great Yogi" and "Great Master" in the Mahābhārata and the Purāṇas

There is a division of labor in puranic depictions of the cosmic cycles, according to which the universe emitted by Viṣṇu at the beginning of a cosmic eon is then ordered and maintained by the god Brahmā (the puranic deification of the vedic *brahman*) for the duration of the eon before being resorbed by a form of Śiva named Time (Kāla), the "Fire of Time" (Kālāgni) or "Rudra of the Fire of Time" (Kālāgnirudra), at the eon's end. However, already in the MBh's late thirteenth book, a long hymn of praise (*stuti*) to Śiva portrays him in terms redolent of the BhG's identification of Kṛṣṇa with exemplary forms of every god, person, place, and thing in the universe.[94] He is the Master of Yoga (*yogeśvara*), the Great Master (*maheśvara*) of the Masters (*īśvarāṇām*), and Master of the Person (*puruṣeśvara*) who emits the hierarchized samkhyan universe of twenty-six *tattvas*.[95] He emits Brahmā and Viṣṇu from his right and left sides, respectively,[96] and at the end of a cosmic age (*yuga*), he emits Rudra who destroys the world and all its creatures. "Becoming Time (Kāla), he burns as brightly as the fire of dissolution. [Then] this [same] god Mahādeva emits the world and all its moving and inert beings [once more], and when the eon comes to an end, he [alone] remains, having struck down the memory of every one of them."[97] This is the sole mythological feat attributed to Śiva in this long epic panegyric.

The "Īśvara Gītā" section of the *Kūrma Purāṇa* (KP)—inserted by Pāśupata redactors, toward the beginning of the eighth century, into what had earlier been a Pāñcarātra work[98]—expands further on this theme, identifying Śiva as the guru of yogis seated in the hearts of yogis, as well as a yogi, Master of Yoga, and the "Great Master of Masters of Yoga (*mahāyogeśvareśvara*), with whom those who know him through yoga are united."[99] Here the description of the yogi god, as beheld by yogis capable of perceiving his form, is reminiscent of both Kṛṣṇa's "yoga of omnipresencing" in the BhG and of the ṚV 10.90 account of the Puruṣa.

> They saw the dancing cosmic creator god, the god with a thousand heads, a thousand shapes, a thousand arms and legs . . . suffusing the entire cosmic egg with his brilliance, blazing with the light of ten million suns, the transcendent being who dwells within the egg and outside of the egg, who is both inside and out, emitting the blazing fire that incinerates the entire universe.[100]

The final chapter of the KP returns to the theme of the yogi god Śiva's cosmic destruction, this time linking his yogic takeover of other bodies to the powers of the sun. At the end of an eon,

> the Fire of Time decides to reduce the entire [universe] to ashes. Entering the self with the self, he becomes the Great Master (Maheśvara) and burns the entire cosmic egg, including its gods, titans, and men. Entering into him, the Great God (Mahādeva) puts

on a fearsome appearance and carries out the destruction of the worlds. Penetrating the solar disk, he multiplies himself into seven times seven true [solar] forms of himself and incinerates the whole world . . . Filling the horizons of space . . . the god whose garland and ornaments are made from the skulls of the gods—that great-armed, gape-mouthed . . . god of a thousand eyes, a thousand shapes, a thousand hands and feet and a thousand rays—stands [alone] engaged in masterful yoga (*yogam aiśvaram*).[101]

The greatest yogi of all and the last god standing, Śiva has employed his "masterful yoga" (*yogam aiśvaram*) to take over the bodies of every being in the universe, wearing the skulls of the most powerful among them as trophies on his divine person. The repeated emphasis in these sources to yogic mastery (*aiśvaryam*) recalls the language of the "Yogavidaḥ" chapter of the MdhP, which identified practitioners of yoga endowed with the power of yoga (*yogabalānvitāḥ*) as masters (*īśvarāḥ*), in the plural.[102] This is, I would argue, the original topos of this usage, with the term *īśvara* ("master") specifically denoting practitioners of yoga who attain mastery (*aiśvaryam*) through their practice.[103] In fact, the term *īśvara* was, prior to the beginning of the common era, not applied to gods but rather to powerful humans—kings, princes, and the like. Through their practice, yogis came to rival kings in their power, exercising their sovereignty over any creature they chose. As noted above, in BhG 11.5–8 Kṛṣṇa termed his divine yoga *aiśvara yoga*, a yoga of mastery—or, as Angelika Malinar has argued, a yoga of sovereignty, intended to appeal to kings who aspired to partake of that yogic god's power in the world.[104] The term *aiśvaryam*, a yogi's abstract quality of "mastery," entered into the lexicon shortly thereafter, as, for example, in Vyāsa's commentary on YS 1.2. In the plural, the term came to be employed in Pāśupata sources as a synonym for the *siddhi*s, the supernatural enjoyments that rendered the Pāśupata practitioner the equal of Śiva.[105]

Likewise, the term *maheśvara* was not applied to a god until the beginning of the common era. An early application of the term to a god occurs in the ŚvU, which says of an unnamed "god in the world who drives the wheel of the *brahman*" that people should know him as the "supreme great master of the masters" (*īśvarāṇaṃ paramaṃ maheśvaram*).[106] In the light of these data, it is clear that *maheśvara* was originally nearly synonymous with the term *mahāyogī*, which was, as we have seen, an epithet applied to several human and superhuman beings in the MBh itself.[107] During the epic period, the name Maheśvara came to be applied to Śiva exclusively, as, for example, in the account of Kāvya Uśanas, in which the great yogi Maheśvara's ascetic energy outmatches that of his titan rival.[108] This is the sole epic account of yogis in which the takeover of another body (that of Kubera) is portrayed as a violent act. It is also the sole epic account in which two yogis are pitted against one another. In both of these respects, it appears to anticipate the medieval literature of "sinister yogis" detailed in the first chapter of this book, a corpus in which Śiva himself seemingly plays the part of the yogi villain, in the exemplary myth of the Little Devotee.

As Mahāyogī or Maheśvara, Śiva's divine personality differs in many respects from that the Yogeśvara Kṛṣṇa. Śiva's yogic modus operandi most often involves taking over other bodies, usually by swallowing them, as he threatens to do with the Little Devotee's son and as he in fact does with Kāvya Uśanas and the entire universe at the end of time. In Kṛṣṇa's case, apart from his theophany in the BhG as a multiheaded being swallowing the sons of Dhṛtarāṣṭra into his numerous mouths,[109] his is generally a creative yoga of self-replication. At the risk of oversimplification, one could characterize Śiva's yoga as that which condenses the many into the one, like that of the practitioner of subtle yoga as described in the NT and like the sun that gathers all living creatures into itself through its rays (MBh 12.289.27), with that of Kṛṣṇa or Viṣṇu-Nārāyaṇa resembling that of the yogi who creates several thousand selves and walks the earth with all of them (MBh 12,289.26), as well as the sun that generates multiple replicas of itself through its multitudinous rays.

As I noted in the previous chapter, the MBh was compiled during a time in which cults of Indo-Iranian solar deities were being reintroduced into the subcontinent by the Kushans and other invaders from Inner Asia. This being the case, the prominence of solar imagery in the mythologies of both of these great gods of the new theism is to be expected. Of course, as has been noted, Viṣṇu's vedic mythology already bore a solar stamp, his three steps being equated with the shadows cast by the gnomon of a sundial. Śiva has no vedic mythology, and there is nothing of the sun in vedic mythology of Rudra. The great yogi Śiva is nonetheless depicted in a solar mode in the myth of Kāvya Uśanas, which concludes with the transformation of Kāvya Uśanas into Śukra—a name that means "semen"—when Śiva ejaculates him. However, Śukra is also the Sanskrit term for the luminous planet Venus, and this narrative, which opens with a series of questions posed to Bhīṣma by Yudhiṣṭhira, should also be read on an astronomical register. As such, this is an account in which another primary sense of the term yoga—as "astronomical conjunction"—is brought to the fore. A question posed by Yudhiṣṭhira in the introduction to this myth ("Why does he, that splendiferous one [i.e., Venus], not move across the middle of the sky?"[110]) refers to the fact that this planet, whose orbit lies within that of the earth, never appears high in the heavens, but is always visible relatively close to the horizon as the morning or evening star.[111] In such a context, this tale of two yogis is possibly an account of that rarest of planetary alignments known as a transit of Venus, in which that planet appears as a black dot as it passes across the disk of the sun.[112]

In such a scenario, the great yogi Kāvya Uśanas would be the planetary deity Venus who, passing through the body of Kubera (another planet?), "carries off his wealth."[113] Kubera appeals to Śiva "of immeasurable splendor" for his assistance, saying that after having robbed him, Kāvya Uśanas has taken his own path (orbit?) "by means of yoga."[114] Visible to the great god from a distance, the great yogi suddenly appears on the tip of Maheśvara's pike (a ray of the sun) and thence is described as entering into his hand, mouth, and belly.[115] The remainder of the myth describes the transit itself, which concludes when Kāvya Uśanas, burning in the belly of the solar furnace, is ejaculated out of the great yogi's body at a low angle of elevation, to become the luminous low-trajectory planet Venus. This corresponds to the fact that the angle of Venus's passage in its transit across the sun's face is very low, diverging by only a few degrees from the angle of the ecliptic.[116] While it is difficult to observe transits of Venus with the naked eye, they can also be predicted or inferred through the observation of the planet's motion with respect to the sun, and it is significant in this regard that the text states that Kāvya Uśanas's position was determined on the basis of his incoming course.[117]

The relationship between Kāvya Uśanas, the planet Venus, and the great god Śiva is further supported by data from the circa third- to sixth-century *Śāntikalpa*, a text belonging to the ancillary literature of the AV. In its first chapter, which is devoted to the ritual pacification of the planetary seizers (*graha*s), a list of the "sons of the gods" who are to be venerated is in fact a list of the heavenly bodies. "The sons of the gods are in fact the planetary seizers [named] Uśanas (Venus), Aṅgiras (Jupiter), Sūrya (sun), the son of Prajāpati (here, Mars), Soma (moon), Budha (Mercury), Śanaiścara (Saturn), Ketu, and Rāhu (the two nodes of lunar and solar eclipses)." The same text stipulates that great yogis should perform this rite in order to obtain success.[118]

In spite of the yogi god Śiva's many associations with the sun in epic mythology, there is little to his solar aspect, beyond the obvious link between his role as cosmic destroyer and the doomsday sun, that survives beyond the epic period (a notable exception being the cult of Mārtāṇḍa Bhairava, a medieval Śaiva sectarian response to the sun god's popularity). In fact, the heavenly body with which Śiva has had the longest-standing connections has been the moon. Lunar astrology is linked to Śiva in the *Atharvaṇapariśiṣṭa*, a ritual "appendix" to the AV composed by the early Śaiva priests who served as *purohitas* to the second century BCE to second century CE Andhra dynasty of southern India.[119] However, as Ronald Inden has demonstrated, vedic lunar astrology was supplanted by a new luni-solar system, the impetus for this shift being the introduction of the Near Eastern solar calendar into the subcontinent in the third and fourth centuries CE via the Sasanians and Kushano-Sasanians. The new astronomy, embraced by such figures as Varāhamihira, the sixth-century author of the *Bṛhat Saṃhitā*, became hegemonic, and in the absence of Śaiva enthusiasm for the new system, the divine figure of Viṣṇu, whose solar connections extending back to the Vedas were many, became the prime repository of solar mythology.[120] Śiva's ancient links to the moon persist in his iconography—he wears the crescent moon in his hair—as well as in the subtle physiology of *haṭha yoga*, which was innovated in a Śaiva milieu. The cranial vault, identified with both Śiva and the full moon, is the locus of bodily immortality, whereas the lower abdomen, identified with destructive goddesses and the sun, is the locus of death.[121]

The principal message of the epic narrative of Kāvya Uśanas-Śukra nonetheless concerns the divine practice of yoga: while there are in the universe many masters (*īśvaras*) and yogis, among which the heavenly luminaries are exemplary, there can only be one great master (*maheśvara*) and great yogi (*mahāyogī*), and that is the solar Śiva. Like the sun, Śiva is hot and fiery, yoking creatures with his multiple rays that are reins and eating them before digesting and releasing them in a new form.

This is but one aspect of Śiva's yoga. In the fourth century CE, the earliest extant sculptural representations appear of Lakulin or Lakulīśa (fig. 2.10), the legendary founder of the Pāśupata order who, according to myth, arose when Śiva himself entered into the body of a burning corpse on a cremation ground at Kāyāvarohaṇa, a toponym identified with Karvan in modern-day Gujarat. That story is told in nearly identical terms in two Purāṇas, the VāP and *Liṅga Purāṇa* (LP), of which the former may date from as early as the third or fourth century CE.[122] The twenty-third chapter of the VāP, entitled "The Yoga of the Great God's Incarnations," is replete with references to the yoga of the Great Master (*māheśvara yoga*). In it, toward the end of a series of *ex cathedra* prophecies, Śiva reveals that

> through the creative power of yoga (*yogamāyayā*), I will then become a [new] self through yoga (*bhaviṣyāmi yogātmā*).[123] [This I will do in] the body of a chaste brahmin student, to the wonder of the world. Seeing a dead body left unprotected on a

cremation ground, I will enter[124] [into it] through the supernatural power of yoga, for the welfare of brahmins . . . Then I will become the one known by the name of Lakulin, and that "Field of Perfected Beings" (*siddhakṣetra*) will thus be called the "Resurrection of the Body" (*kāyāvarohaṇa*).[125]

This myth is, of course, the prototype for the medieval literary accounts, related in chapter one, of Pāśupata yogis entering into and thereby reviving corpses.[126] This is presented as a specifically Śaiva form of yoga in the BA, in which the *parivrājaka* yogi refers to traditions received by "Maheśvara and the other masters of yoga" prior to entering into the dead body of the unfortunate Vasantasenā.[127] Śiva's modus operandi for entering into the body of the burning corpse also recalls Nyāya-Vaiśeṣika discussions of yogi perception, discussed in the preceding chapter. Here it is noteworthy that the sixth-century Nyāya commentator named Uddyotakara belonged to the Bhāradvāja lineage and was Pāśupata teacher.[128] According to B. K. Matilal, "this shows that the Nyāya school was already under the influence of the Pāśupata sect, just as the Vaiśeṣika school was under the influence of the Māheśvara Śaiva sect beginning from [the circa 450–550 CE commentator] Praśastapāda."[129] Matilal's insights allow us to view the Nyāya-Vaiśeṣika commentaries in the new light of their specifically Śaiva sectarian context. They also suggest a possible connection between the Bhārgava hermit Bharadvāja (whose luminosity is also very much in evidence in his MBh account) and later Śaiva lineages on the one hand, and, on the other, the link between yogi perception, as theorized by Praśastapāda and others, and the NT 20 instructions for the "subtle yoga" of entering other people's bodies.[130] The Atharvanic priests who served as *purohitas* for kings from at least the third century BCE forward, who were supplanted in the medieval period by Śaiva tantric priests, were recruited from among the Bhṛgus and the Aṅgirasas.[131]

3. The Deification of Yogis

If only by virtue of the law of transitivity, human yogis whose bodies have become coterminus with the cosmos through their practice are equal (if not identical) to divine yogis whose bodies are by nature coterminus with the cosmos. The cosmi-fication of the yogi is tantamount to his deification. However, whereas postepic scriptural sources provide prescriptive data on how to become a yogi—through initiation or various types of practice[132]—the same sources contain very little descriptive data on the person of the deified yogi. Here the issue can often be one of terminology. When yoga is viewed as the goal of identity or union with the divine or the attainment of god consciousness—as it is in the three major sectarian divisions of Hindu Tantra—a fully realized yogi is no longer a yogi, but rather a god knowing the universe to be himself.[133]

Most often, the term for such a realized practitioner is siddha, "perfected being." However, as noted in chapter three, the matter is not so simple. In the Śaivāgamas and Pāñcarātra Saṃhitās, the scriptures of orthodox Śaiva and Vaiṣṇava Tantra, respectively, *sādhaka* is the term of choice applied to practitioners of yoga whose goals were the *siddhis*, supernatural powers, and siddha (rather than yogi) the term for the fully realized practitioner. As "self-made gods," the siddhas are frequently depicted as the fully realized semidivine denizens of the uppermost regions of the universe.[134] As we have already noted, the term yogi or Master of Yoga was employed extensively, in the Purāṇas in particular, to designate the sons of Brahmā and other residents of the same highly desirable real estate. In the MBh itself, yogis are identified as the "unsurpassed leaders of the Rudras," another indication of their attainment of a heavenly demigod status,[135] which anticipated their role in later Śaiva cosmology as the rulers of eight exalted realms collectively known as the *yogāṣṭaka*, located immediately below the World of Rudra at the summit of the cosmic egg.[136]

A series of chapters from the VāP devoted to *śrāddha*—the offering of food, water, and praise to the ancestors—stipulates that divinities (*devatā*s), ancestors (*pitṛ*s), and great yogis (*mahāyogi*s) are all recipients of the funeral cake (*piṇḍa*).[137] Of particular interest in these chapters are the connections drawn between the practice of yoga and the transformation of the apotheosized yogi into a deified *yogeśvara*.

The ancestors are great-souled beings possessed of a yogic nature, [that is,] beings that arose [to demigod status] through [the practice of] yoga. These ancestral practitioners of yoga cause the moon to swell [and thereby ensure rainfall, harvests, and so forth]. Therefore, a person who has discharged his duty [to the ancestors and] who has that [world of the ancestors] as his goal should offer funeral cakes to [these divine] yogis[138] . . . So it is that these great-souled ones who are venerated and treated with respect in the *śrāddha* rites will fulfill one's every desire a hundred-fold, even a thousand-fold. Leaving behind the triple world of rebirth, and with it the fear of old age and death, these ancestors grant liberation, and likewise yogic mastery (*yogam aiśvaryam*). The subtle-bodied divinities [known as] the ancestors bestow . . . mastery, which is a means to liberation. Yogic mastery is known to be the highest ranked [form of] mastery. There is no way that liberation can be attained without yogic mastery.[139]

The divinized yogis mentioned in this passage nonetheless appear to be a problematic group, who, like the ancestors, can wreak havoc on the living (especially through the destruction of their rites) if they are not appeased through regular offerings made by the living. The dark side of these beings is alluded to in a passage from the JS, a medieval Pāñcarātra scripture. Here the yogis are not only described as cruel beings that abide in the sky and "produce the stars" but are also mentioned together with evildoers (*duṣṭa*s), the demonic dead (*bhūta*s), and zombies (*vetāla*s), who are prone to disturbing religious rites on earth. This is reflected in current attitudes toward yogis, who, unlike the vast majority of South Asians, are not burned at death, but rather interred in tumuli called *samādhi*s. For many South Asians, the presence of their physical remains implies that their restless soul is also tethered to the site, and so yogis are feared as evil spirits.[140]

These scriptural sources have virtually nothing to say about yogis in the world, because from their standpoint, a yogi who had not transcended this world is, for all intents and purposes, a failed yogi. Furthermore, as discussed in chapter three, the history of Śākta-Śaiva Tantra has been one of the progressive marginalization of yoga and its practitioners in favor of gnosis and ritual, that is, the mastery and manipulation of mantras.[141] This was, in part, an effect of increasing institutionalization in the heyday of Hindu Tantra. Instruction in the mantras could only be had through authorized preceptors, and the sociology of knowledge dictated that only authorized postulants from proper backgrounds could receive such instruction. In the case of the Pāśupatas, none but brahmins received instruction or initiation.[142] Yogis, freelance (and often low-caste) seekers of supernatural enjoyments and power in the world, were marginalized because their existence threatened the power of the sanctioned tantric orders, lineages, and so on. As has been noted, the Śaiva *sādhaka* was a likely vestige of the earlier noninstitutionalized yogi who was incorporated into the tantric orders, albeit in a marginal role. Apart from this group, yogis without institutional affiliations—or yogis with the *wrong* institutional affiliation, that is, other people's *sādhaka*s—do appear in scriptural sources, most often under the name of *kāpālika*s, "Skull Bearers" (and, as was noted with reference to the VP, the same figure can often be called both a yogi and a *kāpālika* in nonscriptural sources). Furthermore, with the (in some cases sudden) disappearance of the institutionalized tantric orders in the wake of the Muslim incursions, tantric practice became an increasingly marginalized affair, with the tantric yogi reduced to the roles in which we find him in the Vikrama Cycle tales recounted in the first chapter.[143]

The Śākta-Śaiva Tantras nonetheless allowed that there existed a divine prototype for the human yogi or *sādhaka*: this was the great and fearsome tantric god Bhairava. As we saw in chapter one, it often becomes difficult to distinguish between this god and the yogis who imitate or impersonate him. In the story of the Little Devotee, Śiva visits Ciruttoṇṭar in the disguise of a *vairavar*, a "Bhairava (ascetic)," in other words, as a human replica of himself in his Skull-Bearer form.[144] In a tenth-century passage from the SvT, the yogi's identity with Bhairava (known to tradition as the original divine preceptor of yoga practice[145]) is presented as the paradigm for *jīvanmukti*,

> in this way the yogi rolls on (*vartate*). He is able to displace his identity by means of another [person's body] (*pareṇa*), and death cannot carry him off, not even for a billion eons . . . The yogi, by means of his spontaneous (*svacchanda*) yoga, by living in a world of the spontaneous, joins the ranks of the spontaneous, and becomes identical with "He who is Spontaneous" [i.e., Svacchanda Bhairava].[146]

This goal of the tantric yogi, of becoming a god himself, became institutionalized in a number of late medieval and Mughal period South Asian kingdoms, whose royal epic cycles featured kings who were raised to the throne after taking initiation from Nāth Yogīs . Following their consecration, these kings in turn transformed their yogi mentors into the tutelary deities of their kingdoms, with their royal cultus—centered on a yogi's tumulus, sword, footprints left in stone, or some other material trace of his person—legitimating the dynasty itself. In one case (the kingdom of Jumla), a yogi was revered as the founder of civilization, responsible for draining valleys, introducing rice cultivation, and the principles of government. Materially, this relationship also translated into an exchange of royal protection, land grants, tax-exempt status, and honors for the yogis' supernatural powers of protection, fertility, and increase.[147] On a humbler level, members of the *dalit* community of modern-day Garhwal are fervent devotees of Bhairava, whom they consider to be a god of justice in a world without justice. However, when the god is represented in word descriptions as found in *dalit* songs he appears not as the familiar multiarmed, multiheaded figure of tantric iconography, but rather as a humble two-armed yogi, clad in a loincloth and carrying the fire-tongs, wooden staff, trident, and orange cloth bag of the Nāth Yogīs.[148]

SIX

Mughal, Modern, and Postmodern Yogis

"Die, yogi, die! Dying is sweet, when you die the death by which the dying Gorakh had his vision."[1] This poem, written by a yogi (Gorakhnāth was the founder of the Nāth Yogīs) for the edification of yogis, dates from no later than the fourteenth century and is an early example of Indic vernacular poetry. This is the same period in which literary references to yogis suddenly appear in half a dozen other non-Sanskrit languages, but in this case, the languages are those of foreigners to the subcontinent: the Perso-Arabic languages of India's Muslim conquerors and the Romance and Germanic languages of travelers and traders from Europe. Their etic accounts of yogis differ greatly from those found in the Sanskrit and vernacular literatures of the subcontinent, which while they were also mainly outsider accounts of yogi "others" were nonetheless indigenous, specifically Indic, in their yogi idioms.

1. Yogis in Travelers' Accounts

a. General Observations

I concluded the first chapter of this book with an allusion by the early fourteenth-century Muslim traveler Ibn Baṭṭūṭa to the cannibalistic proclivities of yogis or their female counterparts. Ibn Baṭṭūṭa's is but one among dozens of first-, second-, or thirdhand observations of the yogis and their ways by South Asian "others," that is, by persons who did not profess allegiance to any of the three major Indic religions within which the great bulk of yogi traditions have been embedded: Hinduism, Buddhism, and, to a lesser extent, Jainism. In many respects, the person or persona of the yogi has itself constituted one of South Asia's perennial "others within,"[2] standing as a constructed antitype to the good people of ordered society. In this respect, quite nearly all nonscriptural descriptive and prescriptive accounts of yogis, from Kauṭilya's ĀŚ to Somadeva's KSS, are outsider accounts because they were not written by yogis. There remains, nonetheless, an important difference between medieval and modern Indic accounts of yogis (which continue long-standing cultural attitudes) and those accounts written by recently arrived Muslim observers or by Europeans who were, with few exceptions, merely passing through the subcontinent. I will return to this issue of the yogi in the world (as opposed to yogis in texts) as the quintessential outsider, perhaps even to himself, at the end of this chapter.

Our principal foreign accounts of yogis come from travelers, merchants, scholars, and administrators from the Islamic world and Europe. When one surveys their respective bodies of narrative on yogis, one is struck by the remarkable divergence between them. It is as if the representatives of the two worlds were giving accounts of two entirely different groups of people, whom both term *jogi*s (the vernacular form of the Sanskrit "yogi;" in order to avoid confusion I will continue to use "yogi" in this chapter, except in direct quotations). This was, in fact, the case. Medieval and Mughal-era South Asia was home to a dizzying variety of individual renouncers, ascetics, and wandering hermits, as well as established renunciant monastic orders and institutions, to say nothing of persons who adopted a yogi persona at various periods in their lives. As we will see in this chapter, there were three types of Muslims who had significant interactions with yogis. First and foremost were the Sufis, who entered India in the thirteenth century, precisely the period in which the Nāth Yogīs, an institutionalized yogi religious order founded by Gorakhnāth in the late twelfth century, were on the ascendent. Gorakhnāth was the likely author of many of the foundational Sanskrit-language works on what was at the time a new form of yogic practice (*haṭha yoga*) and the author of a rich collection of mystic poems (*bāṇī*s) on yogic experience.[3] In the Nāth Yogīs, the Sufis found a group whose yogic practice was highly congenial to their own mystic bent, and the two groups quickly coalesced, with the Perso-Arabic terms *faqīr* ("fakir," "poor man"), *dervish* ("mendicant"), and *shaikh* ("chief") and the Indic term jogi becoming virtually synonymous in the minds of the Indian masses. While there clearly were areas of theological disagreement between the two groups and outright competition between Sufi and Nāth Yogī leaders (which often took the form of "miracle contests" in the Sufi hagiographical literature[4]) over patronage and various forms of symbolic capital, relations between the two groups were generally very good, with the Sufis often playing the role of eager pupils to the Nāth Yogīs in matters of yogic practice.[5] In this syncretistic environment, Sufi records of Indian yogis refer nearly exclusively to the Nāth Yogīs and are generally positive. As Gaborieau puts it, "Far from considering them as charlatans, they admitted the authenticity of their mystical experience, the quality of their yoga techniques and the reality of their supernatural powers. They were not so much adversaries as competitors in an already crowded mystic 'market,' but they were respectable competitors, accomplices who could be won over to their side."[6]

During the late Delhi Sultanate and the Mughal period, India's yogis (in the broadest sense of the term) also figure quite prominently in administrative and military documents. Many of the Mughal emperors—most especially Akbar, as we saw in chapter one—were fascinated by the yogis and were so impressed by their knowledge of alchemy and other subjects that they endowed their orders with significant land grants. By and large, Mughal policy toward the yogis was pragmatic: they rarely interfered in their ways but made use of them when such was politically expedient. This translated into the use, by various Mughal emperors, of irregular yogi soldiers in regiments recruited by (often Afghan) middlemen. Muslim scholars and litterateurs tended to be highly respectful in their treatment of yogis, with the literary subgenre known as the "yogi romance" being the nearly exclusive province of Muslim authors. Ibn Baṭṭūṭa's descriptions of India's yogis, which predate the Mughals' rise to power, does not fall into any of these categories and is in many respects closer to those found in European accounts.

The picture that Europeans paint of the yogis (and of their Muslim homologues, the fakirs, with the two terms being used quite indiscriminately and interchangeably) is an entirely different one. I am convinced that this radical divergence stems from the fact that the yogis whom most European travelers met were different from those with whom the Muslims, who were the masters of much of India until the end of the eighteenth century, transacted. In the Muslim case, interactions were between (mainly Sufi) religious order and (mainly Nāth Yogī) religious order, or between the Mughal administration and military and yogi monasteries or fighting troops. As for the early Europeans who recorded their encounters with yogis, these were for the most part either adventurers, seamen, or merchants. These persons, who were incapable of conversing directly with the yogis, tended to meet them in the public spaces where a particular type of yogi congregated, such as temples, pilgrimage sites, or markets.

Then as now, temples and pilgrimage sites were the ideal venues for professional beggars to ply their trade, and individuals dressed in the garb of yogis clustered around them in all manner of ascetic poses and self-mortifying displays in order to fill their bowls with alms. In public markets, troops of yogis would descend on merchants' stalls to extort money and food from them by haranguing customers and disrupting their business until they were paid to go away. Bands of yogis would also harass and prey upon merchant caravans, even when they had been hired to protect them. In these aggressive interactions with the merchant class, the yogi orders were basically running protection rackets, and many European travelers, the British in particular, give outraged accounts of their behavior. What the early European travelers did not yet understand was that underlying these behaviors was a fundamental cleavage in north Indian society. On the one hand, rural society was comprised of the peasantry (from which most of the yogis in the yogi orders were drawn) and the Rajput aristocracy, which was also grounded in the countryside. On the other, urban society was comprised of the intellectual and administrative elites and the merchant classes. The priesthood of rural society was mainly comprised of yogis and their ilk, while that of urban society was brahmanic—and so it was that when yogis preyed on merchants in the towns or on trade routes, they were engaging in a perennial form of class warfare. Warfare, another important activity of yogis in the Mughal era, is also chronicled by a number of Europeans.

b. Yogis in a Chinese Account

Apart from Marco Polo, whose account of yogis I will discuss shortly, the earliest foreign references to persons explicitly termed yogis are found in Chinese sources.[7] The earliest Chinese account of yogis comes to us from an Arabic-language interpreter named Mahuan, himself a Muslim, who traveled to Cochin on the Malabar Coast in 1413 CE. In his circa 1430 *Ying yai shêng lan* (*Description of the Coasts of the Ocean*) he writes that

> there are Choki [yogis] who are something like the *yu-p'o-i* or lay brethren, and who have wives. From the time of their birth their hair is not cut nor combed, but they rub on it butter and plait it in some ten braids and let it hang down behind. They smear their bodies with ashes of cowdung, and wear no clothing, but a rattan holds around

their waists a whitish-green stuff (?or white calico). They carry in their hand a big conch shell which they constantly blow as they go about. Their wives, who cover their nakedness with only a small piece of cotton stuff, follow their husbands about from house to house seeking money and rice.[8]

c. Yogis in Arabic- and Persian-language Accounts

The "discovery" of India by Islamicate cultures had begun several centuries prior to this Chinese account, with a series of invasions, initiated in 997 CE, by Mahmud of Ghazni. Accompanying the invading forces was the scholar Abū-Rajiḥān Muhammad ibn Ahmad Alberuni, whose *Indika* is a remarkable compendium of the state of the Indian sciences, mathematics, and astronomy, most of which he culled from scriptural sources. Alberuni also authored the *Kitāb Pātañjala*, a commentary on the YS. Although he rails in his *Indika* against Indian alchemists whom he considers to be charlatans, he has nothing to say about India's yogis per se.[9] In his sixteenth-century *Ā'īn-i Akbarī*, Abū al-Faḍl 'Allāmī gives a summary of the YS, but like Alberuni makes no mention of contemporary yogis (in spite of the fact that he had a "City of Yogis" built for them at Akbar's order). This is possibly due to his disapproval of his emperor's fascination with them.[10]

A few decades after Mahuan, Ibn Baṭṭūṭa penned his accounts of the yogis he encountered in India. In them, he notes the ability of yogis to survive without food.

These people work wonders. For instance, one of them remains for months without food and drink; many of them dig a pit under the earth which is closed over them leaving therein no opening except one through which the air might enter. There one remains for months and I have heard that some jogis hold out in this manner for a year. In the city of Mangalore I saw a Musalmān who used to take lessons from the jogis. A small stand had been set up for him on which he held himself for twenty-five days without food and drink . . . People relate that the jogis prepare pills of which they take one for a specified number of days or months, and that during this period they need neither food nor drink. They give information about hidden things and the sulṭān honours them and takes them into his company. Some of the jogis confine themselves to a vegetable diet; while others—and they are the majority—never take meat. What appears to be the fact about them is that they subject their bodies to hard exercises and that they have no craving for the world and its trappings.[11]

Ibn Baṭṭūṭa also describes the ability of yogis to levitate, their practice of self-mortification, and their disdain for the things of this world.

I attended [Muhammad ibn Tughluq, the Sultan of Delhi] and found him in a private chamber . . . with . . . two of the jogis. The latter had wrapped themselves with quilts covering their heads because they remove their hair with ashes just as people remove the hair of their arm-pits . . . One of them, then, squatted and lifted himself high up in the air in such a way that he remained over us in a squatting posture . . . His comrade took a slipper from the bag which he had with him and struck it on the ground as if he were in a fury. The slipper rose and hovered over the squatted man's neck which it began to strike; meanwhile, he descended gradually till he sat with us. The sulṭān said to me, "The squatting man is the disciple of the owner of the slipper"[12] . . . [On another occasion], when we landed on this small island [Goa] we met in it a jogi who was leaning against the wall of . . . a house of idols. He stood in the space between two of the idols and bore marks of self-mortification. We addressed him, but he gave no answer. We looked around to see if he had food with him, but we saw none of it. While we were looking around, he uttered a loud cry and at his cry a nut of the coco fell before him which he handed over to us. We were astonished at this and offered him gold and silver coins, which he did not accept. Then we gave him provisions which he rejected . . . We withdrew. I was the last of my comrades to go out. He pulled at my coat and as I turned round to him, he gave me ten dinars.[13]

In 1473, an anonymous Arabic-language travel account describes the self-mortifications of a yogi whom its author had seen on two occasions. Worthy of note is the fact that the yogi in question is a "true" hermit, practicing his extreme asceticism in wild isolation, rather than in public marketplaces or temple precincts.

And in the land of India there are those dedicated to wandering in the jungles and the mountains, meeting few other people, and subsisting on herbs and fruits of the jungles. They place around the penis a ring of iron, in order to prevent interaction with women. Some of them are naked, and others expose themselves to the sun, facing it with no other covering than a tiger skin. I once saw one of these men, just as I have described, and I departed. I returned after sixteen years, and I saw him in the same condition. So I marveled how his eyes were not ruined from the heat of the sun.[14]

Amīn ibn Aḥmad Rāzī, the author of the 1594 Persian-language geography entitled *Haft iqlīm* (*The Seven Climes*), quotes the lost work of a certain Muhammad Yūsuf Harawī in describing the practices of yogis. His narrative includes a graphic account of a yogi's stoic self-immolation in the presence of a king, as well as of the practice of breath control.

Furthermore, in India there is a group of jogis who practice breath control. They carry their unremitting persistence to the point that they take but a single breath every few days, and they consider this skill the height of perfection and the greatest achievement. Among them was a jogi in Benares who had this quality, such that once Khān-i Zamān kept him buried underground for over ten days. Another time he had him spend nearly twelve days under water, like an anchor, but he experienced no harm or injury at all.[15]

Maḥmūd bin Amīr Walī Balkhī, a Central Asian adventurer from Balkh, traveled through India for seven years, between 1624 and 1631. Balkhī was not the member of any religious order, and undertook his journey out of curiosity alone, which may explain his intolerance toward much of what he saw. He is, however, one of the rare foreigners to allude to the power of yogis to enter into foreign bodies. Early in his narrative, he describes the yogis he met on the edge of the Indian subcontinent at Gor Khattrī, a Nath Yogī establishment associated with Bāba Ratan (Rattannāth[16]) located near Peshawar, around the year 1625. There, in a deep underground cell within that yogi establishment, he came upon

some "Exercise-worshippers" sitting in a circle [who] engage themselves in the practices of *jog*, which means "controlling of breath" . . . In this building which is like a temple, a person of the sect of *jogis* sat as the Preceptor . . . The asceticism and endeavour of all these consists in holding back their breath; and seeking the sight in [their mind's] eye, they keep sitting with legs tucked under their bodies. In the view of this wayward sect, the sign of perfection is to take just one breath from one morning to another. When this stage is reached by one of this arrogant sect, they seat him in the position of Preceptor, and the previous Preceptor (*murshid*) is put alive inside one of those buildings the doors of which are sealed with stone and brick so that he dies within a few days, and going to Hell is ensnared in eternal Perdition. In this matter their belief is that since he held perfection in controlling the breath, he would, therefore, transfer his soul to a better body than what he possessed before and return to this world again. [The Sultans] and the Hindus of that area have assigned pensions and lands for the maintenance of this accursed group so that they obtain their subsistence without delay or difficulty . . . There I also saw an old *jogi* among them whose beard was so long that nearly half a yard of it was dragged over the ground and his moustache encircled his neck like the rope of Satan; he had thirteen knots on each side of it. His act of asceticism consisted in this that he had tied to himself a chain weighing ten maunds so that he was unable to move.[17] At that time, a wealthy Hindu, Ram Das by name, passed that way. After offering him a sum of one thousand rupees, he desired that that self-opinionated person should free himself from the [iron] chain. But his answer was that there had to be a generous person who would give twenty thousand rupees and so secure his release from that beard and moustache.[18]

In 1519 the future Mughal emperor Bābūr had also visited this monastery, which he calls Gurh Kattri in his *Bābur Nāma*. Two of his later successors, Akbar and Jahāngīr as well as the Sikh founder Guru Nānak , are said to have visited the monastery as well.[19] There yogis showed Nānak several wonders, making deerskins and stones to fly through the air and causing a wall to run about.[20] Bābur makes no mention of meeting any yogis there but does describe its underground chambers, in which he says there was "an unending pile of hair and beard that had been clipped there,"[21] a puzzling observation given the fact that yogis are generally identified by their great mass of matted hair. However, the yogis whom Ibn Baṭṭūṭa saw in private audience with the Sultan of Delhi were also described as having recently shaven heads, and the late sixteenth-century Carrera distinguishes between "Jogis" who wear their hair long and other wandering ascetics, the "Beragis" (Vairāgīs), whose heads are shaven.[22]

d. Yogis in European Travel Narratives

Most European travel narratives agree on a certain number of points, in no small part because many of these authors copied from one another. These include the yogis (semi)nude appearance with ashes on their bodies and matted hair; their practice of carrying and blowing horns; their iron implements and weapons; and their proclivity for begging alms. In some cases, the European accounts also refer to yogi practices or lifestyles that differentiate them from other types of renouncers as well as from brahmins: yogis are sometimes said to eat meat, bury their dead, and marry or have other sorts of congress with women. With a single exception, Europeans never describe yogis as meditating or adopting any of the postures or techniques of *haṭha yoga*. Most often, they are said to maintain a standing position, with arms upraised for so long that their limbs begin to atrophy. Among the many forms of torment to which they are described as subjecting their bodies, the practice of stopping the breath for fantastic periods of time (as opposed to the measured regulation of the breath, *prāṇāyāma*, enjoined in the various scriptures), sometimes in underground crypts, is often mentioned.

This emphasis on the complete stoppage of the breath may not be a matter of hyperbole. On the one hand, prior to the thirteenth century, the great bulk of prescriptive references to yogic breath control do in fact speak of the practice in terms of stopping the breath. This was the case in the BhG (4.29) and YS (2.49), as well as in the twelfth-century AY, which contains a long discussion of the supernatural powers realized by holding

Figure 6.1 Underground crypt. Detail of a lithograph from Jean-Baptiste Tavernier, *Six Voyages*, ca. 1676.

the breath for up to twenty-four years![23] On the other, the Europeans may have been confused by what they were told they were seeing. The term *samādhi*, which in the context of *pātañjala yoga* means "pure contemplation," has been employed by the Nāth Yogīs with reference to the tumuli beneath which their dead are buried in the ground (figs. 6.1, 6.2). We are fortunate to have an image (fig. 6.1), drawn or commissioned by the mid-seventeenth-century French gem merchant Jean-Baptiste Tavernier, which is identified as "a form of a grave where several times during the year a *Fakir* withdraws . . . nine or ten days without drinking or eating."[24] While Tavernier does not mention the stoppage of breath in the underground crypt, many other Europeans, down into the twentieth century, do so. In the end, what these travelers may have thought was a crypt for living yogis may have been a tumulus for dead yogis—whom their fellow yogis would nevertheless have reported as "living" in the state of suspended animation that the term *samādhi* can connote.

Marco Polo gives the earliest European account of yogis in his description of the kingdom of Maabar in western India, which he passed through in the closing years of the thirteenth century. In his narrative, he speaks of two "yogi religions." His description of the first makes them out to be alchemists, and I quote this account in the following section. The second appears to conflate Śaiva yogis—who smear themselves with cow dung ash and venerate idols—with Jain ascetics, whose nudity and fastidious avoidance of harming life, down to worms and insects, he also details. He concludes his account with a description of a test of sexual dispassion that the *ciugui* are forced to undergo, in which *devadāsīs*, temple prostitutes, appear to be involved. This type of practice is mentioned in several later European accounts, which will be discussed below.

They have their regulars, who live in the temples to serve the idols. And when they are named to a rank or office [in the temple], they are tested in the way that I will describe to you. So, when one of them dies and another has been chosen to take his place, they keep him for a time in their temple and make him live their life. Then, they bring maidens there to offer them to the idol, and have these maidens touch this man who looks after the idols. They touch him here and there over several parts of his body, they

Figure 6.2 Photo of Nāth Yogī tumuli, Mṛgasthali, Kathmandu, ca. 1990. Photo by David Gordon White.

embrace him and kiss him, and subject him to the greatest pleasure in the world. This man, who is touched in this wise by the maidens, if his member does not change in any way, but remains as it had been before the maidens touched it, then he is considered to be good and pure, and they keep him in their Order. As for another man whom the maidens touch, if his member moves and stands up, they in no way keep him, but drive that incontinent one out from the company of monks, saying that they do not wish to keep a lewd man.[25]

Following Marco Polo, one of the earliest Europeans to give an account of India's yogis was the Bolognese traveler Ludovico di Varthema. He describes his meeting, in the first years of the sixteenth century, with a wandering "king of the Ioghe" of Gujarat, whose "country" was constantly at war with Sultan Maḥmūd of Cambay (the modern-day Khambat). His followers

generally carry a little horn at their neck; and when they go into a city they all in company sound the said little horns, and this they do when they wish alms to be given to them . . . Some of them carry a stick with a ring of iron at the base. Others carry certain iron dishes which cut all round like razors, and they throw these with a sling when they wish to injure any person; and, therefore, when these people arrive at any city in India, everyone tries to please them; for should they even kill the first nobleman of the land, they would not suffer any punishment because they say that they are saints.[26]

Some one hundred twenty years later, the Italian traveler Pietro della Valle also describes a meeting with a person whom the Portuguese (who had taken control of much of the west coast of India from its Muslim lords in the mid-sixteenth century) called the "king of Gioghi." His "kingdom" of Cadira (Kadri), located outside of Mangalore, lay over seven hundred miles to the south of Khambat. However, as we will see shortly, Varthema's traveling king of the Gioghi ranged as far down the Malabar Coast as Calicut, which is situated well to the south of Kadri. Della Valle's king of the Gioghi was very likely a Nāth Yogī.

At length I went to see the King of the Gioghi, and found him employed in his business after a mean sort, like a Peasant or Villager. He was an old man with a long white beard, but strong and lusty; in either ear hung two little beads, which seemed to be of Gold, I know not whether empty or full, about the bigness of a Musket-bullet; the holes of his ears were large, and the tips much stretched by the weight; on his head he had a little red bonnet, such as our Galley-slaves wear, which caps are brought out of Europe to be sold in India with good profit. From the girdle upwards he was naked, onely he had a piece of Cotton wrought with Lozenges of several colours cross his shoulders; he was not very low, and, for an Indian, of colour rather white then otherwise. He seemed a man of judgement, but upon tryal in sundry things, I found him not learned. He told me, that formerly he had Horses, Elephants, Palanchinoes [palanquins], and a great equipage and power before, Venk-tapà Naieka [Venkatappa Nāyak] took away all from him, so that now he had very little left . . . I was told by others that he is call'd Batniato [Batināth?]; and that the Hermitage and all the adjacent places is call'd Cadirà [Kadri].[27]

Duarte Barbosa, a Portuguese sailor and adventurer who traveled through the lands bordering on the Indian Ocean during the first decades of the sixteenth century, provides a description of, as well as a putative explanation for, the self-mortifications of the yogis. In his description of the Kingdom of Dely (i.e., the Sultanate of Delhi), Barbosa observes that

[t]his kingdom is of the Moors, and has a Moorish king, a great lord; and in former times this kingdom was of the Gentiles [Hindus], of whom there are still many who live amidst the Moors, with much vexation. And many of them nobles and respectable people, not to be subject to the Moors, go out of the kingdom and take the habit of poverty, wandering the world; and they never settle in any country until their death; nor will they possess any property, since they lost their lands and property, and for that go naked, barefooted, and bareheaded; they only cover their nakedness with coverings of brass . . . Besides this, they carry very heavy chains round their necks, and waists, and legs; and they smear all their bodies and faces with ashes. And they carry a small brown horn at their necks, after the fashion of a trumpet, with which they call and beg for food at the door of any house where they arrive: chiefly at the houses of kings and great lords and at the temples; and they go many together, like the gypsies. They are accustomed to stop very few days in each country. These people are commonly called jogues, and in their own speech they are called zoame [swami], which means servant of God . . . They wear their hair without ever combing it, and made into many plaits, wound round the head. And I asked them many times why they went in this fashion. And they answered me, that they wore those chains upon their bodies as penance for the sin which they committed for allowing themselves to be captured by such bad people as the Moors, and that they went naked as a sign of dishonour, because they had allowed their lands and houses to be lost, in which God brought them up. [28]

Ralph Fitch, a merchant from London who traveled through the southeastern part of the subcontinent in 1585, describes the self-mortifications of the "Iogues" he encountered in a grove in the vicinity of the Catholic church of St. Thomas near Gingee.

The heat forced us to the Grove (though consecrated to an Idoll) the Iogues ambitiously affecting applause by tolerating in the open Court the most intolerable Sun-beames, sometimes at noone (but sildome) interposing a thinne Vaile. Wee saw one of them, which being shut up in [an] Iron Cage had there made himselfe perpetuall prisoner, so walking with his head and feet out, that he never could sit nor lie downe. At the sides of the Cage hung forth an hundred Lampes, which at certaine times four Iogues [who were] his attendants lighted.[29] [Fitch also notes the presence of yogis at the monumental Śiva temple at Chidambaram:] "The next day wee went away, which we had not done, had any told us of a strange Spectacle that day there to bee seene, which wee after came certainly to know. There were twentie Priests which they call Iogues, which threw themselves from the highest pinnacle of the Temple for this cause."[30]

Fitch is mistaken in identifying his Iogues as Chidambaram temple priests, given the fact that this office has been perennially filled there by Smārta Brahmins. Suicide by leaping from high places was most closely associated throughout this period with the yogi devotees of Bhairava.[31] Pietro della Valle, who traveled through India between 1623 and 1625, also identified "Gioghi" as temple officiants at a Mahadeu (Mahādeva) temple in Ahmedabad (Gujarat).

Within the Temple continually stand many naked Gioghi, having onely their privities (not very well) cover'd with a cloth; they wear long Hair dishevel'd, dying their Foreheads with spots of Sanders [sandal paste], Saffron, and other colours suitable to their superstitious Ceremonies. The rest of their bodies is clean and smooth, without any tincture or impurity; which I mention as a difference from some other Gioghi, whose Bodies are all smear'd with colours and ashes, as I shall relate hereafter. There is, no doubt, but these are the ancient Gymnosophists so famous in the world; and, in short, those very Sophists who then went naked, and exercis'd great patience in sufferings, to whom Alexander the Great sent Onesicritus to consult with them . . . The assistant Gioghi give every one that comes to worship some of the Flowers, which are strew'd upon, and round about the Idols; receiving in lieu thereof good summs of Alms.

Della Valle is careful to differentiate these temple officiants from other yogis, "of more austere lives."

Coming out of this Temple, and ascending up the wall of the City, which is hard by, we beheld from that height the little River call'd Sabermeti [Sabaramati], which runs on that side under the walls without the City. Upon the bank thereof, stood expos'd to the Sun many Gioghi of more austere lives, namely such, as not onely are naked, like those above describ'd, but go all sprinkled with ashes, and paint their bodies and faces with a whitish colour upon black, which they do with a certain stone that is reduc'd into powder like Lime: Their Beards and Hair they wear long, untrim'd, rudely involv'd, and sometimes erected like horns. Painted they are often, or rather dawb'd with sundry colours and hideous figures; so that they seem so many Devils, like those represented in our Comedies. The ashes wherewith they sprinkle their bodies are the ashes of burnt Carkasses; and this, to the end they may be continually mindful of death. A great crew of these with their Chief or Leader, (who conducts them with an extravagant banner in his Hand, made of many shreds of several colours, and to whom they all religiously obey) sat by the Rivers side. [32]

Writing at Cambay a short time thereafter, Della Valle continues:

Their Habitations are the Fields, the Streets, the Porches, the Courts of Temples, and Trees, especially under those where any Idol is worshipt by them; and they undergo with incredible patience day and night no less the rigor of the Air than the excessive heat of the Sun, which in these sultry Countries is a thing sufficiently to be admir'd. They have spiritual exercises after their way, and also some exercise of Learning, but . . . both their exercises of wit and their Learning, consist onely in Arts of Divination, Secrets of Herbs, and other natural things, and also in Magick and Inchantments, whereunto they are much addicted, and boast of doing great wonders. I include their spiritual exercises herein . . . because by the means of those exercises, Prayers, Fastings, and the like superstitious things, they come to Revelations; which indeed are nothing else but correspondences with the Devil, who appears to, and deludes them in sundry shapes.[33]

Tavernier, whose many voyages took him to India and Indonesia throughout the mid-seventeenth century, had many meetings with yogis and fakirs. His general observations on their ways are found in his account of a voyage that took him from Surat, on India's west coast, to Batavia (Sumatra).

It is estimated that there are in India 800,000 Muhammadan *Fakirs* and 1,200,000 among the idolaters, which is an enormous number. They are all vagabonds and idlers, who blind the eyes of the people by a false zeal, and lead them to believe that all that escapes from their own mouths is oracular . . . There are other [Hindu] *Fakirs* who are clad in garments of so many pieces of different colours that one is unable to say what they are. These robes extend half way down their legs and conceal the miserable rags which are beneath. These *Fakirs* generally travel in company, and have a chief of superior over them who is distinguished by his garment, which is poorer and made up of more pieces than those of the others. He, moreover, drags a heavy iron chain which he has attached to one leg; it is 2 cubits long and thick in proportion. When he prays it is with great noise; this is accompanied by an affected gravity, which attracts the veneration of the people. However, the people bring him and his followers food to eat, which they serve him in the place where he stops, generally some street or public place . . . There are *Fakirs* who have more than 200 disciples, whom they assemble by the sound of the drum and a horn similar to the horns of our huntsmen. When marching, the disciples carry their standard, lances, and other arms, which they stick in the ground near their master when he halts to rest anywhere.[34]

Tavernier returns to his topic a few pages later, providing a mythological origin account of the fakirs, as the descendents of the demon-king Rāvaṇa, a notion that is echoed in a number of other travel narratives:[35]

As for Rávana, he passed the remainder of his days as a poor *Fakir*, his country being altogether ruined by the troops of Rámá . . . and it is from this Rávana that this incredible number of *Fakirs*, whom one sees in peregrination throughout India, have taken their origin . . . These *Fakirs* ordinarily travel in troops, each of which has its Chief or Superior. As they go perfectly nude, winter and summer, always lying on the ground, and since it is sometimes cold, the young *Fakirs* and other idolaters who have most devotion, go in the afternoon to search for the droppings of cows and other animals, which are dried by the sun, with which they kindle fires . . . Wealthy idolaters consider themselves happy, and believe that their houses receive the blessings of heaven, when they have as guests some of these *Fakirs*, whom they honour in proportion to their austerity; and the glory of a troop is to have some one in it who performs a notable penance. [36]

Following this, Tavernier plunges into a detailed cataloging of the various yogi or fakir penances to which he had been privy, which are illustrated in a remarkable lithographed montage of yogis arrayed in small groups around a cluster of shrines in a forest setting. The illustrated penances include what Tavernier takes to be a live burial, as well as yogis standing suspended by a cord for years at a time; maintaining arms upraised for years at a time, during which the fingernails grow to incredible lengths; and so on.[37] Tavernier's insight is a valuable one: that for the yogi orders in this period, prodigious acts of self-mortification were the means by which their wandering bands could attract notoriety and alms. The sole scriptural precedents for these practices of self-mortification are the biographies of figures like the Buddha and Mahāvīra, who were never considered to be yogis. Self-mortification was a fashion of Mughal times that has endured down to the present, a fashion that continues to be exploited by "yogi entrepreneurs" in the crowded South Asian beggars' market.

Already in the seventeenth century, yogis, fakirs, and traveling magicians were grouped together (perhaps because they were the same people)

Figure 6.3 Indian Fakirs; detail of a lithograph from Jean-Baptiste Tavernier, *Six Voyages*, ca. 1676.

as performers of the illustrious "Mango Trick," with its scenario of bodily dismemberment, and also hathayogic techniques.[38] This transition is documented *in media res* by John Fryer, an English physician who traveled through Persia and India between 1672 and 1681.

[A]t the Heel of these [Fakiers] may be reckoned the *Bengal* Juglers, Mountebanks, and Conjurers, as also the Dancing People; these are Vagrants, that travel to delude the Mobile [mob] by their *hocus Pocus* tricks (living promiscuously like our Gypsies); among whom I saw one who swalloed a Chain . . . and made it clink in his Stomach. . . Others presented a Mock-Creation of a Mango-Tree . . . [At this point, Fryer describes a "trick" which, on the basis of his description, could only have been a demonstration of the hathayogic practice of *uḍḍīyāna bandha*] [B]y Suction or drawing of his Breath [one of these] so contracted his lower Belly, that it had nothing left to support it, but fell flat to his Loins, the Midriff being forced into the *Thorax*, and the muscles of the *Abdomen* as clearly marked out by the stiff Tendons of the *Linea Alba*, as by the most accurate Dissectio could be made apparent, he moving each Row like living Columns by turns.[39]

Fryer's general account of the "Fakiers," whom he identifies with the "Jougies," is particularly damning.

A *Fakier* is a holy man among the *Moors*; for all who Profess that Strictness (for such it should be) they esteem them Sacred; and though before apparent Traytors, yet declaring for this kind of life, and wearing a patch'd Coat of a Saffron Colour, with a pretended careless neglect of the World, and no certain Residence, they have Immunity from all Apprehensions, and will dare the *Mogul* himself to his Face: of this Order are many of the most Dissolute, Licentious, and Prophane Persons in the World, committing Sodomy, will be drunk with *Bang* [*bhāṅg*, a drink made from cannabis], and Curse God and *Mahomet* . . . these People Beg up and down like our *Bedlams* with an Horn and Bowl, so that they enter an House, take what likes them, even the Woman of the House; and when they have plaid their mad Pranks, away they go to repeat them elsewhere. Under this Disguise many pass as Spies up and down, and reap the best Intelligence for the benefit of the Prince that Employs them.[40]

The French traveler Jean de Thevenot, who traveled across north India in from 1666 to 1667, describes the behaviors of "Faquirs" he observed at Halabas (Allahabad), which was, then as now, a principal Hindu site of pilgrimage.

It many times happens that a *Banian* [a Hindu or Jain merchant] will give a *Faquir* considerable sums of Money, because he has the boldness to place himself near his Shop, and to protest that he'll kill himself if he be not supplied with what he demands: the *Banian* promises fair, and brings it him; but because the fantastical *Faquir* understands that several have contributed to that Charity, he openly refuses it, and goes about to execute what he hath threatened, if the *Banian* alone not furnish the Sum; and the *Banian* knowing that some *Faquirs* have been so desperate as to kill themselves on like occasion, is so much a fool as to give it out of his own Purse, and to give the others back again what they had contributed. These *Faquirs* . . . cannot be better compared (if you'll set aside the Penances they do) than to *Gypsies*, for their way of Living is like theirs; and I believe their Profession has the same Original, which is *Libertinism* . . . They are many times to be seen in Troops at *Halabas*, where they Assemble for Celebrating of some Feasts (for which they are obliged to wash themselves in the *Ganges*) and to perform certain Ceremonies. Some of them as do no hurt, and show signs of Piety, are extreamely honoured by the Gentiles; and the Rich think they draw down blessings upon themselves, when they assist those whom they call Penitents. Their penance consists in forbearing to eat for many days, to keep constantly standing upon a Stone for several weeks, or several months; to hold their Arms a cross behind their head, as long as they live, or to bury themselves in Pits for a certain space of time. But if some of these *Faquirs* be good Men, there are also very [many] Rogues among them; and the *Mogul* princes are not troubled, when such of them as commit violences are killed. One may meet with some of them in the Countrey stark naked with Colours and Trumpets, who ask Charity with Bow and Arrow in hand; and when they are the strongest, they leave it not to the discretion of Travellers to give or refuse. These wretches have no consideration even for those that feed them; I have seen some of them in the *Caravans*, who made it their whole business to play tricks, and to molest Travellers, though they had all their subsistence from them. Not long since I was in a *Caravane*, where some of these *Faquirs* were, who took a fancy to suffer no body to sleep: All night long they did nothing but Sing and Preach; and instead of banging them soundly to make them hold their peace (as they ought to have been served) the Company prayed them civilly, but they took it ill; so they doubled their Cries and Singing, and they who could not Sing, laugh'd and made a mock of the rest of the *Caravane*. These *Faquirs* were sent by ther Superiours, into I know not what Countrey full of *Banians*, to demand of them Two thousand *Roupies*, with a certain quantity of Rice and *Mans* [maunds] of Butter; and they had orders not to return without fulfilling their Commission. This is their way all over the *Indies*, where by their *Mummeries*, they have accustomed the Gentiles to give them what they demand, without daring to refuse.[41]

Giovanni Francesco Gemelli Careri, an Italian nobleman who journeyed around the world in the late seventeenth century, passed part of the year 1695 in India, where he encountered "Fachires" at Broach, on the coast of Gujarat.

I went to see the Tree of the *Gentils*, we call *Banians* [banyans], under which they have the Pagods of their Idols, and Meet to perform their Ceremonies . . . Under this Tree and in the neighboring Parts there are many Men, who have enjoyn'd themselves and do perform such dreadful Penances, that they will seem fabulous to the Reader, and impossible to be gone through without the assistance of the Devil. You may see one hanging by a Rope ty'd under his Arms and to the Tree, only his Feet touching the Ground, and the rest of his Body being Bow'd, and this for many Years without changing Place or Posture Day or Night. Others have their Arms lifted up in the Air, so that in process of Time there grows such a Stiffness or Hardness on the Joynts that they cannot bring them down again . . . In short, they are in such Postures, that sometimes a Man can scarce believe his Eyes, but fancies it is an Illusion. Thus they continue Naked all Seasons of the Year, with vast long Hair, and Nails grown out, expos'd to the Rain, and burning Rays of the Sun, and to be stung by Flies, whom they cannot drive away. Other *Fachires* who take that Employment supply their Necessities of Eating and Drinking. These Penitents are not asham'd to go quite Naked, as they came out of their Mothers Wombs.[42]

Later in his narrative, Careri gives a general account of the "Jogis."

The Gentils pay so great a Respect to these Penitents, that they think themselves happy, who can Prostitute Daughters, Sisters, or Kins-women to their Leudness, which they believe lawful in them; and for this Reason there are so many Thousands of Vagabond *Fachires* throughout *India*. When the *Fachires* meet with *Baraghis* (which is another sort of Penitents, differently habited, with their Hair and Beard shav'd) they Fight desperately. They never Marry, and Eat in the Houses of all Sects, except the *Polias* [Pulayans, an outcaste group]. They go into the Kitchin, and take what they will, tho' the Master be not at Home. They come together like Swine by beat of a Tabor, or at the blowing of a Horn, and march in Companies with Banners, Lances and other Weapons, which, when they rest, they lay down by their Master . . . [T]hese vagabonds . . . are look'd upon as Saints, and Live a loose Life, with the Priviledge of committing any Crime their Brutality suggests.[43]

François Bernier, French physician to the Mughal court and man of letters who lived in India throughout the entire final decade of the seventeenth century, also gives a long and quite balanced account of the "Fakires" and "Jauguis," condemning those who are ostentatious in their practices of self-mortification or lacking in true piety and professing guarded admiration for those whose quiet meditation affords them a light-filled vision of the divine.

Among the infinite numbers & great diversity of Fakires, or, as one would say, of the Poor, Dervishes, Monks, or Gentile Santons of the Indies, there is a significant number who have a sort of Order, in which there are Superiors, & in which they take a kind of Vow of Chastity, Poverty & Obedience, & who lead a life that is so strange, that I do not know if you will be able to believe it. Ordinarily, these are the people known as Jauguis, which means united with God; one sees throngs of them entirely naked seated or lying down day & night on ashes & generally beneath one of the great trees, as are found on the banks of Talabs or ponds, or in the Galleries surrounding their . . . Idol Temples . . . In many places I have seen them holding an arm & sometimes both of them raised and perpetually extended over their heads, & who had nails twisted around their fingertips that were longer, according to my measurements, than half the length of my pinky finger; their arms were stunted and thin . . . No Fury from Hell is as horrible to behold as these naked people with their black skin, mass of hair, stumps of arms . . . and long, twisted nails. In the countryside, & especially in the lands of the Rajas, I have often met bands of these naked Fakires . . . I saw a famous one of their number named Sarmet, who had lived for a long time in Delhi and who went about naked in the streets, & who would in the end have preferred to have his throat cut than to put on clothes, [in response to] some of the threats and promises that Aureng-Zebe [Aurangzēb] had made to him. I have seen many among them who, out of devotion, went on long pilgrimages entirely naked and weighted down with great iron chains, like those that are put on the feet of Elephants . . . Sometimes I have only seen brutality & ignorance in them, who appeared to me to be more like trees that occasionally bestirred themselves from one place to another than creatures with reason; or, I have regarded them as people intoxicated by their Religion; but . . . without the slightest degree of true Piety; I have also said to myself that their lazy, slothful & non-conformist beggarly lives must be in some way attractive [to them] . . . Among all of these [types] that I have just described, there are some whom people believe to be truly enlightened Saints & perfect Jaugues, or people perfectly united with God. These are people who have completely forsaken the world, & who normally secret themselves to some distant Garden, like the Hermits, without ever coming into the City . . . & people believe that they live by the grace of God during their fasts & in perpetual austerities, & especially when they are lost in meditation; I say lost, because they go so deep into it that they pass hours at a time in an enraptured state of ecstasy, their outer senses having no function, & (what would be most admirable if it were true) seeing God himself as a sort of very white, very bright and inexplicable light, with a joy & a satisfaction no less ineffable, followed by a disdain & a total detachment from this world, if it is true what one of those who claimed to be able to enter into such a state of ecstasy & and had done so several times, said of it.[44]

2. Yogis as Alchemists, Healers, Poisoners, and Purveyors of Aphrodisiacs

The earliest foreign traveler to speak of the yogis per se was Marco Polo, who in his account of his travels through India in the waning years of the thirteenth century includes mentions of the "ciugi," whom he says he met on the Malabar Coast.

[T]hey have among them regulars and orders of monks who are called *ciugi*, and who certainly live more than all the others in the world, for they live for one hundred to two hundred years . . . And again I tell you that these *ciugi* who live as long as I have said, eat that which I shall explain . . . I tell you that they take quicksilver and sulphur and mix them together with water and make a drink out of it. Then they drink it and they say it lengthens their life. They do so twice a month . . . and without mistake those who live as long as I have said make use this drink of sulphur and quicksilver.[45]

The late seventeenth-century Englishman John Marshall, whose "Joguee-Eckbar" narrative was reproduced in chapter one, also speaks of the longevity of the "Fuckeers," as well as their knowledge of botanical and mineral elixirs.

It is reported by these Moores and Hindus that upon the Hills by Casmeere [Kashmir] and also by Neopoll [Nepal] . . . there are people [who] live to 4 and 500 yeares of age. They can hold in their breath and ly as it were dead for some yeares, all which time their bodies are kept warme with oyles, &ca. They can fly, and change souls with each other or into any beast. They can transforme their bodies into what shapes they please and make them so plyable that [they] then can draw them thorow a little hole, and wind and turne them like soft wax. They are mighty temperate in diet . . . At first they use themselves to hold in their breaths for a very little time when young, and so more by little and little . . . Tis very credibly reported that yearly some Fuckeers come from said [Kashmir] hills to Pattana, where they wash in Ganges, [who] by their eating only herbs and roots, have such reamidies in Physick as hath not been heard of. They have at some times given powders to people when they have come, that have recovered them when almost dead, and hath in few howers made them as well as ever.[46]

Also in the late seventeenth century, Sujān Rāi Bhandārī mentions the alchemical practices of the "jogis," echoing an early Sufi account by the Chishtī saint Burhān al-Dīn Gharib (d. 1337) of a yogi alchemist whom the saint believed was supplementing his potions with drugs and the assistance of spirits.[47] In his description of a yogi encampment he saw in the vicinity of the Khajuraho temples (Madhya Pradesh) in the same period, Ibn Baṭṭūṭa also speaks of the expertise of the "jogis" in preparing life-enhancing medicinal pills.

[At] Kajarrā [Khajuraho] . . . there is a great pond about a mile in length . . . At the four corners of the pond are cupolas in which live a body of the jogis who have clotted their hair and let them grow so that they become as long as their bodies . . . Many Musalmans follow them in order to take lessons from them. It is said that whoever is subjected to a disease like the leprosy or elephantiasis lives with them for a long period of time and is cured by the permission of God. It was in the camp of the Sulṭān Tarmashīrīn, king of Turkistan, that I saw these people for the first time. They were about fifty in number, and a subterranean cavern had been dug for them wherein they lived and would not come out except to satisfy their needs. They have a kind of horn, which they blow at daybreak, at the close of the day and at nightfall. And their whole condition was extraordinary. One of them made pills for Sulṭān Ghiyāṣ-ud-dīn al-Dāmghānī, king of Ma'bar—pills which the latter was to take for strengthening his pleasure of love . . . Their effect pleased the sulṭān, who took them in more than necessary quantity and died. He was succeeded by his nephew Nāṣir-ud-dīn, who honored this jogī and raised his rank.[48]

One may view images of Khajuraho yogis, inscribed in the stone of the 954 CE Lakṣmaṇa Temple, where four of the yoga-born sons of Brahmā are depicted as emaciated figures with matted hair, carrying distinctive regalia and what appear to be weapons of the type described by Varthema: razor-edged disks flung by a sling (fig. 5.4).

Another consumer of aphrodisiacs of yogi manufacture was the Mughal emperor Aurangzēb (fl. 1659–1707), who, in an imperial edict, offered his continued protection to a Nāth Yogī monastery and its land grants in the Punjab in exchange for treated quicksilver.[49] Nearly as notorious as Aurangzēb was for their destruction of Hindu temples, the Khaljis, the fourteenth- to fifteenth-century rulers of Malwa in western India, also took an interest in yogi expertise in these matters. Certain members of the Khalji aristocracy of Malwa, attracted by the longevity promised by yoga, are said to have lived with yogis in order to acquire the yogic techniques and drugs used for mastering the health of the body as well as prowess in sexual practices.[50] Of course, improperly prepared mercury is a poison, which is a possible explanation for the demise of the king of Ma'bar as recounted by Ibn Baṭṭūṭa, and one cannot help but wonder whether the king's nephew, who rewarded the Khajuraho yogi for his deadly aphrodisiacs, had not colluded with the yogi in administering the king's overdose. That yogis were notorious for their knowledge of poisons is corroborated by Pietro della Valle, who attributes the sudden death of an elephant who had eaten a leaf from a forbidden tree in a temple at Surat to their arts.[51] If the Khajuraho yogi had intentionally poisoned the king of Ma'bar, he was not the last of his ilk to take part in a palace intrigue of this sort. In his account of the "miraculous" rise to power of Mān Singh of Jodhpur, Colonel James Tod related that

> Bheem Singh [Bhīm Singh, one of Mān Singh's fellow junior princes] had destroyed almost every branch of the blood-royal . . . and young Māun [Mān Singh] . . . was reduced to the last extremity, and on the eve of surrendering himself and Jalore to this merciless tyrant, when he was relieved from his perilous situation. He attributed his escape to the intercession of the high priest of Marwar, the spiritual leader of the Rathors. This hierarch bore the title of divinity, or *Nāt'hji*: his praenomen of Deo or Déva was almost a repetition of his title; and both together, Deonāt'h, cannot be better rendered than by "Lord God." Whether the intercession of this exalted personage was purely of a moral nature, as asserted, or whether Raja Bheem was removed from this vain world to the heaven of Indra by other means less miraculous than prayer is a question on which various opinions are entertained . . . [Referring to Deonāt'h:] Such prophets are dangerous about the persons of princes, who seldom fail to find the means to prevent their oracles from being demented. A dose of poison, it is said, was deemed a necessary adjunct to tender efficacious the prayers of the pontiff; and they conjointly extricated the young prince from a fate which was deemed inevitable, and placed him on the regal cushion of Marwar. The gratitude of Mān Singh knew no limits . . . and the throne itself was exalted when Deonāt'h condescended to share it with his master.[52]

Deoraj, the founder of the Rāwal dynasty of Jaisalmer, was raised to power through the intervention of a yogi possessed of a vessel containing the alchemical elixir (I will return to his story shortly). It will also be recalled that the yogi in the Joguee-Eckbar account related by John Marshall first alighted on a balcony of the Mughal emperor Akbar's palace while flying through the air with the aid of a pill of mercury held in his mouth. According to Marshall's sources, Akbar's reaction to the yogi's presence in his harem was not anger, but rather curiosity: he wanted the yogi to teach him some of his tricks. This account is of a piece with Akbar's general fascination with yogis, which began in 1584. In the words of Badauni, an orthodox critic of what he perceived to be the emperor's apostasy,

> [h]is majesty [had] built outside the town [of Agra] two places for feeding poor Hindus and Musalmans, one of them being called *Khairpura*, and the other *Dharmpurah* . . . As an enormous number of *Jogis* also flocked to this establishment, a third place was built, which got the name of *Jogipurah*. His majesty also called on some of the Jogis, and gave them at night private interviews, enquiring into abstract truths; their articles of faith; their occupation . . . the power of being absent from the body; or into alchemy, physiognomy, and the power of omnipresence of the soul. His Majesty even learned alchemy, and showed in public some of the gold made by him. On a fixed night, which came once a year, a great meeting was held of Jogis from all parts. This night they called *Sivrat* [Śivarātrī]. The emperor ate and drank with the principal Jogis, who promised him that he should live three or four times as long as ordinary men.[53]

3. Yogis as Soldiers, Spies, Long-Distance Traders, Power Brokers, and Princes

Akbar's support of the yogis had not always been so unconditional, as a well-known account of a pitched battle between "yogis" and "sannyasis," which took place at Ambala (Punjab) in 1567, would indicate. Chancing upon a skirmish between two groups of armed ascetics, the young emperor threw his support to the losing sannyasi side, and the yogis were quickly routed and their leader beheaded.[54] The battle that Akbar observed prior to his decisive intervention appears not to have been fought at the behest of any royal or imperial commander, in which case it is appropriate to conclude that this was a settling of scores between rival orders of warrior ascetics, a not unusual occurrence for the times.[55] As was noted in chapter two, irregular armies of yogis were a perennial fixture in the Mughal-era South Asian military labor market. For the most part, these fighting yogis were drawn from two different sorts of labor pools. On the one hand, there were the yogi orders and monastic institutions themselves, where "in the slave culture implicit in Śaiva warrior asceti-

Figure 6.4 Nāth Yogī; wall painting from *haveli* of Sukhdev Das Ganeriwala, Mukundgarh, Rajasthan, circa 1880. Photo courtesy of Francis Wacziarg and Aman Nath.

cism . . . hundreds and even thousands of men would be inculcated from youth in complete submission to and incorporation in the social world of the *akhara* [confraternity] at the head of which stood the master/commander."[56] On the other, there were the fighting gangs of north Indian villagers who often adopted yogi personas when recruited by warlords and other dealers in military manpower to fight as mercenaries in the armies of the highest bidders.[57]

The fluidity of the Mughal-era north Indian military labor market, and of the ease with which fighters changed allegiances and identities, emerges with great clarity in a description that Tavernier gives of a group of *Fakirs* that he met near Sidhpur in Gujarat in the 1640s.

The following day I had another experience, which was a meeting I had with a party of *Fakirs* or Muhammadan *Dervishes*. I counted fifty-seven of them, of whom he who was their Chief or Superior had been master of the horse to Sháh Jahángir [the Mughal emperor], having left the court when Sultan Boláki, his grandson, was strangled by the order of Sháh Jahán [the Mughal emperor who succeeded Jahángir in 1628] his uncle . . . There were four others who, under the Superior, were Chiefs of the band, and had been the first nobles of the court of the same Sháh Jahán . . . The other *Dervishes* had for their sole garment a cord, which served as a waistband, to which there was attached a small scrap of calico to cover . . . the parts which should be concealed. Their hair was bound in a tress about their heads, and made a kind of turban. They were all well armed, the majority with bows and arrows, some with muskets, and the remainder with short pikes, and a kind of weapon which we have not got in Europe. It is a sharp iron, made like the border of a plate which has no centre, and they pass eight or ten over the head, carrying them on the neck like a ruff. They withdraw these circles as they require to use them, and when they throw them with force at a man, as we make a plate to fly, they almost cut him in two. Each of them had also a sort of hunting horn, which he sounds, and makes a great noise with when he arrives anywhere . . . During the same evening, after they had supped, the Governor of the town came to pay his respects to these principal *Dervishes*.[58]

Later in his travels, Tavernier describes the conditions that likely drove persons from rural poverty into military service or renunciation (or more likely, both, as the occasion required).

You may see in India whole provinces like deserts, from which the peasants have fled on account of the oppression of the Governors. Under cover of the fact that they [the Governors] are themselves Muhammadans, they persecute these poor [Hindu] idolaters to the utmost, and if any of the latter become Muhammadans it is in order not to work any more; they become soldiers or *Fakirs*, who are people who make profession of having renounced the world, and live upon alms; but in reality they are all great rascals.[59]

In the decades following Tavernier, Thevenot and Careri also note the fact that the yogis they encountered were often armed.[60] It is clear from the historical record that South Asia's warrior ascetics belonged to, or were recruited into, a significant number of different orders (*sampradāya*s, *panth*s), confraternities (*ākhāḍa*s), or lodges (*maṭh*s). What is unclear, and insoluble, are the shifting uses of terminology among these orders, particularly given the relative paucity of internal documentation. So, for example, Marshall, in the late seventeenth century, states that "these Jougees or Sunossees (Sannyasis) are Fuckeers (fakirs) or beggars, which are Hindu."[61] However, on the basis of Mughal and British records, as well as travelers' accounts from the period, it is possible to draw up a list of the terms that were unsystematically employed for them. These include Sannyasi, Bairagi (*Vairāgī*), Naga, Gosain, Kāpālika, Fakier, and Jogi. The term Gosain, in particular, was employed both emically and etically for Vaiṣṇavas and Śaivas,[62] while Naga ("naked") was a term appropriately applied to the many military confraternities within the Vaiṣṇava and Sannyāsī (later termed *Dasnāmī*) orders.[63] Śaṅkara, who is traditionally identified as the founder of the Sannyasi orders, is described in his hagiographies, many of which date from the Mughal period, as having confronted and defeated legions of Kāpālikas in gruesome and magical combats.[64]

As has been noted, in many accounts from between the fourteenth and twentieth centuries, yogis become conflated with the Nāth Yogīs, who have been referred to frequently in these pages. While there were likely many renouncers and ascetic warriors who referred to themselves as yogis, and far more who were referred to as such by outsiders, the Nāth Yogīs are the sole organized religious order in South Asia to have referred to themselves as a yogi order and to have employed the term yogi as a title—even if, by the mid-twentieth century, the pejorative overtones of the term yogi were such that Digvijaynāth, the *mahant* of the Nāth Yogīs' principal monastery at Gorakhpur, eschewed the term *Kānphaṭa* ("Split-Eared") *Yogī* in favor of *Nāth*.[65] A power to be reckoned with militarily as well as politically and economically, the Nāth Yogīs were, together with the various Naga orders, among the most readily recognizable institutional faces of militant asceticism in the Mughal period. Time and again, they figure in accounts of the fighting, trading, and power-brokering ascetics with whom the Mughals, British, and other imperial or royal powers transacted.

We see traces of an early British learning curve, when the emerging masters of India commissioned the *Silsila-i jūgiyān* (*Order of Jogis*), a Persian-language survey of yogis, in the year 1800. While this work employs the term *jogi* in a generic sense, it also reserves the specific sense of the term for the Nāth Yogīs.

The first person who was the originator of this path was Mahādeva, and after him Gorakhnāth and Machhindirnāth [Matsyendranāth]; they established and made current the rules of yoga. The leaders of this sect were people who lived in ancient times with revelations and miracles, powerful ones who held the choices of life and death, old age and youth. They had the power to fly to heaven, to disappear from sight, and similar wonders and marvels. Those who may be found in our day practice the following external religious path: whenever a jogi takes a disciple, he cuts open the side of the disciple's ear and inserts a ring of whalebone (Hindi *kachkara*) or crystal or something else of this type, because with this sign of splitting the ear, he can never again become worldly. They practice ordering of the heart, restraint of breath, and bodily discipline. Smearing their bodies with ash, they wear a hat, patchwork cloak, colorful clothes, and an iron bar on the neck. They spend their youth in servitude. Some are attendants of Bhairoṅ [Bhairava] and Hanuman, and these do not refrain from consuming meat and wine; their retreats are mostly devoted to immorality and debauchery.[66]

In spite of this piece of evidence to the contrary, "jogi" remained throughout this period the most widely employed term for an itinerant and often warrior ascetic, whether unaffiliated with any particular sect or affiliated with a sect other than the Nāth Yogīs. So, for example, a Nirvāṇī Ākhāḍa chronicling of that confraternity's 1664 battle against Aurangzēb's army at Benares lists the name of one of its heroic warriors as Jogindra, the "Lord of Yogis."[67] The fifteenth-century *Ṕṛthvirāja Raso*, an Old Hindi chronicle-legend that relates events that transpired in the twelfth century, states that the Rajput prince Rāwal Samar Singh of Mewar was addressed as "Jogindra" (*yogīndra,* the "Lord of Yogis"). Another Rajput warrior, identified as the leader of the Janghāra clan, is described as a terrifying human form of the yogi god Śiva.

The Janghára, appearing like the Lord of Yogis, was armed with a dagger; his ensigns were an axe in his hand and a tall trident, and a leather cloak. With a coil of matted hair on his head, and a musical horn, and ashes of cow dung, he was altogether like Hara (Śiva), the destroyer of all. With a powerful voice he cried and from his odd eye he scattered masses of fire. On his throne he might be seen (sitting) in the midst of his own congregation (of Yogis), bearing on his head the moon with the nectar of the immortals.[68]

The early sixteenth-century Italian traveler Ludovico di Varthema, whose first meeting with the "King of the Gioghi" was related above, had a second encounter with this same figure in Calicut (Kerala) in 1605 or 1606, where the local Muslim ruler had paid the sum of one hundred ducats to the king, "who was at that time in Calicut with three thousand Gioghi," in payment for their killing of two suspected Portuguese spies. The yogis' assassination of the two men culminates in an act of cannibalism. As Varthema tells it,

the king of the Gioghi immediately sent 200 men to kill the said two Christians, and when they went to their house, they began by tens to sound their horns and demand alms. And when the Christians . . . began to fight . . . these Gioghi cast at them certain pieces of iron which are made round like a wheel, and they threw them with a sling and struck Ioan-Maria on the head and Pierre Antonio on the head, so that they fell to the ground; and then they ran upon them and cut open the veins of their throats, and with their hands they drank their blood.[69]

Tavernier, who claims to have personally slain a fakir who had "run amuck" in Java, offers another account of the ferocity of a yogi warrior. Debarking at Suwali, the port of Surat (Gujarat), from a pilgrim's ship returning from Mecca in 1642, a fakir "had no sooner said his prayers than he took his dagger and ran to attack some Dutch sailors . . . Before they saw him and were able to put themselves on their defence, this maddened *Fakir* wounded seventeen, of whom thirteen died."[70] Descriptions of Naga warriors portray them as a terrifying force, with faces and bodies painted to give them an unearthly appearance and emitting blood-curdling yells and rushing at their enemies in a drug-induced frenzy. Experts in hand-to-hand combat (the primary sense of the term *ākhāḍa* is "wrestling ground"), these warrior ascetics also carried bows, arrows, shields and swords, cakras (the disks described in Varthema's account), and, as weaponry became more sophisticated, firearms.[71] A poem spuriously attributed to Kabīr (d. 1518), but undoubtedly dating from after the 1526 Battle of Panipat when such weapons were first used on a large scale on Indian soil, describes the "yogis" in the following terms:

Never have I seen such yogis, Brother.
They wander mindless and negligent
Proclaiming the way of Mahādeva.
For this they are called great *mahants.*
To markets and bazaars they bring their meditation,
False siddhas, lovers of *māyā.*
When did Dattātreya attack a fort?
When did Śukadeva join with gunners?
When did Nārada fire a musket?
When did Vyāsadeva sound a battle cry?
These make war, slow-witted.
Are they ascetics or archers?
Become unattached, greed is their mind's resolve.
Wearing gold they shame their profession,
Collecting stallions and mares and
Acquiring villages they go about as tax collectors.[72]

When the military labor market was at its height in the Mughal period, these yogi warriors who fired muskets, traded in horses, and occasionally drank the blood of their enemies at the behest of their "kings"—whether monastic *yogīrāj*s, warlords, or actual landed rulers—numbered in the hundreds of thousands. For several centuries, the routes taken by military marauders, pilgrims, and long-distance traders were one and the same, as a flood of adventurers, mercenaries, and voluntary and "compulsory renouncers"[73] ebbed and flowed across the Indian subcontinent. The activities of yogi spies, or of spies dressed in the garb of yogis, is well documented in prescriptive works such as the AŚ, as well as in travelers' accounts. Fryer notes that they "reap the best Intelligence for the benefit of the Prince that Employes them," while the seventeenth-century Italian physician and soldier of fortune Niccolao Manucci provides a long narrative of how he was nonplussed by a yogi spy.[74] Two hundred years later, in a reversal of roles, an Englishman plays the yogi spy in Rudyard Kipling's *Kim*.

In the eighteenth century, with Mughal power on the wane, "Gosain" corporations of Hindu ascetics and mercenaries emerged as a mainstay of the north Indian economy, combining pilgrimage, plunder, and transport of goods over a vast territory.[75] These ascetic traders were not alone, however, in their efforts to dominate trade in the area: the British East India Company, seeking monopoly control over all commerce in the region, was their increasingly powerful rival. As Chris Bayly has noted,

> [t]he Gosain corporations of Hindu ascetics and mercenaries . . . also emerged as some of the most powerful trading people of the century. When the British encountered them on one leg of their great nomadic cycles of pilgrimage and trade on the borders of Bengal, they were seen as marauders and robbers. But in upper India . . . they helped maintain the urban economy and the growing external trade . . . The ascetic institutions . . . were able to provide their own protection regardless of established political authority. This came in two forms. First, there was the Gosains' sheer military power, which they sold to other magnates such as the Nawab of Awadh, and used to protect their own trade routes and revenue grants. Second, their capacity to protect, in part, derived from their status as holy men "divorced from the world." . . . Fear of physical and spiritual retribution together had a salutary effect . . . Their armed pilgrimage cycle from the Hardwar fair through the main towns of the Gangetic plain to Bengal and Jagannath-Puri provide[d] a "ready-made trading network." Using a combination of military and commercial power, they could link up areas of supply and demand in the stable and productive zones and provide their own protection on the difficult routes between them. Their corporate savings and investment habits enabled them to form and direct the uses of capital with great efficiency. By the 1780s, ascetics had become the dominant money-lending and property-owning group in Allahabad, Benares, and Mirzapur . . . Their privileged social status in Hindu society provided the ascetics with unique advantages. They received dispensations from full customs rates in some king-

Figure 6.5 Detail from the illustrated manuscript, *Hamzanama (The Stories of Hamza): Mesbah the Grocer Brings the Spy Parran to His House*, Islamic, Mughal period (1526–1858), Akbar (1556–1605), sixteenth century. Ink, watercolor, and gold on cotton, 27 7/8 x 21 5/8 inches. Courtesy of the Metropolitan Museum of Art, Rogers Fund, 1924 (24.48.1). Image © The Metropolitan Museum of Art.

doms, since it was illogical to take from holy men if the justification of rule was to protect *dharma*; it was also dangerous.[76]

Documentation from fourteenth- to nineteenth-century sources indicates that the Nāth Yogīs were particularly powerful in the political economies of western Indian kingdoms, as well as in the Himalayan and sub-Himalayan zones of the subcontinent. At first traders in horses and elephants, they expanded their economic positions through land grants, control of temples and pilgrimage sites, warfare, and, eventually, banking.[77] With expanded wealth came enhanced political influence, which saw the Nāth Yogīs successfully outmaneuvering their political and monastic rivals to place their chosen princes on the thrones of Marwar, Nepal, and several lesser principalities and to increase their influence over the rulers of several other kingdoms. In Nepal, the Śāh Dynasty—whose two-hundred-forty-year rule was brought to an end in the spring of 2008—was founded through an alliance between a young Gurkha prince named Pṛthivinārāyaṇ Śāh and a Nāth Yogī named Bhagavantnāth. Legends of the prince's conquest change the name of the prince's wonder-working advisor to Gorakhnāth, who, together with the goddess Taleju, was the titulary deity of the Śāh dynasty. In recent decades, his name figured on the Nepali one rupee coin.[78]

As with yogis, the power, protection, and even the jurisdiction of fakirs over specific kingdoms and territories, both in life and after death, was a feature of South Asian Islamicate polities even before the advent of the Mughals. The ideology of this role was explicitly formulated in a 1349 CE epic poem glorifying the Muslim rulers of India, the *Futūḥ al-salāṭīn* (*Conquests of the Sultans*) of Khwaja 'Abd al-Malik Iṣāmī. Arguing that the Chishtī Shaikh Nizām al-Dīn's (Nizāmuddīn) physical presence there had been responsible for the wellbeing of the capital city of Delhi and all the territories of the Delhi Sultanate for so long as he had lived there, he wrote:

In every realm although there is a ruler (*amir*)
He is under the protection of a *faqir*;
Although the rulers may be at the head of the kingdom
The *faqirs* are the drinkers (averters) of disaster of the kingdom.[79]

An early nineteenth-century bardic account of the foundation of the Rāwal dynasty of Jaisalmer by Deorāj (b. 836 CE) epitomizes the combination of supernatural power and political shrewdness that were the bywords of yogi strategy, in western India in particular, and casts new light on the literary theme of the prince who becomes a yogi already seen in the legends of Bhartṛhari and Gopīcand. The young prince, whose entire family had been massacred by his Baraha enemies, has seen his landholdings reduced to

> such a quantity of land as he could encompass by the thongs cut from a single buffalo's hide . . . Deoraj immediately commenced erecting a place of strength . . . Soon as the Boota chief heard that his son-in-law was erecting, not a dwelling, but a castle, he sent a force to raze it. Deoraj despatched his mother with the keys to the assailants, and invited the leaders to receive the castle with his homage; when the chief men, to the

number of a hundred and twenty, entering, they were inveigled, under pretence of consultation ten at a time, and each party put to death and their bodies thrown over the wall. Deprived of their leaders, the rest took to flight. Soon after, the prince was visited by his patron, the Jogi who had protected him from the Barahas, and who now gave him the title of *Sid* [siddha, a perfected yogi]. This Jogi, who possessed the art of transmuting metals, lodged in the same house where Deoraj found protection on the massacre of his father and kindred. One day, the holy man had gone abroad, leaving his *jirghir-kantha* or "tattered doublet," in which was the *Rascoompa* [*rasa kumbha*] or "elixir-vessel," a drop of which having fallen on the dagger of Deorāj and changed it to gold, he decamped with both, and it was by the possession of this he was enabled to erect Deorawul [his fortress]. The Jogi was well aware of the thief, whom he now came to visit; and he confirmed him in the possession of the stolen property, on one condition, that he should become his *chela* and disciple, and, as a token of submission and fidelity, adopt the external signs of the Jogi. Deoraj assented and was invested with the Jogi robe of ochre. He placed the *moodra* [*mūdra*, the thick earrings worn by Nāth Yogīs and other Śaiva orders] in his ears, the little horn [*siṅgnād*] around his neck, and the bandage (*laṅgoti*) about his loins; and with the gourd (*cupra*) in his hand, he perambulated the dwellings of his kin, exclaiming *Aluc! Aluc!* [*Alakh! Alakh!*]. The gourd was filled with gold and pearls . . . the *teeka* [*ṭīkā*] was made on his forehead, and exacting that these rites of inauguration should be continued to the latest posterity, the Baba Ritta (for such was the Jogi's name) disappeared.[80]

This synergy between a king and a yogi is also seen in the literary subgenre of the "yogi romance," a marked departure from the portrayals of yogis found in the earlier Sanskrit-language literature reviewed in chapter one. The themes of these romances flowed from two sources. There were the vernacular *bārahmāsa* song tradition, in which village wives separated from their husbands (*virahinīs*) poignantly sang of their longing for their return. More significant was the political reality of princes taking initiations with yogis and thereby being ritually transformed into yogis. Fusing the two, yogi romances, written exclusively by Muslim authors, transformed the humble itinerant yogi soldiers of the *bārahmāsa* songs into princes, who, in order to win the hands of their beloveds and prove themselves as rulers and men, underwent extended periods of exile and adventure as in yogi guise. In some respects, these were Mughal-era variations on the old epic theme of the forest exile of the Pāṇḍavas or of Rāma and his family, with an overlay of the Sufi mysticism also found in the poetry of the Punjabi Sufi Bullhe Śāh (d. 1758), who employed folklore motifs to portray the archetypal yogi as the mystical beloved.[81] Vāriṣ Śāh, another Sufi from the Punjab, used the same device in his 1766 CE poem *Hīr Rāñjhā*. Here Rāñjhā, the princely hero of the piece, is made a yogi when he is initiated by Bālnāth at Tilla, the Nāth Yogī monastery shrine located in the Salt Range, in the Jhelum district of the Punjab. In his yogi disguise, he escapes with his beloved Hīr, who had been forced into marriage with Saidā, an ally of her family's clan. A plague of fire that takes Saidā's life convinces Hīr's family to accept her marriage to Rāṅjhā, but they poison her before the wedding can take place, and Rāṅjhā dies of grief. The two lovers are at last united in death.[82]

By far the most celebrated work of this genre is the 1540 CE Avadhī-language *Padmāvat* of Malik Muhammad Jāyasī, who was himself a Sufi in the Chishti order.[83] Padmāvatī, the poem's eponymous heroine, is a beautiful princess of Siṃhala, whose parrot falls into the hands of King Ratansen of Chittor. Learning from the parrot of the princess's beauty, Ratansen puts on the garb of a yogi as he departs, together with his yogi entourage, for the distant and inaccessible fortress of Siṃhala. In the meantime, Padmāvatī has fallen in love with Ratansen, who has penetrated her mind through his yogic powers. In the portion of the narrative that describes the mutual longing of the yet to be united lovers, two terms are used interchangeably for Ratansen's ascetic journey: *yog* and *viyog*. *Yog* is, of course, his arduous self-mortifying struggle to realize union with his beloved. As for *viyog*, this is employed by Jāyasī as a synonym for *virah*, the "love in separation" of Sanskrit poetics. No sooner has the spark of *virah* ignited his longing for Padmāvatī than does he put on the yogi's garb, together with his companions. This includes the ochre robe, matted locks, ash-besmeared body, little horn, *rudrākṣa* rosary, tattered cloak, thick earrings—as well as a *dhadharī* (more commonly referred to as a *gorakh-dhāndhā*), a contraption made of iron rings and rods which may have served as a weapon.[84]

> Barons and princes, they all became *viyogis*; sixteen thousand young princes all became yogis . . . The army of yogis began to move. With all of them clad in ocher robes, it was as if a carpet of [turmeric-colored] *ṭesu* flowers had been spread over twenty leagues![85]

Ratansen's yoga ends in his union with his beloved, but it is a fleeting one. Condemned to die by impalement, he cries out his eternal love for Padmāvatī. Saved in extremis by Śiva, he marries his beloved, and the two return to Ratansen's capital of Chittor, where he is later slain in battle. Padmāvatī commits *satī* on his pyre and the two are united forever in death. Significantly, when he is taking leave of the queen mother to depart in his quest for the hand of Padmāvatī, Ratansen evokes the names of the exemplary kings-turned-yogis Bhartṛhari and Gopīcand, whose stories were summarized in chapter one.[86] There can be no question that Jāyasī's work was something more than an account of a prince who becomes a yogi, after the fashion of hundreds of thousands of young men seeking a fast track to fame and fortune in this period. It was also an allegory of yogic ascent in the Hindu sense of the term (with Jāyasī mystically identifying Padmāvatī with the supreme guru Gorakhnāth at one point), as well as of the mystic journey of the soul in the Sufi sense of the term.[87]

4. Yogis and the Indian Peasantry

We have already noted the demographic reality of peasant males taking on yogi personas for the periods in which they were on the road, active in trade or the military labor market. We have also seen that full-fledged members of the yogi orders were a highly mobile group, as in the case of Varthema's "king of the Ioghe," whom he saw, together with his entourage of two hundred fighters, over a thousand miles from his base in Gujarat. While roving bands of yogis would have been highly visible to foreign travelers, many of their number, whether individuals or members of established orders, would have nonetheless had a base of operations, to which they returned periodically (if only in the rainy season), in their home villages or in monasteries scattered across the South Asian countryside. This reality is expressed in a Hindustani saying: "[A man who is] a yogi in his own village, [is] a [deified] siddha in the next."[88] Throughout much of the north and west of the Indian subcontinent, one finds countless instances of immortalized yogis, siddhas, *pīrs*, and *shaikh*s being venerated in their *samādhi*s, shrines, and tombs as the demigod protectors of the specific locale in which they had been active in life. This role does not begin at death, however, but is rather the continuation of a relationship with a locality that had begun in life. Drawn mainly from peasant stock, these were men of the people who spoke the language of the people and administered to their needs in exchange for alms. As Vaudeville has noted,

> [i]t was their particular form of yoga, blended with the cult of the indigenous *devīs* ("mother goddesses"), which, propagated by innumerable wandering *jogīs*, formed the foundation of popular religion and culture in all of these western regions [of the subcontinent] . . . Here, the brahmin appears as a negligible quantity, even mocked

and abused by the Siddhas and Nāth Yogīs who, part preachers and part magicians spoke the language of the people and were objects of universal admiration and trust . . . The tantric yoga current and the Sufi current, which were at first parallel, tended to converge in the minds of the masses, and one is tempted to conclude that this confusion, carefully cultivated by the Sufis themselves, likely constituted an important if not decisive factor in the rapid conversion of a certain number of artisan and pastoral castes to Islam.[89]

Down to the present day, yogis are called upon as exorcists, driving away disease and evil spirits with their traditional tools: spells, amulets, salves, blood, red ochre, threads, earrings, drums, ashes, fire-tongs, peacock feather fans, and so on. As is so often the case, they are also notorious for using the same powers to destructive ends in the practice of black magic and sorcery.[90] Their powers extended to control over nature as well, with yogis reputed, down to the present day, for their capacity to control wild animals and serpents,[91] divert hailstorms and other natural calamities,[92] and ensure fertility in livestock as well as human women. Throughout the regions where they exerted their political influence over earlier centuries, deceased Nāth Yogīs have continued to be venerated by local populations for their powers of protection and fertility. As was noted in chapter one, even following the disappearance of these kingdoms of yore, the divinized guru Gorakhnāth and his yogi disciples continue to be venerated at communal village fire pits (*dhūnī*s) in sub-Himalayan Kumaon, Garhwal, and western Nepal, where they are made to possess spirit mediums in nighttime vigils (*jāgar*s). Gorakhnāth and other illustrious Nāth Yogīs are worshiped in shrines across northern and western India.[93]

a. Yogis and Sexuality

The special relationship between yogis and women was noted by a number of European travelers, beginning with Marco Polo,[94] and including Marshall, Tavernier, Thevenot, and Careri in the seventeenth century and Sonnerat in the eighteenth.[95] As Marshall describes it,

the Hindoo women will go to them and kiss the Jougee's yard. Others ly somthing upon it when it stands, which the Jougees buy victuells with; and severall come to stroke it, thinking there is a good deale of virtue in it, noe [nothing] having gone out of it as they say, for they ly not with women nor use any other way to vent their seed . . . They have often given things which never failed to cause women to bring forth, and also to make old men quite dried up to be able to ly with young women everie night for some years together, without any injury done to their bodies.[96]

Careri also links this practice to the yogis' presumed powers of fertility: "[o]thers run a ring through their prepuce, and hang a little Bell to it; which, when the silly barren Women hear, they run to see, and touch him, hoping by that means to become Fruitful."[97] The power of ascetics to retain their seed, and thereby to possess superhuman sexual energy, is a South Asian commonplace, as epitomized by the divine Śiva, the erotic ascetic of the ever-erect phallus. Among human ascetics, it would appear that the proof of their practice is a flaccid member, and Nirad Chaudhuri is correct when he argues that the hordes of naked Nagas who parade before crowds of women at the Kumbhā Melā bathing festivals retain their sexual composure due to their rigorous practice.[98] But like Śiva, the sexual powers of yogis are not always transmitted in latent form. Referring to the sorts of tantric *yoginī* practices that were evoked in the tale of *Bhairavānand Yogī*, Della Valle reports that

> there are certain Immortal, Spiritual, Invisible Women, to the number of forty, known to them and distinguisht by various forms, names, and operations, whom they reverence as Deities, and adore in many places with strange worship . . . by long spiritual exercises [a Gioghi] can come to have an apparition of any of these Women, who foretells him future things, and favours him with the power of doing other wonders, is accounted in the degree of perfection; and far more if he happen to be adopted by the Immortal Woman for her Son, Brother, or other Kinsman; but above all, if he be receiv'd for a Husband, and the Woman have carnal commerce with him; the Giogho[99] thenceforward remaining excluded from the commerce of all other Women in the world, which is the highest degree that can be attain'd to; and then he is call'd a spiritual Man, and accounted of a nature above humane, with promise of a thousand strange things, which for brevities sake I pass over. Thus doth the Devil abuse this miserable people.[100]

Concerning yogis' relations with human women, Della Valle observed that "[t]hey marry not, but make severe profession of Chastity at least in appearance; for in secret 'tis known many of them commit as many debaucheries as they can." This assessment is shared by the eighteenth-century compiler of the "Chritro Pakhyan" anthology, which attests to the general climate of debauchery among the yogis of the Punjab.[101] Similar opinions are found among the British two centuries later, as well as a Pakistani villager in the 1990s: "They take whatever pleases them—especially pretty girls."[102] While there can be no doubt that the yogis' reputation for lechery was not without foundation, it should also be noted that sexual *yoginī* practices were among the most powerful techniques employed by tantric practitioners for the realization of *siddhi*s. When, following the sexual initiation that makes him a yogi, a tantric practitioner succeeds in his *yoginī* practice, that supernatural feminine entity grants him the powers he seeks.[103] In this respect, Della Valle's report is quite accurate.

Nāth Yogī hagiography is rife with accounts of barren women who, through a yogi's boon—often in the form of grains of rice or a pinch of ash which the woman in question is made to eat—father children who are replicas or "incarnations" of themselves. Nāth Yogī legend casts Gorakhnāth himself as such a child, born from a woman to whom his later guru Matsyendranāth had offered a gift of rice.[104] Edmund Demaitre, a freelance author writing in the 1930s gives the following secondhand report of the powers of the yogis' sexual prowesses:

> One of my friends from the Central Provinces told me that a *sadhu* visited his village periodically, offering his favors with extraordinary zeal to the brave village women who, for reasons that I ignore, seemed to lose their minds as soon as the *sadhu* made an appearance. Far from concealing the aim of his visit, the *sadhu* said to anyone who had ears to hear that, thanks to his "intervention," he could not only cure sterility but also guarantee the birth of male offspring. When my friend asked him for an explanation of his miraculous faculties, the *sadhu* asserted with all possible seriousness that far from being a mere ascetic, he was in fact the reincarnation of [Śiva's] Bull Nandi. Under these circumstances, it was easy to understand why husbands, who are normally so jealous in India, incited their wives to spend a few hours in the company of the reincarnated divinity, whose embodiment, having fulfilled his pleasant duty, received payment in coin for his small services.[105]

b. Yogis in the World, in Their Own Words

Mastnāth, the eighteenth-century Nāth Yogī revered as the founder of the Asthal Bohar monastery in Rohtak (Hariyana), was, according to his hagiography, the *Śrī Mastnāth Carit* (ŚMC), born through the miraculous intervention of Gorakhnāth, who projected himself into an infant body at the request of a childless couple.[106] The ŚMC is a precious source, inasmuch as it is a fully emic yogi *exemplum* and account of the ways of the Nāth Yogīs. Written in the late nineteenth or early twentieth century by a Nāth Yogī from the monastery that Mastnāth had himself founded, the work interweaves historical events with perennial Nāth Yogī mythemes.[107] The picture that emerges is one of a wonder worker who treats the high and the humble in the same evenhanded way, granting boons to those who respect his powers and bringing down plague and disaster upon those who do not.[108] His life is a succession of miracles, his "supernatural play" (*adbhūt līlā*), which take him from the village of his childhood to the pinnacle of imperial power near the end of his hundred-year life. As a child, he shows himself to be possessed of multiple bodies, simultaneously appearing in his village to play with his friends and tending his flocks in the forest.[109] He causes rain to fall in a time of drought and supplies milk to an entire wedding party from a single inexhaustible pail.[110] After he has taken initiation and begun his life as a wandering yogi, Mastnāth begins to attract people from village and city alike, all of whom are hungry for his miracles. He restores the body of a limbless, hunchback women to wholeness, causes the blind to see, bestows three sons on an elderly barren woman, and raises cows from the dead.[111]

As Mastnāth's reputation spreads, he moves from rural into urban contexts, where he finds himself in competition with members of other religious orders for economic resources and symbolic capital, that is, alms. In these situations, in which Mastnāth and his band of disciples are treated as "outsiders," his supernatural displays take on a darker tone. A visit to a town in the "country of Patiala" brings him into conflict with the abbot of a nearby monastery who prohibits the townspeople from offering alms of any sort to the yogi and his disciples. Mastnāth has his disciples dump piles of tattered cloth in the middle of the town and orders the townspeople to take that rubbish to the monastery or suffer the consequences. The abbot of the monastery refuses to allow the rags in his establishment, and the townspeople are compelled to carry everything back to the town center. There a group of boys sets about tightly wrapping strips of the cloth into balls, with which they begin to play games. As they throw the balls at one another, each child begins to cough up blood, and returning to their homes, they spread fever and plague, the fruit of Mastnāth's curse. The town is entirely depopulated, and the monastery that was responsible for the townspeople's stinginess reduced to a state of penury.[112] This pattern repeats itself in another town, where a *sādhu* named Devīdās, jealous of Mastnāth's renown, demands that the wild yogi perform a miracle before he will advise the townspeople, who are loyal to him, to offer alms to him and his entourage. With the exception of one person, whom Mastnāth spares, the hapless townspeople obey their local holy man; and the miracle that Mastnāth then performs is to set fire to the entire town. When Devīdās is unable to quell the flames, the townspeople rebuke him and rue the day they had taken him into their midst. They repent and venerate Mastnāth, who then restores the town he had reduced to ashes.[113]

Following this, Mastnāth decides to play a prank on Sūrat Singh, the king of Bikaner. At a great feast that the king has thrown for the brahmins of his kingdom, Mastnāth has one of his disciples place a camel bone into the communal soup pot. When the brahmins see the camel bone, they are enraged, and the king seeks to find the culprit who has spoiled his feast. His soldiers bring Māstnāth before the king, who demands an explanation. However, when a brahmin brings the incriminating evidence before Mastnāth and the king, all see that the bone has been turned to gold. The citizens of Bikaner flock to worship the wonder-working yogi, who transforms melon seeds into pearls, enriching all who have come to him. Urging him to remain in his kingdom, Sūrat Singh offers Mastnāth a land grant and his protection, which the yogi accepts.[114]

5. The Yogis and the British

One of Mastnāth's most remarkable acts takes the form of an *ex cathedra* prophecy, concerning no less a person than the Mughal emperor himself. After he has arrived in the imperial capital of Delhi, word of Mastnāth's miracles reach the ears of Śāh Ālam II, the ruler of a failing empire. Curious to meet the naked yogi, the emperor sends an emissary to him, bearing the gift of a shawl with which to cover his nakedness in a city where Aurangzēb's dress code remains in effect. Mastnāth refuses both the gift and an audience in the imperial court by casting the shawl into the fire of his *dhūnī*. Unaccustomed to such cheekiness, the emperor sends his man back to Mastnāth, demanding that his shawl be returned, at which point the yogi pulls shawl after shawl out of his *dhūnī*, mockingly asking the emissary to identify the one he had given to him previously. Hereupon, Mastnāth instructs his assembled disciples to "play their horns upside down" (*ulaṭā nād bajāo yogī*), saying that by doing so, they will be empowered to foretell, even determine, the future. Then, at the urging of one of his disciples, Mastnāth begins to prophesy the fall of the Mughal Empire "on the third day of the month." Together with his disciples, he then departs for Chittor, in Rajasthan, and immediately events in Delhi take a turn for the worse. The emperor is blinded by a warlord named "Gulam Kokar" (Gulam Qādir) and, as Mastnāth's hagiographer tells it, "the English made the Kingdom of Delhi their own."[115] In fact, Gulam Qādir's blinding of Śāh Ālam II occurred in 1788, with the British taking over what little remained of his empire in 1803.

While the extent to which yogis were players on India's greatest political stage is debatable, they were, as has been noted, capable of effecting regime change in a number of other South Asian kingdoms, a fact that was not lost on the British. From the time they established their first outpost at Fort William (the future Calcutta), the British were forced to acknowledge the ascetic orders as their economic, political, and even moral rivals for the wealth, power, and soul of India. As we have seen, the Nāth Yogīs were especially powerful in those regions of South Asia that had remained relatively independent of Mughal and British rule in the latter half of the second millennium, serving as power brokers in several kingdoms. Whereas the Mughal emperors—not only Akbar and Aurangzēb, but also Bābur and Jahāngīr[116]—took a pragmatic approach to the powerful ascetic orders, conferring with and often negotiating with them for aphrodisiacs, military manpower, and the circulation of goods and services, the attitudes and policies of the British toward them were generally adversarial.

As they did in every aspect of their empire-building ventures, the British sought to know their enemies through good intelligence. In the late eighteenth and early nineteenth centuries, however, there was a paucity of information on yogis, which may explain in part the East India Company's and later the imperial government's failure to chart an effective policy toward them. Clearly, the British found the yogis to be unworthy rivals, considering their lifestyles to be repugnant and deficient vis-à-vis their own Eurocentric standards of morality and decorum. In this, they placed them at the lower end of a spectrum, only a rung or two above the abominable Thugs and Aghoris[117] and far below the orders that had embraced the *bhakti*-style religiosity that was so congenial to their own Victorian-age spirituality.[118] A source that the British considered significant in the early years of their presence in India was Sujān Rāi Bhandārī's *Khulāṣat-ut-Tawārīkh* (*The Essence of Histories*), a Mughal imperial gazetteer completed in 1695–96. Near the turn of the eighteenth century, the British had this work translated into Urdu by the chief Hindustani instructor at Fort William, following which they used it as a standard text for training officials of the East India Company in the Hindustani language. Its chapter on the Indian fakirs, which includes descriptions of Sannyasis, Jogis, Beragis, and Nānak Panthīs, makes the following observations concerning the yogis:

> They spend their time day and night in recalling their God to memory, and, by holding in their breath (*ḥabs-i dām*) for a longtime, live for hundreds of years; by reason of their strict austerities (*riyāḍat*, i.e., yoga), their earthly garment (i.e., their body) is so light, that they fly in the air and float on the water, and by the power of their actions, they can cause their souls to flee away whenever they please, assume whatever form they like, enter the body of another person, and tell all the news of the hidden world; from putting copper in ashes, they can turn it into gold, and by the power of their magic, fascinate the hearts of the whole world; they can make a sick man, on the point of death, well in one moment, and can instantaneously understand the hearts of

other people, and their custom is to have no cares or acquaintances; it is true that "the jogi is no man's friend;" and although, in magic and sorcery, alchemy and chemistry, "Sannyasis" have great skill, still the art of the jogis in these matters is more widely famous.[119]

In the course of the same decade, John Gilchrist, the Scottish pioneer of Hindustani lexicography, commissioned the poets Kazim 'Ali and Lalluji Lal to undertake translations of two other texts, in this case from Braj bhāṣa into Hindustani, once again for the Hindustani-language instruction of Company agents. Here the works in question were none other than the *Baitāl Pachīsī* and the *Siṅhāsan Battīsī*, the Hindustani versions of the VP and SD, those medieval tales, surveyed in chapter one, in which dastardly yogis of the ilk of Kṣāntaśila figured so prominently. The translators' introduction to the 1801 Fort William edition of the *Siṅhāsan Battīsī*, the first mass-produced publication of the work in the Hindustani language (and in both the Devanagari and Arabic scripts), made the following argument for its pedagogical usefulness:

Now in the reign of Emperor Shah Alam, by order of the illustrious John Gilchrist, in the year 1215 A.H., 1801 A.D., the poet Kajim Ali, whose pen name is 'Javañ,' with the aid of the poet Lallu Ji Lal, wrote it in the general current idiom of the people of India—so that it should be simple for the learning and understanding of the new sahibs, and they should understand everyone's daily speech, and know the language of Hindus and Muslims, urban and rural, high and low, and not be dependent on others' explanations.[120]

Forty years later, E. B. Eastwick, the editor of an English-language interlinear translation of the 1805 Fort William edition of the *Baitāl Pachīsī*, made a similar argument, noting in his introduction that "the *Baitál Pachísí* has been selected as one of the test-books in the examination of candidates for the Military service of the Hon. East India Company, and is admirably adapted for this purpose. The frequent recurrence of the ordinary forms of colloquial expression makes it also an excellent class-book for the use of Students of Hindústáni."[121] While it is the case that the Hindustani language of these two compendia is pellucid and uncomplicated and would have enabled agents of the Company and the Empire to comprehend and converse with much of the north Indian populace, one cannot help but wonder about the extent to which their contents might have contributed to the strong antiyogi bias of the British in India.

To be sure, the British had other reasons to despise the yogis, given the fact that in places like Jodhpur, the capital of the Rathor Rajput kingdom of Marwar, the yogis had completely stymied them. I have already quoted a portion of Tod's acerbic account of the Nāth Yogī Deonāth's (Āyas Dev Nāth's) strategic intervention in raising young prince Mān Singh to the throne.[122] Tod concludes his narrative with the following jeremiad:

Lands in every district were conferred upon the Nāt'h, until his estates, or rather those of the church of which he was the head, far exceeded in extent those of the proudest nobles of the land; his income amounting to a tenth of the revenues of the state. During the few years he held the keys of his master's conscience, which were conveniently employed to unlock the treasury, he erected no less than eighty-four *mindurs* [temples] . . . with monasteries adjoining them, for his well-fed lazy *chelas* or disciples, who lived at free quarters on the labour of the industrous . . . This [Cardinal] Wolsely of Marudes [*mārudeśa*, i.e.. the western desert] exercised his hourly-increasing power to the disgust and alienation of all but the infatuated prince. He leagued together with the nominal minister, Induraj, and together they governed the prince and the country. Such characters, when exceeding the sphere of their duties, expose religion to contempt.[123]

Here we may safely parse Tod's righteous indignation at Āyas Dev Nāth and his yogis as a case of British sour grapes, given the fact that Bhīm Singh—the victim of the dose of poison so mysteriously administered in the eleventh hour for the rescue of young Mān Singh—was the man the British had been backing as the successor to the vacant throne.[124] In addition, Mān Singh had offered asylum for no fewer than eleven years to Madhu Rāj Bhonsle (Appa Sahib) of Nagpur in open defiance of the British—housing him throughout that period in the Mahāmandir temple, the centerpiece of the Nāth Yogī presence in Jodhpur—and this following his signature of a treaty with the British![125] Well after Āyas Dev Nāth's 1815 murder, the Nāth Yogīs remained a thorn in the side of the British in Marwar. After having used a show of armed force to persuade Mān Singh to remove the yogis from positions of power in the kingdom in 1839, they found them back in power again in 1841.[126]

The Rajput princely states of western India and the sub-Himalayan and Himalayan zones that the British were unwilling or unable to conquer were, nonetheless, exceptions to a more general rule of British hegemony over the yogis and their ilk. The most celebrated (or notorious) example of the British ability to crush these groups who so troubled their imperial tranquility were Sleeman's successful propaganda and law and order campaigns against the Thugs.[127] The quashing of the so-called Sanyasi and Fakir Rebellion in Bengal in the final decades of the eighteenth century was a case in which the British acted militarily to defeat militarized ascetics.[128] British counterinsurgent tactics were not, however, limited to military retaliation alone. A combination of legislation and police action proved to be far more effective weapons against the yogis. With a stroke of the pen in 1773, Warren Hastings transformed the yogis entering or traversing Company-controlled territories from members of religious orders to vagrants and criminals.[129] There are a number of interesting caveats in Hastings' proclamation, including an exemption to Rāmānandis and Gorakhnāthis "who have for a long time been settled and receive a maintenance in land money . . . from the Government or the Zemindars of the province," as well as Sannyasis "for executing religious offices."

6. The Passing of the Yogis

In the course of the nineteenth century, however, things took a turn for the worse for the Nāth Yogīs, since, according to the 1891 British imperial census, the Jogis, including the Gorakhpanthis, were listed under the category of "Miscellaneous and Disreputable Vagrants."[130] The *cār sau bīs jogī* had been born. And so they are described by H. A. Rose in his survey of the tribes and castes of northwest India, which was based on the Punjab census reports for 1883 and 1892.

> [T]hat miscellaneous assortment of low caste *faqīrs* and fortune-tellers, both Hindu and Musalmān . . . are commonly known as Jogīs. Every rascally beggar who pretends to be able to tell fortunes or to practice astrological and necromantic arts, in however small a degree, buys himself a drum and calls himself, and is called by others, a Jogī . . . They are a thoroughly vagabond set, and wander about the country beating a drum and begging, practicing surgery and physic in a small way, writing charms, telling fortunes, and practicing exorcism and divination; or, sitting in the villages, eke out their earnings from these occupations by the offerings made at the local shrines of the malevolent godlings of the Sayads and other Musalmān saints; for the Jogī is so impure that he will eat the offerings made at any shrine. These people, or at least the Musalmān section of them, are called Rāwal in the Panjab. Rāwal corresponds to Nāth.[131]

To be sure, the criminalization of the yogis was not a pure British fabrication: many if not most yogis likely did engage in the sorts of activities Rose condemns here, once their ability to engage in long-distance trade or soldiering was curtailed. Furthermore, even prior to the demilitarization of the yogi orders, itinerant begging had clearly been part of the yogi lifestyle, whether the yogi in question was a yogi by profession or circumstance. The British ideology underlying their criminalization of the yogis has been summarized by Pinch.

The modern state in India could not countenance recalcitrant sadhus wandering about the countryside armed, dangerous, often naked, and claiming to represent an alternate locus of authority. The Company needed a modern sadhu: a priestly monk unconcerned with worldly power and given over to religious contemplation and prayer . . . In retrospect, it can be argued that with the gradual removal of armed monks from territories controlled by the Company in the late eighteenth and nineteenth centuries, north Indian monasticism turned inward, away from worldly martial pursuits and toward more aesthetic, devotional, and literary accomplishments. In the Vaishnava context, this would have meant a greater emphasis on *rasik*-oriented bhakti, or "devotional aestheticism," which had constituted a powerful strand of both Ram and Krishna worship since the sixteenth century.[132]

In fact, the inward turn of Indian monasticism had begun in some parts of the subcontinent even before Company policy made warrior asceticism illegal. One sees evidence for this in the strong condemnations that South Asian religious reformers make of the martial practices and general lifestyles of yogis. We have already seen this in the poem attributed to Kabīr, who excoriates the yogis for their arrogance and mercantile and military ways. So too, Guru Nānak (d. 1539), the founder of the Sikh faith, urges Gorakhnāth and his ilk to abandon the yogi path for that of the one God: "Listen divine yogi, make the divine vision your sect, your earrings, pouch and patched cloak . . . The mind turned away from the world is our [the Sikhs'] begging bowl; the realization of the five higher senses the yogi's cap . . . True yoga praxis in absorption in holy truth lies. Yogis by delusion of *maya* in twelve sects and *sannyasi*s in ten are divided."[133] In spite of the fact that he calls God a divine yogi,[134] the condemnations of human yogis by Guru Gobind Singh (d. 1708), the last of the Sikh gurus, are more pointed, with the path of devotion to God being proclaimed as the sole authentic form of practice. In his *Bachittar Nāṭak* (BN), God declares:

Then I created Datt[ātreya],
who also started his own path,
His followers have long nails in their hands,
And matted hair on their heads,
They do not understand the ways of the Lord.
Then I created Gorakh,

Who made great kings his disciples,
His disciples wear rings in their ears,
And do not know the love of the Lord . . . [135]
I [Gobind Singh] neither wear matted hair on the head
nor bedeck myself with ear-rings,
I meditate on the name of the Lord, which helps me in all my errands.
Neither [do] I close my eyes, nor exhibit heresy,
Nor perform evil actions, nor cause others to call me a person in disguise . . .
Those who exhibit various guises in the world and win people on their side,
They will reside in hell, when the sword of death chops them.[136]

The rejection of the ways of the yogis with their claims of supernatural powers in favor of an all-powerful god is dramatized in a Vaiṣṇava legend concerning the sixteenth-century struggle, between power-seeking Nāth Yogīs and the Rāmānandi devotees of Kṛṣṇa, for the control of Galta, an important shrine near Jaipur. Following the plot of tales from the Vikrama Cycle, Tāranāth, the champion of the yogis, transforms himself into a tiger to attack the Rāmānandi Paihāri Kṛṣṇadās. Speaking the words "what a jackass," Paihāri Kṛṣṇadās turns Tāranāth into a donkey; at the same time, the distinctive earrings of his disciples fall from their ears, causing the terrified yogis to flee to the hills. As a result—and here we move back into the realm of history—the local ruler, Pṛthivirāj, previously a patron of the yogis, threw his support behind Paihāri Kṛṣṇadās, who established a Rāmānandi monastic lineage there.[137] As Pinch has argued, this legend is an account of the beginnings of a paradigm shift in Rajput religiosity on the edge of the western Indian region that had long been the yogis' power base:

Love of God (*bhakti*) itself was not new. But the harnessing of *bhakti* to Mughal imperial expansion, or more precisely, to the widely dispersed Rajput clans . . . who provided the lion's share of the military manpower of the Mughal state, was . . . The key difference that separated [Tāranāth from Paihāri Kṛṣṇadās] was the manner in which they conceived of and related to God. Tāranāth affected a yoga-tantric asceticism, the sole purpose of which was to cultivate supernormal power within—in effect, to turn himself into a god. Paihāri Kṛṣṇadās, by contrast, only appeared to conjure Tāranāth's transformation into a jackass. In fact, this was the work of a distant yet ever-present Lord, his God as a thing apart, God with an upper-case 'G'—a being who inspired total self-abandonment and offered a sheltering refuge of love in return.[138]

In other words, Kṛṣṇa, the "Master of Masters of Yoga" had defeated a "Master of Yoga" through the vessel of his nonyogi devotee. In concrete terms, as a result of this legendary encounter, Galta would become a Vaiṣṇava stronghold with the yogis reduced to the menial task of providing firewood for the new masters of the site.[139] Interestingly, the yogis would regain the upper hand there in the late nineteenth century, through the rhetorical and debating skills of a certain Lakṣmaṇnāth; but this was, in many respects, a last hurrah.[140] Overtaken by the brave new world of Rajput devotionalism and the Pax Brittanica, the political power and influence of the yogis quickly evaporated. In postindependence India, when their last remaining princely patrons fell, virtually all of South Asia's yogis were reduced to beggar status. No longer moving commercial goods along their annual pilgrimage cycles, their capital was reduced to songs of yogi glories past, such as those sung by the impoverished Bhartṛhari yogis that Mahadevprasad Singh heard and recorded at his village in Bihar in the middle of the twentieth century. A comic, but nonetheless poignant testimony to the yogis' diminished status is found in E. M. Forster's autobiographical *Hill of Devi*, in which the author describes the 1913 observance of an annual event in the court of the miniscule princely state of Dewas Senior: "Those saddhus would sometimes come to Dewas and bless the Palace, and demand a hundred rupees each. Malrao would speak to them as fair as he could and give each of them one rupee. Then they cursed the Palace and returned to Ujjain."[141]

7. Modern and Postmodern Yogis

Whereas patriotic asceticism lay at the core of Mahatma Gandhi's strategies for the Indian independence movement, modern yoga was a principal platform of the Hindu reform campaign spearheaded by Swami Vivekananda (1863–1902). Like his fellow reformers, Vivekananda felt that Hinduism had departed from its rational, philosophical, and scientific roots as affirmed in the Vedas and Upaniṣads into little more then a "kitchen religion" for manipulating petty supernatural powers.[142] As Peter Van der Veer has argued, yoga as reinterpreted by Vivekananda was, before all else, nonsectarian, a "unifying sign of the Indian nation—and not only for national consumption but for consumption by the entire world."[143] I have already briefly discussed the sources of Vivekananda's idiosyncratic synthesis,[144] which set the agenda for the modern yoga movement; for an exhaustive treatment of the subject, I refer the reader to Elizabeth De Michelis's *A History of Modern Yoga*.[145] Vivekananda's lectures and writings on the YS were highly congenial to the religious Zeitgeist of the Victorian period, which found expression in India mainly through the rationalist spirituality of Neo-Vedanta. So it was that Vivekananda defined *rāja yoga* as the supreme contemplative path to self-realization, in which the self so realized was the supreme self, the absolute *brahman* or god-self within. As such, Vivekananda publicly rejected out of hand the legitimacy of the extraordinary powers of yogis or of any sort of "miracle."[146] In a word, yogi practice was made out to be the antitype of yoga, and the yogis of the twentieth century the degenerate heirs to the practitioners of the true yoga of yore. Writing in 1919, the American psychologist of religion James Leuba encapsulated the modernist condemnation of India's yogis.

> The emaciated, bewildered ascetic, reduced to the dimmest spark of life, equally incapable for lack of energy of committing good or evil is . . . but a shrunken caricature of what man ought to be. . . The Yogin . . . is much deceived in the magical powers he ascribes himself. His self-deception, the corresponding self-deception of the user of drugs . . . constitute[s] one of the most pathetic chapters of human history. To aim so high, and to fall so low, is in truth both deep tragedy and high comedy. Yet the stupefied Yogin is one of the blundering heroes and martyrs who mark the slow progress of humanity.[147]

However, like postmodern man, who has in recent decades been smitten by a sort of remorse and nostalgia for the various plant and animal species he is responsible for having annihilated, in the latter half of the nineteenth century the British in India began to romanticize the yogis whose lifestyles and livelihoods their policies had largely contributed to wiping out. In urban middle-class society in particular, the bogey of the wild, naked, drug-crazed warrior ascetic was gradually airbrushed into the far more congenial image of a forest-dwelling meditative, spiritual renouncer, something far closer to the ideal of the sages of vedic lore. This romanticization—indeed, this reinvention—of the yogi and his yoga occurred not only among the British but also within an increasingly Anglicized Indian urban society, and most especially among the *bhadralok*, the "gentlefolk" of late nineteenth-century Bengal. These groups' reimaginings of yogis and yoga took a number of forms, including the "patriotic asceticism" championed by Bankim Chandra Chatterjee in his greatly influential 1882 novel *Ānandamaṭh* ("The Monastery of Bliss").[148]

During the first decades of the twentieth century, Indian and Western representations of the yogis range from Leuba's wholesale condemnation to expressions of confusion. An example of the latter may be found in the opening chapter of the Englishman John Campbell Oman's 1908 *Cults, Customs, and Superstitions of India*, entitled "Yogis and Mahatmas, the Sages of India." Acknowledging that the yogis whom the Indian masses continued to revere remained capable of the miracle of extracting from the hands of stingy merchants the food that they in turn fed to the multitudes of their devotees, Oman nonetheless asserts that the people's embrace of them was in fact grounded in a general fear of their supernatural powers. Furthermore, the sole true yogis were those who lived a life of contemplation in the splendid isolation of the Himalayas, far from the town and marketplace. However, the yogis of India "form a distinct order [and] hold peculiar doctrines," which Oman identifies with the teachings of the YS. Yet, at the same time, Oman is dismayed to note that the Theosophist Madame Blavatsky, whose staged demonstrations of the powers of the same yoga were little more than conjuring tricks, had attracted followers not only among educated Hindus but also from "the best educated class of Europeans in India."[149] Then, in a mocking aside concerning imposters, he relates the case of "a yogi, who believed himself possessed of a commanding influence over wild animals [and] put his powers to the test, attempt[ing] some familiarities with the tiger in the Lahore Zoological Gardens. [He] got himself so mauled that his arm had to be amputated."[150]

A year prior to the publication of Oman's book, Richard Schmidt brought out *Fakire und Fakirtum im Alten und Modernen Indien*, a balanced and sympathetic work that combined travelers' descriptions of yogis with a comprehensive account of yoga philosophy and *haṭha yoga*. Schmidt's inclusion of eighty-seven reproductions of Indian watercolor illustrations of the yogic postures detailed in two hathayogic works, the *Haṭhayogapradīpikā* and *Gheraṇḍa Saṃhitā*, would inspire such early Indian pioneers of yoga as Kuvalayananda and Krishnamacarya in their respective innovations of what would become modern yoga practice.[151] Oman's mixed feelings about India's yogis are echoed by the American Reverend W. M. Zumbro, whose 1913 *National Geographic* article, "Religious Penances and Punishments Self-Inflicted by the Holy Men of India," reproduces, this time with photographs, many of the images found in the seventeenth- and eighteenth-century works of Tavernier and other European travelers. While condemning "Sadhuism" as the outmoded lifestyle of "an army of five million idlers," Zumbro nonetheless distinguishes the yogis from the other ascetics and vagrants he catalogs, identifying their postures and practice of breath control as "indisputable means of obtaining a state of pure intelligence, with which comes emancipation and the union of the soul with the Universal Spirit." Furthermore, Zumbro singles out the yogis as "the least offensive of the ascetics . . . according to occidental notions."[152]

Are we to see in Zumbro's measured assessment a softening of Indian and Western attitudes toward the yogis? Evidence that the category of the yogi was being revised may be adduced from Paramahansa Yogananda's *Autobiography of a Yogi*, which, while it was not published until 1946, records a mission of teaching in the United States that lasted for over thirty years, from 1920 until his death in 1952. The yoga of Yogananda's teachings is unabashedly a yoga of yogis, especially that of his guru Swami Sri Yukteswar Giri, who was himself the disciple of a reincarnating saint named Babaji, who "is ever in communication with Christ; together they send out vibrations of redemption and have planned the spiritual technique of salvation for this age."[153] Yogi practice and miracles form the warp and weft of Yogananda's autobiography, which includes accounts of levitation, the production of multiple bodies, and so on.

In his autobiography, Yogananda explains that he has offered his guru's gospel of "Kriya Yoga" to a modern disenchanted world in order to show that "the highest yogic attainments are not barred to the family man."[154] Alongside Swami Kuvalayananda (1883–1966) and Swami Sivananda (1887–1935), it is the life and teachings of Yogananda that have had the greatest impact on modern-day conceptions of yoga as a marriage between the physical and the spiritual, the human and the superhuman. Yogananda's greatest legacy may in fact lie in the early influence he had on the lives and teachings of three modern-day yoga gurus whose own "brands" of physical yoga have defined modern yoga practice in both India and the West. Here, I am speaking of B. K. S. Iyengar, K. Pattabhi Jois, and T. K. V. Desikacar, all of whom were disciples (and in some cases relatives) of Krishnamacarya. More than the content of his teachings, it was Yogananda's style and charismatic ability to attract Western disciples that were most influential in the transformation of these figures from Indian teachers of physical culture to international yoga celebrities. Krishnamacarya, the Mysore Palace's resident instructor of "martial athletics," created his own synthesis, combining *haṭha yoga* (mainly gleaned from Theosophical Society publications) with British military calisthenics and the regional gymnastic and wrestling traditions of Karnataka.[155] Krishnamacarya nonetheless recognized his innovations for what they were—an improvised tradition—and yearned to discover the original and true yoga teachings, which had been utterly lost to India and were only being practiced by yogis living in the pure climes of distant Tibet.[156] At the time, Iyengar was a disciple of Krishnamacarya (who was his elder brother-in-law), and the techniques of *haṭha yoga* that both he and Pattabhi Jois have innovated over the past decades clearly bear the stamp of their guru's synthesis.

The gospel of yoga that Iyengar heard from the mouth of "the esteemed visitor from California" differed from Krishnamacarya's martial athletics in every respect. In order to demonstrate his own yoga program to Yogananada, Krishnamacarya had the young Iyengar undertake a difficult posture called the *hanumān āsana*. "His eyes fell on me," Iyengar relates, "and he asked me whether I would accompany him to America."[157] Krishnamacarya would not permit his pupil to depart; however, shortly after Yogananada's departure—and perhaps inspired by Yogananda's example—the master demonstrated the "Tibetan" techniques that he had theretofore hidden from even his own disciples to two foreigners. Two French doctors placed electrodes on the body of Krishnamacarya, who proceeded to stop his heartbeat, change the rhythm of his pulse, and hold his breath for as many as five minutes. "The encounter," writes Elizabeth Kadetsky,

> burst open Iyengar's world. . . Like the visit from the swami [Yogananda], it pulled him from his mentor. The gap between what the doctors gleaned from the master and what the master taught to his quarry [Iyengar and his fellow pupils] was large. The science of these Western visitors was as spectacularly suggestive of inaccessible worlds as the divine bearing of the yogi Yogananda. Krishnamacharya was training Iyengar in a yoga of "physical culture," something associated more closely with wrestling and gymnastics. The secrets of Tibet had been withheld. Their spiritual core was not evident. To a disappointed young Iyengar, yoga seemed something he could pursue with the "mercenary" intent of making a living.[158]

In 1952, Iyengar became the personal yoga trainer of the violinist Yehudi Menuhin, and his fortune was made. Over the decades that have followed, Iyengar and his two fellow *guru bhais*, Pattabhi Jois and Desikacar, have trained countless thousands of disciples, mainly Western, in their innovative physical yoga techniques. Like the modern yoga tradition spawned by Vivekananda and others, their innovations developed out of a modern context in which their teacher had, in the 1930s, himself bemoaned the fact that yoga had disappeared from India and could only be rediscovered outside of India's borders. Yet the authentic yoga that he brought back with him from Tibet bore little resemblance to any of India's indigenous yoga or yogi traditions. In other words, the bedrock of the West's modern-day, billion-dollar yoga industry, with its celebrity gurus (most of whom claim one of Krishnamacarya's three disciples as their master), glossy journals, fashion accessories, trademarks, franchises, and lawsuits, is Indian yoga, but a reinvented Indian yoga that dates from no earlier than the 1930s.[159]

How have Indian yoga and Indian yogis fared in the midst of the yoga industry's many reinventions and expropriations of their own traditions? On the one hand, India is taking steps to safeguard the intellectual property of its yoga traditions. The Traditional Knowledge Digital Library (TKDL) is being developed as a tool "to prevent foreign entrepreneurs from claiming Indian traditions as novel, and thus patenting it." One of the catalysts for the TKDL was the patent granted by the United States in 2004, on a sequence of twenty-six *āsanas*, to the Indian-American yoga celebrity Bikram Chaudhury.[160] While the TKDL is seeking to protect India's yoga traditions (or at least the selected traditions it considers to be yogic), the survival of its yogis is another matter. Are India's yogis an endangered species? In fact, the Nāth Yogīs, India's most visible modern-day yogi order, have been making a comeback of sorts, in no small part by reinventing themselves to conform to the expectations of their newest benefactors, urban merchants and industrialists who have seen fit to funnel some of their newfound wealth into Nāth Yogī institutions. This has particularly been the case in the Shekhavati region of eastern Rajasthan, where the yogis are once again well fed, well dressed, and well housed. In return, the Nāth Yogīs are building ashrams, which they place at the disposition of their benefactors who come there for vedic rituals, devotional singing, and other activities that would have been utterly anathema to Nāth Yogīs at any other time in their history.[161]

8. Postmortem Yogis, followed by a Postmortem on Yogis

One of the most interesting chapters in the legal history of British India concerns an individual who returned from the dead, as it were, in the guise of a yogi. This was the case of Kumar Ramendra Narayan Ray of Bhawal—the second son of the raja of Bhawal, a petty prince of eastern Bengal—which has been painstakingly reconstructed by Partha Chatterjee in his 2002 book *A Princely Imposter?* In 1909, the young "Kumar of Bhawal" suddenly died and was cremated under the cover of night and under strange circumstances far from home in Darjeeling. Some time in late 1920 or early 1921, a "sannyasi" appeared in Dhaka, dressed in the garb of an itinerant ascetic. Soon after his arrival there, word began to spread that he was none other than the deceased Kumar of Bhawal. Recognized as her brother by the princess Jyotirmoyee Devi, but claiming no memory of his earlier life as a prince, he took up residence at the family estate in Jaidebpur, sitting on its verandah in ordinary clothes. So great was popular curiosity that the railway company began to run special trains to the place, and on May 15, 1921, as many as 50,000 people assembled there to view the reanimated prince.[162] As he settled into "his old life," the "prince" began to recall "his past," and initiated the legal process of reclaiming his name and his inheritance.

Over the months and years that followed, there were several challenges to the authenticity of the so-called prince's claim to be the person he said he was. This was not the first time in British Indian legal history that an itinerant ascetic had made such a claim.[163] In one of these, Pratapchand, the son of Tejchandra, an important *zamindar* of the Burdwan Raj, had in 1821 died under mysterious circumstances and been cremated on the night of his death. His father, the sole witness to his death and cremation, himself died in 1833. Two years later, a sannyasi going by the name of Alok Shah appeared, claiming to be Pratapchand, and asserting that he had faked his illness and death scene fourteen years earlier through the practice of *haṭha yoga*. Garnering political support against the claims of the sole surviving pretender to the throne, he made public his intention to raise an army of 100,000 men to fight the English. In 1836, he was tried and convicted of "assembling a tumultuous body of armed men and setting at defiance of the Constituted Authorities," and in 1838, he was convicted a second time, for the crime of "fraudulent impersonation." He lived out the rest of his life as a religious cult leader, with a great following, mainly female, in rural western Bengal.[164] The "Landhaura Case" had a similar story line.

> In 1874, there was a great sensation when a fakir appeared . . . and declared himself to be Raja Raghubir Singh [who had taken over Landhaura estate at age 18, in 1866, dying in 1868 of tuberculosis]. He claimed that he had been poisoned, but fortunately had managed to escape from the scene of his cremation. [The District Magistrate John Markham] concluded that the man posing as a fakir was actually someone called Mahal Singh hailing from Hoshiarpur in the Punjab. The alleged Raghubir Singh was jailed for "cheating by false impersonation."[165]

In both of these nineteenth-century cases, the charge against the "sannyasi" or "fakir" defendant was fraudulent or false impersonation. In the second of these, which was tried under the then new Penal Code enacted by the British in 1860, the imposter was charged under section 420.[166] In the case of the Kumar of Bhawal, the testimony of the ascetics whom he claimed had saved him from the pyre was crucial. In the trial, two *udāsi*s testified in court that while staying in Darjeeling together with their guru Dharamdas, they had rescued the plaintiff—whom they called Sundardas—from the funeral pyre. However, in his statement to the court,

Dharamdas, who recognized the plaintiff as his disciple Sundardas, denied that he had ever been to Darjeeling, saved anyone from a funeral pyre, or had ever known any *sadhu* by the name of Dharamdas![167]

Here a word on terminology is in order. Throughout his book, Chatterjee alternates between the terms "sannyasi" and "sadhu" to designate the so-called Kumar of Bhawal. These would have been the terms employed in early twentieth-century Bengal, which had about 150 years earlier been the theater of the "Sanyasi and Fakir Rebellion." In the heavily Islamic context of east Bengal, "sannyasi" would have borne the same nonspecific meaning as "sadhu," to signify a non-Muslim itinerant beggar, holy man, ascetic, renouncer, and so on. However, the three men who testified in the Kumar of Bhawal's case concerning his escape from the pyre and the twelve years he had passed in their midst identified themselves as *udāsi*s, a term specifically applied to persons from the Sikh fold who embrace the renunciant life. The *udāsi*s first came to prominence in the seventeenth century as the antitype within the Sikh community to members of the warrior Khalsa. One of the most important markers of the *udāsi*s was their dress: a cap, a rosary of flowers, a cotton bag, a vessel made of dried pumpkin, ash for smearing the body, a chain worn around the waist, and a deerskin upon which to practice *haṭha yoga*.[168] With some variations, these are the marks of the yogi, and as Harjot Oberoi has argued, the social role that the *udāsi*s played at the village level in the Sikh Punjab was analogous to that played by the Sufis (and by extension the yogis) elsewhere in South Asia.[169] Like the yogis, the *udāsi*s were associated with goddesses, local shrines, miracles, sorcery, and the practice of yoga, and like the yogis and Sufis in their respective traditions, the *udāsi*s were increasingly marginalized, in their case by nineteenth- and twentieth-century reform Sikhism.[170] We may therefore conclude that the erstwhile *udāsi* Sundardas was, in many respects, a yogi. On August 4, 1936, at the end of the 608-day trial, one of the longest in British Indian legal history, the judge ruled in favor of the plaintiff.[171] Vindicated, the Kumar of Bhawal died shortly thereafter.

In his analysis of these multiple cases of princes who returned from the dead as "sannyasis," "fakirs," or "sadhus" to claim their birthright, Chatterjee draws up a typology of their return narratives, which includes a botched cremation and other recurring elements. Here Chatterjee notes that

> the prince usually returns as a holy man. At one level, this signifies the moral strength of his claim—the fact that he has been purified of the sins and corruptions of the aristocratic lifestyle, and that he now has an aura of renunciation. Moreover, a period of

living in disguise and in exile has been, ever since the *Rāmāyaṇa* and the *Mahābhārata*, a well known trope of ordeal in the lives of exemplary rulers. But at another level, it also helps explain the period of disappearance in the narrative. The life of the mendicant is a life outside society. It allows the missing prince to hide his real identity without getting into any new social entanglements.

In their treatment of a similar case from the seventeenth century, Flores and Subrahmanyam also focus on the person of the prince or king, noting that the theme of the royal "double" is a powerful one that potentially possesses the capacity to transcend cultural divisions.[172] Of course, in the light of the preceding chapters, these authors' analyses are shown to be lacking, given the episteme of the yogi who inhabits other people's bodies, sometimes raising them from the dead, or who reduplicates his body to create doubles of himself for his personal use. Amidst the welter of elite, textualist perspectives that Chatterjee introduces to contextualize the Kumar of Bhawal case, those of the *udāsi* renouncers themselves, with whom "Sundardas" had crisscrossed north India for a dozen years, never appear. In a subchapter entitled "An Excursus on the Subaltern," he asks the rhetorical question of where the people—the thousands who thronged to see the prince after his return to Jaidebpur or who filled the courts and bought all the special editions of the newspapers following the trial—stood in all of this.[173] He gives no answer (and this is his point) because their views were not recorded for posterity.

In the light of the rich yogi traditions we have surveyed in these pages, I would argue that had "the people" (and the *udāsi*s) been consulted, they would have ruled that the prince who had returned to life as a yogi was in fact a yogi who had returned to life as a prince. Less than a century earlier, agents of the British East India Company might have at least entertained such as possibility, given the fact that its agents were reading tales of sinister yogis from the Vikrama Cycle in order to learn the Hindustani language. But, as Chatterjee notes, Pannalal Basu, the judge in this case, had been trained in English schools and, like Vivekananda before him, only had a superficial knowledge of things Indian. Indian philosophical theories of identity and categories of valid cognition (which Chatterjee reviews extensively, unfortunately neglecting to discuss the category of yogi perception) were nearly completely omitted from the trial.[174] In fact, in the reformist spirit of the times, so widely embraced by urban Bengali elites, the rejection of nearly all things Indian would have been a badge of honor for Judge Basu. In the same way that Vivekananda could lecture the world on yoga without ever thinking to consider yoga's relationship to India's yogis, Basu was able to render a judgment on a claim made by a yogi without ever considering the meaning of a *yogi-pratyakṣa* in the Indian philosophical tradition. Ironically, the judge's 1936 ruling overturned Hastings's Minute and Proclamation of 1773. For, whereas Hasting's edict criminalized India's jogis, Basu's ruling found in favor of India's yogis.

Far more than a literary device or marginal religious phenomenon, the person or persona of the sinister yogi is a South Asian cultural episteme. Even today, naughty South Asian children find themselves threatened by their parents that if they won't be quiet and go to sleep "the yogi will come and take them away," just as the yogi came and took the second Kumar of Bhawal away. As a recent newspaper story reports, the yogi may have come to take another illustrious Bengali away in more recent times. "Netaji" Subhas Chandra Bose, who was, alongside Gandhi and Nehru, one of the most prominent leaders of the Indian independence movement against the British Raj, is thought to have died in a plane crash over Taiwan in August of 1945. However, as the *Deccan Herald* reported in 2003, in a story entitled "Tests to decide if *sadhu* was Netaji":

> [A] one-man commission, probing the disappearance of Netaji Subash Chandra Bose, will collect blood samples from two direct maternal descendants of Netaji within a week to ascertain whether there was any link with the DNA of late Gumnami Baba, an ascetic who ran an ashram at Faizabad in UP [Uttar Pradesh] and believed by many to be Subhas Chandra Bose . . . According to the status report, the remnants of the sealed specimen of teeth and blood samples of Gumnami Baba were taken back from CDFD, Hyderabad on completion of DNA fingerprinting and handed over to the Central Forensic Science Laboratory here for preservation and to obtain a second opinion.[175]

In his analysis of the Kumar of Bhawal trial, Chatterjee notes that the entire case hinged on the issue of identity, on the epistemological foundations for any individual to claim his or her unique personhood.[176] As I noted at the end of chapter four, the body, person, or self as constructed in South Asian ways of knowing is a highly permeable, open system, bristling with conduits through which it transacts with other bodies, persons, or selves. So it is that the act of seeing involves an extension of the contours of one's body outward from the eye, via a ray of perception, to the object of perception, and that the shadow cast by an impure individual can physically alter the composition of the body of the person upon whom that shadow falls.

The person of the yogi encapsulates all of the epistemological and ontological conundrums that such constructions entail. What is the "self" of a person whose body has been appropriated by a yogi who has applied his enhanced powers of vision to take it over for "himself"? When yogis appropriate multiple bodies, do these constitute individual selves, or a single collective self? Both the South Indian literary record and scriptural and philosophical canons portray yogis as extending their own lives by taking the lives of others. The language of the SvT and NT is telling here: a yogi lives forever because he "is able to displace his identity by means of another person's body"; yet, whenever he enters another body, he does so "from another body" in the potentially endless series of bodies he has inhabited in the course of his life.[177] In this respect, the yogi is also "another" to "himself,"—that is, an alter ego—even as he is the antitype of the self of anyone who is not a yogi, whence Praśastapāda's definition of yogis as "those who are different than ourselves."[178]

Throughout these pages, we have seen the real world instantiations of these philosophical treatments of the personhood of the yogi. When, in the Mughal and colonial periods, a north Indian peasant left home and family to soldier in the armies of north India in the Mughal and colonial periods, he assumed a yogi identity, only becoming "himself" once more upon his return. Throughout their history, India's yogis have assumed alternate identities through a number of strategies, including "charismatic impersonation," by which a living yogi claims to be an illustrious yogi of the past, such as a Gorakhnāth or a Dattātreya.[179] Combined with the tantric strategy of dissimulation and the Shia principle of *taqīyya*—according to which Hindu yogis have assumed undercover identities as nonyogis while Muslim *dāīs* have adopted the personas of Hindu yogis—the identity of the yogi remains an enigma.[180] In many respects, yogis are persons who play on all of these registers of the fluid Indic categories of personhood and identity, introducing themselves (uninvited and often unbeknownst to their "hosts") into other people's bodies, other people's countries (as spies), and other people's villages, markets, caravans, and marriage beds. If the yogi is the archetypal "other" to the South Asian "self," then it is appropriate to identify its yogi gods as the "wholly other" in the sense intended by Rudolf Otto in his groundbreaking study of the idea of the holy.[181] No Indic description of a yogi god better captures the combination of majesty, mystery, and terror that typifies Otto's holy than that of Kṛṣṇa—the arch-yogi whose role it is to take over the bodies of all creatures—when he reveals his universal form to Arjuna at the climax of the BhG.

[Kṛṣṇa,] the great master of yoga revealed . . . his supreme masterful form, with countless mouths and eyes, countless supernatural aspects . . . and countless weapons uplifted . . . If the light of a thousand suns were to rise simultaneously in the sky, such

> would be the light of that expansive self. Then [Arjuna] beheld the entire manifold universe gathered together in the body of the god of gods[182] . . . The Lord then said: "Now I am become Death, the destroyer of worlds."[183]

Thousands of years later, the yogi god's words would be recalled by Robert Oppenheimer to describe the supernatural military powers of the universe's emerging new masters. The date was July 16, 1945, and the United States had just tested its first nuclear weapon at the White Sands Missile Range.

Notes

PREFACE

1. MBh 12.289.24–28.
2. An important exception, which laid the groundwork for a far broader approach to the subject, was Mircea Eliade's *Yoga: Immortality and Freedom*. Unfortunately, this work cast too broad a net in its treatment of the subject, treating such disparate topics as spirituality, shamanism, asceticism, Islamic *dhikr*, alchemy, and so on. On this "yoga is everywhere" approach, see Larson and Bhattacharya 2008, 30–31.
3. It may be argued that the moniker Nāth Yogī constitutes an exception to this rule; however, this term refers to a sectarian group or monastic order. The Nāth literature never refers to its practices as "nātha yoga": rather, *haṭha yoga* and *siddha yoga* are its operative terms.
4. JS 8.19; 19.27, cited in Rastelli 2000, 357.

CHAPTER ONE

1. See below, n. 17; chap. 4, n. 157; and chap. 6, n. 101.
2. Singh n.d., 1. The preceding text is an abridged translation of Singh's tale.
3. The most widely used Indian dating system is named after Vikramāditya. Its year 0 corresponds to 58 BCE. On the relationship of this system to the Vikrama Cycle, see Edgerton 1926, vol. 1, lviii–lxiii.
4. Although it has been a scholarly convention to translate the Sanskrit *vetāla* as "vampire," ever since the earliest Western editions of the VP, "zombie" constitutes a more accurate translation of the term because the narrator of the stories is a spirit that has enlivened the body of a corpse.

5. The history of these recensions is briefly summarized in Emeneau 1935, 59, and Renou 1963, 15–17.
6. The history of these recensions is summarized in Edgerton 1926, 2: xxix–xlvii, lii–lviii; and Haksar 1998, xiii–xv.
7. On the translation and adaptation of these two anthologies into vernacular South Asian languages, see Pritchett 1985, 56–78; and Renou 1963, 17–18. See also below, n. 69.
8. See below, n. 34.
9. YV 6.1.70–73, discussed in O'Flaherty 1984, 162.
10. Bloomfield 1917, 15–43.
11. This is a single manuscript (G) of Śivadāsa's Sanskrit recension of the VP, which has been edited and translated into German by Uhle (1869, 443–52). This story, which is appended in Uhle's manuscript to the last of the standard series of Vampire Tales, is very close in nearly every respect to the version found in the Jain *Prabandhacintāmaṇi*. See below, n. 33.
12. Haksar 1998, xvii.
13. Eleven of these are referenced in Pritchett 1985, 72–74.
14. Four of these are referenced in Bloomfield 1917, 15.
15. This was the Fort William College version. See chap. 6, n. 120.
16. Pritchett 1985, 72.
17. Ibid., 71; Bindra 2002, vol. 1, 86, 101, 303–4, 388–90; vol. 2, 567–68, 574–75, 668. On the place of the Chritro Pakhyān in the *Dasam Granth*, see Kohli 2005, xlii.
18. Bloomfield (1917, 21) surmises that both versions draw on an earlier, unidentified source. See below, n. 33.
19. What follows is an abridgement of Lescallier's 1817 French translation from the Persian of the seventh tale of the throne (vol. 1, 130–57). Bloomfield (1917, 16–18) also provides an English summary. I have retained Lescallier's use of italics and spelling of proper names. On the history of this and other Persian- and Urdu-language versions of the SD, see Pritchett 1985, 58, citing Narang 1962, 92–94.
20. The long and witty exchanges between Vikrama as parrot and his queen (rather than his treasurer's daughter) form the bulk of the narrative of the PC version of the story, reproduced in Bloomfield 1917, 21–42.
21. Several of the vernacular tales of Vikram referenced in Pritchett (1985, 72–74) involve his transformation into a parrot. Pritchett (ibid., 74) also cites a ca. 1400 CE work in Dakkani Urdu, in which the parrot-king is named "Raja Kidam Ra'o."
22. Trungpa, et al. 1982, 162–76.
23. Wangyal 1982.
24. White 2003, 39–53, 188–95, 204–12; Gray 2007, 322–83.
25. Mayaram 1999, 107, 110–11.
26. Meister 1986, 233–46.

27. This is the goal of Bhairavācārya, the tantric practitioner in Bāṇabhaṭṭa's *Harṣacarita* (HC) who enlists the aid of King Puṣpabhūti in subduing a *vetāla* in order to become a Vidyādhara: Kane 1965, vol. 1, 46–47.
28. In Kumaon, for example, as documented in Krengel 1999, 265–88; and Gaborieau 1975, 147–72.
29. Krengel 1999, 268.
30. Crooke 1968, vol. 1, 195.
31. Jørgensen 1939: 265–68.
32. The later PC (3.105–324) retains the name of the mountain, but calls the master living there Siddheśvara, "Lord of the Siddhas": Bloomfield 1917, 24. On Sriparvata (or Srisailam) and its close associations with the siddhas, see White 1996, 110–12.
33. The PC has certainly borrowed this theme from the *Prabandhacintāmaṇi* or from a source common to both works. The VP manuscript edited and translated by Uhle (1869) also casts a brahmin as the villain; however, it is the god Śiva himself, and not a figure named Bhairavānanda, who reveals the supernatural power to Vikrama. See above, n. 11.
34. Tawney's (1982, 9–10) translation, quoted in Bloomfield 1917, 19–20. A similar version in which an unnamed yogi teaches the art of entering into other people's bodies to King Mukunda of Līlāvatī is found in certain recensions of the PT. In this version, a hunchback who has overheard the spell takes over the king's body, but Mukunda recovers it when the hunchback briefly enters the body of the queen's dead parrot: Bloomfield 1917, 13–14.
35. Keith 1924, 248.
36. Sanskrit edition: Suru 1960; edition and English translation: Konow and Lanman 1901. Cf. Chattopadhyaya 1994, 227–28.
37. *Karpūramañjarī* 1.22–23, translated in Davidson 2002, 179.
38. See Servan-Schreiber (1999a, 10) for a map of the Bhojpuri-speaking region.
39. Singh n.d., 10.
40. Servan-Schreiber 1999a, 25–26.
41. Vaudeville 1962, 352–54. See chap. 6, n. 89.
42. Their bardic annals and histories are chronicled in Tod 1957–72.
43. Servan-Schreiber 1999a, 16–19, 106–8.
44. Sax 1995, 137–43.
45. Unbescheid 1980, 169–83; Bouillier 1991, 3–21; Bouillier 1997, 166–73.
46. White 1996: 90–101.
47. Oman 1908, 13. All of the photos of yogis in this book are of Nāth Yogīs.
48. See chap. 6, nn. 65–66.
49. Toffin 1996, 219–20. This is Toffin's English translation of a French version from Toffin 1993: 101–2. My translation follows Toffin's (1996) in nearly every respect; however, I replaced the term "yogin" from the English translation with "yogi," which is how Toffin renders the term in the French.
50. AB 7.15.1–5. See chap. 4, n. 157.

51. AB 7.13–18; *Śāṅkhāyana Śrauta Sūtra* 15.17–27. Versions of the Śunaḥśepa myth are found in the MBh, Rām, and several Purāṇas. For bibliography and discussion, see White 1986, 227–62, and White 1991, 80–86.
52. Gopīcand's story is invoked in the 1540 CE *Padmāvat*: see chap. 6, n. 86. Three *bāṇīs*, entitled *Gopīcand jī kī Sabadī*, *Rājā Rāṇī Sambād*, and *Rāg Rāmagrī*, offer fragmentary accounts of the Gopīcand legend: Dvivedi 1980, 6–11 (vv. 47–125). The language of these poems dates from "later than the fifteenth or sixteenth century": ibid., 10 of foreword. Complete legend cycles of Gopīcand are found in the seventeenth-century Nepali *Gopīcandra Nāṭaka* and Bengali *Gorakṣa Vijaya* and *Mīn Cetan*. On these traditions, see White 1996, 295–97. An oral Punjabi version is recorded in Temple 1998, vol. 2,1–77 (legend 18).
53. This summary is based on the Rajasthani oral version recorded by Gold 1989, 774–76, and Gold 1992, 161–310.
54. See, for example, KSS 1.6.78–82, tr. in White 2003, 191.
55. See chap. 4, n. 256.
56. Pinch 2006, 116, 150.
57. Lescallier 1817, 1:179–83.
58. Neogi 1912, 92–95.
59. *Mallinātha Caritra* 1.29–31, summarized in Bloomfield 1924, 220–21.
60. *Kathāratnākara* of Hemavijaya, stories 187 and 69, summarized ibid., 222–23.
61. KSS 12.32.17–19.
62. KSS 12.31.75. He is also called a *śramaṇa* in the VP frame story of the 1037 CE *Bṛhatkathāmañjarī* of Kṣemendra. The two frame stories are virtually identical, which has led most scholars to accept a common source, the lost *Bṛhatkathā* of Guṇāḍhya, who lived in the region of Ujjain several centuries earlier: Renou 1963, 10.
63. Uhle 1881, 5 (vv. 24, 32), 6 (vv. 3, 7, 9, 18, 31, 33). In the same volume, Uhle's "Anonymous Recension of Manuscript F" (ibid., 69, 92) only uses the term "yogi."
64. Emeneau 1934, 6, 8, 10, 152, 154.
65. Riccardi 1971, 50, 118. Riccardi notes (ibid., 8, 12) that this, the sole extant manuscript version of Kṣemendra's Sanskrit-language VP, is a "synoptic" manuscript, with parallel Sanskrit and Nepali *ślokas* on each page. The Sanskrit of this manuscript (University of Pennsylvania Collection No. 746) differs from that of all other manuscript recensions. This is the sole vernacular version of Kṣemendra's VP; all other vernacular versions of the text, in Braj bhāṣā, Avadhi, Bengali, Marathi, and Tamil, derive from other Sanskrit recensions (ibid., 7). See above, nn. 6–7, for other references to the recension history of this collection.
66. Edgerton 1926, 14. See chap. 5, n. 143.
67. See, for example, Uhle's "Manuscript A" of Śivadāsa's recension of the VP (1881, 1–4). This and other Sanskrit versions of the prologue are discussed

in Emeneau 1935, especially pp. 62–66. Emeneau provides a critical edition of one of these versions (found in India Office MSS 2688c): Emeneau 1935, 70–87.

68. See chap. 6, n. 120.
69. This was the capital of the great king Bhoja, himself a commentator on the YS and the subject of an alchemical tale: White 1996, 49–50.
70. Eastwick 1845, 1–16.
71. Uberoi 1937, 16.
72. While elites of this religious order prefer the term Nāth Siddha (terminology I adopted in White 1996, 6–9, they are best known as Nāth Yogīs or simply Yogis in vernacular South Asian traditions.
73. Servan-Schreiber 1999a, 29–35. All of Singh's tales and transcriptions of the canon of Bhojpuri-language song cycles have gone into multiple printings in identical editions issued by two chapbook publishers, Loknath Pustakalay of Calcutta and Thakur Prasad and Sons Booksellers of Benares: ibid., 21–24. Cf. Servan-Schreiber 1999b, 81–105.
74. The HV (96.13–15) employs the terms *yoga-puruṣa* and *yogakanyā* (or *yogastrī*) to designate male and female "secret agents" whose covers are the guise of yogis and their female counterparts: Couture and Schmid 2001, 179, n. 14. On yogi spies in the AŚ, see below, n. 99 and chap. 6, n. 74.
75. See Lescallier (1817, 1:28; 2:62) for the SB episodes in which King *Békermadjiet* disguises himself as a yogi; for the Newari narrative, see above, n. 31.
76. Pritchett 1985, 76, 78. Cf. Servan-Schreiber 1999a, 35–51; and Gold 1992, 105–58.
77. Eastwick 1845, 2. See chap. 6, nn. 81–84.
78. See above, nn. 3, 62.
79. The Nepali-language *Nepālī Dāntya Kathā*, an anthology of folktales by B. V. Adhikari, went into ten printings in the twenty years following its original publication. In Adhikari's adaptation, the story of the prince's defeat of the yogi is fused with a second narrative in which the hero saves a princess from a clan of ogres: Bouillier and Cabaud 1989, 23, 32. Cf. Haksar 1998, xiii.
80. Bouillier and Cabaud 1989, 26. Cf. *Daśakumāracarita* 12.3.
81. PC 3.161–73, in Bloomfield 1917, 27–28.
82. PC 3.196–324, in ibid., 30–43.
83. KSS 1.4.98, 103. A similar account is found in the *Prabandhacintāmaṇi*. See Tawney 1982, 170.
84. KSS 1.4.105–8.
85. KSS 1.4.108–25.
86. Possession by *yakṣas* (as well as other demigods) is a common occurrence, for which symptomologies and clinical treatments are discussed in SS 6.60.11 and elsewhere in the Indian medical literature. For a general discussion, see Braverman 2003, 46–67.
87. Bloomfield 1917, 10.

88. On this alchemical *siddhi*, see White 1996, 315, 336–37, 349–52.
89. "Jougee-Eckbar," in Khan 1927, 371; summarized in Pinch 2006, 53–54.
90. This is a direct quote from Marshall's notebook, quoted in Pinch 2006, 54.
91. Ibid., 212–13.
92. RCM 1.158–75, in Poddar 1938, 168–84.
93. RCM 1, dohas 160 and 162, in ibid., 172–73.
94. RCM 1, chaupai 168.2, in ibid., 177.
95. RCM 1, chaupai 169.2–3, in ibid., 178.
96. RCM 1, doha 171 and chaupai 172.1a, in ibid., 180–81.
97. RCM 1, chaupai 166.3 and 167.3, in ibid., 176–77.
98. This is the title of Heinrich Zimmer's study of the frame story of the VP, contained within an anthology of the same name: Zimmer 1948/1993.
99. AŚ 5.6.21–22, in Olivelle 1987, 55, 57.
100. Tod 1957–72, vol. 1, 565. Cf. ibid., 562, 567, and ibid., vol. 2, 115–16, 122. See chap. 6, n. 52.
101. Gold 1995, 120–21, 128–29.
102. There is no evidence for the use of the term Daśanāmi (or Dasnāmi) or any attachment of the term with the name of Śaṅkara prior to the nineteenth century: Pinch 2006, 37.
103. Renou 1963, 11.
104. ŚDV 9.44–10.72, in Padmanabhan 1985–86, vol. 2, 52–82.
105. ŚV 58–60, in Tarkapancanana 1868, 244–47.
106. Ungemach 1992, 81–89.
107. Summaries of these versions are found in Wilke 1995, 164, and Smith 2006, 295–96.
108. ŚDV 9.104b-106b.
109. According to the ŚDV (10.11–18), he attains carnal knowledge through love-play and conversation with *all* of the ladies of the royal harem.
110. balaṃ dikṣu preṣayamās satvaram yatra kutra śarīrāṇi jīvahīnāni bhūmiṣu: Tarkapancanana 1868, 245.
111. MBh 12.289.24–27. See chap. 4, nn. 185–87.
112. ŚDV 10.8.
113. Ungemach 1992, 150–51; Gautam 1981, 62, 96–97; Dvivedi 1981, 48–49.
114. Temple 1998, vol 2, 21 (v. 208 of the story of Gopīcand); Gautam 1981, 51–55; Dvivedi 1981, 48.
115. Gautam 1981, 96–97.
116. ŚMS 4.51–52, in Ungemach 1992, 82.
117. ŚDV 9.30; GSS, 17, in Lorenzen 1972, 34, 36.
118. Tarkapancanana 1868, 21. The ŚV recounts Śaṅkara's "refutation of the Śaiva doctrine" immediately after its account of the philosopher's birth and its discussion of the fundamentals of his *advaita* philosophy, and before his refutation of the doctrines of any of his seventy other rival sects. This account is the longest in the entire work.
119. MBh 12.337.59, 62.

120. These include the *Kūrma*, especially, as well as portions of the *Varāha*, *Padma*, and *Garuḍa Purāṇas*: Hazra 1975, 21, 58, 62–68, 101, 119, 143.
121. Davidson 2002, 341–43.
122. *Pāśupata Sūtra* (PSū) 1.21–26 with the *Pañcārthabhāṣya* (PBh) commentary (attributed to Kauṇḍinya), p. 6, vv. 8–9; p. 41, vv. 17–18, and p. 148, v. 18, cited in Hara 2002, 34–35.
123. KSS 12.30.21ab, 23ab, 37a. This story forms a portion of the twenty-third Vampire Tale.
124. KSS 12.30.21ab, 23b.
125. KSS 12.30.31b-35b. A nearly identical account is found in Jambhaladatta's version of the VP; Śivadāsa tells the same story but transforms the Pāśupata into a Vaiṣṇava figure named Nārāyaṇa: Smith 2006, 327, and 341, n. 12.
126. KSS 8.2.3,31–53.
127. KSS 8.2.54–61. Cf. Trungpa (1982, 97) for nearly identical terminology in a sixteenth-century Tibetan Buddhist text and Khan (1927, 199) for a similar account in the writings of the seventeenth-century John Marshall. See chap. 4, nn. 115, 119.
128. KSS 8.2.67–68,78–80.
129. KSS 8.2.115–27.
130. The BA was edited by Achan 1925. A study containing a Hindi-language translation of the work is Bhatta 2000, 57–109. The play is summarized in Smith 2006, 328–30.
131. For example, BA 14, in Achan 1925, 45: yogapravṛtteratītānāgatavartamā natattva-darśanaṃ bhavati/ etebhyo 'ṣṭaguṇamaiśvaryaṃ labhate//.
132. See chap. 5, n. 127.
133. BA 27, in Achan 1925, 77: tadasya pratyayotpādanaṃ kariṣyāmīdṛśo yoga iti/ asyā gaṇikāyāḥ śarīre ātmānaṃ yojayāmi//.
134. BA 29, in Achan 1925, 81–82.
135. BA 32, in Achan 1925, 86: aye atrabhavān yogī parivrājakaḥ krīḍati/ kimidānīṃ kariṣye/ bhavatu dṛṣṭam/ asyā gaṇikāyā ātmānaṃ parivrājakaśarīre nyasya avasite karmaṇi yathāsthānaṃ yojayiṣyāmi//.
136. BA 33, in Achan 1925, 87–88.
137. dvāv imau puruṣau loke sūryamaṇḍala bhedinau/ parivrāḍyogayuktaśca raṇe cābhimukho hataḥ//. *Parivrāḍ* is an alternate reading for the more common *parivrāj* and *parivrājaka*.
138. ĀpDhSū 2.21.15, in Bronkhorst 2007, 86. For further discussion, ibid. 85–91.
139. *Udumbarikā Sīhanāda Suttanta* of the DN, cited in Eliade 1973, 188.
140. Roy 1983, 212, 245–48.
141. Hart 1979, 217–36.
142. In addition to Hart 1979, see Shulman 1993, 18–86, and Hudson 1989, 373–404.
143. Shulman 1993, 21. The same dynamic is found in a contemporary *dalit* myth from Garhwal, in which Bhairava appears as a Nāth Yogī: Sax 2008, 32–35.

144. SvT 7.258, 260; Jayaratha ad *Tantrāloka* (TĀ) 1.7, in Dwivedi and Rastogi 1987, vol. 2, 24. See chap. 5, n. 145.
145. Shulman 1993, 67–80. As Shulman acknowledges (ibid., 48), the entire third chapter of his book represents the collaborative work of himself and Velcheru Narayana Rao.
146. Ibid., 75.
147. Ibid., 76.
148. Parwan may be the same town as Baroi, which the sixteenth-century *A'īn-i-Akbarī* locates in the *sarkar* of Nārwār and the province of Agra: Husain 1976, 163.
149. *Reḥla* of Ibn Baṭṭūṭa 4.35, translated in Husain 1976, 163–64.
150. Bindra 2002, vol. 2, 440–41. See above, n. 57.
151. Smith 2006, 296–97, 310.

CHAPTER TWO

1. See Bryant 2009, 5–6, for a discussion of this commentarial convention.
2. Fitzgerald (2004, 139–41) argues convincingly that the BhG is later than much of the didactic content of the epic's twelfth book, specifically the teachings found in its Rājadharma and MdhP sub-parvans, which are themselves a late portion of the epic. It therefore dates from 200–400 CE. On the date of the definitive compilation of the YS, see Larson and Bhattacharya 2008, 21–22.
3. ĀpDhSū 1.23.3–7. Although short discussions of yoga are also found in the *Baudhāyana Dharma Sūtra* (4.1.22–25) and the *Vasiṣṭha Dharma Sūtra* (25.5–8), these are, as Olivelle (1999, 127, 244) has indicated in his critical apparatus, late additions to these texts.
4. I generally follow the dates determined by Olivelle (1996, xxxvi–xxxvii) for the classical Upaniṣads. However, see chap. 3, section 2, for discussion of the time frame of the long discussion of yoga found in the MU's sixth book.
5. Before they became hardened into philosophical schools, Yoga as a tradition of practice and Sāṃkhya as a "common tradition" (*samānatantra*) of knowledge were closely intertwined. On this, see chap. 5, section 1. Cf. Larson and Bhattacharya 2008, 22–23, 33–36; Bronkhorst 2007, 30; and Fitzgerald 2009, 185–212.
6. Griffiths 1981, 605–24.
7. Malinar 2007, 144–56.
8. BhG 6.46–47.
9. BhG 6.20a: yatroparamate cittaṃ niruddhaṃ yogasevāya. Note the similarity to the celebrated formula of YS 1.2: yogaścittavṛttinirodhaḥ.
10. BhG 6.23a: taṃ vidyād duḥkhasaṃyogaviyogaṃ yogasaṃjñitam. An entirely different identification of *yoga* and *viyoga* is found in the ca. 1569 CE *Padmāvat*, a "yogi romance": see chap. 6, nn. 81–87.

11. BhG 5.4, 5.26, 6.27, discussed in Gerow 2007, 146–47.
12. "Pure contemplation" is Barbara Stoler Miller's (1996) felicitous translation of the term. "Com-position," a quite literal translation of the verb *dhā preceded by the prefixes sam-ā, does not satisfactorily render the semantic field of the term.
13. Pāṇini, *Dhātupāṭha* 4.68, 7.7, cited in Larson and Bhattacharya 2008, 28. Śaiva theoreticians, from among both the early Pāśupatas and the orthodox Śaivasiddhāntins, took issue with this reading, defining yoga as union or identity with Śiva, and rejecting Vācaspatimiśra's interpretation: Brunner 1994, 429. For other "non-pātañjala" definitions of yoga, see Vasudeva 2000, 176–79.
14. Larson and Bhattacharya, 115, 294.
15. Quarnström 2003, 131–33, citing the *Tattvārtha Sūtra* of Umāsvāti and Haribhadra's *Yogadṛṣṭisamucchaya* (1.11).
16. Grinshpon 1997, 559–62; Edgerton 1924, 38–39 and n. 44.
17. BrSūBh 2.1.3; Bronkhorst 1981, 309.
18. In this, I take issue with Michel Angot (2008, 32) who assumes the identity between yoga and meditation, asserting that the Buddha and Mahāvīra "practiced yoga," and whose genealogy of the post-patañjalian history of "classical yoga" is generally restricted to philosophical works. Whicher (1998, 7–8) briefly reviews theories of yoga that acknowledge the yoking paradigm.
19. De la Vallée Poussin 1936–37b, 226.
20. AN 3.355.9–10, quoted in De la Vallée Poussin 1936–37a, 191. Further discussion is found in Eliade 1973, 174–76; Griffiths 1981, 616; and Sarbacker 2005, 87, 101. I have adopted Eliade's translation of the two Pali terms.
21. This use of terminology is embedded in discussions of the respective theories and practices of the two systems. It is found especially in MBh 12.229; 12.289–90; 12.294–96; 12.306.
22. See chap. 2, sections 5 and 6.
23. ŚvU 6.13.
24. Gonda 1963, 18, 289–301.
25. See chap. 4, sections 1a and 5.
26. YS 3.18–19.
27. Sarbacker 2005.
28. YS 1.41–46. Although, as Sarbacker (ibid., 127 and passim) has rightly emphasized, *samādhi*, the final goal of *pātañjala-yoga* practice, comprises both the numinous and cessative modes of yogic and meditative practice.
29. Sénart 1900, 255, 261. See chap. 5, section 2a.
30. Vivekananda 1946, 119–314, reproduces a series of lectures made to the New York Vedanta Society and devoted to the topic of *rāja yoga*. On the influences of Blavatsky on Vivekananada's interpretations, see DeMichelis 2004, 178.

31. Jason Birch and Olle Quarnström have recently discovered a series of verses shared in common between the AY and the YŚ of the Jain author Hemacandra (fl. 1089–1172 CE). According to their analysis, Hemacandra borrowed a number of verses from the AY: e-mail message from Jason Birch, October 28, 2007. If the historical Gorakhnāth lived in the twelfth to thirteenth centuries, as I have argued (White 1996, 95), then he could have authored a work referenced by Hemacandra in the latter half of the twelfth century.
32. AY 2.3–5 identifies *rāja yoga* with "inner yoga" and an "inner seal" and etymologizes the term by stating that its practitioner becomes "the illustrious king (*rāja*) of the embodied ones": Birch 2006, 68–69, 78.
33. White 1996, 199–201; White 2003, 81. Cf. *Haṭharatnāvalī* 2.105.
34. The author of the *Aparokṣānubhūti* enumerates the fifteen steps to true knowledge in verses 100–44. He draws a sharp contrast between the two forms of yoga in verse 143 and mentions *rāja yoga* alone in verses 114 and 144 (the final verse of the work). On the question of authorship and dating, see Bouy 1994, 62–63.
35. While four types of yoga, including *haṭha yoga* and *rāja yoga*, are listed at verse 19, most of the remainder of this text (from v. 24) is devoted to *haṭha yoga*. According to Bouy (1994, 9, n. 3, 113, 117), the YTU is a composite work that borrows heavily from the HYP and the *Yogayājñavalkya* (YYāj), which is a tenth- to fourteenth-century work. However, he indicates that its title is included in a listing of fifteen Upaniṣads that may date from "before the twelfth century": ibid., 65. For an extended discussion of this and the other Yoga Upaniṣads, see also Ruff 2002.
36. Bouy 1994, 19.
37. APr 4b: yaścittavṛttirahitaḥ sa tu rājayogaḥ//.
38. APr 5: oṣadhyo 'dhyātmakaśceti rājayogo dvidhā kvacit/ haṭho 'pi dvidvidhaḥ kvāpi vāyubinduniṣevaṇāt//.
39. *Kālacakra Tantra* 4.119, with the Vimalaprabhā commentary.
40. HYP 1.2–3; 4.8. Elsewhere, this text underscores the complementarity of the two (2.76).
41. In Jha 1992, 39, 55.
42. Sarbacker (2005, 90) evokes a similar conundrum in Buddhist studies, "where there has been difficulty understanding why such an important ['numinous'] part of Buddhist meditation theory (*samatha*) has become not only a marginal practice but one that might even receive ridicule by some practitioners."
43. Wood 1959, 82, 98, 168, 188, cited in DeMichelis 2004, 179, n. 38.
44. See chap. 4, section 4a.
45. The seal is so numbered in Mackay 1937–38, vol. 1, 335; vol. 2, pl. XCIV and C (F).
46. Marshall 1931, vol. 1, 52–54.
47. Filliozat 1955, 368.

48. Eliade 1973, 355; Werner 1975, 180; Hiltebeitel 1978, 768–69; O'Flaherty 1981, 9; Kramrisch 1981, 10–11.
49. These are the seals numbered 222 and 230, in MacKay 1937–38, vol. 1, 335, and vol. 2, pl. LXXXVII.
50. Kenoyer 1998, 113–15, and figs. 6.24 and 6.25.
51. Coomaraswamy 1956, plate 40, fig. 124. The medallion is discussed ibid., 83. She is named "Sirima" (Śrīmā) on the railing inscription.
52. MBh 12.124.46.
53. MBh 1.189.9–48, especially vv. 9, 11, and 39.
54. Errington and Cribb 1992, 63, figs. 27 and 28. On the Maues coin, see also Rosenfeld 1967, 283, n. 3. The seated royal figure is on the reverse of the Maues coin and the obverse of the Azes coin. Both coins are held in the British Museum, London (1859-3-1-68 and 1894-5-6-604).
55. Fleischer 1973, 91.
56. Jensen 2003, 206–21; Duval 1981, vol. 1, 152.
57. Duval 1981, vol. 1, 152; Klindt-Jensen 1961, 11.
58. Klindt-Jensen 1961, 50; Puhvel 1987, 35.
59. Czuma 1985, 64, fig. 12. This sculpture is housed in the Museum of Fine Arts, Boston, Massachusetts, David Pulsifer Kimball Fund 25.437.
60. Ibid., 53, fig. 3 . This sculpture is housed in the State Museum, Lucknow J. 250.
61. Figure 2.7 is shown in Czuma 1985, 197, fig. 108. Cleveland Museum of Art, Bequest 61.418. A first through third century CE Maitreya from Gandhara is pictured in Schwartzberg 1992, 23 (pl. III.C4e).
62. A study that simply juxtaposes seal 420 with images of T. K. V. Desikachar practicing the *mūlabandha* posture, and concludes that the image on the seal is therefore that of a yogi, is Dhyansky 1987, 89–108.
63. Duval 1981, 152.
64. Bronkhorst 1993, 19, 23.
65. Ibid., 1–5.
66. Ibid., 22–24.
67. Kumoi 1997, 415–18; De la Vallée Poussin 1936–37a, 189–90, n. 1. Silk notes (2000, 281) that the term *yogācāra* appears nowhere in the Pali Canon.
68. MU 6.20.
69. White 1996, 158–59.
70. MU 6.18.
71. See chap. 3, n. 37.
72. While *tarka* remains the fifth member of many later Hindu enumerations, it is replaced by *anusmṛti* ("recollection") in several Buddhist accounts of six-limbed yoga: see chap. 3, nn. 61–68.
73. Errington and Cribb 1992, 169, fig. 167.
74. Stein 1907/1975, vol. 1, 279, and pl. LXI. Stein (ibid., 277) has established that the panel cannot date from later than 790 CE; the iconographic

program of the multi-headed Śiva image on the obverse cannot date from before the sixth century: Granoff 1979, 75–76.

75. Soper 1949, 263–64; Watson 1983, 556. Soper notes (ibid., 271, n. 44) that the kings of Khotan had close ties with the Kushan kings.
76. Brunner, Oberhammer, and Padoux 2000, 209, s. v. "āsana."
77. Rosenfield 1967, 14–15 and pl. I, fig. 6. Rosenfeld notes the resemblance in composition between this and the Indo-Scythian coins described above (n. 54). Like those coins, that of Kujala Kadphises also bears Greek and Kharoshti inscriptions.
78. Ibid., 23–24 and pl. II, no. 20. The same coin is discussed in Soper 1949, 270, and fig. 3. See chap. 4, n. 28.
79. Errington and Cribb 1992, fig. 199, p. 200. Cribb maintains that the frontal representations of such early Buddha images on Kushan coinage are indications that they were copied from Gandharan sculpture. Seated figures are extremely rare in Kushan coinage, accounting for fewer than five percent of all finds, with the lion's share of seated figures representing Kaniṣka's successor, Huviṣka. For an encyclopedic treatment, with exhaustive iconography, of the Kushan coins, see Göbl 1984.
80. The ŚvU appears to identify yoga with *tapas* when it states (2.12) that a body "cooked in the fire of yoga" will no longer experience old age or suffering. On the vedic origins of *tapas* as the prime means for a sacrificer to purify himself in his initiation (*dīkṣā*) or as a form of penance; and on *prāṇāyāma* as a *tapas*-generating form of penance, see Kaelber 1989, 50–60.
81. See chap. 1, n. 137.
82. MBh 5.33.52 (*178 in the critical edition, following 5.33.52 in the K2.4.5; D8.10; K1; and D2.7 manuscripts).
83. In the VV (in Sastri 1983–84, vol. 1, 4, lines 21–22) of the ca. 950 CE Nyāya-Vaiśeṣika commentator Vyomaśiva. Here, Vyomaśiva is quoting *Parāśara Smṛti* 3.37.
84. Settar and Sondheimer 1982, 274; Singh 1957, vol. 4, chap. 61, vv. 180, 288, 312, and 321. I am grateful to Cynthia Talbot for these references.
85. KhV 3.51–54, text and translation in Mallinson 2007, 106–7, 132–33. This dynamic becomes internalized with the hathayogic technique of *sūryabheda*, discussed in HYP 2.48–50.
86. YājS 1.324, quoted in Hara 2001a, 337. On the dating of this text, see Lingat 1967, 118.
87. AB 6.35 and MS 4.4.10, discussed in Biardeau and Malamoud 1976, 191–92.
88. ṚV 2.8.1, cited in Renou 1953, 179, who also argues that the compound *ṛta yoga* ought to be read as the "chariot of sacrifice."
89. ŚB 9.4.4.15, discussed in Biardeau and Malamoud 1976, 191.
90. AB 18.7, discussed in Lévi 1966, 89.
91. It is perhaps due to the prestige of this god's vedic mythology of the "three steps" that the verb *kram is used so frequently in the contexts I will describe, even when another verb, such as *car, or *ruh might have been

more appropriate. On Viṣṇu's steps and the motion of the sun, see chap. 4, section 1d.

92. ŚB 1.9.3.8–9,11, discussed in Lévi 1966, 89–90.
93. Biardeau and Malamoud 1976, 192–94.
94. Lévi 1966, 130–32. See also Malamoud 1989, 115–36.
95. Biardeau and Malamoud 1976, 195.
96. The Brāhmaṇas already distinguish, ambiguously, between the worlds of the ancestors, the gods, and the kingdom of Yama to which the dead go: Lévi 1966, 96, 98–99.
97. ŚB 2.3.3.7–8, discussed in Lévi 1966, 96–97.
98. Biardeau and Malamoud 1976, 75, n. 1; Whicher 1998, 7–8.
99. Oguibénine 1984, 85, citing Grassman (1873/1976), *Wörterbuch zum Rig-Veda*, Sp. 1115.
100. Ibid., 87, 89, 93.
101. ṚV 10.114.10, cited ibid., 92.
102. ṚV 4.16.21; 4.37.6; 4.56.4; 7.93.3; 8.4.20, etc. Cf. Heesterman (1985, 1993), who has argued convincingly that vedic ritual, as presented in the vedic Saṃhitās and Brāhmaṇas, is an overwriting of agonistic sacrifice performed by chariot warriors.
103. ṚV 5.46.1, quoted in Oguibénine 1984, 88.
104. ṚV 7.70.2, cited ibid., 96.
105. "Driving into battle." Oertel 1926, 226.
106. ṚV 6.25.3, quoted in Oguibénine 1984, 89. Several other citations from both the ṚV and AV are found in Renou 1953, 178, 179.
107. Watkins 1985, 79, s.v. "yeug" (the Indo-European root).
108. BṛU 4.3.10. Cf. AV 6.91.1, in which "yokes of eight" and "yokes of six" draft animals are evoked.
109. ChU 8.12.3.
110. KU 3.3–9; Plato, *Phædrus* 246a–256e. Plato's charioteer journeys up into the transcendent World of Ideas and thereby escapes rebirth—if he can control his horses.
111. Renou 1953, 178, citing ṚV 5.37.5; 5.54.3; 7.86.8; 10.89.10.
112. Like the later "original" MU, the MS is linked to the Black Yajurveda: Van Buitenen 1962, 71. See chap. 3, n. 20.
113. Oertel 1926, 224.
114. MS 3.2.2 (pp. 16, 14), tr. in Oertel 1926, 223.
115. Filliozat 1967, 80–88; Hara 2001a, 140–41; Weinberger-Thomas 1999, 14–19.
116. Rām 7.110.21, 24.
117. In ṚV 6.75.6, *raśmayaḥ* simply refers to the reins of a chariot.
118. ṚV 1.50.9, quoted in Oguibénine 1984, 96.
119. The term is found in a number of didactic passages, including seven mentions in the BhG, in which its archaic literal meaning is generally lost: see chap. 3, nn. 84–88. It is used in a literal, nonmetaphorical sense in MBh

7.19.18, in which the warrior Pragjyotiṣa mounted on his elephant is compared to the full moon, hitched up to its rig of the stars of the Pleaides (*kṛttikā yoga-yuktena*).

120. AB 6.35 and MS 4.4.10, discussed in Biardeau and Malamoud 1976, 191–92. Cf. ŚB 13.2.10.1.
121. Parallel beliefs among Etruscans and Romans of the same period are evidenced in the bas reliefs found on numerous sarcophagi, on which dead warriors and members of the nobility are depicted as traveling to the world of the dead on horse-drawn chariots.
122. Schreiner 1999b, 755–77.
123. The Nārāyaṇīya Parvan, a formulation of Bhāgavata doctrine, which predates that found in the BhG, forms a portion of the MdhP, comprising chapters 321–39 of the MBh's twelfth book.
124. An illuminating study is Heimann 1939, 125–35, especially pp. 130–31.
125. MBh 13.154.3–6. See below, n. 147 and chap. 3, nn. 178–80.
126. Mbh 16.5.18–25.
127. MBh 17.1.28, 44; 17.2.1.
128. MBh 16.5.21–23.
129. MBh 12.319.5b–24b. See below, nn. 151–61.
130. MBh 9.49.1–62. See below, nn. 163–64 and chap. 4, nn. 130, 132–33.
131. MBh 12.350.8–12.351.1.
132. Schreiner 1999a, 141, and Schreiner 1988, 12–18. Cf. Sullivan 2006, 61–80, who approaches these deaths from the perspective of the epic ethic of suicide.
133. MBh 9.54.6; 11.2.6–11; 12.22.14; 12.29.11; 12.98.31 and elsewhere. For discussion, see Hara 2001b, 336–38.
134. See chap. 3, n. 162, on the adaptation of a warrior's *prāya* by the Jain monk seeking to abandon his body.
135. MBh 7.118.16b, 17a–18b. Here I am translating *mahopaniṣad* ("great setting to rest," "death") in a way analogous to the usage of *mahāprasthāna* ("great departure"), which is employed, in MBh 17.1–3 and elsewhere, to signify departing from life, i.e., dying. However, the term could be a reference to the esoteric teachings of the Upaniṣads on liberation. Cf. Mbh 6.114.112a, with reference to Bhīṣma.
136. MBh 7.165.35.
137. Bharadvāja's yoga is described chap. 4, n. 136. A number of vedic and upanishadic figures named Bhāradvāja (or, as a group, the Bhāradvājas) are linked to the sun: see Chenet 1993, 328, 338. However, Bharadvāja/Bhāradvāja is a common clan or *gotra* name, going back to one of the seven sages, so these are likely different individuals.
138. MBh 7.165.39a–41a, 41c–42b.
139. MBh 17.1.28; 17.2.1.
140. MBh 17.1.42; 17.2.3a.
141. Hiltebeitel 2001, 271.

142. MBh 17.2.1b–2a. Pāṇḍu, the father of the five Pāṇḍavas, attempts to do the same with his wives. The account of their climb employs the verbs *ati-kram* and *para-ā-kram*: MBh 1.110.43; 1.111.2.
143. MBh 17.2.3b. A passage from the VāP (73.1–10) employs the term *bhraṣṭayogā*, this time with reference to a female Apsaras named Ācchodā, who falls from a heavenly aerial car, her rig fallen due to her excessive libido.
144. For the use of this term in the heavenly ascent of the vedic sacrificial patron, see above, n. 120.
145. MBh 16.5.18–20.
146. MBh 16.5.21–23.
147. MBh 13.154.2–6. While Bhīṣma has been forced to fight on the Kaurava side in the war, he is nonetheless very much a Pāṇḍava ally in word and deed, as proven by the fact that he indicates to the Pāṇḍavas how they must kill him!
148. See chap. 3, n. 32.
149. BhP 12.6.9–10.
150. See chap. 4, section 4.
151. Śuka's story is recounted in detail in Hiltebeitel 2001, 278–322, and Shulman 1993, 108–32.
152. Mbh 12.312.8.
153. MBh 12.312.12–14, 16b.
154. MBh 12.314.26b, 27b.
155. MBh 3.38.27–29. In this case, Arjuna does not continue on his journey up to or through the sun, since the narrative logic of the epic requires that he remain in this world to fight the Kauravas in the great battle.
156. MBh 12.315.28–31. The "seven winds" (*maruts*), which are sometimes described as luminous, are an epic variation on the vedic theme of the seven solar rays: see chap. 3, nn. 34 and 105. They are also mentioned in the context of meditative ascent in MBh 12.290.72: see chap. 5, n. 17.
157. MBh 12.318.53.
158. MBh 12.319.2, 6.
159. MBh 12.319.16b, 17b.
160. MBh 12.320.3b.
161. Hazra 1975, 13.
162. VāP 73.32–33.
163. MBh 9.49.6. The compound *yogayukta* is found in all southern recensions of this verse.
164. MBh 9.49.24–61. See chap. 4, nn. 162–63. MBh 12.222.3–24 comprises a teaching by Jaigīṣavya to Asita Devala on the path to liberation.
165. MBh 12.349.7.
166. Dharmāraṇya calls himself *yogayukta* (12.349.7), yet he neither undergoes apotheosis nor has he been described as practicing yoga of any type.
167. MBh 12.350.9–10, 13, 15.

168. Mbh 12.228.7: evam hy etena yogena yuñjāno 'py ekam antataḥ/api jijñāsamāno hi śabdabrahmātivartate//.
169. The Sanskrit terms *pṛṣṭhatas* and *pārśvatas* employed here are also applied to the location of chariot guards on war chariots: Hopkins 1901, 354.
170. MBh 12.228.11–16.
171. Hopkins 1901, 354. This passage is also discussed in Wynne 2007, 38.
172. Hopkins 1901, 353, 354.
173. Monier-Williams 1984, 519, s.v. "dhṛ"(with *raśmīn* or *prahāran*). In a celebrated hymn from the AV (19.53), the solar chariot driven by Time (Kāla) is controlled by seven reins/rays: see chap. 4, n. 46.
174. They are so identified by the commentator Nīlakaṇṭha: Hopkins 1901, 352.
175. MBh 12.228.16. Cf. the coeval *Śāntikalpa* 3.2 (in Bolling 1913, 268), which evokes a *mahāyogī's* attainment, through yoking, of *karmasiddhi.*
176. MBh 12.228.21–22.
177. MBh 12.228.37.
178. See chap. 1, n. 122.
179. Proferes 2007, 17. Cf. Oberlies 1998, 337–47, who notes a corresponding alternation between the cults of the war god Indra and those of Varuṇa and the Ādityas as gods of order.
180. Heesterman 1982, 255.
181. Ibid., 268, 269.
182. TU 3.10.2.
183. Kumoi 1997, 409, quoting *Suttanipāta* 425.
184. KU 2.2; BhG 2.45, 9.22, discussed ibid., 410–11.
185. Oertel 1926, 226.
186. *Yogakṣema* appears to be a copulative (*dvandva*) compound; yet it has the masculine singular ending of a *tatpuruṣa*: ibid., 227, 230–31.
187. Kolff 1990, 85.
188. Ibid., 77.
189. Ibid., 195.
190. Ibid., 82.
191. The Brāhmaṇas are traditionally dated to the eighth century BCE; however, in the light of Bronkhorst's (2007, 258) revision of the chronology of the Brāhmaṇas and early Upaniṣads, a far later date is possible.
192. TB 3.3.3.3–4: yad yoktraṃ sa yogo yad āste sa kṣemaḥ//yogakṣemasya kḷptyai.
193. divasaṃ prapadair nayet sthānāsanavihārair vā yogābhyāsena vā punaḥ//.
194. Hopkins 1901, 369.
195. BhG 6.11–14; 3.6–7. Cf. Fitzgerald 2004, 139–41.
196. Gnoli 1977, vol. 1, 113.
197. Shah 1984, 96–97 and pl. 79, 80.
198. Ibid., 96, 100.
199. Ibid., pl. 81–83 and 86–93.

200. Monier-Williams 1984, s.v. "yoga-paṭṭa," cites the fifth- to sixth century CE *Padma Purāṇa* (PP), the ca. 625 CE HC, and Hemādri's (1260–1309) *Caturvargacintāmaṇi*. SvT 7.290–91, which dates from the tenth century, follows an enumeration of three of the first four *āsanas* listed in Vyāsa's commentary on YS 2.46 with a mention of the *yoga-paṭṭa*.
201. *Nei-yeh* 16.1–6, 17.14–4, 24.1–4, 7–9 in Roth 1999, 76, 78, 92.
202. Harper 1995, 381, 390.
203. White 2003, 187; Filliozat 1969, 73–74.
204. The Indian penal code, which has remained virtually unchanged since it was drawn up by the British in 1860, is accessible through the Indian Ministry of Home Affairs Web site: http://mha.nic.in/home.asp. Such uses of the expression *car sau bīs* gained great popularity following the 1955 Raj Kapoor movie *Shri 420*: e-mail communication from Partha Chatterjee, June 29, 2008.

CHAPTER THREE

1. Fort 1994, 379–90.
2. The ChU and other early Upaniṣads are traditionally dated to the sixth to third centuries BCE: Olivelle 1996, xxxvi–xxxvii. However, in the light of the recent forward revision of dates of the historical Buddha to some time between 500 and 380 BCE (Cousins 1996, 57–63), the dates of all of the early Upaniṣads should also be moved forward: Fitzgerald 2004, 111, n. 134. Bronkhorst 2007, 127–30, 258 argues quite convincingly for still later dates, pushing the date of the final composition of the BṛU forward to the time of Pāṇini (ca. 400 BCE). However, Bronkhorst's principal hypothesis remains: that the bulk of upanishadic speculation on karma and rebirth dates from the time of the Buddha.
3. On this translation of the term, see chap. 5, nn. 26–27.
4. BṛU 1.4.9–10. Vāmadeva's declaration repeats the opening verse of ṚV 4.26: Roebuck 2003, 397, n. 57.
5. See below, n. 37 and chap. 5, nn. 81–85.
6. ChU 7.25.2; 7.26.1.
7. ChU 8.1.1–6.
8. See chap. 5, section 1.
9. ChU 8.6.2, 5.
10. ChU 8.6.1–2, 4–6.
11. *Prāyaṇāntam*: PU 5.1.
12. PU 1.6; 5.5.
13. See chap. 2, n. 97.
14. KU 6.18. The "definition" of yoga offered in KU 6.11 evokes that of YS 1.2. See chap. 2, n. 9.
15. Malinar 2007, 142; Biardeau 1968, 39–45.
16. KU 6.7–8, 9b. KU 6.7–8 is identical to KU 3.10–11. See below, n. 32.

17. Cf. MBh 5.44.4, which paraphrases these verses. The circa second-century CE Buddhist *Patisambhidamagga* (2.210) employs the same language in its instructions for creating a "mind-made body" (Clough 2008, 6).
18. KU 6.16–17. Cf. KU 4.12–13.
19. In his commentary (in Joshi 1981, 982–83), he does not take issue with BrSū 4.2.18, which states that all who die follow the sun's ray.
20. Van Buitenen 1962, 71.
21. Ibid., 21–23.
22. Ibid., 24–28.
23. Ibid., 5.
24. MU 6.19–22.
25. Here I am referring to the Upaniṣads that precede the so-called Yoga Upaniṣads, none of which predate the thirteenth century. On this corpus, see Bouy 1994; Ruff, 2002; and Larson and Bhattacharya 2008, 591–629.
26. See chap. 2, n. 69.
27. HYP 4.85–86.
28. MU 6.30.
29. See chap. 4, section 1c.
30. KU 6.7–8, 16–17. See above, n. 18 and chap. 2, n. 2.
31. KU 3.9–11. See chap. 2, n. 110.
32. MU 1.4: rājāno miṣato bandhuvargasya mahatīṃ śriyāṃ tyaktvā 'smāllokādamuṃ lokaṃ prayātā.
33. MU 1.4: tvaṃ no gatistvaṃ no gatiḥ.
34. MU 2.1. "Marut" is derived from the same Sanskrit root as "marici," which means "ray" or "beam of light." Monier-Williams (1984), s.v. "marut." Nonetheless, the term "marut" is frequently associated with wind, which is the likely source of the association of the seven winds with the seven solar rays. See chap. 2, n. 156.
35. MU 6.24 speaks of reaching "the darkness that is pervaded by non-darkness," by the piercing of which one comes into the presence of the effulgent *brahman* which, blazing like a whirling circle of light, has the color of the sun, and whose light is also visible in the moon, fire, and lightening.
36. In the *dharmasūtra* literature, which dates from several centuries before the common era, *prāṇāyāma* denoted a type of penance and religious rite for removing the taint attached to acts and omissions that were condemned by the society of the time. At this stage, *prāṇāyāma* had not been identified as a component of yogic practice: Kane 1968–77, vol. 5, part 2, p. 1436. *Prāṇāyāma* is defined in both the YS (2.49) and the BhG (4.29) as the complete *cessation* of breathing, rather than controlling the in- and out-breaths.
37. The sons of Brahmā-Prajāpati (Sanatkumāra, Sanatsujāta, etc.) are commonly identified as the liberated denizens of the world of *brahman*: on this, see above, n. 5 (on Sanatkumāra), below, n. 184 (on Sanatsujāta), and chap. 5, nn. 81–85.
38. MU 6.30.

39. At MU 2.3, a deeper level of embedded discourse is opened up when Śākāyanya introduces "what was taught to us by the blessed Maitri." Presumably, all that follows, from MU 2.4 until the end of MU 6.28, is Śākāyanya's retelling of Maitri's earlier teaching.
40. ChU 3.12.7–8; 3.13.7; 3.14.3. ChU 3.19.1–3 identifies the *brahman* with the sun and then proceeds to describe a cosmogony that is simultaneously an embryology, with the "embryo" identified with the cosmic egg.
41. See chap. 4, section 6.
42. This is, in fact, the final verse of MU 6.27.
43. Cf. ChU 7.24.1.
44. See below, n. 57 for similar language in the BhG.
45. See chap. 2, section 5. As we will see, this language also evokes the supernatural power of perception possessed by yogis who are "yoked," as described in Nyāya-Vaiśeṣika philosophy. See chap. 4, n. 203.
46. MBh 6.114.88–89; 13.3b. See chap. 2, nn. 123 and 147, and below, n. 178.
47. This is of a piece with vedic traditions, which are quite consistent in their assertion that one looked *down* into the night sky, such that the highest heaven was situated below, at the bottom or back of the sky: Hiltebeitel 2001, 153–54. In later Vaiṣṇava cosmology, Viṣṇu's eye is situated at the southern celestial pole, from which he "panoptically" views the entire cosmos: Kloetzli 1985, 142. This appears to be an early expression of what would later become a commonplace of Vaiṣṇava cosmology.
48. Dhruva is also the name of the Pole Star, with which Viṣṇu is identified in later sectarian sources: see below, n. 105. So, too, is Rudra, in Śaiva traditions: see below, n. 125. In the third-century BCE Buddhist DN (1.223), *nirvāṇa* is cast as an infallible (*acyuta*) and fixed (*dhruva*) place to which one could travel: Wynne 2007, 114–15.
49. I have translated the term *bhuvana* twice, since the term means both "realm" and "living being" and because in all that has preceded the *brahman* has been simultaneously portrayed as both internal and infinitesimal and all encompassing and infinite.
50. However, the expression "two, indeed, threefold" (*dvistridhā hi*) appears to be a reference to the *puruṣa*, which is said to be twofold, but is actually threefold, in the JUB 1.25.1–10; BhG 15.16–18; and elsewhere. See chap. 4, nn. 41–45.
51. The *brahman* is called an "ocean of light" in MU 6.37.
52. See chap. 2, n. 81.
53. Bronkhorst 2007, 31.
54. ChU 7.6.1–2.
55. Gonda 1963, 292–95. See chap. 2, n. 11.
56. *Muṇḍaka Upaniṣad* (MuU) 2.2.6; ŚvU 1.10–11; PU 5.1–5. Cf. ChU 8.12.6, which employs the term *upāsanā*.
57. Here, nityayuktasya yoginaḥ. Cf. MU 6.28: yuktasya nityamuktasya dehinaḥ. This language appears to be reprised by Kauṇḍinya in his PBh

commentary on the PSū, which speaks of the appearance of a yogi's supernatural powers (*aiśvaryam*) after six months: āha ṣaṇmāsān nityayuktasya . . . pravartanta (PBh 117.14–118.12, quoted in Oberhammer 1994, 82); as well as in *Parākhyatantra* 4.104–5, see below, n. 168.

58. See above, nn. 10–11.
59. BhG 8.13–14.
60. Malamoud 1989, 298.
61. Beyer 1977, 336.
62. Karlsson 1999, 69. Ruegg (1967, 157–61) argues—on the basis of the contents of the untitled Inner Asian manuscript from Qïzïl—that *anusmṛti* was also a technique of the Sarvāstivādin school of Kashmir in this period: see chap. 4, n. 148.
63. Sarbacker 2005, 56, 72.
64. VM 4.26–30, discussed in Griffiths 1981, 610. See chap. 4, n. 207.
65. Described in a Chinese-language Buddhist meditation manual, the *Ssu-wei liu-yao fa* (*Short Method of Meditation* [T. 617]), quoted in Beyer 1977, 337.
66. Chenet 1987, 50.
67. Yamabe 2002, 124. See chap. 4, n. 149.
68. Soper 1950, 69 and fig. 5.
69. Howard 1986, xix, 61–63. The DN's fourth book is the textual source for the "cosmological Buddha": ibid., 6–12. Howard notes (ibid., xix, 54–57) that in the Central Asian cave paintings as well as in the earliest representations of Viṣṇu's universal form, the cosmos was projected out from the body of the Buddha onto the walls of the caves; later representations of the cosmological Buddha, mainly from China, inscribe the cosmos on the Buddha's garment.
70. On the orthodox Śaiva meditation program, see Brunner 1994, 442–43.
71. Wallace 2001, 26. *Smaraṇa* is the fifth limb of the five-limbed yoga system of the VāP (10.76). See chap. 2, n. 72.
72. Kapani 1992–93, vol. 1, 287. See chap. 4, section 1a.
73. Malamoud 1989, 304; YS 3.18. See chap. 1, n. 127, and chap. 4., nn. 115, 133.
74. Strickmann 1996, 50; Nabokov 2000.
75. Primiano 1995; Smith 2006.
76. Beyer 1977, 333–35.
77. Ibid., 339.
78. *Lakṣmī Tantra* (LT) 55.7–19. Cf. LT 6.38; 12.56; 31.70–76.
79. *Uttarabhāvanākrama* of Kamalaśīla, translated from Tucci 1971, 4–5, by Gimello 1978, 184–85. Cf. Chenet 1987, 50–55; Sackrider 2005, 19–22; and Gonda 1985, 456.
80. BhG 6.11–13.
81. BhG 4.29–30; 5.27. See above, n. 36.
82. BhG 5.13.
83. BhG 8.9–10. See chap. 3, section 6.

84. BhG 6.5,6,21; 6.29; 8.8,27; 9.28.
85. See chap. 4, n. 204, for uses of this compound in Indic theories of perception.
86. See chap. 5, section 1, on the *sāṃkhya-yoga* dyad, as presented in chapters 289 and 290 of the MdhP.
87. BhG 5.10–15.
88. BhG 5.12,27; 6.23; 8.8; 9.28.
89. Both Hudson (1995, 137–82) and Bryant (2002, 51–80) argue that portions of this Purāṇa are "archaic," whereas other parts date from the ninth century CE and later. The data in BhP 2.2 appears to be coeval with that found in the YBh (see below, nn. 157–59) and the NTS (see below, nn. 126–29).
90. This chapter employs several terms for "virtuoso practitioner": *kavi* (2.2.3), *siddha* (2.2.6), *yogeśvara* (2.2.10,23), *yati* (2.2.15), *muni* (2.2.19), and *yogī* (2.2.29).
91. BhP 2.2.8.
92. BhP 2.2.8a–10a. Cf. JS 10.58–68, tr. in Flood 2000, 517.
93. BhP 2.2.13, 16, 18. Cf. ViṣP 1.6.38. One may also translate *paraṃ padaṃ vaiṣṇavam* as the "highest Viṣṇu foot." This reading makes sense when placed in the context of Vaiṣṇava metaphysics, which locates Viṣṇu's eye at the southern celestial pole (see above, n. 47) and his foot at the place of the Pole Star, at the summit of the universe. See White 2002, 201–2.
94. BhP 2.2.21–22, 32.
95. MBh 3.160.17–18, 21–23.
96. BhP 2.2.10, 23. See above, nn. 40, 48. Cf. Mbh 12.290, in the MdhP (discussed in chap. 5, section 1).
97. BhP 2.2.23.
98. BhP 2.2.24–26. Dhruva, identified with *brahman*, is termed the navel of the universe in *Hiraṇyakeśi Gṛhya Sūtra* 1.23.1: Brereton 1991, 5.
99. BhP 2.2.28–30. These stages or hierarchized metaphysical categories are enumerated, in reverse order, in Mbh 12.290.87–91. See chap. 5, nn. 19–20.
100. BhP 2.2.31.
101. Hudson 1993, 146.
102. Ibid., 149.
103. Ibid., 162–64.
104. MBh 12.290.96. See above, n. 48.
105. Pingree 1981, 12–13, cited in Roebuck 2003, 467, n. 18. See chap. 2, nn. 156 and 173.
106. *Sūryaśataka* 22, 29, cited in Chenet 1993, 358.
107. See chap. 4, nn. 165–67; chap. 5, nn. 94–97.
108. Biardeau 1968, 19–45. An English-language version is Biardeau 1991, 43–50.
109. The highest categories of the samkhyan hierarchy are those enumerated in KU 3.10–11 and 6.7–8. See above, n. 16.

110. On the upanishadic origins of speculations on *dhruva*, see Brereton 1991, 5–7.
111. For the Pāśupatas, this meant placing Rudra above the individual soul, as the twenty-sixth *tattva*, analogous to the samkhyan *puruṣa*: Sanderson 2006, 193.
112. The list also includes the names Viṣṇu, Nārāyaṇa, Prajāpati, and a dozen other deities or metaphysical principles.
113. ŚvU 3.7–16.
114. MBh 12.337.59, 62 and Sanderson 2006, 210.
115. Hara 1999, 593–94.
116. Ibid., 595.
117. PBh 6.8–9; 41.13; 42.1–3; 110.19; 118.2; 122.1; 124.9–10 (quoted in Oberhammer 1994, 77, 80).
118. See chap. 5, nn. 102–5.
119. Sanderson 2006, 146–47.
120. Sanderson (ibid., 158) cogently argues for the adoption, in Indological usage, of the term Atimārga for "group[ing] these [Pāśupata] systems and certain other satellites which need to be distinguished as a unity over and against agamic Śaivism."
121. The core text of the SvT dates from the sixth to seventh century; however, portions of the work, including the seventh chapter, are later interpolations.
122. Ibid., 160.
123. On the dating of this work, see Goodall and Isaacson 2007, 4–6.
124. Sanderson 2006, 152, 160–74. Sanderson (ibid., 152) lists the manuscripts included in this codex. In his translation, he also drawns on the *Niśvāsakārikā*, a portion of the *Niśvāsasaṃhitā* missing from the Nepali codex but extant in southern manuscripts.
125. Ibid., 169–70, 174.
126. *Niśvāsamukha* 4.96 (ibid.,163). Mbh 12.224.53–59 appears to present the same alternative soteriologies with the important difference that asceticism (*tapas*) is made out to be the path to the higher worlds and "yoga" the path for reaching the highest self: e-mail from James Fitzgerald dated December 6, 2007.
127. Sanderson 2006, 188–192.
128. Ibid., 193.
129. Ibid., 193–98.
130. See above, n. 48.
131. The Śaivāgamas employ the term *dhyāna* to denote the mental construction of an image of Siva, which is subsequently worshiped (Brunner 1994, 442). Cf. KP 2.11.59–60 for Pāśupata use of the same terminology.
132. Sanderson (2006, 202) argues that this tradition is inherited from both of the branches of the *atimārga*. Brunner (1994, 452) calls the MPĀg, as well as two other Upāgamas, the MĀg and *Sardhatriśatikalottarāgama* "late," dating them before the ninth century CE.

133. A nearly identical description, embedded in a discussion of "pāśupata yoga," is found in KP 1.11.61–64, 67, which dates from the early eighth century: see chap. 5, n. 98.
134. MPĀg, caryāpada 9.9–11, 13, 21–27, translated in Sanderson 2006, 205–6 (I have emended Sanderson's translation of v. 13). As Sanderson notes (ibid., 207), "gradual ascent through the levels of the cosmos is the essence of the *Niśvāsamukha*'s account of the Lākulas' path to liberation, and Kṣemarāja describes the systems of the Mausulas and Kārukas [forerunners of the *atimārga* sects] in similar terms as methods for reaching (*prāpti*) the Rudras of their highest world-levels."
135. Goodall 1998, 163–64, n. 10, citing KT 8.121, Kṣemarāja's commentary on SvT 10.891, and Rāmakaṇṭha's commentary on MĀg 23.45–47.
136. Brunner 1994, 434–35, 454, 456; Brunner 1975, 411–43.
137. On the relationship between *sādhakas* and yogis in chapter 33 of this text, see Rastelli 2000, 338, 343, 357–59, and passim.
138. On the rare and problematic usage of this idealized tetrad and the fact that yoga was discussed most often in the Āgamas' ritual sections, see Brunner 1994, 427.
139. Gonda 1977, 184, 186, 188, on the MĀg and *Kiraṇāgama*. However, see below, section 6, for a discussion of *utkrānti*, a yogic practice described in the *yoga-pada* of certain Āgamas.
140. Sanderson 2006, 202, and Sanderson 2007, 241. I disagree, however, with Sanderson's tacit assumption that the original sense of the term yoga would have been limited to "meditative ascent," including in the *atimārga* and other esoteric tantric circles.
141. However, see Hiltebeitel 2001, 97, n. 19.
142. MVUT 4.27–41. Cf. TĀ 15.18–19.
143. Vasudeva 2000, xxxiv.
144. MVUT 2.1–9, translated and summarized ibid., 138–40. See chap. 4, section 5, on the Nyāya-Vaiśeṣika definition of yogi perception as the means by which yogis can see within themselves as well as into the most distant reaches of the universe.
145. See above, n. 32. Eyewitness observation (*pratyakṣa*) is the most widely accepted of the *pramāṇas* (valid cognitions) in the Indian philosophical schools: see chap. 4, section 1a.
146. Summarized in Gimello 1978, 182–83. See, however, Przyluski (1933, 153–54), who links the threefold hierarchy of the form realms, formless realms, and cessation in early Buddhist texts to the three states of consciousness and their cosmological homologues, as theorized in BṛU 4.3.9: see chap. 4, n. 45.
147. De la Vallée Poussin 1936–37a, 212; Sarbacker 2005, 57–58; Gimello 1978, 182–86.
148. See chap. 2, nn. 27–28.
149. Gimello 1978, 187–88.

150. *Vimuttimagga* ("Path of Liberation"), quoted in Gimello 1978,183–84.
151. Sarbacker 2005, 33.
152. Griffiths 1981, 617.
153. Ibid., 616. Cf. De la Vallée Poussin 1936–37a, 197, and Sarbacker 2005, 90.
154. YS 3.37, 50–55 and commentaries. Cf. White 2003, 220.
155. Whicher 1998, 214–15.
156. This is a point made by the earliest western historians of yoga, including Oldenberg, Sénart, and De la Vallée Poussin: Sarbacker 2005, 79. The powers are discussed at length in VM 12 (in Nanamoli 1991, 369–401).
157. *Prakṛtilaya* is also referred to in *Sāṃkhya Kārika* 45. My analysis of the YS's and YBh's treatments of *prakṛtilaya* is entirely based on Malinar 2008.
158. See chap. 4, nn. 213–16.
159. Malinar 2008.
160. Vasudeva 2000, 342. In his translation of *Parākhyatantra* 14.104–5, Goodall (2004, 382) translates *tasya yogayuktasya yoginaḥ . . . utkrāntiṃ yogataḥ . . . prakuryāt* as "Such a yogin engaged in yoga . . . should perform yogic suicide": for similar language, see above, n. 57. The tantric Buddhist homologue to this practice, termed the yoga of "consciousness transference to a higher realm," is "equivalent to suicide" if applied prematurely: Mullin 2006, 67. This practice is termed "completion" (*niṣṭhā*) in Pāśupata sources: Sanderson 2006, 207.
161. Full references in Brunner, Oberhammer, and Padoux 2000, 226, s.v. "utkrānti"; and Brunner, Oberhammer, and Padoux 2004, 301. Cf. Goudriaan 1983, 112, n. 10, and *Kiraṇāgama*, 4.2 (discussed in Gonda 1977, 188), which uses the term *kālotkrānti*.
162. ĀP 11.94–98, 111, in Jain 1963, 235–37. Cf. Dundas 1991, 173–74. Jain monks who undertake to fast unto death are also compared to battlefield warriors eager to die in battle in the *Bhagavatī Ārādhanā*: Granoff 2007, 80–81.
163. Vasudeva 2000 is an exposition of one such "yoga" system: that of the MVUT.
164. MPĀg, yoga-pada 7.42b–45a. See above n. 50.
165. RĀg, yoga-pada 9.9–11. However, in spite of the fact that it is situated at the end of this text's *yoga-pada*, where all discussions of *utkrānti* are found in this literature, the outcome of this practice differs from that of *utkrānti* per se.
166. RĀg, *yoga-pada* 9.12–14. Cf. BhP 5.20.42, which states that only masters of yoga (*yogeśvaras*) are able to pass beyond the barrier of *lokāloka* in the cosmic egg.
167. SvT 10.613a–614a; *Tantrasadbhāva* (TSB) 10.646–48. Cf. Kaviraj 1984, 115.
168. *Parākhyatantra* 14.71–77 (tr. in Goodall 2004, 371–74).
169. The use of missile-spells, or spell-incanted missiles (*astra*), is common enough in the epics, but solely in the context of weaponry. So, for ex-

ample, the powerful Viśvāmitra, the warrior-sage, provides Rāma and his brother Lakṣmaṇa with a host of spell-incanted missiles, in Rām 1.27–28.

170. MVUT 17.29–32. The actual mantra, decoded in Vasudeva (2000, 345) is the onomatopoetic *skṛk*. Vasudeva notes that this mantra, whose sound "imitate[s] the breaking of the body," closely resembles the mantra *krrrk phaṭ*, employed for magical murder in the *Siddhavartīmata* (24.7).
171. The KM's account of two forms of *utkrānti* (KM 23.98–130) is the subject of Goudriaan 1983, 92–117.
172. Here it would appear that the MVUT's redactor stumbled upon a headache the Buddha had over a thousand years earlier: see chap. 2, n. 65.
173. MVUT 17.25–32, translated in Vasudeva 2000, 343–45.
174. *Parākhyatantra* 14.105, with Goodall's discussion of alternate readings (2004, 382–83, n. 846). Cf. Vasudeva 2000, 346. In KM 23.142 (in Goudriaan 1983, 106), the practitioner describes himself as sorrowful, wishing to abandon [life], and *bhraṣṭa*, the same term as was used in MBh 17.2.3b to describe Draupadī's failed yoga: see chap. 2, n. 143.
175. See above, n. 19.
176. TĀ 14.32–45, discussed in Vasudeva 2000, 346–49.
177. Ibid., 349.
178. Mbh 6.114.112a, mahopaniṣadaṃ caiva yogasthaṃ vīryavān. Cf. MBh 7.118.18b, which describes the yogic death of Bhūriśravas, discussed chap. 2, n. 135.
179. TĀ 14.39b. In his commentary on TĀ 14.32, Jayaratha quotes BhG 8.12, which describes the abandonment of the body through yogic practice.
180. MBh 13.154.5–6.
181. MBh 14.17. On this chapter, see Smith 2007, 93. 98.
182. MBh 14.17.15–17. Cf. RĀg, yoga-pada 9.8a, 12a, which employs the same terminology.
183. MBh 12.207.25.
184. MBh 5.44.16. On Sanatsujāta and his brothers, see Monier-Williams 1984, 1141 (s.v. "sanaka" and "sanat").
185. Weinberger-Thomas 1999, 160–66.
186. LP 1.100.16; ŚP 2.2.30.3–8. Cf. RCM 64.4, in which Satī reduces herself to ashes with her *jog agini*.
187. ŚP 2.2.30.4–5.
188. KāP 16.48–49. This language is repeated at 17.16. Cf. *Parākhyatantra* 14.106b, which instructs the yogi to "burst the door" (*sphoṭayed dvāram*): Goodall 2004, 384, 385, n. 847.
189. Weinberger-Thomas 1999, 113, 116, 119. Fig. 3.2 is taken from her book (fig. 31).
190. BhG 6.37–45; YV 6.1.126.57.
191. Pinch 2006, 54, n. 52.
192. YS 3.38, 39.
193. See above, nn. 28 and 38 (MU 6.21). Cf. MU 2.2 (*ūrdhvam utkrānta*).

194. For example, in RĀg, *yoga-pada* 9.11–13, 16–17.
195. See above, nn. 10–11.
196. Monier-Williams 1984, 176–77 (s.v. "ut-kram").
197. NT 20.29b, 35a.

CHAPTER FOUR

1. See chap. 2, n. 159.
2. Potter 1977, 32.
3. See Matilal's distinction (1986, 226) between the etymological ("sensory experience") and the conventional ("perception") meaning of the term. Matilal favors the latter.
4. King 1999, 150. Several definitions of *pratyakṣa* are presented in Verpoorten 2005, 92–93, n. 6.
5. Matilal 1977, 54, 78.
6. Matilal 1986, xiv; Potter 1977, 282.
7. Four *pramāṇas* (perception, inference, comparison, and verbal testimony) are listed in NS 1.1.3. The root VS does not list its four *pramāṇas* (perception, inference, recollection, and cognition of the vedic seers) together, although it treats them separately. They are listed together as the fourfold *vidyā* in PADhS 98: vidyāpi caturvidhā pratyakṣa-laiṅgika-smṛty-ārṣa-lakṣaṇā (in Jha 1997, 441). The YS (1.7) admit three *pramāṇas*: perception, inference, and scriptural testimony (*āgama*).
8. MBh 12.187.12; YS 2.17–18; Cakrapāṇi ad CS 4.1.21.
9. VS 1.1.3.
10. NS 4.2.38: [tattvabuddhiḥ] samādhiviśeṣābhyāsāt.
11. NS 4.2.42, 46.
12. For a discussion, see Potter 1977, 32.
13. Dignāga terms this *yogijñāna*: Woo 2003, 439.
14. VS 5.2.16, with the commentary of Śaṅkaramiśra (in Sinha 1911/1974, 182). Cf. Potter 1977, 32.
15. King 1999, 148. The term is used and discussed, for example, by Bhāsarvajña in his *Nyāyasāra* and *Nyāyabhūṣaṇam* auto-commentary (in Yogindrananda 1968, 94). According to Roşu (1978, 201), citing ṚV 6.9.5–6 and 10.119.6, the *prāpyakāri* theory of perception has its origin in the Vedas. Cf. Gonda 1969, 19–20, for other citations from the Vedas and Brāhmaṇas.
16. *Vedāntaparibhāṣā*, trans. in Gupta 1991, 167–68, quoted in King 1999, 148.
17. Sinha 1986, vol. 1, 21.
18. NS 3.1.35: raśmyarthasannikarṣaviśeṣāt grahaṇam.
19. Yogindrananda 1968, 95: cakṣureva raśmidvāreṇārthadeśaṃ gatvā pradīpavatsambadhyate tadraśmyaścānudbhūtarūpatvāt na dṛśyante.
20. Matilal 1986, 224.

21. ātmaivāsya jyotirbhavati (BṛU 4.3.6), cited in King 1999, 147. Cf. KU 5.14–15.
22. This passage expands on KU 4.1,6.
23. SS 1.21.10, discussed in Roşu 1978, 201–2.
24. Humbach 1978, 229–53, especially 239. Chenet (1993, 342, 349–59) discusses the adstratal sources of the so-called Saura cult in South Asia. Circa 550 CE mentions of the Magas (Persian sun priests, whose name in Sanskrit is the cognate of the Biblical *magi*) and of the sun god's so-called northern attire in the Purāṇas marks the consolidation of a specifically non-Indic sun cult on the subcontinent.
25. Inden 1992, 570.
26. Michon 2007, 203, 206. On the history of the Yuezhi prior to their 15 CE confederation that inaugurated the Kushan empire, see Schwartzberg 1992, 20–21, 174–75.
27. Michon 2007, 239, 242, and fig. 77.
28. Soper (1949, 272) sees a direct link between the portrayal of the emperor on this coin and that of the Persian Mithra.
29. Chenet 1993, 328.
30. Chenet 1993, 330–31, citing ṚV 1.154.4; 5.47.2, 4.
31. The eye is linked to the sun in dozens of passages from the Brāhmaṇas. These, as well as the ṚV passages cited here, are listed in Gonda 1969, 6, n. 16.
32. ṚV 5.40.8; 5.59.3, 5; AV 9.9.14; 13.1.45; 18.1.10, listed ibid.
33. BṛU 1.3.7–14.
34. ChU 3.18.5a.
35. See chap. 2, n. 97.
36. ŚB 10.5.2.8, 13, quoted in Malamoud 2002, 14–15. According to the BhP, Viṣṇu's feet are also placed on the heart: see chap. 3, n. 92.
37. BṛU 4.4.1, 2. On the relationship of the BṛU to the ŚB, see Limaye and Vadekar 1958, 174.
38. The sun is truth because it is the homologue of the eye, and visual perception is, according to this early source, superior to acoustic perception: BṛU 5.14.4. Cf. BṛU 3.1.4: "What the eye is, the sun is."
39. BṛU 5.5.2. The macrocosmic "man who is seen in the sun" is homologized with the microcosmic "man who is seen within the eye" in ChU 1.6.6 and 1.7.5. *Brahma Sūtra* 1.2.13, 17 makes the same link (Apte 1960, 111, 116), which is repeated by Śaṅkara in his BrSūBh 1.4.12 (ibid., 246).
40. JUB 1.25.1–10.
41. JUB 1.26.1–4. As with the case of the sun, the "black" of the eye is not linked explicitly to either death or immortality here.
42. Here, I translate *vidyut*, which most often denotes "lightening," as "ray": the term literally means "that which irradiates," with the prefix *vi-* bearing a dispersive sense, by which a single solar lamp proliferates into an infinity of rays.

43. JUB 1.26.5, 8; 1.27.1–3, 4a, 5a, 6a.
44. See chap. 5, section 5b. Cf. White 2003, 177.
45. Przyluski, 1933: 148–49. See chap. 3, n. 146.
46. AV 19.53.1. Sāyaṇa identifies time's rays with "cords" (*rajjvaḥ*) and the number seven with the seasons in his commentary on this verse (in Visvabandhu 1962, vol. 4, part 1, pp. 1971–72). JUB 1.28–29 is ostensibly a praise of the god Indra; however, the sun is the explicit center of attention throughout.
47. AV 19.53.6.
48. JUB 1.28.7–8.
49. JUB 1.30.1.
50. ChU 8.12.4, 5, 6. Cf. MU 6.6: "Seated in the eye, the *puruṣa* moves among all of the sense objects."
51. Gonda 1963, 276–80.
52. JUB 1.43.10 and 4.24.13 identify the man in the eye with both Indra and Prajāpati, the one who shines beyond the heavens and a host of other beings and qualities. The husband-wife pair is identified as "Indra" and "his wife" in MU 7.11. BṛU 4.2.2 itself states that "people call him Indra."
53. BṛU 2.1.19. Cf. PU 5.5 on the celestial citadel (*puriśayam*) in which the *puruṣa* dwells (see chap. 3, n. 12).
54. AV 10.2.30. The same passage continues by evoking a "casing" (*kośa*), which containing the self, is enclosed in this citadel, but that also "goes to heaven." This language reappears in MU 6.27, 28, 38, discussed in chap. 3, nn. 42–44, 48.
55. BṛU 2.5.18.
56. See chap. 4, section 6.
57. See also the discussion of upanishadic subtle body physiology in chap. 3, sections 1 and 2.
58. See Lévi 1966, 90, 93, on the other world as the ground for the sacrifice that is performed in this world.
59. BṛU 4.3.9 states that the *puruṣa* who is "illuminated by his own light" has two "sites" (*sthāna*), this world and the world beyond.
60. BṛU 4.4.23; BhG 13.54. The classic study of these compounds is Ingalls 1959, which relies heavily on Śaṅkara's commentary on the BhG.
61. ŚB 1.9.3.10, with the commentary of Sāyaṇa. See chap. 2, n. 92, and chap. 5, n. 139.
62. BrSūBh 4.2.18–19, entitled "raśmyadhikaraṇam" (in Joshi 1981, 982–83; tr. in Apte 1960, 830–32). Cf. *Brahmāṇḍa Purāṇa* 1.2.21.56–57 (quoted in Smith 2006, 222): "As the sun sets, the luster of the sun gradually enters the sacrificial fire. As a result of this the sun shines from afar at night. When the sun rises again, the luster of the fire takes possession of it."
63. BrSūBh 4.2.20–21 (tr. in Apte 1960, 833).
64. See chap. 3, sections 2–5, and chap. 5, sections 1a and 1b.

65. See chap. 3, nn. 50 and 91.
66. Falk 1987, 120–21.
67. Monier-Williams 1984, 702, s.v. *prādeśa*.
68. Falk 1987, 122; Filliozat 1962, 339–40.
69. Falk 1987, 123.
70. ṚV 1.154.1–6; TĀr 3.1. Viṣṇu's name is derived from the vedic root *vay, "to draw lines, guide straight, make a framework." Bailey (1975, 11–12 and n. 24) identifies the vedic Viṣṇu as a "surveyor" god.
71. Shamasastry 1938, 120–22. The same device was used to determine the lengthening and shortening of daylight in the course of the year on or near the Tropic of Cancer. See AŚ 2.20.41–42 (with Kangle's notes: Kangle 1969, vol. 2, 161) and Falk 1987, 128.
72. ŚB 6.6.2.12: prādeśamātro vai garbho viṣṇurātmasammitām. Cf. ŚB 6.6.3.17.
73. MBh 3.186–87; HV, appendix 1.41; and BhP 12.9 (in Couture 2007, *passim*); MP 167–68 (in O'Flaherty 1984, 111–14).
74. Brereton 1991, 1–17.
75. ṚV 1.22.16–21, in Falk (1987, 128–30), who also notes the connection between the seven steps taken by the bride in the Hindu marriage ritual (ibid., 126). Cf. Shamasastry 1938, 123.
76. AŚ 2.20.10. This source uses the term *vitasti*, rather than *prādeśa* for "span."
77. The same terminology was innovated by Thales, the Greek father of mathematics, who was able to calculate the height of the Pyramid of Cheops by measuring "the great with the small," in this case, his shadow against that of the monument. Thales called his unit of measurement the "thales," because it was his own height: Guedj 1998, 49, 67.
78. AŚ 2.20.39–40.
79. AŚ 2.20.17–18; Falk 1987, 124.
80. These sources are also identifying the god with the *puruṣa* of Sāṃkhya metaphysics.
81. Falk 1987, 126–27. The translation is my own.
82. Shamasastry 1938, 200–3.
83. Mus 1968, 548–49, 558.
84. ṚV 1.154.4, cited in Chenet 1993, 331.
85. BṛU 4.2.9–16; ChU 5.4.1–5.10.10.
86. MU 6.1.
87. MU 6.2.
88. For an extended discussion, see White 1996, 19–32. Cf. Wujastyk 2004, 347–69.
89. CS 1.6.3–51; SS 1.6.1–38; AH 1.3.2–58. The CS and SS date from between the third century BCE to fifth century CE: Wujastyk 1998, 39–41, 104–5. The AH is a sixth- to seventh-century work.
90. An important study of this terminology is Zimmermann 1975, 87–105.
91. CS 1.11.42–43. For a discussion, see Zimmermann 1975, 92.

92. Here the moon has replaced Varuṇa, the god of the waters, as the principle of hydration in the ecosystem described in MU 6.14. The sun doubles for fire here.
93. AH 1.3.2–6.
94. The oily (*snigdha*) flavor is out of place. The other three flavors mentioned here, together with the three listed in verse 4a, constitute the standard "six flavors" of ayurvedic diet.
95. CS 1.6.5.
96. CS 1.6.27a. Cf. SS 1.6.8a; YV 6.1.81.94–95.
97. Zimmermann 1975, 94.
98. MBh 3.3.5–9. The fact that this passage concludes with a reference to the six flavors, also evoked in the AH excerpt quoted above, establishes that its context is ayurvedic. Cf. MBh 1.223.16, on the relationship between fire in the world and the sun in heaven.
99. RĀg 8.3–4, 6.
100. Sax 2002, 22. This is Sax's translation of a song sung in the village of Sutol in the Garhwal region of Uttarakhand.
101. YV 5.84–85. This portion of the YV does not belong to the original "Mokṣopaya" core of the YV, which dates from ca. 950 CE: Hanneder 2006, 15, 55. It may date from as late as the thirteenth century.
102. YV 5.85.26. The term *piṅgalā* is best known from tantric subtle body physiology, in which it signifies the "solar" right channel (*nāḍī*), the complement to the "lunar" left channel, called the *īḍā*.
103. Demaitre 1936, 154.
104. MU 6.21, 30. See chap. 3, n. 28.
105. A general answer to this question is given by Kaviraj 1977–79, vol. 2: see below, nn. 255–57.
106. See below, nn. 140–41.
107. Śuka is also so-called, in MBh 12.311.9 and 12.319.6, but his is a yoga of bodily ascent. See chap. 2, n. 158.
108. MBh 12.278.13–28; MBh 3.80.126–27. Cf. MBh 3.81.142.
109. MBh 12.274.57.
110. MBh 12.320.40, 13.18.1.
111. MBh 1.101.3.
112. MBh 6.102.53.
113. MBh 3.290.9a, 3.291.23ab. Cf. MBh 1.114.2–3, in which Dharma puts on a yogic image of himself to father Yudhiṣṭhira on Draupadī. I am grateful to Kendall Busse for alerting me to this and other epic passages that discuss the *yoga-mūrtis* of the gods: Busse 2007.
114. Tertullian, "Incarnation of the Logos," (*Apologia* xxi), translated in Bettenson and Maunder 1999, 34.
115. MBh 15.33.24–29.
116. MBh 12.308.7b, 10a, 12ab. For a discussion, see Fitzgerald 2002, 641–77.

117. MBh 12.308.17ab.
118. MBh 12.308.16b.
119. MBh 12.308.58, 189. See chap. 1, n. 127, on the KSS's description (8.2.61) of entering into other bodies "as if going from house to house."
120. BhP 9.13.13.
121. Mbh 12.312.12. See chap. 2, n. 153.
122. MU 2.1 calls Bṛhadratha the "banner of Ikṣvāku," whose lineage is traced through Janaka in BhP 9.13.14–15. Śākāyanya is himself listed in one of two lineage lists of upanishadic teachers: BṛU 4.6.2. For a discussion, see Bronkhorst 2007, 220–21.
123. BṛU 3.1.1–4.4.25: these two books are called the Yājñavalkya Kāṇḍa.
124. BhP 9.13.27.
125. Bronkhorst argues (ibid., 258) that the BṛU, and by extension all of the Upaniṣads in their final recensions, postdate the time of the Buddha and Mahāvīra: see chap. 3, n. 1.
126. By "Greater Magadha," Bronkhorst is referring to the Gangetic basin east of the confluence of the Ganges and Yamuna rivers: ibid., 2–3.
127. Bronkhorst 2007, 53, 71, 268–69, and passim.
128. These include an asceticism grounded in the cessation of activity, a feature of early Jainism: ibid., 15–28.
129. MBh 12.211.4.
130. MBh 12.306.57–60. Also listed are Parāśara, Asita Devala, Śuka, Sanatkumāra, and Śukra (Kāvya Uśanas). On Pañcaśikha, see chap. 5, n. 50.
131. MBh 12.313.14–51.
132. See chap. 2, n. 163.
133. BC 12.67.
134. VM 12.8–12, discussed in Clough 2008, 10–11. The early Buddhist literature does contain accounts of the Buddha himself performing "yogic" feats (see chap. 5, section 2a), but these do not conform to the two paradigms of yogic practice found in the MBh.
135. MBh 12.353.1–3.
136. MBh 13.31.27–31.
137. A rich listing of references to this term in Kashmir Śaiva texts and commentaries is in Hara 1966, 212. See above, n. 106.
138. TĀ 29.186–289 comprises an extended discussion of tantric initiation. See especially 29.253–276, whose description of *paravedha* ("supreme penetration") resembles the NT's instructions for the hostile takeover of a foreign body: see section 6, chap. 4.
139. Brunner 1994, 450–51. *Nāḍīsaṃdhāna* is evoked several times in the SvT (2.130, 257; 3.49–53, 83, 95; 4.65–67). See Sanderson 2004b, 22, for a description.
140. Kaviraj 1977–79, vol. 1, 287.
141. TĀ 23.33–35, discussed in Muller-Ortega, 1989, 168.
142. RĀg 47.16–17; *Uttarakāmikāgama* 24.53–55. Cf. Bhatt 1988, viii.

143. Rastelli 2003, 137–38, quoting *Īśvara Saṃhitā* 21.134–36, and *Viṣṇu Saṃhitā* 10.51. A Śaiva equivalent is *nayana-dīkṣā*, summarized in Gonda 1969, 54.
144. RĀ 1.54; *Kaulasūtra* f. 1, v. 4, translated in Sanderson 2007, 348.
145. As in the case of Tibetan Buddhist *guru yoga*: Mullin 2006, 103–4.
146. See chap. 3, nn. 61–62 and 76.
147. Birnbaum 2004, 196.
148. Ruegg 1967, 157.
149. See chap. 3, nn. 67–69.
150. Ruegg 1967, 162, 164; Kloppenborg and Poelmeyer 1987, 85. On the provenance and history of the term *yogācāra,* see Silk 2000, 265–314, especially 274, 281.
151. Schlingloff 1964, 177–78 (165R1–3); Kloppenborg and Poelmeyer 1987, 86.
152. Ruegg 1967, 162.
153. Davidson 2002, 124, citing Schlingloff 1964, 41, 194–95.
154. Yiengpruksawan 2004, 230. See Yamabe 2002 for the relationship between this text and cave paintings from the Turfan region of Chinese Turkestan.
155. Wallace 2001, 187.
156. Ibid., 194. A nearly identical practice is described in *Sarvadurgapariśodhana Tantra* 28a–30a (in Skorupski 1983, 28–29, 164–65). Cf. Kloppenborg and Poelmeyer 1987, 87–94.
157. MBh 13.40.23, 28–38. Cf. ṚV 6.47.18.
158. This verse is an insertion following MBh 13.40.55, found in only four Devanagari manuscripts.
159. MBh 13.40.56–57.
160. MBh 13.41.11ab, 12b.
161. See below, n. 183.
162. MBh 12.289.28.
163. See Fitzgerald 2009, 196–97. Cf. Gonda 1985 , 131–63, especially p. 158. See chap. 5, nn. 102–5.
164. MBh 12.278.8–9.
165. MBh 12.278.12.
166. MBh 12.278.18–20. By virtue of this act, the text explains, Śiva transforms his pike into his famous "Pināka" bow.
167. MBh 12.278.28–30.
168. MBh 12.278.32. In fact, this entire account is narrated in answer to the question (12.278.4) of how Kāvya Uśanas became Śukra, a term that means both "semen" and "the planet Venus." See chap. 5, nn. 110–17.
169. On the relationship of this seminal mantra to the content of several Upaniṣads, see Roebuck 2003, 389.
170. MU 6.7. In the *Ārṣeya Upaniṣad,* a certain Bhāradvāja affirms the superiority of the sun god. This opinion is condemned by another sage who relates sun worship to non-Hindu populations, including, perhaps, peoples living beyond the western borders of the subcontinent: Chenet 1993, 338.
171. Monier-Williams 1984: s.v. "bhargas," "bhṛj," "bhrāj."

172. Chatterji 1967, xvi, citing *Farvardin Yast* 94 and ṚV 10.14.6.
173. Ibid., xxxv.
174. Modak 1993, 32.
175. Goldman 1977, 81–128.
176. Ibid., 99. On the identity between the Bhārgavas and the Aṅgirasas, whom the AV associates with black magic and destructive charms and spells, see ibid., 146, and Bloomfield 1967, xxvi–xxvii.
177. TĀr 4.38: tvā bhṛgūṇāṃ cakṣuṣā prekṣe, discussed in Gonda 1969, 37.
178. Dumézil 1986, 147–49; 153–56. Dumézil discusses the epic myth of Kāvya Uśanas's transformation into "Śukra" ibid., 201–2.
179. Kellens 1978, 269–70. Dumézil's (1981, 24) claim that the term *kavi* signified a prince or king is based on late Sasanian royal ideology, which applied the term to the mythic kings who were the founders of civilization.
180. Dumézil 1986, 173–205; 274–315. Chatterji (1967, xii-xv) argues that the MBh 12.323 myth of Vasu Uparicara portrays that king as a devotee of Ahura Mazda (Harimedhas).
181. See chap. 2, nn. 105–6.
182. See chap. 5, n. 115.
183. MBh 12.289.24–27.
184. Recall here Bharadvāja's promise to Divodāsa that through his son, whom he yogically penetrates, he will be able to conquer "a thousand sons of Vītahavya." See above, n. 184 and chap. 5, nn. 39–43.
185. BrSūBh 1.3.27 (in Joshi 1981, 320), which is also cited in the critical edition's notes on alternate readings for MBh 12.289.26–27. See chap. 5, n. 55. Cf. BrSūBh 1.3.40, 4.2.17–4.3.5, and 4.4.15–22; and Vedavyāsa's commentary on YS 3.37, which states that "the yogi draws his mind-stuff out from his own body and casts it into other bodies (śarīrāntareṣu nikṣipati)."
186. See chap. 1, n. 110.
187. Matilal 1977, 60.
188. Smith 2006, 297–98.
189. Lindquist 1935, 22–24. While his is a very useful compendium of primary text material on the *siddhis* of yoga practitioners, Lindquist's reductionist analysis that all may be explained by reference to hypnosis is not helpful.
190. Cf. Śaṅkara's commentary on BrSū 2.3.25, tr. in Apte 1960, 462: "[A] lamp is but the "effulgence substance" (*teja-dravyam*) with its particles in a massed condition, and the same *teja* particles when they are in a loose condition, are "light."
191. Smith 2006, 301, who notes that this position is also held in the subcommentaries of the ca. thirteenth-century Śrīkaṇṭha and of Appayya Dīkṣita (1554–1626). See below, n. 229 for the Nyāya-Vaiśeṣika commentator Vyomaśiva's use of the same principle to explain how yogis are able to quickly burn away lifetimes of karma by simultaneously appropriating multiple bodies.

192. BrSūBh 4.4.15, in Joshi 1981, 1015–16. See chap. 5, nn. 52–55.
193. MĀg, yoga-pāda 10.
194. Smith 2006, 298. According to traditional Indic theories of cognition, the *antaḥkaraṇa* is a combination of the heart (as the locus of emotional experience), the mind, intellect, and ego. As such, it is the closest Indic cognate to the Western concept of "consciousness"; ibid., 46, citing Vallabhācārya, *Antaḥkaraṇaprabodha,* and commentaries.
195. Smith 2006, 299 (on Nimbārka's sub-commentary); 301 (on Śrīkaṇṭha's sub-commentary).
196. See chap. 2, n. 118.
197. MU 6.31. See Goudriaan 1992, 167–68, and Goudriaan 1983, 113, n. 28.
198. TĀ 5.91b, with Jayaratha's commentary. Cf. TĀ 3.166 and Brunner, Oberhammer, and Padoux 2004, 127, s. v. "kulamātaraḥ" and ibid., 246, s. v. "cinmarīci."
199. Peabody 2003, 61.
200. MBh 12.197.13–15, quoted in Goudriaan 1992, 169.
201. *Nyāyamañjarī* of Jayantabhaṭṭa, in Varadacharya 1969, vol. 1, 268: [darśanātiśayaḥ] . . . ataśca yatrāsya paraḥ prakarṣaḥ te yogino gīyate/ darśanasya ca paro'tiśayaḥ sūkṣmavavahita-viprakṛṣṭabhūtabhaviṣyadādi-viṣayatvam/.
202. VS 9.1.11–13. Here I have translated constructions in *sam-ā-dhā* as literally as possible, preferring "com-pose" and its resulting verbal forms to the more descriptive "concentrate" or "meditate."
203. PADhS 99, glossed in NK 166 as: ātmano manasā saṃyogo manasa indriyeṇa indriyasyārthena (in Jha 1997, 443–44, and Jetly and Parikh 1991, 436–37).
204. PADhS 99 (in Jha 1997, 464–65, and Jetly and Parikh 1991, 455).
205. Faddegon 1918/1969, 293. Early *sāmkhya* commentaries employ the terms *para-pratyakṣa* and *abāhya-pratyakṣa;* Bryant 2009, 37–38, 145–46.
206. Mbh 6.16.5–8.
207. Gonda 1963, 307–17; Eckel 1992, 129–52; VM 13.75, 95, 100, cited in Clough 2008, 10, 13, and 14.
208. VS 9.2.13: ārṣaṃ siddhadarśanañca dharmebhyaḥ.
209. PADhS 122 (in Jha 1997, 627–29, and Jetly 1971, 245–46).
210. *Vākyapadīya* 2.152 with Bhartṛhari's auto-commentary, cited in Timilsina 2008, 12.
211. YS 3.32.
212. See Gonda (1963, 318–48) for a rich discussion of this technical term.
213. Vedavyāsa *ad* YS 3.32. I accepted and elaborated on Vedavyāsa's reading in White 2003, 185–87.
214. Praśastapāda uses similar language in his commentary on VS 9.1.13. Cf. VM 13.8–12.
215. *Saṃyama,* "co-restraining," is a term widely employed in the YS and its commentaries to denote the three final phases of eight-limbed yoga (or,

I would argue, meditative) practice: *dhyānam*, *dhāraṇā*, and *samādhi*. The three are to be practiced conjointly.

216. Vedavyāsa ad YS 3.26, in Rukmani 1987, 109–13.
217. YS 3.19, 21.
218. Whicher 1998, 214.
219. BhP 3.11.17.
220. On the rich tradition of Buddhist philosophical inquiry into *yogipratyakṣa*, see Woo 2003 and 2005.
221. Two Kashmirian commentaries on the NS also provide lengthy discussions of yogi perception: the mid-tenth-century *Nyāyasāra* of Bhāsarvajña (together with an auto-commentary, the *Nyāyabhūṣaṇam*) and the late ninth-century *Nyāyamañjarī* of Jayanta Bhaṭṭa. All four of these authors' dates and locations are discussed in Matilal 1977, 68–69, 92–94.
222. Ibid., 85. This would explain the references made in Jain doxographical literature to Naiyāyikas and Vaiśeṣikas as Śaiva and Pāśupata "yogis" and to their teachings as "yoga"; Halbfass 1988, 278.
223. NK 166 (in Jha 1997, 446, and Jetly and Parikh 1991, 437): ata eva dūrādavyaktagrahaṇam gacchataś cakṣūraśme antarāleviśīrṇānām avayavāntarāṇāmarthaprāptyabhāvāt.
224. yogaḥ samādhiḥ. Here, as well as in his interpretation of the terms *yukta* and *viyukta*, Śrīdhara appears to be directly influenced by Vedavyāsa's commentary on YS 1.2. On this, see chap. 2, n. 12.
225. The *Nyāyasāra*, Bhāsarvajña's tenth-century commentary on the NS, generates the same division between types of yogic perception, preferring the terms *yuktāvasthā* ("yoked condition") and *ayuktāvastha* ("unyoked condition"): Yogindrananda 1968, 170.
226. NK 172 (in Jha 1997, 464–66, and Jetly and Parikh 1991, 455–57).
227. SvT 5.84–85. See chap. 4, section 4b.
228. LT 49.111–28 (in Sanjukta Gupta 1972, 331–34). Cf. Smith 2006, 388–89; 411, n.66.
229. Sastri 1983-84, vol. 1, 3.
230. Sastri 1983–84, vol. 1, 156.
231. MBh 14.17.30–31, discussed in Smith 2007, 93.
232. Cakrapāṇidatta *ad* CS 4.2.35, in Trikamji Acharya 1992, 305. I am grateful to Martha Selby for this reference.
233. MS 4.8.2, cited in Gonda 1969, 17, who lists many other examples (ibid., 18–27).
234. A power mentioned by Ibn Baṭṭūṭa: see chap. 1, n. 149.
235. MBh 11.15.6–7.
236. NS 23.79–80; 35.26–27, in Ghosh 1951–61, vol. 2, 422, and vol. 1, 216–17. I am grateful to Bruce Sullivan for these references.
237. The same technique, called *saṃkrānti*, is briefly described in the coeval MVUT 21.9–19, which indicates that a *yogayukta* yogi may practice it on either a dead or living body.

238. On this date, see Sanderson 2004a, 273–76.
239. NT 20.9b–10a.
240. NT 20.27ab.
241. NT 7.1.
242. These are discussed at length in White 1996, 184–334, and White 2003, 220–34.
243. NT 20.29b-36a. Abhinavagupta refers to this technique in TĀ 21.29 and elsewhere.
244. Dwivedi 1985, 9. It is probable that Kṣemarāja's Kallaṭa was the same as the eponymous disciple of Vasugupta, because Kṣemarāja followed him in writing a commentary on the same *Spandakārikās*.
245. Kṣemarāja *ad* NT 20.28a–29a, in Shastri 1926–39, vol. 2, 226–27. Cf. SvT 11.85, on the *puryaṣṭakam* (that which is comprised of eight fortresses, i.e., the eight constituents of the subtle body: the five subtle elements, mind, intellect, and ego). Goudriaan (1992, 175, n. 34) relates this to the upanishadic "fortress" or citadel of the heart in the Upaniṣads. See above, nn. 53–55.
246. Kṣemarāja ad NT 20.30, in Shastri 1926–39, vol. 2, 227.
247. One may read *cakṣurādiraśmi* either as "a ray originating from the eye" or "a ray of the eye, etc." In the latter case, "etcetera" would refer to the fact that every one of the five sense organs perceives through the contact of a ray and its object.
248. Kṣemarāja ad NT 20.32b–33a, in Shastri 1926–39, vol. 2, 229.
249. See Strong 1983, 151, for a Buddhist parallel.
250. YV 6.1.82.28–34: see Smith 2006, 292–93 for a translation.
251. YŚ 5.264–71, tr. in Quarnström 2002, 141–42; *Svopajñavṛtti* commentary tr. in Smith 2006, 289.
252. GS 14.258–60.
253. Tr. in Mullin 2006, 37–38.
254. Mullin 1996, 217–18.
255. Clémentin-Ojha 1990, 87–90; Singh 1968, 207.
256. Kaviraj 1977–79, vol. 2, 25–32. The long excerpt that follows is an abridged rendering of this chapter.
257. sūtrākār tejomay padarth ke dvāra juḍe rahte haiṃ.
258. Mus 1968, 562.
259. Marriott 1976, 111.

CHAPTER FIVE

1. See chap. 4, n. 194, on the term *antaḥkaraṇa*.
2. BṛU 1.4.10. See chap. 3, n. 4.
3. KU 3.9; MU 6.38 and elsewhere. See chap. 3, nn. 33 and 47.
4. ŚvU 3.2–3, 8,9. This last hemistich (3.9c) is a possible reference to the *puruṣa* as gnomon: see chap. 4, section 1d.

5. These terms are used interchangeably in the Upaniṣads, with all three being identified in BṛU 2.5.1–14 and KU 5.8; 6.1; 6.17.
6. MBh 12.318.59, 12.320.19b.
7. ChU 3.14.3. See chap. 3, n. 40. ChU 3.19.1–3 identifies the *brahman* with the sun and then proceeds to describe a cosmogony that is simultaneously an embryology, with the "embryo" identified with the cosmic egg.
8. See chap. 3, n. 134.
9. See chap. 3, n. 144.
10. Fitzgerald 2009, 186.
11. Ibid., 187 (table 1). My translations of these two passages draw on those of Fitzgerald, who kindly shared his work in progress with me at the University of Tennessee, Knoxville, on April 19–21, 2006, as well as in several e-mail communications between 2006 and 2008.
12. Fitzgerald 2009, 186. Fitzgerald opines (ibid., 189) that the passages translated here were perhaps late additions made by the same redactor who inserted the Nārāyaṇīya into the Mokṣadharma.
13. Fitzgerald (ibid., 186, n. 7) identifies the concluding portions of both chapters of this text pair as "codas," elegantly constructed statements, written in *triṣṭubh* meter, of the doctrines espoused in the bodies of the respective chapters, which also subordinated the two to Vaiṣṇava doctrine.
14. MBh 12.289.7.
15. In the fourth- to sixth-century Śaiva *Niśvāsaguhya* (7.293–98), the goddess named Suṣumṇā is said to be white, with the shape of a lotus stalk, and to "emerge from the body of Śiva": Hatley 2007, 136, n. 9. The *Niśvāsaguhya* belongs to the Nepali codex analyzed by Sanderson (2006, 152): see chap. 3, n. 124.
16. Cf. MBh 12.289.24, according to which the yogi may "obtain the realms of the sense objects." See chap. 4, sections 1a and 1b, on *prāpyakāri* perception.
17. This is also a reference to the seven rays of the sun, as attested in AV 19.53 and a host of other sources: see chap. 2, nn. 118 and 173. On the relationship between the term *marut* and luminosity, see chap. 3, nn. 34 and 105.
18. Although the term *nabhas* is used in both cases, this (290.72) is a higher level or path than that of 290.69. In 290.69, the sun is the agent of motion, whereas in 290.72, it is the highest of the seven winds.
19. Mbh 12.290.86b.
20. Mbh 12.290.91, 96b, 99b–100b.
21. This is mirrored in the use of the term *sāṃkhya* in these two chapters. So, for example, MBh 289.2a literally reads: "The twice-born 'sāṃkhyas' praise sāṃkhya, [while] the twice-born 'yogas' praise yoga."
22. Or three, in the light of Fitzgerald's claim that the coda to this chapter was the work of a different hand, whose agenda it was to force its content into a Vaiṣṇava or Nārāyaṇīya mould: see above, n. 10.
23. MBh 12.289.21b, 26b.

24. MBh 12.289.39–40. Cf. YS 3.27–34 and White 2003, 224–29.
25. MBh 12.289.58–61, 62b.
26. Monier-Williams 1984, 794 (s.v. "mah").
27. Fitzgerald (2009, 199, n. 39) argues for a similar reading of the term here.
28. ChU 6.12.
29. Kapani 1992–93, vol. 2, 413.
30. See chap. 3, n. 95.
31. A comparison of the Indic *mahān ātmā* with the Platonic "world soul" may be in order here.
32. YŚ 11.49, 51–52, with the author's *Svopajñavṛtti* auto-commentary inserted in [brackets], translated in Quarnström 2002, 183–84.
33. YŚ 11.57–58, ibid., 185–86.
34. Varenne 1976, 30–40; Banerjea 1983, 30, 137; White 1996, 218–62.
35. For translations and studies, see Michaël 2007 and White 2002. Cf. LT 55.1–19; *Yogadarśana Upaniṣad* 4.39–60, in Varenne 1976, 210–12.
36. On-line *Oxford English Dictionary* (http://dictionary.oed.com) s.v. "microcosm" and "microcosmos."
37. SSP 3.1 in Mallik 1954, 14.
38. SSP 6.15, 21 in Mallik 1954, 33, 34.
39. *Kathāvatthu* 18.1.2, cited in Kaviraj 1922, 50. This entire section relies heavily upon Kaviraj's article. I am grateful to Gérard Colas for indicating this article to me.
40. Strong 2001, 107–9.
41. The names of many of these realms, which are found in many Buddhist Abhidhamma works, are identical to those found in Vedavyāsa's YBh on YS 3.26.
42. Strong 1983, 199–203. The passage translated by Strong is from pp. 30–34 of Mukhopadhyaya's annotated 1963 edition. I have emended his translation of the clause *nirmitam visarjayati*. A similar description is found in the introduction to the Mahāyāna *Saddharmapuṇḍarika*.
43. Strong 2002, 159.
44. Ibid., 160–61.
45. Quarnström 2003, 133. See chap. 4, n. 113.
46. ṚV 6.47.18.
47. Kaviraj 1922, 47.
48. Sarbacker 2005, 33.
49. Pañcaśikha is called a *bhikṣu* in this passage. See chap. 4, n. 130.
50. Kaviraj 1922, 56.
51. In Ghosh 2003, 239.
52. See chap. 4, nn. 190–92.
53. Quoted in chap. 4, n. 183.
54. VM 12.57-65 (in Nanamoli 1991, 383–85). For discussion, see Kaviraj 1922, 49, and Lindquist 1935, 12–18. An early Buddhist discussion of the power to generate thousands of *nirmāṇakāyas* through the use of a tantric mantra

is found in the seventh- to eighth-century *Cakrasaṃvara Tantra* (1.4–8, with the commentary of Bhavabhaṭṭa); Gray 2007, 204–5. See also chap. 3, n. 17.

55. BrSūBh 1.3.27, in Joshi 1981, 320.
56. Goodall 1998, 292.
57. *Saṃvitprakāśa* 1.28, cited in Dyczkowski 2004, 77.
58. MBh 6.62.20, quoted in Malinar 2007, 151, n. 148. I have slightly altered her translation.
59. See chap. 3, nn. 84–85, on the altered meaning of this term in the BhG.
60. BhG 6.29–31.
61. BhG 11.4. Kṛṣṇa is also termed a *yogeśvara* in the concluding verses of the BhG. (18.75, 78).
62. BhG 11.5–8. Cf. Malinar 2007, 146–48, 156–63.
63. See chap. 2, n. 4.
64. BhG 10.7.
65. BhG 10.16, 18.
66. BhG 10.19, 40–41.
67. BhG 11.12.
68. BhG 11.20ab, 24a.
69. BhG 11.19b, 21a.
70. BhG 11.30.
71. Rām 7.111.11–13.
72. BhG 11.13.
73. For a discussion, see Heimann 1939, 127–28.
74. gṛhṇāti hi īśvaro 'pi kāryavaśāt śarīramantarāntarā darśayati ca vibhūtimiti//. Kaviraj (1922, 49) quotes this passage, citing the fifth book of the *Kusumañjali* of Udayana. I am unable to locate this verse.
75. BhP 10.33.3. Cf. 10.29.42.
76. BhP 10.32.14. See chap. 3, n. 92.
77. BhP 10.69.1–45. Kṛṣṇa is called a *yogeśvara* three times in this chapter, which also alludes to the practice of yoga repeatedly.
78. BhP 10.22.8, 10.44.7. Cf. McGregor 1984, 81, 188.
79. BhP 9.15.19.
80. BhP 10.84.9.
81. BhP 9.2.32.
82. See chap. 3, n. 184.
83. See chap. 3, n. 37.
84. MBh 5.42.1–5.45.28.
85. MBh 5.45.24.
86. BhP 2.2.10, 23; 9.13.27. See chap. 3, nn. 98–100.
87. BhP 3.5.6.
88. See chap. 3, nn. 16 and 31.
89. Biardeau 1968, 19–45.
90. VāP 1.5.30.

91. KU 6.11.
92. MP 166.1–4. Cf. ViṣP 6.3.17 ("Viṣṇu dwells in the sun's seven rays"), discussed in Couture 2007, 124, n. 24. See above, n. 11 and chap. 2, nn. 118 and 173.
93. HV, appendix 1, no. 41, line 1397. The "Manifestation of the Lotus" was appended to the HV sometime between the eleventh and fifteenth centuries CE: Couture: 2007, 24.
94. MBh 13.14.150–89. See above, n. 66.
95. MBh 13.14.163b, 181b, 182b, 190b.
96. MBh 13.14.183ab.
97. MBh 13.14.183c–185b.
98. Hazra 1975, 71.
99. KP 2.4.16, 19, 30, 32.
100. KP 2.5.3, 8–11. See chap. 3, n. 97.
101. KP 2.44.2–5, 8–10.
102. MBh 12.289.24. See chap. 4, n. 163 and below, n. 139.
103. MBh 12.228.14, 21.
104. Malinar 2007, 146.
105. Bisschop 2005, 552. Cf. SvT 11.181b; LT 5.25–26, etc. YS 3.49 speaks of *adhiṣṭātṛtvam*, a synonym of *aiśvaryam* as a supernatural power arising from knowledge of the distinction between *buddhi* and *puruṣa.*
106. ŚvU 6.1,7.
107. See chap. 4, nn. 107–12.
108. On the application of the term Maheśvara to Śiva as a yogi, see Mallmann 1964, 77, and Renou and Filliozat 1949–53, vol.1, 513–14.
109. BhG 11.26–27.
110. MBh 12.278.5a.
111. MBh 12.278.5a, with the interpolated verse from C_8.
112. Only seven such events have occurred since the invention of the telescope (1631, 1639, 1761, 1769, 1874, 1882, and 2004). It is only possible for such transits to occur in the months of December and June (in which case it is likely that which is described in this MBh passage occurred in June, during a time of great heat). The next transit of Venus will occur on June 6, 2012. For further information and images of Venus transiting the sun, see http://www.transitofvenus.org; http://www.dsellers.demon.co.uk/venus/ven_ch_frames.htm and http://sunearth.gsfc.nasa.gov/sunearthday/2004/vt_observe_2004.htm.
113. MBh 12.278.9.
114. MBh 12.278.12.
115. The sun's rays are likened to hands or arms. In the epic tale of the "brahmin gleaner," the sun reaches out with its hand to pull the brahmin, by the hand, into its orb: MBh 12.350.12.
116. http://www.phy6.org/stargaze/Svenus1.htm.

117. MBh 12.278.15. From an emic perspective, such transits, while not visible to the naked eye, would be so through yogi perception.
118. *Śāntikalpa* 1.3.3 and 1.11.1, in Bolling 1913, 268, 273.
119. Inden 1992, 568, 570.
120. Ibid., 569–70.
121. This topic is comprehensively treated in White 1996, 240–58.
122. The VāP, perhaps the earliest of the great Purāṇas, may be coeval with the didactic portions of the MBh: Hazra 1975, 13.
123. See chap. 1, n. 83, on the figure named Yogananda, "he who became Nanda through the practice of yoga."
124. The text literally reads "I was entered [into it]" (*praviṣṭaḥ*). Tense shifts such as this are frequent in *ex cathedra* prophecies, which project events that have already transpired into a future time.
125. VāP 23.219a–220b, 221b–222b. Cf. LP 1.24.127a–128b, 129b–130b.
126. See chap. 1, nn. 123–24.
127. See chap. 1, n. 133.
128. Uddyotakara is the author of the *Nyāyavārttika*, an extensive sub-commentary on Vātsyāyana's *Nyāyabhāṣya*: Matilal 1977, 85. See above, n. 51.
129. Matilal 1977, 85.
130. See chap. 4, section 6.
131. Inden 1992, 562, citing *Kauśika Sūtra* 94.2–4; Sanderson 2004a, 233–58.
132. *Kaulajñānanirṇaya* 18.7–14, tr. in White 2003, 108; Brunner 1994, 430–35.
133. Brunner 1994, 428–29; Muller-Ortega 2000, 573–86; Flood 2006, 113–18.
134. I have discussed this subject extensively in White 1996, 323–34, and White 2003, 169–84.
135. MBh 12.304.5.
136. Goodall 1998, 163–64, n. 10, citing KT 8.121, Kṣemarāja's commentary on SvT 10.891, and Rāmakaṇṭha's commentary on *Mataṅgāgama* 23.45–47.
137. VāP 74.16.
138. VāP 76.26–27.
139. VāP 73.65–68. See above, nn. 102–4.
140. JS 8.19 and 19.27, cited in Rastelli 2000, 357. Cf. Bouillier 1989, 208–9, and Bouillier 1997, 154.
141. See chap. 3, nn. 140–42.
142. See chap. 3, n. 119.
143. See chap. 1, n. 67. Cf. White 2000, 28–36.
144. Shulman 1993, 21. See chap. 1, n. 143.
145. Jayaratha ad TĀ 1.7, in Dwivedi and Rastogi 1987, vol. 1, 24.
146. SvT 7.258, 260.
147. See Bouillier 1989, 196–98, and Bouillier 1997, 167–224, for the Himalayan and sub-Himalayan regions of India and Nepal; White 1996, 118–22, and Bouillier 2008, 14, for western India and Orissa.
148. Sax 2008, 4.

CHAPTER SIX

1. Marau be jogi marau maraṇ hai mīṭhā/tis maraṇī marau jis maraṇī goraṣ mari dīṭhā//: Gorakhnāth, *Sabadi* 26 (in Barthwal 1971, 10).
2. White 1991, 91.
3. White 1996, 90–101.
4. Digby 1970, 1–35; Digby 2000, 221–33.
5. Vaudeville 1960, 354; Bouillier 2004, 252; Ernst 2005, 23, 27; Digby 2003, 238.
6. Gaborieau 1989, 233.
7. Here I am leaving aside the accounts by the ancient Greeks and Romans to India's *gymnosophists* ("naked philosophers") and that left by the seventh-century Chinese Buddhist traveler Hsuan-tsang on the renouncers he encountered in western India, because neither employs the term yogi per se.
8. Rockhill 1915, 69–72, 450–51. A circa 1630 miniature from an album of the Mughal emperor Śāh Jahān portrays a group of yogis wearing this style of garb: Beach 1978, pl. 62.
9. Gelblum 2008, 261–66.
10. See "Patañjali" in the index to Sachau 1910/1983, vol. 2, 418, for Alberuni's many references to the YS. On Abū al-Faḍl 'Allāmī, see Ernst 2007, 413. See below, n. 53.
11. Husain 1976, 164.
12. Ibid., 165.
13. Ibid., 177–78.
14. Sulaymān, *Akhbār as-Sin wa-l-Hind*, par. 52, pp. 22–23, quoted in Ernst 2007, 411.
15. Ernst 2007, 414–16.
16. On this figure, see Bouillier 1997, 55–87.
17. An improbable figure, given that the Indic measure of one *maund* is equivalent to twenty-five kilograms or more.
18. Husain 1992, 142–43.
19. Ibid., 142, n. 1.
20. Briggs 1982, 137.
21. Thackston 1996, 285.
22. See above, n. 12, and below, n. 43.
23. AY 1.50–98, discussed in White 1996, 316–17.
24. Ball 1889, vol. 2, 199. Tavernier refers (ibid., 201) to "other pictures of the same penitents, which I have drawn, on the spot, after nature." The lithograph shown in figure 6.2 is a reproduction based on Tavernier's sketch, but is not by Tavernier's own hand.
25. Hambis 1955, 270.
26. Penzer 1924–28, 46–47.
27. Della Valle 1665, 176–77. Pyrard de Laval (in Gray 1887, 343), who visited the Malabar coast in the first decade of the seventeenth century, juxtaposes

but distinguishes between Joguies and wandering charlatans, dancers, acrobats, and mountebanks.

28. Stanley 1866, 99–100.
29. Purchas 1625, vol. 2, 1748.
30. Ibid., 1745.
31. Weinberger-Thomas 1999, 69.
32. Della Valle 1665, 51–53.
33. Ibid., 55–56.
34. Ball 1889, vol. 2, 178–79.
35. Including Thevenot (in Sen 1949, 93).
36. Ball 1889, vol. 2, 196–97.
37. Ibid., vol. 2, 199–201.
38. Discussed extensively in Siegel 1991.
39. Crooke 1967, 104–5.
40. Ibid., 113–14.
41. Sen 1949, 93–94.
42. Ibid., 164–65.
43. Ibid., 258.
44. Bernier 1709, vol. 2, 121–24 (quoted in full in Schmidt 1907, 124–27).
45. White 1996, 50; Hambis 1955, 268. Bernier makes similar observations: White 1996, 50–51.
46. Khan 1927, 197–98.
47. *Khulāṣat-ut-Tawārīkh*, cited in Husain 1992, 144; Ernst 1992, 328, n. 361.
48. Husain 1976, 166.
49. Goswamy and Grewal 1967, 120–22. The Jakhbar monastery had originally secured protection and a land grant from Akbar: Richards 1995, 92.
50. Ernst 2007, 412.
51. Della Valle 1665, 21.
52. Tod 1957–72, vol. 1, 562–63. For a discussion, see White, forthcoming. See chap. 1, nn. 100–1, and below, n. 123.
53. Pinch 2006, 51–52. Cf. Pyrard de Laval's account (in Gray 1887, 343), from the first decade of the seventeenth century, of the Nair "king of Calecut" (Calicut), who had a Joguie "by him" whom he treated as a saint, and for whom he constructed a "monastery or hospital" for the lodging of wandering yogis "two musket-shots from the king's palace."
54. Pinch 2006, 28–44.
55. Bouillier 1994, 216–22.
56. Pinch 2006, 116. Cf. Farquhar 1925, 446.
57. Kolff 1990, 30, 65.
58. Ball 1889, vol. 1, 81–84.
59. Ibid., vol. 1, 391–92.
60. See above, nn. 41 and 43.
61. Khan 1927, 201.
62. Peabody 2003, 57; Pinch 1996, 43–44.

63. Bedi 1991, 74–75, 79, 82–86.
64. Lorenzen 1972, 31–48.
65. Shirreff 1944, 88. However, the great Nāth Yogī scholar Narharināth, whom I met in Kathmandu in 1984, always published under the name Narharināth Yogī.
66. *Silsila-i jūgiyān*, fols. 19a, 20a, tr. in Ernst 2007, 421–22.
67. Bouillier 1994, 218.
68. Tod 1957–72, vol. 1, 81, 208; Hoernle 1881, 49–50. Elsewhere, the same source describes a column of warriors as a line of *jogindas*.
69. Tod 1957, vol. 1, 101. A nearly identical account, dated March 4, 1506, is given, with additional detail, by another Italian traveler, Pietro Martire d'Anghiera (1577, 414–15). If the two men were present there at the same time, it is surprising that neither mentions the other; yet both accounts appear authentic, with no sign of the one copying from the other.
70. Ball 1889, vol. 2, 363.
71. Farquhar 1925, 16. See above nn. 26, 32, and 58.
72. Lorenzen 1978, 61.
73. Pinch 2006, 150. See chap. 1, n. 56.
74. AŚ 1.11.13–20; 1.12.22, quoted in Olivelle 1987, 49–52; Crooke 1967, 114; Pinch 2006, 47–49. See chap. 1, n. 74.
75. Bayly 1993, 29, 142–43.
76. Ibid., 142–43. Cf. Sondheimer 1989, 96–97.
77. White 1996, 344.
78. Bouillier 1991, 1–21.
79. Digby 2003, 250. 'Iṣāmī diverges from the general theory, that a deceased *shaikh* continues to protect his *wilāyat* from his tomb after death, attributing the decline of the Delhi Sultanate to Nizamuddin's "departure" from Delhi to the next world: ibid., 242.
80. Tod 1957–72, vol. 2, 187–88.
81. Ernst 2005, 33.
82. Matringe 1988, 18–20; Shackle 2000, 63. Cf. Lath 1981, 162–63, who mentions two other seventeenth-century yogi romances written by Muslim authors.
83. McGregor 1984, 68.
84. *Padmāvat* 122–28 (in Grierson and Dvivedi 1896, 238).
85. *Padmāvat* 136 (in ibid., 263). Cf. Vaudeville 1962, 359.
86. *Padmāvat* 132, 134 (in Grierson and Dvivedi 1896, 249, 256). See chap. 1, nn. 53 and 76.
87. *Padmāvat* 187, cited in Vaudeville 1962, 362–66; McGregor 1984, 70.
88. āpne gaon kā jogī ān gaon kā sidh, quoted in Yule and Burnell 1968, s.v. «jogee», p. 462.
89. Vaudeville 1962, 353–54. Cf. Gilmartin and Lawrence 2000, 32–33.
90. Briggs 1982, 127–29.
91. Ibid., 132–36.

92. White 1996, 121; Briggs 1982, 129.
93. See also chap. 1, n. 29. Cf. Briggs 1982, 137–39; Bouillier 1997, 89–134.
94. See above, n. 25.
95. Sonnerat 1788–89, vol. 1, 175–76.
96. Khan 1927, 196–97. A similar description is found in Thevenot's account of *fakirs* he observed at Surat: Sen 1949, 165.
97. Sen 1949, 258. Cf. Tavernier's account: Ball 1889, vol. 2, 179.
98. Chaudhuri 1965, 180–81.
99. Like many of his Italian contemporaries, Della Valle understood the term *jogi* (Gioghi) to be the plural form of an imagined singular, **jogo* (Giogho).
100. Della Valle 1665, 56.
101. Ibid., 55; Uberoi 1937, 32–33. See chap. 1, n. 17.
102. Mujtaba and Shah 1992, 84. See above, n. 40.
103. *Kaulajñānanirṇaya* 18.7–14, tr. in White 2003, 108. For background, see ibid., 94–122.
104. White 1996, 288.
105. Demaitre 1936, 34.
106. Sankarnath Yogisvar 1969, 6.
107. White 2001, 144–45.
108. Bouillier 1989, 204–5; Bouillier 1994, 215–16.
109. Sankarnath Yogisvar 1969, 10–12.
110. Ibid., 15–16.
111. Ibid., 44–47, 79–82, 94–95.
112. Ibid., 68–77. See Sax 2008, 36–37, who relates a myth in which Bhairav takes the form of a Nāth Yogī to destroy livestock and spread a cholera epidemic among disrespectful villagers.
113. Sankarnath Yogisvar 1969, 112–18.
114. Ibid., 119–29.
115. Ibid., 103–12. See also above, n. 44. A remarkably similar prophecy by "a Bengali who went about in the garb of a Jogue," this time concerning the fall of Goa, is recorded by the mid-sixteenth-century Portuguese traveler João de Barros (in Cidade 1945, 202).
116. Schimmel 2004, 109, 113–14; Ernst 2007, 413; Husain 1992, 143.
117. Barrow 1893.
118. Pinch 2003; Van der Veer 2001.
119. Quoted in Ernst 2007, 420.
120. Quoted in Pritchett 1985, 58. According to Pritchett (ibid., 77), most modern north Indian editions of this collection adhere closely to this 1801 "original."
121. Eastwick 1845, vi.
122. See above, n. 52.
123. Tod 1957–72, vol. 1, 563.
124. Mehta and Mehta 1985, vol. 1A, 263.
125. Parihar 1968, 181–92.

126. Gold 1995, 120, 128–29. For further discussion, see White, forthcoming.
127. Van Woerkens 2002; Pinch 2006.
128. Pinch 2006, 82–93.
129. The full text is reproduced ibid., 84–86.
130. Gross 1992, 120.
131. Rose 1990, vol. 2, 389.
132. Pinch 1996, 25, 31.
133. "Rāga Rāmkālī" (*Guru Granth Sahib* 939, 941), in Talib and Singh 1987, 1923–24, 1930.
134. BN, bhujang prayāt 6, 10, in Kohli 2005, 111, 112.
135. BN, chaupai 23–24, in ibid., 126.
136. BN, rasāval 51–52; dohira 56, in ibid., 128.
137. Pinch 2006, 18–19.
138. Ibid., 19.
139. Ibid.
140. Clémentin-Ojha 1999, 144–52, 160–66.
141. Forster 1953, 65.
142. Kadetsky 2004, 71.
143. Van der Veer 2001, 73–74.
144. See chap. 2, section 2.
145. DeMichelis 2004. Another pioneer of modern yoga was the Bengali Sri Aurobindo who lived and wrote in the same period as Vivekananda; Alter 2004, 27.
146. Singer 1972, 30–31, citing a letter written by Vivekananda to the *Detroit Free Press* in 1890. However, in his commentary on YS 3.39, Vivekananda (1946, 281) admits the possibility of a yogi entering into another body.
147. Leuba 1919, 205, quoted in Bryant 2009, 331.
148. Pinch 2006, 237, 240–42.
149. Oman 1908, 6–8, 13, 16, 20–21, 27.
150. Ibid., 27.
151. Kadetsky 2004, 198. Schmidt was able to rely on the HYP and *Gheraṇḍa Saṃhitā* because the theretofore "lost" texts had been recently edited by the Theosophical Society.
152. Zumbro 1913, 1265, 1291, 1298, 1305.
153. Yogananda 1992, 299.
154. Ibid., 314.
155. Sjoman 1996, cited in Alter 2004, 23, and Jacobsen 2007, 149.
156. Kadetsky 2004, 76–79. This notion was shared by a number of Indian and Western seekers, including Theos Bernard, a Californian scholar and adventurer who died in Tibet in the 1930s while searching for the yogic grail; Alter 2004, 17; Hackett 2008.
157. Kadetsky 2004, 83.
158. Ibid., 85.

159. Michael O'Neill's 2007 *Vanity Fair* "photo shoot" of yoga celebrities—including Iyengar and Pattabhi Jois, as well as Rodney Yee, Sting, and "the model yogini" Christy Turlington—may be viewed at http://www.vanityfair.com/culture/features/2007/06/yoga_slideshow200706.
160. Das 2006, 7.
161. Bouillier 2008, 199–260, especially 212–14. See also images 1 through 76 of the color illustrations following p. 183 that document the new wealth of these Nāth Yogī establishments more powerfully than any word description possibly could.
162. Chatterjee 2002, 2–5, 10, 12.
163. Other cases, dating from the sixteenth and seventeenth centuries, are documented and Flores and Subrahmanyam 2004, 80–121.
164. Chatterjee 2002, 99–104.
165. Ibid., 107–8.
166. E-mail communication from Partha Chatterjee, June 29, 2008.
167. Chatterjee 2002, 183, 228.
168. Oberoi 1994, 78–79.
169. Ibid., 128.
170. Ibid., 332, 407, 421.
171. Chatterjee 2002, 236, 271.
172. Flores and Subrahmanyam 2004, 82.
173. Chatterjee 2002, 379.
174. Ibid., 115–37.
175. *Deccan Herald*, November 28, 2003. I am grateful to Catherine Clémentin-Ojha for this reference.
176. Chatterjee 2002, 115–37.
177. SvT 7.258a; NT 20.28b.
178. See chap. 4, n. 203.
179. Digby 1970, 31; Ernst 2005, 37.
180. White 2003, 157–59; Khan 1997, 76.
181. Otto 1980.
182. BhG 11.12–13.
183. BhG 11.32a.

Bibliography

Achan, P. Anujan, ed. 1925. *Bhagavadajjukīyam: A Prahasana of Bodhayana Kavi*. Jayantamangalam: Office of the Paliyam Mss. Library.

Ādi Purāṇa. See Jain 1963.

Aitareya Brāhmaṇa. See Samasrami 1895–98.

Alter, Joseph S. 2004. *Yoga in Modern India: The Body between Science and Philosophy*. Princeton: Princeton University Press.

Amanaska Yoga of Gorakhnāth. See Birch 2006.

Amaraughaprabodha of Gorakhnāth. See Mallik 1954.

Angot, Michel. 2008. *Le yoga-sūtra de Patañjali: Le yoga-bhāṣya de Vyāsa: Avec des extraits du yoga-varttika de Vijñāna-Bhikṣu*. Paris: Belles Lettres.

Aparokṣānubhūti. See Tookaram 1901.

Āpastamba Dharma Sūtra. See Olivelle 1999.

Apologia of Tertullian. See Bettenson and Maunder 1999.

Apte, V. M., trans. 1960. *Brahma-Sūtra Shānkara-Bhāshya: Bādarāyaṇa's Brahma-Sūtras*. With Shankarāchārya's commentary. Bombay: Popular Book Depot.

Aranya, Swami Hariharananda, ed. and trans. 1981. *Yoga Philosophy of Patañjali*. Containing his Yoga aphorisms with the commentary of Vyāsa in the original Sanskrit and annotations thereon with copious hints on the practice of yoga. Calcutta: University of Calcutta.

Arthaśāstra of Kauṭilya. See Kangle 1969.

Aśokāvadāna. See Mukhopadhyaya 1963.

Assayag, Jackie, and Gilles Tarabout, eds. 1999. *La Possession en Asie du Sud: Parole, Corps, Territoire (Puruṣārtha 21)*. Paris: Editions EHESS.

Aṣṭāṅgahṛdayasaṃhitā. See Das 1998.

Atharva Veda. See Sastri 1960–64; Bloomfield 1967.

Bāburnāma. See Thackston 1996.

Bachittar Nāṭak of Guru Gobind Singh. See Kohli 2005.

Bailey, H. W. 1975. "The Second Stratum of the Indo-Iranian Gods." In *Mithraic Studies. Proceedings of the First International Congress of Mithraic Studies*, 2 vols. Edited by John R. Hinnells, vol. 1, 1–20. Manchester: Manchester University Press.

Baitāl Pacīsī. See Eastwick 1845.

Ball, Valentine. 1889. *Travels in India by Jean Baptiste Tavernier, Baron of Aubonne*, 2 vols. Translated from the original French edition of 1676 with a biographical sketch of the author, notes, appendices, etc. London and New York: Macmillan and Co.

Banerjea, Aksaya Kumar. 1983. *Philosophy of Gorakhnath with Goraksha-Vacana-Sangraha*, 2nd ed. New Delhi: Motilal Banarsidass. (Orig. pub. 1962. Gorakhpur: Mahant Dig Vijai Nath Trust.)

Banerjee-Dube, Ishita, and Saurabh Dube, eds. 2009. *Ancient to Modern: Religion, Power, and Community in India*. New York: Oxford University Press.

Barrow, H. W. 1893. "On Aghoris and Aghorapanthis." *Anthropological Society of Bombay* 3, no. 4: 197–251.

Barthwal, Pitambaradatta. 1971. *Gorakh Bāṇī*, 4th ed. Allahabad: Hindi Sahitya Sammelan.

Bayly, Christopher A. 1993. *Rulers, Townsmen, and Bazaars: North Indian Society in the Age of British Expansion, 1770–1870*. Delhi: Oxford University Press. (Orig. pub. 1983. Cambridge: Cambridge University Press.)

Beach, Milo Cleveland. 1978. *The Grand Mogul: Imperial Painting in India, 1600–1660*. Williamstown, MA: Sterling and Francine Clark Art Institute.

Bedi, Rajesh. 1991. *Sadhus, the Holy Men of India*. New Delhi: Brijbasi Printers.

Bernier, François. 1709. *Voyages de François Bernier* . . . contenant la description des États du Grand Mogul, de l'Hindoustan, du royaume de Kachemire, & c; où il est traité des richesses, des forces de la justice & des causes principales de la decadence des États de l'Asie, & de plusieurs évenemens considerables. Et où l'on voit comment l'or & l'argent après avoir circulé dans le monde, passent dans l'Hindoustan, d'où ils ne reviennent plus, 2 vols. Amsterdam: P. Marret.

Bettenson, Henry, and Chris Maunder. 1999. *Documents of the Christian Church*, 3rd ed. London and New York: Oxford University Press.

Beyer, Stephen. 1977. "Notes on the Vision Quest in Early Mahāyāna." In *Prajñāpāramitā and Related Systems: Studies in Honor of Edward Conze*. Edited by Lewis Lancaster, 329–40. Berkeley: Berkeley Buddhist Studies Series.

Bhagavadajjukīya. See Achan 1925; Bhatta 2000.

Bhagavadgītā. See Van Buitenen 1981.

Bhāgavata Purāṇa. See Goswami and Sastri 1971; Bryant 2003.

Bhatt, N. R. 1988. *Rauravāgama*, vol. 3. Publications de l' Institut Français d'Indologie, no. 18,3. Pondicherry: Institut Français d'Indologie.

Bhatta, Umesadatta. 2000. *Prahasana paramparā aura Bhagavadajjukīya*. Allahabad: Nisanta Pandeya.

Bhattacharyya, Janaki Vallabha, trans. 1978. *Jayanta Bhaṭṭa's Nyāyamañjarī* [The Compendium of Indian Speculative Logic], vol. 1. Delhi: Motilal Banarsidass.

Biardeau, Madeleine. 1968. "Études de mythologie hindou. I. Cosmogonies purāṇiques." *Bulletin de l'Ecole Française d'Extrême Orient* 54: 19–45.

———. 1991. "Purāṇic Cosmogony." In *Asian Mythologies*. Compiled by Yves Bonnefoy. Translated under the direction of Wendy Doniger, 43–50. Chicago: University of Chicago Press.

Biardeau, Madeleine, and Charles Malamoud. 1976. *Le sacrifice dans l'Inde ancienne*. Paris: Presses Universitaires de France.

Bindra, Pritpal Singh. 2002. *Chritro Pakhyaan: Tales of Male-Female Tricky Deceptions from Sri Dasam Granth*, 2 vols. Amritsar: B. Chattar Singh Jiwan Singh.

Birch, Jason. 2006. "Amanaska Yoga: A Critical Edition, Translation, and Dissertation." B.A. Honours Thesis (Sanskrit), University of Sydney.

Birnbaum, Raoul. 2004. "Light in the Wutai Mountains." In *The Presence of Light: Divine Radiance and Religious Experience*. Edited by Matthew T. Kapstein, 195–226. Chicago: University of Chicago Press.

Bisschop, Peter. 2005. "Pañcārthabhāṣyam on Pāśupatasūtra 1.37–39 Recovered from a Newly Discovered Manuscript." *Journal of Indian Philosophy* 33: 529–51.

Bloomfield, Maurice. 1917. "On the Art of Entering Another's Body: A Hindu Fiction Motif." *Proceedings of the American Philosophical Society* 56: 1–43.

———. 1924. "On False Ascetics and Nuns in Hindu Fiction." *Journal of the American Oriental Society* 44: 202–42.

———, trans. 1967. *Hymns of the Atharva Veda: Together with Extracts from the Ritual Books and Commentaries*. Sacred Books of the East, vol. 42. New Delhi: Motilal Banarsidass.

Bolling, George Melville. 1913. "The Çāntikalpa of the Atharvaveda." *Journal of the American Oriental Society* 33: 265–78.

Bouillier, Véronique. 1989. "Des Prêtres du Pouvoir: Les Yogī et la Fonction Royale." In *Prêtrise, pouvoirs et autorité en Himalaya (Puruṣārtha 12)*. Edited by Véronique Bouillier and Gérard Toffin, 193–213. Paris: Éditions de l'Ecole des Hautes Études en Sciences Sociales.

———. 1991. "The King and His Yogī: Pṛthivinārāyaṇ Śāh, Bhagavantanāth and the Unification of Nepal in the Eighteenth Century." In *Gender, Caste, and Power in South Asia: Social Status and Mobility in A Transitional Society*. Edited by John P. Neelsen, 3–21. Delhi: Manohar.

———. 1994. "La violence des non-violents ou les ascètes au combat." In *Violences et Non-violences en Inde* (*Puruṣārtha 16*). Edited by Denis Vidal, Gilles Tarabout, and Éric Meyer, 213–43. Paris: Éditions de l'École des Hautes Études en Sciences Sociales.

———. 1997. *Ascètes et rois: Un monastère de Kanphata Yogis au Népal*. Paris: CNRS Éditions.

———. 2004. "Samādhi et dargāh: hindouisme et islam dans la Shekhavati." In *De l'Arabie à l'Himalaya, Chemins croisés: En hommage à Marc Gaborieau.*

Edited by Véronique Bouillier and Catherine Servan-Schreiber, 251–71. Paris: Maisonneuve & Larose.

———. 2008. *Itinérance et vie monastique: Les ascètes Nâth Yogîs en Inde contemporaine*. Paris: Editions de la FMSH.

Bouillier, Véronique, and Marie-Christine Cabaud. 1989. "La version népalaise des Aventures du Prince Dikpal." *Cahiers de l'Asie du Sud-Est* 25: 19–42.

Bouillier, Véronique, and Catherine Servan-Schreiber, eds. 2004. *De l'Arabie à l'Himalaya, Chemins croisés: En hommage à Marc Gaborieau*. Paris: Maisonneuve & Larose.

Bouillier, Véronique, and Gérard Toffin, eds. 1989. *Prêtrise, pouvoirs et autorité en Himalaya (Puruṣārtha 12)*. Paris: Éditions de l'Ecole des Hautes Études en Sciences Sociales.

Bouy, Christian. 1994. *Les Nātha-yogin et les Upaniṣads*. Paris: De Boccard.

Brahmāṇḍa Purāṇa. See Shastri 1983.

Brahmasūtra Bhāṣya of Śaṅkara. See Apte 1960; Joshi 1981.

Brahmasūtra of Bādarāyaṇa. See Apte 1960; Joshi 1981.

Braverman, Marcy Alison. 2003. "Possession, Immersion, and the Intoxicated Madnesses of Devotion in Hindu Traditions." Ph.D. Dissertation, University of California, Santa Barbara.

Brereton, Joel. 1991. "Cosmographic Images in the *Bṛhadāraṇyaka Upaniṣad*." *Indo-Iranian Journal* 34: 1–17.

Bṛhadāraṇyaka Upaniṣad. See Limaye and Vadekar 1958; Olivelle 1996; Roebuck 2003.

Briggs, George Weston. 1982. *Gorakhnāth and the Kānphaṭa Yogis*. Delhi: Motilal Banarsidass. (Orig. pub. 1938. Calcutta: YMCA Publishing House.)

Brockington, John. 2003. "Yoga in the *Mahābhārata*." In *Yoga: The Indian Tradition*. Edited by Ian Whicher and David Carpenter, 13–24. London: RoutledgeCurzon.

———, ed. 2009. *Battles, Bards, Brāhmans. Papers from the Epics Section of the 13th World Sanskrit Conference: Edinburgh, 10th–14th July 2006*. Delhi: Motilal Banarsidass.

Bronkhorst, Johannes. 1981. "Yoga and Seśvara Sāṃkhya." *Journal of Indian Philosophy* 9: 309–20.

———. 1993. *The Two Traditions of Meditation in Ancient India*. Delhi: Motilal Banarsidass.

———. 1998. *The Two Sources of Indian Asceticism*, 2nd ed. Delhi: Motilal Banarsidass.

———. 2007. *Greater Magadha: Studies in the Culture of Early India*. Leiden: Brill.

Brunner, Helène. 1974. "Un Tantra du nord: Le Netra Tantra." *Bulletin of the School of Oriental and African Studies* 37: 125–97.

———. 1975. "Le sādhaka, personnage oublié du śivaïsme du Sud." *Journal Asiatique* 263: 411–43.

———. 1994. "The Place of Yoga in the Śaivāgamas." In *Pandit N. R. Bhatt Felicitation Volume*. Edited by Pierre-Sylvain Filliozat, S. P. Narang, and C. P. Bhatta, 425–61. Delhi: Motilal Banarsidass.

Brunner, Helène, Gerard Oberhammer, and André Padoux, eds. 2000. *Tāntrikābhidhānakośa I: A Dictionary of Technical Terms from Hindu Tantric Literature*. Beiträge zur Kultur- und Geistesgeschichte Asiens, no. 35. Vienna: Verlag der Österreichischen Akademie der Wissenschaften.

———, eds. 2004. *Tāntrikābhidhānakośa II: A Dictionary of Technical Terms from Hindu Tantric Literature*. Beiträge zur Kultur- und Geistesgeschichte Asiens, no. 44. Vienna: Verlag der Österreichischen Akademie der Wissenschaften.

Bryant, Edwin F. 2002. "The Date and Provenance of the *Bhāgavata Purāṇa* and the Vaikuṇṭha Perumāl Temple." *Journal of Vaishnava Studies* 11, no.1 (September): 51–80.

———, trans. 2003. *Krishna: The Beautiful Legend of God: Śrīmad Bhāgavata Purāṇa, Book X*. With chapters 1, 6, and 29–31 from Book XI. London: Penguin Books.

———, ed. and trans. 2009. *The Yoga Sūtras of Patañjali. A New Edition, Translation, and Commentary, with Insights from the Traditional Commentators*. New York: North Point Press.

Buddhacarita of Aśvaghoṣa. See Cowell 1977.

Bühnemann, Gudrun, ed. 2003. *Maṇḍalas and Yantras in the Hindu Tradition*. Leiden: Brill.

Busse, Kendall. 2007. "Mūrtis, Vigraha, and Sacred Abodes: Observations on the Bodies of the Gods in Epic India." M.A. Thesis, University of California, Santa Barbara.

Cakrasaṃvara Tantra. See Gray 2007.

Caraka Saṃhitā. See Trikamji Acharya 1992.

Chāndogya Upaniṣad. See Limaye and Vadekar 1958; Olivelle 1996; Roebuck 2003.

Chatterjee, Partha. 2002. *A Princely Imposter? The Kumar of Bhawal and the Secret History of Indian Nationalism*. Princeton, NJ: Princeton University Press.

Chatterji, Jatindra Mohan. 1967. *Hymns of the Atharvan Zarathushtra*. Calcutta: Parsi Zoroastrian Association.

Chattopadhyaya, Brajadulal. 1994. *The Making of Early Medieval India*. Delhi: Oxford University Press.

Chaudhuri, Nirad C. 1965. *The Continent of Circe: Being an Essay on the Peoples of India*. London: Chatto & Windus.

Chenet, Francois. 1987. "Bhāvanā et Créativité de la Conscience." *Numen* 34, no.1 (June): 45–96.

———. 1993. "Les Sauras de l'Inde: le brilliant échec d'une identité religieuse inclusiviste?" *Journal Asiatique* 281, no. 3–4: 317–92.

Cidade, Hernani, ed. 1945. *Ásia de João de Barros: Dos feitos que os portugueses fizeram no descobrimento e conquista dos mares e terras do Oriente*, vol. 2. Lisbon: Agência geral das Colónias.

Clémentin-Ojha, Catherine. 1990. *La divinité conquise: Carrière d'une sainte*. Nanterre: Société d'Ethnologie.

———. 1999. *Le trident sur le palais: Une cabale anti-vishnouite dans un royaume hindou à l'époque coloniale*. Paris: Presses de l'Ecole Française d'Extrême-Orient.

Clough, Bradley S. 2008. "Remembering Lives and Reading Minds: The Importance of Yogic Powers in Early Theravada Buddhism." Paper read at the Annual Meeting of the American Academy of Religion. Chicago, November 3.

Coomaraswamy, Ananda K. 1956. *La sculpture de Bharhut*. French translation by Jean Buhot. Paris: Editions d'Art et d'Histoire.

Cousins, Lance Selwyn, 1996. "The Dating of the Historical Buddha: A Review Article." *Journal of the Royal Asiatic Society*, 3rd series, 6, no.1 (April): 57–63.

Couture, André. 2005. "The Meaning of the Words *yoga* or *yogin* in the Puṣkaraprādurbhāva Section of the *Harivaṃśa*." In *Epics, Khilas, and Purāṇas: Continuities and Ruptures*. Edited by Petteri Koskikallio, 389–409. Zagreb: Croatian Academy of Sciences and Arts.

———. 2007. *La vision de Mārkaṇḍeya et la manifestation du lotus: Histoires anciennes tirées du* Harivaṃśa, éd. cr., Appendice I, no. 41. Geneva: Librarie Droz.

Couture, André, and Charlotte Schmid. 2001. "The *Harivaṃśa*, the Goddess Ekānaṃśā, and the Iconography of the Vṛṣṇi Triads." *Journal of the American Oriental Society* 121, no.2 (April-June): 173–92.

Cowell, Edward B. 1977. *The Buddha-karita or Life of Buddha by Asvaghosha, Indian Poet of the Early Second Century After Christ*. Sanskrit Text, edited from a Devanagari and two Nepalese manuscripts, with Variant readings and English translation. New Delhi: Cosmo Publications. (Orig. pub. 1894.)

Crooke, William, ed. 1967. *A New Account of East India and Persia being Nine Years' Travels 1672–1681, by John Fryer*, vol. 2. Nendeln/Lichtenstein: Kraus Reprint Limited. (Orig. pub. 1912. London: Hakluyt Society.)

———. 1968. *The Popular Religion and Folklore of Northern India*, 2 vols. Delhi: Munshiram Manoharlal. (Third reprint of second edition. Orig. pub. 1896.)

Czuma, Stanislaw J. 1985. *Kushan Sculpture: Images from Early India*. Cleveland: Indiana University Press.

D'Anghiera, Pietro Martire, Richarde Eden, and Richarde Willes. 1577. *The history of trauayle in the VVest and East Indies, and other countreys lying eyther way, towardes the fruitfull and ryche Moluccaes*. London: Richarde Iugge.

Das, Anupreeta. 2006. "India: Breathe in and Hands Off Our Yoga." *Christian Science Monitor*. February 9: 7.

Das, Rahul Peter, ed. 1998. *Vāgbhaṭṭa's Aṣṭāṅgahṛdayasaṃhitā*. The romanized text accompanied by line and word indexes. Groningen: Egbert Forsten.

Dasam Granth. See Kohli 2005.

Davidson, Ronald M. 2002. *Indian Esoteric Buddhism: A Social History of the Tantric Movement*. New York: Columbia University Press.

De, S. K. 1939. "Sanskrit Literature Under the Pāla Kings of Bengal." In *A Volume of Indian and Iranian Studies presented to Sir E. Denison Ross, Kt., C. I. E. on his 68th brith-day [sic], 6th June 1939*. Edited by S. M. Katre and P. K. Gode, 79–98. Bombay: Karnatak Publishing House.

De la Vallée Poussin, Louis. 1936–37a. "Musīla et Nārada. Le chemin du nirvāṇa." *Mélanges chinois et bouddhiques* 5 (July): 189–222.

———. 1936–37b. "Le Bouddhisme et le yoga de Patañjali." *Mélanges chinois et bouddhiques* 5 (July): 223–42.

Della Valle, Pietro. 1665. *The travels of Sig: Pietro della Valle, a noble Roman, into East-India and Arabia Deserta in which, the several countries, together with the customs, manners, traffique, and rites both religious and civil, of those Oriental princes and nations, are faithfully described : in familiar letters to his friend Signior Mario Schipano : whereunto is added a relation of Sir Thomas Roe's Voyage into the East-Indies*. London: J. Macock, for John Place.

Demaitre, Edmund. 1936. *Fakirs et yogis des Indes*. Paris: Librarie Hachette.

DeMichelis, Elizabeth. 2004. *A History of Modern Yoga: Patañjali and Western Esotericism*. New York and London: Continuum.

Dhyansky, Yan Y. 1987. "The Indus Valley Origin of a Yoga Practice." *Artibus Asiae* 48, no. 1–2: 89–108.

Digby, Simon. 1970. "Encounters with Jogīs in Indian Sūfī Hagiography." Typescript of paper read at the School of Oriental and African Studies, London, January 27.

———. 2000. *Wonder-Tales of South Asia: Translated from Hindi, Urdu, Nepali, and Persian*. Jersey: Orient Monographs.

———. 2003. "The Sufi Shaikh as a Source of Authority in Medieval India" *India's Islamic Traditions, 711–1750*. Edited by Richard M. Eaton, 234–62. Delhi: Oxford University Press.

Divanji, P. C. 1939. "Yogavasiṣṭhha on the Means of Proof." In *A Volume of Indian and Iranian Studies presented to Sir E. Denison Ross, Kt., C. I. E. on his 68th brith-day [sic], 6th June 1939*. Edited by S. M. Katre and P. K. Gode, 102–12. Bombay: Karnatak Publishing House.

Duchesne-Guillemin, Jacques, et al., eds. 1978. *Études Mithriaques. Actes du 2è Congrès International, Téhéran, du 1èr au 8 septembre 1975*. Leiden: Brill; Tehran: Bibliothèque Pahlavi.

Dumézil, Georges. 1981. *Mythe et épopée III: Histoires romaines*, 3rd ed. Paris: Gallimard.

———. 1986. *Mythe et épopée II: Types épiques indo-européens: un heros, un sorcier, un roi*. Paris: Gallimard.

Dundas, Paul. 1991. "The Digambara Jain Warrior." In *The Assembly of Listeners: Jains in Society*. Edited by Michael Carrithers and Caroline Humphrey, 169–86. Cambridge and New York: Cambridge University Press.

Duval, Paul-Marie. 1981. "Cernunnos, le dieu aux bois de cerf." In *Dictionnaire des Mythologies et des religions des sociétés traditionnelles et du monde antique*, 2 vols. Sous la direction de Yves Bonnefoy. Paris: Flammarion.

Dvivedi, Hazariprasad, ed. 1980. *Nāth Siddhoṃ kī Bāniyāṃ*, 2nd ed. Benares: Kasi Nagarapracarini Sabha.

———. 1981. *Nāth-sampradāy*, 3rd ed. Allahabad: Lokabharati Prakasan.

Dwivedi, R. C., and Navjivan Rastogi. 1987. *The Tantrāloka of Abhinavagupta*, 2nd ed., 8 vols. With commentary by Rājānaka Jayaratha. Delhi: Motilal Banarsidass. (Orig. pub. 1918–38. Allahabad: Indian Press.)

Dwivedi, Vajravallabh, ed. 1985. *Netratantram [Mṛtyuñjaya Bhaṭṭāraka]*. With the commentary Udyota of Kṣemarājācārya. Delhi: Parimal Publications.

Dyczkowski, Mark. S. N. 2004. *A Journey in the World of the Tantras*. Benares: Indica Books.

Eastwick, Edward Backhouse, ed. 1845. *The Baital Pachisi; or Twenty-five tales of a demon*. A new edition of the Hindí text, with each word expressed in the Hindústání character immediately under the corresponding word in the Nágarí, with a perfectly literal English interlinear translation, accompanied by a free translation in English at the foot of each page, and explanatory notes by W. Burckhardt Barker, M.R.A.S. Hertford: Stephen Austin.

Eaton, Richard M., ed. 2003. *India's Islamic Traditions, 711–1750*. New Delhi: Oxford University Press.

Eckel, Malcolm David. 1992. *To See the Buddha: A Philosopher's Quest for the Meaning of Emptiness*. San Francisco: Harper SanFrancisco.

Edgerton, Franklin. 1924. "The Meaning of Sāṃkhya and Yoga." *American Journal of Philology* 45, no. 1: 1–47.

———, ed. and trans. 1926. *Vikrama's adventures; or, The thirty-two tales of the throne, a collection of stories about King Vikrama, as told by the thirty-two statuettes that supported his throne*, 2 vols. Cambridge: Harvard University Press.

Eliade, Mircea. 1973. *Yoga: Immortality and Freedom*, 2nd ed. Princeton: Princeton University Press. (Orig. pub. 1958. New York: Pantheon Books.)

Emeneau, Murray Barnson. 1934. *Jambhaladatta's Version of the Vetālapañcaviṃśati: A Critical Sanskrit Text in Transliteration*. With an introduction and an English translation. American Oriental Society, vol. 4. New Haven: American Oriental Society.

———. 1935. "The Story of Vikrama's Birth and Accession." *Journal of the American Oriental Society* 55, no. 1 (March): 59–88.

Ernst, Carl. 1992. *Eternal Garden: Mysticism, History, and Politics at a South Asian Sufi Center:* Albany NY: SUNY Press.

———. 2005. "Situating Sufism and Yoga." *Journal of the Royal Asiatic Society*, series 3, 15, no. 1: 15–43.

———. 2007. "Accounts of Yogis in Arabic and Persian Historical and Travel Texts." *Jerusalem Studies in Arabic and Islam* 33: 409–26.

Errington, Elizabeth, and Joe Cribb. 1992. *The Crossroads of Asia: Transformation in Image and Symbol in the Art of Ancient Afghanistan and Pakistan*. An exhibition at the Fitzwilliam Museum, Cambridge, 6 October—13 December 1992. Cambridge: Ancient India and Iran Trust.

Faddegon, B. 1918/1969. *The Vaiçeṣika-System, Described with the Help of the Oldest Texts*. Wiesbaden: Dr. Martin Sändig oHG.

Falk, Harry. 1987. "Viṣṇu im Veda." In *Hinduismus und Buddhismus: Festschrift für Ulrich Schneider*. Edited by Harry Falk, 112–33. Freiburg: Hedwige Falk.

Farquhar, John Nicol. 1925. "The Fighting Ascetics of India." *Bulletin of the John Rylands Library* 9: 431–52.

Filliozat, Jean. 1955. "Review of Mircea Eliade: *Le Yoga; Immortalité et liberté*." *Journal Asiatique* 243, no. 3: 368–70.

———. 1962. "Notes d'astronomie ancienne de l'Iran et de l'Inde (I, II, et III)." *Journal Asiatique* 250 no. 3: 325–50.

———. 1967. "L'Abandon de la vie et les suicides du criminel et du héros dans la tradition indienne." *Arts Asiatiques* 15: 65–88.

———. 1969. "Taoïsme et yoga." *Journal Asiatique* 257: 41-87.

Filliozat, Pierre-Sylvain, S. P. Narang, and C. P. Bhatta, eds. 1994. *Pandit N. R. Bhatt Felicitation Volume*. Delhi: Motilal Banarsidass.

Fitzgerald, James L. 2002. "Nun Befuddles King, Shows *Karmayoga* Does Not Work: Sulabhā's Refutation of King Janaka at Mbh 12.308." *Journal of Indian Philosophy* 30: 641–77.

———, trans. 2004. *The Mahābhārata: 11. The Book of the Women: 12. The Book of the Peace, Part One*. Chicago: University of Chicago Press.

———. 2009. "The Sāṃkhya-Yoga 'Manifesto' at MBh 12.289-290." In *Battles, Bards, Brahmans. Papers from the Epics Section of the 13th World Sanskrit Conference. Edinburgh, 10th–14th July 2006*. Edited by John Brockington, 185–212. Delhi: Motilal Banarsidass.

Fleischer, Robert. 1973. *Artemis von Ephesos und Verwandte Kultstatuen aus Anatolien und Syrien*. Leiden: Brill.

Flood, Gavin. 2000. "The Purification of the Body." In *Tantra in Practice*. Edited by David White, 509–20. Princeton, NJ: Princeton University Press.

———. 2006. *The* Tantric *Body: The Secret Tradition of Hindu Religion*. London: I. B. Taurus.

Flores, Jorge, and Sanjay Subrahmanyam. 2004. "The Shadow Sultan: Succession and Imposture in the Mughal Empire, 1628–1640." *Journal of the Economic and Social History of the Orient* 47, no. 1: 80–121.

Forster, E. M. 1953. *The Hill of Devi*. Harmondsworth: Penguin.

Fort, Andrew O. 1994. "Going or Knowing? The Development of the Idea of Living Liberation in the Upaniṣads." *Journal of Indian Philosophy* 22: 379–90.

Fowler, Harold North, trans. 1990. *Plato: Euthyphro, Apology, Crito, Phædo, Phædrus*. Loeb Classical Library 36. Cambridge, MA: Harvard University Press. (Orig. pub. 1914).

Franco, Eli, and Karin Preizendanz. 1997. *Beyond Orientalism: The Work of Wilhem Halbfass and its Impact on Indian and Cross-Cultural Studies*. Poznan Studies in the Philosophy of the Sciences and the Humanities, vol. 59. Amsterdam and Atlanta: Rodopi.

Gaborieau, Marc. 1975. "La transe rituelle dans l'Himalaya Central: folie, avatār, meditation." *Puruṣārtha* 2: 147–72.

———. 1989. "Pouvoirs et autorité des soufis dans l'Himalaya." In *Prêtrise, pouvoirs et autorité en Himalaya (Puruṣārtha 12)*. Edited by Véronique Bouillier and Gérard Toffin, 215–38. Paris: Éditions de l'Ecole des Hautes Études en Sciences Sociales.

Gautam, Camanlal. 1981. *Śrī Gorakhnāth Caritr*. Bareilly: Samskrti Samsthan.

Geenens, Philippe. 2000. *Yogayājñavalkyam: Corps et Ame, le yoga selon Yājñavalkya*. Paris: Gallimard.

Gelblum, Tuvia. 2008. "Al-Bīrūnī, *Book of Patañjali*." *Yoga: India's Philosophy of Meditation. Encyclopedia of Indian Philosophies*, vol. 12. Edited by Gerald Larson and Ram Shankar Bhattacharya, 261–66. Delhi: Motilal Banarsidass.

Gerow, Edwin. 2007. "La dialectique de la Bhagavadgītā." *Journal Asiatique* 295, no.1: 133–54.

Ghanekar, Bhaskara Govinda, ed. 1980. *Suśruta Saṃhitā*, 5th ed. With the commentary of Atrideva. Delhi: Motilal Banarsidass.

Ghosh, Manmohan, trans. 1951–61. *The Nāṭyaśāstra ascribed to Bharata-muni*, 2 vols. Bibliotheca Indica 272, issue numbers 1559, 1581. Calcutta: Royal Asiatic Society of Bengal; Calcutta: Asiatic Society.

Ghosh, Raghunath, ed. 2003. *Nyāyadarśana of Gotama*. With Sanskrit text, Vātsyāyana Bhāṣya, Sanskrit commentary, English summary, and English translation. Translated by Satish Chandra Vidyabhusana. Delhi: New Bharatiya Book Corporation.

Gilmartin, David, and Bruce Lawrence, eds. 2000. *Beyond Turk and Hindu: Rethinking Religious Identities in Islamicate South Asia*. Gainesville: University of Florida Press.

Gimello, Robert. 1978. "Mysticism and Meditation." In *Mysticism and Philosophical Analysis*. Edited by Steven T. Katz, 170–99. London: Sheldon Press.

Gnoli, Raniero. 1977. *The Gilgit MSS of the Saṅghabhedavastu*, 2 vols. Rome: Istituto Italiano per il Medio ed Estremo Oriente.

———. 1999. *Abhinavagupta, Luce dei tantra: Tantrāloka*. Milan: Adelphi Edizioni.

Göbl, Robert. 1984. *System und Chronologie der Münzprägung des Kuśānreiches*. Wein: Verlag der Österreichishcen Akademie der Wissenschaften.

Gold, Ann Grodzins. 1989. "The Once and Future Yogi: Sentiments and Signs in the Tale of a Renoucer-King." *Journal of Asian Studies* 48, no. 4 (Nov.): 770–86.

———. 1992. *A Carnival of Parting: The Tales of King Bharthari and King Gopi Chand as Sung and Told by Madhu Natisar Nath of Ghatiyali, Rajasthan*. Berkeley: University of California Press.

Gold, Daniel. 1995. "The Instability of the King: Magical Insanity and the Yogi's Power in the Politics of Jodhpur, 1803–1843." In *Bhakti Religion in North India: Community Identity & Political Action*. Edited by David Lorenzen, 120–32. Albany, NY: SUNY Press.

Goldman, Robert. 1977. *Gods, Priests, and Warriors: The Bhṛgus of the Mahābhārata*. New York: Columbia University Press.

Gonda, Jan. 1963. *The Vision of the Vedic Poets*. The Hague: Mouton & Co.

———. 1969. *Eye and Gaze in the Veda*. Amsterdam and London: North-Holland Publishing Company.

———. 1977. *Medieval Religious Literature in Sanskrit*. History of Indian Literature, vol. 2, fasc. 1. Wiesbaden: Harassowitz.

———. 1985. *Change and Continuity in Indian Religion*. New Delhi: Munshiram Manoharlal.

Goodall, Dominic. 1998. *Rāmakaṇṭha's Commentary on the Kiraṇatantra*, vol. 1 (Chapters 1–6). Pondicherry: Institut Française d'Indologie.

———, ed. and trans. 2004. *The Parākhyatantra: A Scripture of the Śaiva Siddhānta*. Pondicherry: Institut Français de Pondichéry.

Goodall, Dominic, and Harunaga Isaacson. 2007. "Workshop on the *Niśvāsatattvasaṃhitā:* The Earliest Surviving Śaiva Tantra?" *Newsletter of the Nepal German Manuscript Cataloguing Project* 3: 4–6.

Goodall, Dominic, and André Padoux, eds. 2007. *Tantric Studies in Memory of Hélène Brunner*. Pondicherry: Institut Français de Pondichéry.

Gorakṣa Saṃhitā. See Pandeya 1976.

Gorakṣasiddhāntasaṃgraha. See Pandeya 1973.

Goswami, C. L., and M. A. Sastri, ed. and trans. 1971. *Śrīmad Bhāgavata Mahāpurāṇa*, 2 vols. Gorakhpur: Gita Press.

Goswamy, B. N., and J. S. Grewal. 1967. *The Mughals and the Jogis of Jakhbar: Some Madad-i-Ma'ash and Other Documents*. Simla: Indian Institute of Advanced Study.

Goudriaan, Teun. 1983. "Some Beliefs and Rituals Concerning Time and Death in the Kubjikāmata." In *Selected Studies on Ritual in the Indian Religions: Essays to D. J. Hoens*. Edited by Ria Kloppenborg, 92–117. Leiden: Brill.

Goudriaan, Teun, and Jan Schoterman, eds. 1988. *Kubjikāmata Tantra, Kulālikāmnāya Version*. Orientalia Rheno-Traiectina, 30. Leiden: Brill.

———. 1992. "The Pluriform Ātman from the Upaniṣads to the Svacchanda Tantra." *Wiener Zeitschrift für die Kunde Sudasiens* 36: 163–86.

Gough, Archibald Edward, ed. and trans. 1975. *The Vaiśeṣika Aphorisms of Kanâda*. With comments from the Upaskâra of Śankara Miśra and the Vivritti of Jaya-Nârâyaṇa Tarkapañcânana. New Delhi: Oriental Books Reprint Corporation. (Orig. pub. 1873. Benares: E. J. Lazarus & Co.)

Granoff, Phyllis. 1979. "Maheśvara/Mahākāla: A Unique Buddhist Image from Kaśmīr." *Artibus Asiae* 41, no. 1: 64–82.

———. 2007. "Fasting or Fighting: Dying the Noble Death in Some Indian Religious Texts." In *Heroes and Saints: The Moment of Death in Cross-cultural Perspectives*. Edited by Phyllis Granoff and Koichi Shinohara, 73–100. Newcastle: Cambridge Scholars Publishing.

Grassmann, Hermann. 1873/1976. *Wörterbuch zum Rig-Veda*. Leipzig: F.A. Brockhaus. Reprint Wiesbaden: Harrassowitz.

Gray, Albert, trans. 1887. *The Voyage of François Pyrard of Laval to the East Indies, the Maldives, the Moluccas, and Brazil*, vol. 1. London: Hakluyt Society. (Reprint 1964. New York: Burt Franklin).

Gray, David B. 2007. *The Cakrasaṃvara Tantra (The Discourse of Śrī Heruka) Śrīherukābhidhāna. A Study and Annotated Translation.* New York: Columbia University Press.

Grierson, George, and Sudhakara Dvivedi, ed. 1896. *The Padumawāti of Malik Muhammad Jaisī.* Bibliotheca Indica, n.s. 877. Calcutta: Baptist Mission Press.

Griffiths, Paul. 1981. "Concentration or Insight: The Problematic of Theravāda Buddhist Meditation-Theory." *Journal of the American Academy of Religion* 49, no. 4: 605–24.

Grinshpon, Yohanan. 1997. "Experience and Observation in Traditional and Modern Pātañjala Yoga." In *Beyond Orientalism: The Work of Wilhem Halbfass and Its Impact on Indian and Cross-Cultural Studies.* Poznan Studies in the Philosophy of the Sciences and the Humanities, vol. 59. Edited by Eli Franco and Karin Preizendanz, 557–66. Amsterdam and Atlanta: Rodopi.

Gross, Robert Lewis. 1992. *The Sādhus of India: A Study of Hindu Asceticism.* Jaipur: Rawat Publications.

Guedj, Denis. 1998. *Le théorème du perroquet.* Paris: Seuil.

Gupta, Anand Swarup, ed. 1972. *The Kūrma Purāṇa, with English Translation.* Translated by Ahibhushan Bhattacharya, Satkari Mukherji, Virendra Kumar Varma, and Ganga Sagar Rai. Benares: All-India Kashiraj Trust.

Gupta, Bina. 1991. *Perceiving in Advaita Vedānta: Epistemological Analysis and Interpretation.* Lewisburg: Bucknell University Press.

Gupta, Sanjukta, trans. 1972. *Lakṣmī Tantra: A Pāñcarātra Text.* Leiden: Brill.

Guru Granth Sahib. See Talib and Singh 1987.

Hackett, Paul G. 2008. "Barbarian Lands: Theos Bernard, Tibet, and the American Religious Life." Ph.D. Dissertation, Columbia University.

Haksar, Aditya Narayan Dhairyasheel. 1998. *Siṃhāsana Dvātriṃśikā: Thirty-two Tales of the Throne of Vikramaditya.* Delhi: Penguin Books India.

Halbfass, Wilhelm. 1988. *India and Europe: An Essay in Understanding.* Albany, NY: State University of New York Press.

Hambis, Louis. 1955. *Marco Polo, La description du monde: Texte intégrale en français moderne avec introduction et notes.* Paris: Librairie C. Klincksieck.

Hanneder, Jürgen. 2006. *Studies on the Mokṣopāya.* Abhandlungen für die Kunde des Morgenlandes, no. 58. Wiesbaden: Harrassowitz.

Hara, Minoru. 1966. "Review of Lillian Silburn, *La Bhakti.*" *Indo-Iranian Journal* 9, no. 3: 211–18.

———. 1999. "Pāśupata and Yoga: *Pāśupata-sūtra* 2.12 and *Yoga-Sūtra* 3.37." *Asiatische Studien/Études Asiatiques* 53: 593–608.

———. 2001a. "Apsaras and Hero." *Indo-Iranian Journal* 29: 135–53.

———. 2001b. "The Death of the Hero." *Journal of the International College for Postgraduate Buddhist Studies* 4 (March): 315–40.

———. 2002. *Pāśupata Studies.* Edited by Jun Takashima. Vienna: Institut für Südasien-, Tibet-, und Buddhismuskunde.

Harivaṃśa. See Vaidya 1969–71.

Harper, Donald. 1995. "The Bellows Analogy in *Laozi* V and Warring States Macrobiotic Hygiene." *Early China* 20: 381–91.

Harṣacarita of Bāṇabhaṭṭa. See Kane, P. V. 1965.

Hart, George W., III. 1979. "The Little Devotee: Cekkilār's Story of Ciurttoṇtar." In *Sanskrit and Indian Studies in Honor of J. H. H. Ingalls*. Edited by M. Nagatomi, B. K. Matilal, J. M. Masson, and E. Dimock, 217–36. New York: Reidel Publishing Company.

Haṭharatnāvalī of Śrīnivāsabhaṭṭa Yogīndra. See Reddy 1982.

Haṭhayogapradīpikā of Svātmarāman. See Iyengar 1972.

Hatley, Shaman. 2007. "The *Brahmayāmalatantra* and the Early Śaiva Cult of Yoginīs." Ph.D. Dissertation, University of Pennsylvania.

Hazra, R. C. 1975. *Studies in the Purāṇic Records on Hindu Rites and Customs*, 2nd ed. Delhi: Motilal Banarsidass.

Heesterman, Johannes Cornelius. 1982. "Householder and Wanderer." In *Way of Life: Essays in Honour of Louis Dumont*. Edited by T.N. Madan, 251–71. New Delhi: Vikas.

———. 1985. *The Inner Conflict of Tradition*. Chicago: University of Chicago Press.

———. 1993. *The Broken World of Sacrifice*. Chicago: University of Chicago Press.

Heimann, Betty. 1939. "Terms in Statu Nascendi in the Bhagavadgītā." In *A Volume of Indian and Iranian Studies presented to Sir E. Denison Ross, Kt., C. I. E. on his 68th brith-day [sic], 6th June 1939*. Edited by S.M. Katre and P. K. Gode, 125–35. Bombay: Karnatak Publishing House.

Hillebrandt, Alfred. 1981. *Śāṅkhāyana Śrauta Sūtra*. With commentary of Varadattasuta Ānartīya and Govinda. New Delhi: Meharchand Lachhmandas Publications.

Hiltebeitel, Alf. 1978. "The Indus Valley 'Proto-Śiva,' Reexamined through Reflections on the Goddess, the Buffalo, and the Symbolism of *vāhanas*." *Anthropos* 73, no. 5–6: 767–97.

———, ed. 1989. *Criminal Gods and Demon Devotees: Essays on the Guardians of Popular Hinduism*. Albany: SUNY Press.

———. 2001. *Rethinking the Mahābhārata: A Reader's Guide to the Education of the Dharma King*. Chicago: University of Chicago Press.

Hoernle, A. F. Rudolf, trans. 1881. *The Prithirája Rásau of Chand Bardáí*. Bibliotheca Indica, new series, no. 452. Calcutta: Baptist Mission Press.

Hopkins, E. Washburn. 1901. "Yoga-technique in the Great Epic." *Journal of the American Oriental Society* 22: 333–79.

Howard, Angela. 1986. *The Cosmological Buddha*. Studies in South Asian Culture, 13. Leiden: Brill.

Hudson, D. Dennis. 1989. "Violent and Fanatical Devotion among the Nāyanārs: A Study in the *Periya Purāṇam* of Cekkilār. In *Criminal Gods and Demon Devotees: Essays on the Guardians of Popular Hinduism*. Edited by Alf Hiltebeitel, 373–404. Albany: SUNY Press.

———. 1993. "Vāsudeva Kṛṣṇa in Theology and Architecture: A Background to Śrīvaiṣṇavism." *Journal of Vaiṣṇava Studies* 2, no. 1 (Winter): 139–70.

———. 1995."The Śrīmad Bhāgavata Purāṇa in Stone: The Text as an Eighth-Century Temple and its Implications." *Journal of Vaiṣṇava Studies* 3, no. 3 (Summer): 137–82.

Hulin, Michel, trans. 1980. *Mṛgendrāgama, sections de la doctrine et du yoga: Avec la vṛtti de Bhaṭṭanārāyaṇakaṇṭha et la dīpikā de Aghoraśivācārya*. Pondicherry: Institut Français d'Indologie.

Humbach, H. 1978. "Mithra in India and the Hinduized Magi." In *Études Mithriaques. Actes du 2è Congrès International, Téhéran, du 1èr au 8 septembre 1975*. Edited by Jacques Duchesne-Guillemin et al., 229–54. Leiden: Brill; Tehran: Bibliothèque Pahlavi.

Husain, Iqbal. 1992. "Hindu Shrines and Practices as Described by a Central Asian Traveller in the First Half of the 17th Century." In *Medieval India 1: Researches in the History of India, 1200–1750*. Edited by Irfan Habib, 141–49. Delhi: Oxford University Press.

Husain, Mahdi, trans. 1976. *Reḥla (India, Maldive Islands, and Ceylon)*. Gaekwad's Oriental Series, 122. Baroda: Oriental Institute.

Ibn Baṭṭūṭa. 1976. See Husain 1976.

Inden, Ronald. 1992. " Changes in Vedic Priesthood." In *Ritual, State, and History in South Asia*. Edited by A. W. van den Hoek, et al., 556–77. Leiden, Brill.

Ingalls, Daniel H. H. 1959. "Ātmanātmānam." In *Jñānamuktāvalī: Commemoration Volume in Honor of Johannes Nobel, on the Occasion of His 70th Birthday Offered by Pupils and Colleagues*. Edited by Claus Vogel. Delhi: International Academy of Indian Culture.

Iyengar, Srinivasa, ed. and trans. 1972. *Haṭhayogapradīpikā of Svātmarāman*. With the commentary of Brahmānanda. Madras: Adyar Library and Research Centre.

Jacobsen, Autumn. 2007. "Contemporary Yoga Movements." In *Yoga: India's Philosophy of Meditation, Encyclopedia of Indian Philosophies*, vol. 12. Edited by Gerald Larson and Ram Shankar Bhattacharya, 148–58. Delhi: Motilal Banarsidass.

Jaiminīya Upaniṣad Brāhmaṇa. See Oertel 1894; Limaye and Vadekar 1958.

Jain, Pannalal, ed. 1963, *Ādipurāṇa [first part] of Āchārya Jinasena*, 2nd ed. With Hindi translation, introduction, and appendices. Benares: Bharatiya Jnanapitha.

Jayākhya Saṃhitā. 1967. *Jayākhya Saṃhitā of Pāñcarātra Āgama*. Edited by E. Krishnamacharya. Gaekwad's Oriental Series, 54. Baroda: Oriental Institute.

Jensen, Jørgen. 2003. *Danmarks Oldtid, Aeldre Jernalder 500 f. Kr.—400 e. Kr.* Copenhagen: Gyldendal.

Jetly, J. S., ed. 1971. *Praśastapādabhāṣyam*. With the commentary Kārakāvalī of Udayanācārya. Baroda: Oriental Institute.

Jetly, J. S., and Vasant G. Parikh. 1991. *Nyāyakandalī, being a commentary on Praśastapādabhāṣya, with Three Sub-commentaries*. Gaekwad's Oriental Series, no. 174. Baroda: Oriental Institute.

Jha, Durgadhara, ed. 1997. *Praśastapādabhāṣyam (Padārthadharmasaṅgraha) of Praśastapādācārya*. With the commentary Nyāyakandalī by Śrīdhara Bhaṭṭa along with Hindi translation. Ganganathajaha-Granthamala, vol. 1. Varanasi: Sampurnanand Sanskrit University.

Jha, Ganganatha, trans.1982. *Padārthadharmasaṅgraha of Praśastapāda with the Nyāyakandalī of Śrīdhara*. Chaukhambha Oriental Series, 4. Varanasi: Chaukhambha Orientalia. (Orig. pub. 1916. Benares: Allahabad.)

———, ed. and trans. 1992. *Yogasārasaṃgraha: Vijñānabhikṣupranīta*. Delhi: Chaukhamba Sanskrit Pratisthana. (Orig. pub. 1933. Madras: Theosophical Publishing House.)

Jha, Ramchandra, ed. 1991. *Pañcatantram*, 6th ed. Vidyabhavan Sanskrit Grantha Mala, 17. Benares: Chowkhamba Vidyabhavan.

Jørgensen, Hans. 1939. *Batīsaputrikākathā: The Tales of the Thirty-two Statuettes; A Newārī Recension of the Siṃhāsanadvātriṃśatikā*. Kgl. Danske Videnskabernes Selskab, Historisk-filologiske Meddelelser XXIV, 2. Copenhagen: Ejnar Munksgaard.

Joshi, K. L., ed. 1981. *Brahmasūtra Śāṅkara Bhāṣya*, 2 vols. With the commentaries of Bhāmatī, Kalpataru, and Parimala. Ahmedabad and Delhi: Parimal.

Joshi, L. V. 1986. *A Critical Study of the Pratyakṣa Pariccheda of Bhāsarvajña's Nyāyabhūṣaṇa*. Research-Thesis Work Publication Series—22. Ahmedabad: Gujarat University.

Kadetsky, Elizabeth. 2004. *First There Is a Mountain: A Yoga Romance*. Boston: Little, Brown and Company.

Kaelber, Walter O. 1989. *Tapta-Mārga: Asceticism and Initiation in Vedic India*. New York: State University of New York Press.

Kālikā Purāṇa. See Shastri 1992.

Kane, Pandurang Vaman, ed. 1965. *The Harṣacarita of Bāṇabhaṭṭa with Exhaustive Notes [Ucchvāsas I—VIII]*, 2nd. ed., 2 vols. New Delhi: Motilal Banarsidass. (Orig. pub. 1918. Bombay: P. V. Kane.)

———. 1968–77. *History of Dharmaśāstra*, 2nd ed., 5 vols. Poona: Bhandarkar Oriental Research Institute.

Kangle, R. P. 1969. *The Kauṭilya Arthaśāstra*, 2 vols. Bombay: University of Bombay.

Kapani, Lakshmi. 1992–93. *La notion du saṃskāra*, 2 vols. Publications de l'Institut de Civilisation Indienne, no. 59. Paris: De Boccard.

Kapferer, Bruce, ed. 1976. *Transaction and Meaning: Directions in the Anthropology of Exchange and Symbolic Behavior*. Philadelphia: Institute for the Study of Human Issues.

Kapstein, Matthew T., ed. 2004. *The Presence of Light: Divine Radiance and Religious Experience*. Chicago: University of Chicago Press.

Karlsson, Klemens. 1999. "Face to Face with the Absent Buddha: The Formation of Aniconic Buddhist Art." Ph.D. Dissertation, Uppsala University.

Karpūramañjarī of Rājaśekara. See Konow and Lanman 1901; Suru 1960.

Kaṭha Upaniṣad. See Limaye and Vadekar 1958; Olivelle 1996; Roebuck 2003.

Kathāratnākara of Hemavijaya. See Municandrasuri 1997.

Kathāsaritsāgara of Somadeva. See Sastri 1970; Penzer 1924–28.

Katre, S. M., and P. K. Gode (eds.). 1939. *A Volume of Indian and Iranian Studies presented to Sir E. Denison Ross, Kt., C. I. E. on His 68th Brith-day [sic], 6th June 1939*. Bombay: Karnatak Publishing House.

Kaviraj, Gopinath. 1922. "Nirmāṇa Kāya." *Princess of Wales Sarasvati Bhavana Studies* 1, no. 1. Edited by Ganganatha Jha, 47–57.

———. 1977–79. *Bhāratīya Saṃskṛti aur Sādhanā*, 2nd ed., 2 vols. Patna: Bihar Rashtrabhasha Parishad.

———. 1984. *Bhāratīya Sādhanā kī Dhārā*. Bihar: Rashtrabhasha Parishad.

Keith, Arthur Berriedale. 1924. *The Sanskrit Drama in its Origin, Development, Theory, & Practice*. Oxford: Clarendon Press.

Kellens, Jean. 1978. "Caractères differéntiels du Mihr Yast." In *Études Mithriaques. Actes du 2è Congrès International, Téhéran, du 1èr au 8 septembre 1975*. Edited by Jacques Duchesne-Guillemin et al., 261–70. Leiden: Brill; Tehran: Bibliothèque Pahlavi.

Kenoyer, Jonathan Mark. 1998. *Ancient Cities of the Indus Valley Civilization*. Karachi: Oxford University Press.

Khan, Dominique-Sila. 1997. *Conversions and Shifting Identities: Ramdev Pir and the Ismailis in Rajasthan*. New Delhi: Manohar.

Khan, Shafaat Ahmad, ed. 1927. *John Marshall in India: Notes and Observations in Bengal 1668–1672*. London: Oxford University Press.

Khecarīvidyā of Ādinātha. See Mallinson 2007.

King, Richard. 1999. *Indian Philosophy: An Introduction to Hindu and Buddhist Thought*. Washington, D.C.: Georgetown University Press.

Kiraṇa Tantra. With the commentary of Rāmakaṇṭha. See Goodall 1998.

Kiraṇāvalī of Udayanācārya. See Jetly 1971.

Klindt-Jensen, Ole. 1961. *Gundestrupkedelen*. Copenhagen: Nationalmuseet.

Kloetzli, W. Randolph. 1985. "Maps of Time—Mythologies of Descent: Scientific Instruments and the Purāṇic Cosmograph." *History of Religions* 25: 120–45.

Kloppenborg, Ria, and Ronald Poelmeyer. 1987. "Visualizations in Buddhist Meditation." In *Effigies Dei: Essays on the History of Religions*. Edited by Dirk Van der Plas, 83–95. Leiden: Brill.

Kohli, Surindar Singh. 2005. *The Dasam Granth: The Second Scripture of the Sikhs Written by Sri Guru Gobind Singh*. New Delhi: Munshiram Manoharlal.

Kolff, Dirk H. A. 1971. "Sannyasi Trader-Soldiers." *Indian Economic and Social History Review* 8: 213–20.

———. 1990. *Naukar, Rajput, & Sepoy: The Ethnohistory of the Military Labour Market in Hindustan, 1450–1850*. Cambridge: Cambridge University Press.

Konow, Sten, ed. 1901. *Raja-Çekhara's Karpūra-mañjarī: A Drama by the Indian Poet Rājaçekhara (about 900 A.D.)*. Harvard Oriental Series, vol. 4. Translated by Charles Rockwell Lanman. Cambridge: Harvard University Press.

Kramrisch, Stella. 1981. *The Presence of Śiva*. Princeton: Princeton University Press.

Krengel, Monika. 1999. "Spirit Possession in the Central Himalayas. *Jāgar*-Rituals: An Expression of Customs and Rites." In *La Possession en Asie du Sud: Parole, Corps, Territoire (Puruṣārtha 21)*. Edited by Jackie Assayag and Gilles Tarabout, 265–88. Paris: Editions EHESS.

Kubjikāmata. See Goudriaan and Schoterman 1988.

Kumoi, Shozen. 1997. "The Concept of Yoga in the Nikayas." In *Bauddhavidyāsudhākaraḥ: Studies in Honour of Heinz Bechert on the Occasion of His 65th Birthday*. Edited by Heinz Bechert, Petra Kieffer-Pülz, and Jens-Uwe Hartmann, 407–20. Swisttal-Odendorf: Indica et Tibetica Verlag.

Kūrma Purāṇa. See Gupta, Anand Swarup. 1972.

Lakṣmī Tantra. See Gupta, Sanjukta. 1972.

Larson, Gerald, and Ram Shankar Bhattacharya, eds. 2008. *Yoga: India's Philosophy of Meditation. Encyclopedia of Indian Philosophies*, vol. 12. Delhi: Motilal Banarsidass.

Lath, Mukund. 1981. *The Ardhakathanaka / Half a Tale: A Study of the Interrelationship between Autobiography and History*. Jaipur: Rajasthan Prakrit Bharati Sansthan.

Lescallier, Daniel (Baron). 1817. *Le trône enchanté*, 2 vols. in one tome. New York: J. Desnoues.

Leuba, James H. 1919. "The Yoga-System of Mental Concentration and Religious Mysticism." *Journal of Philosophy and Scientific Methods* 18, no. 1: 197–206.

Lévi, Sylvain. 1966. *La doctrine du sacrifice dans les Brāhmaṇas*. Paris: Presses Universitaires de France. (Orig. pub. 1898. Paris: E. Leroux.)

Limaye, V. P., and R. D. Vadekar, eds. 1958. *Eighteen Principal Upaniṣads*. Upaniṣadic text with parallels from extant Vedic literature, exegetical, and grammatical notes. Poona: Vaidika Samsodhana Mandala.

Lindquist, Sigurd. 1935. *Siddhi und Abhiññā. Eine Studie über die klassischen Wunder des Yoga*. Uppsala: A. B. Lundequistska Boghandeln.

Liṅga Purāṇa. See Shastri 1980.

Lingat, Robert. 1967. *Les sources du droit dans le système traditionnel de l'Inde*. Paris and The Hague: Mouton.

Lopez, Jr., Donald S., ed. 1995. *Religions of India in Practice*. Princeton, NJ: Princeton University Press.

Lorenzen, David. 1972. *The Kāpālikas and Kālāmukhas: Two Lost Śaivite Sects*. New Delhi: Thomson Press.

———. 1978. "Warrior Ascetics in Indian History." *Journal of the American Oriental Society* 98: 61–75.

———. 1989. "New Light on the Kāpālikas." In *Criminal Gods and Demon Devotees: Essays on the Guardians of Popular Hinduism*. Edited by Alf Hiltebeitel, 231–38. Albany: SUNY Press.

———, ed. 1995. *Bhakti Religion in North India: Community Identity & Political Action*. Albany, NY: SUNY Press.

Mackay, John Henry. 1937–38. *Further Excavations at Mohenjo-Daro*, 2 vols. New Delhi: Archaeological Survey of India.

Madan, T. N., ed. 1982. *Way of Life: Essays in Honour of Louis Dumont*. New Delhi: Vikas.

Mahābhārata. See Sukthankar 1933–60; Fitzgerald 2004.

Maitrāyaṇī Saṃhitā. See Von Schroeder 1881–86.

Maitri Upaniṣad. See Limaye and Vadekar 1958; Van Buitenen 1962; Roebuck 2003.

Malamoud, Charles. 1989. *Cuire le monde: Rite et pensée dans l'Inde ancienne*. Paris: Editions de la Découverte.

———. 2002. *Le jumeau solaire*. Paris: Éditions du Seuil.

Malinar, Angelika. 2007. *The Bhagavadgītā: Doctrines and Contexts*. Cambridge: Cambridge University Press.

———. 2008. "Something Like Liberation: On *prakṛtilaya* in the *Yogasūtra*." Unpublished paper presented at "Erlöst Leben oder sterben, um befreit zu werden? Tagung an der Abteilung für Indologie der Universität Zurich anlässlich der Emeritierung von Professor Dr. Peter Schreiner" Conference, Zurich, Switzerland, May 2.

Mālinīvijayottaratantra. See Shastri 1922; Gnoli 1999; Vasudeva 2000.

Mallik, Kalyani, ed. 1954. *Siddha Siddhānta Paddhati & Other Works of the Nath Yogis*. Poona: Oriental Book House.

Mallinātha Caritra. See Bloomfield 1924.

Mallinson, Sir James. 2007. *The Khecarīvidyā of Ādinātha*. A critical and annotated translation of an early text of haṭhayoga. London: Routledge.

Mallison, Françoise, ed. 2001. *Constructions hagiographiques dans le monde indien: Entre mythe et histoire*. Paris: Honoré Champion.

Mallmann, Marie-Therèse de. 1964. "Divinités hindoues." *Ars Asiatiques* 10, no. 1: 67–86.

Mandalika, Narayana Visvanatha, ed. 1893–94. *Padmapurāṇam*, 4 vols. Bombay: Anandasrama-mundranalaya.

Manu Smṛti. See Nene 1970.

Marriott, McKim. 1976. "Hindu Transactions: Diversity without Dualism. In *Transaction and Meaning: Directions in the Anthropology of Exchange and Symbolic Behavior*. Edited by Bruce Kapferer, 109–42. Philadelphia: Institute for the Study of Human Issues.

Marshall, Sir John. 1931. *Mohenjo-daro and the Indus Civilization: Being an Official Account of Archaeological Excavations at Mohenjo-daro Carried out by the Government of India between the Years 1922 and 1927*, 2 vols. London: Arthur Probsthain.

Matilal, Bimal Krishna. 1977. *Nyāya-Vaiśeṣika: A History of Indian Literature*, vol. 6, fasc. 2. Wiesbaden: Otto Harrassowitz.

———. 1986. *Perception: An Essay on Classical Indian Theories of Knowledge*. Oxford: Clarendon Press.

Matringe, Denis. 1988. *Hīr Vāriṣ Śāh, poème panjabi du XVIIIe siècle: Introduction, translittération, traduction et commentaire: Tome I, strophes 1 à 110*. Pondicherry: Institut Français d'Indologie.

Matsya Purāṇa. See Pushpendra 1984.

Max Müller, Friedrich, ed. 1966. *Rig-Veda-Saṃhitā: The Sacred Hymn of the Brāhmans, Together with the Commentary of Sāyaṇācārya*, 4 vols. Benares: Chowkhamba Sanskrit Series Office. (Orig. pub. 1890–92. London: H. Frowde.)

Mayaram, Shail. 1999. "Spirit Possession: Reframing Discourses of the Self and Other." In *La Possession en Asie du Sud: Parole, Corps, Territoire (Puruṣārtha 21)*. Edited by Jackie Assayag and Gilles Tarabout, 101–31. Paris: Editions EHESS.

McGregor, Ronald Stuart. 1984. *Hindi Literature from its Beginnings to the Nineteenth Century*. Wiesbaden: Otto Harrassowitz.

Mehta, J. M, et al., eds. 1960–75. *The Vālmīki-Rāmāyaṇa: critically edited for the first time*. Baroda: Oriental Institute.

Mehta, Markand Nandshankar, and Manu Nandshankar Mehta. 1985. *The Hind Rajasthan or Annals of the Native States of India*, 2 vols. New Delhi: Usha Publications. (Orig. pub. 1896. Baroda: Ahmedabad Times Press.)

Meister, Michael W., ed. 1984. *Discourses on Śiva: Proceedings of a Symposium on the Nature of Religious Imagery*. Philadelphia: University of Pennsylvania Press.

———. 1986. "Regional Variations in Mātṛkā Conventions." *Artibus Asiae* 47, no. 3–4: 233–46.

Michaël, Tara, trans. 2007. *La centurie de Gorakṣa suivi du Guide des Principes des Siddha*. Paris: Éditions Almora.

Michaels, Axel, Cornelia Vogelsanger, and Annette Wilke, eds. 1995. *Wild Goddesses in India and Nepal: Proceedings of an International Symposium, Berne and Zurich, November 1994*. Bern: Peter Lang.

Michon, Daniel Merton. 2007. "Material Matters: Archaeology, Numismatics, and Religion in Early Historic Punjab." Ph.D. Dissertation, University of California, Santa Barbara.

Miller, Barbara Stoler, trans. 1996. *Yoga: Discipline of Freedom. The Yoga Sutra Attributed to Patanjali*. Berkeley: University of California Press.

Modak, B. R. 1993. *The Ancillary Literature of the Atharva-Veda: A Study with Special Reference to the Pariśiṣṭas*. New Delhi: Rashtriya Veda Vidya Pratishthan.

Monier-Williams, Sir Monier. 1984. *A Sanskrit-English Dictionary Etymologically and Philologically Arranged with Special Reference to Cognate Indo-European Languages*. Delhi: Motilal Banarsidass. (Orig. Pub. 1899. London: Oxford University Press.)

Mṛgendrāgama. See Sastri 1928; Hulin 1980.

Mujtiba, Hasan, and Nafisa Shah. 1992. "Taming of the Serpent." *Newsline* (Pakistan), August: 80–86.

Mukherji, Tarapada. 1970. *Gopīcandra Nāṭaka*. Calcutta: University of Calcutta Press.

Mukhopadhyaya, Sujitkumar. 1963. *The Aśokāvadāna*. New Delhi: Sahitya Akademi.

Muller-Ortega, Paul Eduardo. 1989. *The Triadic Heart of Śiva*. Albany, NY: State University of New York Press.

———. 2000. "On the Seal of Śambhu: A Poem by Abhinavagupta." In *Tantra in Practice*. Edited by David Gordon White, 573–86. Princeton: Princeton University Press.

Mullin, Glenn H., ed. and trans. 1996. *Tsongkhapa's Six Yogas of Naropa by Tsongkhapa Lobzang Drakpa*. Ithaca, NY: Snow Lion Publications.

———, ed. and trans. 2006. *The Practice of the Six Yogas of Naropa*. Ithaca, NY, and Boulder, CO: Snow Lion.

Muṇḍaka Upaniṣad. See See Limaye and Vadekar 1958; Olivelle 1996; Roebuck 2003.

Municandrasuri, Vijaya, ed. 1997. *Śrī Hemavijayagaṇiracitaḥ Kathāratnākara [258 kathātmaka]*. Banasakantha: Omkarasahitya Nidhi.

Mus, Paul. 1968, "Où finit Puruṣa?" In *Mélanges d'Indianisme à la mémoire de Louis Renou*. Edited by Charles Malamoud, 539–63. Paris: De Boccard.

Nabokov, Isabella. 2000. *Religion Against the Self: An Ethnography of Tamil Rituals*. New York: Oxford University Press.

Nanamoli (Bhikkhu), trans. 1991. *The Path of Purification (Visuddhimagga) by Bhadantācariya Buddhaghosa*, 5th ed. Kandy: Buddhist Publication Society. (Orig. pub. 1956.)

Narang, Gopi Cand. 1962. *Hindustānī qissoṃ se makhuz Urdū masnaviyāṃ*. Delhi: Maktaba Jamia.

Naro Choe Druk of Lama Jey Tsongkhapa. 1996. See Mullin 1996.

Nāṭya Śāstra of Bharata. See Ghosh 1951–61; Sharma and Upadhyaya 1980.

Neelsen, John P., ed. 1991. *Gender, Caste, and Power in South Asia: Social Status and Mobility in A Transitional Society*. Delhi: Manohar.

Nei-yeh. See Roth 1999.

Nene, Gopala Sastri, ed. 1970. *Manu Smṛti*. With the commentary of Kullūka Bhaṭṭa. Kashi Sanskrit Series, no. 114. Benares: Chowkhamba Sanskrit Series Office.

Neogi, Dwijendra Nath. 1912. *Tales, Sacred, and Secular*. Calcutta: Mukhopadhyay & Sons.

Netra Tantra. See Shastri 1926–39; Dwivedi 1985.

Nyāya Sūtra. See Ghosh 2003.

Nyāyabhūṣaṇam of Bhāsarvajña. See Yogindrananda 1968.

Nyāyakandalī of Śrīdharācārya. See Jha 1982; Jetly and Parikh 1991; Jha 1997.

Nyāyamañjarī of Jayantabhaṭṭa. See Varadacharya 1969; Bhattacharyya 1978.

Nyāyasāra of Bhāsarvajña. See Vidyabhusana 1910; Yogindrananda 1968.

Oberhammer, Gerhard. 1994. *La délivrance, dès cette vie (jīvanmukti)*. Paris: De Boccard.

Oberlies, Thomas. 1998. *Die Religion des Ṛgveda*, vol. 1. Vienna: Institut für Indologie der Universität Wien.

Oberoi, Harjot. 1994. *The Construction of Religious Boundaries: Culture, Identity, and Diversity in the Sikh Tradition*. Chicago: University of Chicago Press.

Oertel, Hanns. 1894. "The *Jaiminīya* or *Talavakāra Upaniṣad Brāhmaṇa*: Text, Translation, and Notes." *Journal of the American Oriental Society* 16, no. 1: 79–260.

———. 1926. *The Syntax of Cases in the Narrative and Descriptive Prose of the Brāhmaṇas: 1. The Disjunct Use of Cases*. Heidelberg: Carl Winter's Universitätsbuchhandlung.

O'Flaherty, Wendy Doniger. 1981. *Śiva, the Erotic Ascetic*. New York: Oxford University Press.

———. 1984. *Dreams, Illusion, and Other Realities*. Chicago: University of Chicago Press.

Oguibénine, Boris. 1984. "Sur le terme *yóga*, le verbe *yuj-* et quelques-uns de leurs dérivés dans les hymnes védiques." *Indo-Iranian Journal* 27: 85–101.

Olivelle, Patrick. 1987. "King and Ascetic: State Control of Asceticism in the *Arthaśāstra*." *Festschrift Ludo Rocher*. *Adyar Library Bulletin* 51: 39–59.

———, trans. 1996. *Upaniṣads*. Oxford and New York: Oxford University Press.

———, trans. 1999. *Dharmasūtras: The Law Codes of Ancient India*. Oxford and New York: Oxford University Press.

Oman, John Campbell. 1908. *Cults, Customs, & Superstitions of India*. (London: T. Fisher Unwin.

O'Neill, Michael. 2007. "The Yoga Portfolio: Spiritual Stretching." In Outtakes. *Vanity Fair*, May 2. http://www.vanityfair.com/culture/features/2007/06/yoga_slideshow200706.

Otto, Rudolf. 1980. *The Idea of the Holy: An Inquiry into the Non-Rational Factor in the Idea of the Divine and Its Relation to the Rational*, 2nd ed. Translated from the German by John W. Harvey. London: Oxford University Press.

Oxford English Dictionary. Online subscription, http://dictionary.oed.com. Oxford: Oxford University Press.

Padārthadharmasaṅgraha of Praśastapāda. See Jetly 1971; Jha 1982; Jha 1997.

Padma Purāṇa. See Mandalika 1893–94.

Padmanabhan, K., ed. and trans. 1985–86. *Śrīmad Śaṅkara Digvijayam*, 2 vols. Madras: n.p.

Padmāvat of Malik Muhammad Jāyasī. See Grierson and Dvivedi 1896; Shirref 1944.

Pañcārthabhāṣya of Kauṇḍinya. See Sastri 1940.

Pañcatantra. See Jha 1991.

Pandeya, Janardana, ed. 1973. *Gorakṣasiddhāntasaṃgraha*. Benares: Sampurnanand Sanskrit Visvavidyalaya.

———. 1976. *Gorakṣa Saṃhitā (Part One)*. Sarasvatibhavana Granthamala, vol. 110. Benares: Sampurnananda Sanskrit Visvavidyalaya.

Pansikar, Wasudeva Laxmana Sastri, ed. 1918. *The Yogavâsiṣṭha of Vâlmîki*, 2 vols., 2nd ed. With the commentary Vâsiṣṭhamahārāmāyaṇatâtparyaprakâsha. Bombay: Nirnay-Sagar Press.

Parākhya Tantra. See Goodall 2004.

Parihar, G. R. 1968. *Marwar and the Marathas*. Jodhpur: Hindi Sahitya Mandir.

Pārśvanātha Caritra. See Bloomfield 1917.

Pāśupata Sūtra. See Sastri, R. Ananthakrishna 1940.

Peabody, Norbert. 2003. *Hindu Kingship and Polity in Precolonial India*. Cambridge Studies in Indian History & Society, 9. Cambridge: Cambridge University Press.

Penzer, N. M., ed. 1924–28. *The Ocean of Story being C.H. Tawney's translation of Somadeva's Kathā Sarit Sāgara (or Ocean of Streams of Story)*, 10 vols. London: Chas. J. Sawyer, Ltd.

———, ed. 1928. *The itinerary of Ludovico di Varthema of Bologna from 1502 to 1508, as translated from the original Italian edition of 1510, by John Winter Jones, F. S. A., in 1863 for the Hakluyt society; with a Discourse on Varthema and his travels in southern Asia, by Sir Richard Carnac Temple*. London: Argonaut, 1928.

Pinch, William. 1996. *Peasants and Monks in British India*. Berkeley: University of California Press.

———. 2003. "*Bhakti* and the British Empire." *Past & Present* 17:9 (May): 159–96.

———. 2006. *Warrior Ascetics and Indian Empires*. Cambridge Studies in Indian History & Society, 12. Cambridge: Cambridge University Press.

Pingree, David. 1981. *Jyotiḥśāstra: Astral and Mathematical Literature: A History of Indian Literature*, vol. 6, fasc. 4. Wiesbaden: Harrassowitz.

Plato. *Phædrus*. See Fowler 1990.

Poddar, Hanuman Prasadji. 1938. *Śrī Rām Carit Mānas*. Gorakhpur: Gita Press.

Potter, Karl, ed. 1977. *Encyclopedia of Indian Philosophies: Indian Metaphysics and Epistemology: The Tradition of Nyāya-Vaiśeṣika up to Gaṅgeśa*. Princeton NJ: Princeton University Press.

Prabandhacintāmaṇi of Merutuṅga, See Tawney 1982.

Praśna Upaniṣad. See Limaye and Vadekar 1958; Olivelle 1996; Roebuck 2003.

Primiano, Leonard. 1995. "Vernacular Religion and the Search for Method in Religious Folklife." *Western Folklore* 54, no. 1: 37–56.

Pritchett, Frances. 1985. *Marvelous Encounters: Folk Romance in Urdu and Hindi*. Riverdale, MD: Riverdale Company.

Proferes, Theodore N. 2007. *Vedic Ideals of Sovereignty and the Poetics of Power*. New Haven: American Oriental Society.

Pṛthvirāj Raso. See Hoernle 1881; Singh 1957.

Przyluski, Jean. 1933. "Les trois états psychiques et les trois mondes." *Bulletin de l'École Française d'Extrême-Orient* 32: 148–54.

Puhvel, Jaan. 1987. *Comparative Mythology*. Baltimore: Johns Hopkins University Press.

Purchas, Samuel. 1625. *Purchas His Pilgrims In Five Bookes*, vol. 2. London: Fetherston.

Pushpendra (Dr.), ed. 1984. *The Matsya Mahāpurāṇa*. New Delhi: Meharchand Lachhmandas.

Quarnström, Olle, ed. and trans. 2002. *The Yogaśāstra of Hemacandra: A Twelfth Century Handbook on Śvetāmbara Jainism*. Cambridge, MA, and London: Harvard University Press.

———. 2003. "Losing One's Mind and Becoming Enlightened." In *Yoga: The Indian Tradition*. Edited by Ian Whicher and David Carpenter, 130–42. London: RoutledgeCurzon.

Rām Carit Mānas of Tulsīdās. See Poddar 1938.

Rāmāyaṇa of Vālmīki. See Mehta, et al. 1960–75.

Rasārṇavam. See Ray and Kaviratna 1910; White 1995.

Rastelli, Marion. 2000. "The Religious Practice of the *Sādhaka* According to the *Jayākhyasaṃhitā*." *Indo-Iranian Journal* 43: 319–95.

———. 2003. "Maṇḍalas and Yantras in the Pāñcarātra Tradition." In *Maṇḍalas and Yantras in the Hindu Tradition*. Edited by Gudrun Bühnemann, 119–51. Leiden: Brill.

Rauravāgama. See Bhatt 1988.

Ray, Prafulla Chandra, and Hariscandra Kaviratna, eds. 1910. *Rasārṇava*. Bibliotheca Indica, 174. Calcutta: Baptist Mission Press.

Reddy, Medapati Venkata. 1982. *Hatharatnavali of Srinivasabhatta Mahayogindra*. Arthamaru, Vijaywada.

Renou, Louis. 1953. "Quelques termes du Ṛgveda, d. *yoga*." *Journal Asiatique* 241: 177–80.

———. 1963. *Contes du Vampire*. Paris: Gallimard.

Renou, Louis, and Jean Filliozat. 1949–53. *L'inde classique*, 2 vols. Paris: Imprimerie Nationale.

Ṛg Veda. See Max Müller 1966.

Riccardi, Jr., Theodore. 1971. *A Nepali Version of the Vetālapañcaviṃśati:* Nepali text and English translation with an introduction, grammar, and notes. American Oriental Series, vol. 54. New Haven: American Oriental Society.

Richards, John F. 1995.*The Mughal Empire*. New Cambridge History of India 1.5. Cambridge: Cambridge University Press.

Rockhill, W. W. 1915. "Notes on the Relations and Trade of China with the Eastern Archipelago and the Coasts of the Indian Ocean during the Fourteenth Century, Part II." *T'oung pao* 16: 61–159, 236–71, 374–92, 435–67, 604–26.

Roebuck, Valerie. 2003. *The Upaniṣads*. London: Penguin Books.

Rose, H. A. 1990. *A Glossary of the Tribes and Castes of the Punjab and North-West Frontier Province*, 3 vols. Delhi: Asian Educational Services. (Orig. pub. 1914. Lahore: Superintendant, Government Printing, Punjab.)

Rosenfield, John M. 1967. *The Dynastic Art of the Kushans*. Berkeley: University of California Press.

Roşu, Arion. 1978. *Les conceptions psychologuqes dans les texts médicaux indiens*. Paris: De Boccard.

Roth, Harold. 1999. *Original Tao. Inward Training (nei-yeh) and the Foundations of Taoist Mysticism*. New York: Columbia University Press.

Roy, Asim. 1983. *The Islamic Syncretistic Traditions of Bengal*. Princeton, NJ: Princeton University Press.
Ruegg, D. Seyfort. 1967. "On a Yoga Manuscript in Sanskrit from Qïzïl." *Journal of the American Oriental Society* 87 no. 2 (April-June): 157–65.
Ruff, Jeffrey. 2002. "History, Text, and Context of the Yoga Upanishads." Ph.D. Dissertation, University of California, Santa Barbara.
Rukmani, T. S. 1987, ed. and trans. *Yogavarttika of Vijñānabhikṣu*. Text with English translation and critical notes along with the text and English translation of the Pātañjala *Yoga Sūtras* and *Vyāsabhāṣya*, vol. 3. New Delhi: Munshiram Manoharlal.
Sachau, Edward, ed. 1910/1983. *Alberuni's India*, 2 vols. London: Kegan Paul, Trench, and Trubner. Reprint Delhi: Munshiram Manoharlal.
Samasrami, Satyavrata, ed. 1895–98. *The Aitareya Bráhmana of the Ṛg-Veda*. With the commentary of Sáyanāchárya. Calcutta: Satya Press.
Sāṃkhya Kārikas of Īśvara Kṛṣṇa. See Virupaksananda 1995.
Sanderson, Alexis. 2004a. "Religion and the State: Śaiva Officiants in the Territory of the Brahmanical Royal Chaplain." *Indo-Iranian Journal* 47: 229–300.
———. 2004b. "Śaivism, Society and the State." Unpublished paper.
———. 2006. "The Lākulas: New Evidence of a System Intermediate Between Pāñcārthika Pāśupatism and Āgamic Śaivism." *Indian Philosophical Annual* 24 (2003–05): 143–217.
———. 2007. "The Śaiva Exegesis of Kashmir." In *Tantric Studies in Memory of Hélène Brunner*. Edited by Dominic Goodall and André Padoux, 231–442. Pondicherry: Institut Français de Pondichéry.
Śaṅkaradigvijaya of Mādhava-Vidyāraṇya. See Padmanabhan 1985–86.
Śaṅkaramandarasaurabha of Nīlakaṇṭha. See Ungemach 1992.
Śaṅkaravijaya of Ānandagiri. See Tarkapancanana 1868.
Sankarnath Yogisvar, Sri. 1969. *Śrī Mastnāth Carit (Śrī Mastnāth adbhut līlā prakāś)*. Delhi: Dehati Pustak Bhandar.
Śāṅkhāyana Śrauta Sūtra. See Hillebrandt 1981.
Sarbacker, Stuart Ray. 2005. *Samādhi: The Numinous and Cessative in Indo-Tibetan Yoga*. Albany, NY: State University of New York Press.
Sarvadurgatipariśodhana Tantra. See Skorupski 1984.
Sastri, A. Mahadeva. 1968. *Yoga Upanishads*. With the commentary of Sri Upanisad-Brahmayogin. Madras: Adyar Library and Research Centre.
Sastri. Gaurinath, ed. 1983–84. *Vyomavatī of Vyomaśivācārya*, 2 vols. Benares: Sampurnanand Sanskrit University.
Sastri, Jagadish Lal, ed. 1970. *Kathāsaritsāgaraḥ kaśmīrapradeśavāsinā Śrīrāmabhaṭṭanūdbhavena mahākavi Śrī Somadevabhaṭṭena viracitaḥ*. Delhi: Motilal Banarsidass.
Sastri, Jagannath, ed. 1930. *Yājñavalkyasmṛtiḥ*. With the commentary of Mitramiśra. Benares: Caukhamba Sanskrit Series Office.

Sastri, Krsna. 1928. *Śrīmṛgendram Kāmikopāgama, Vidyāyogapādadvayamilitam.* With the commentaries of Bhaṭṭanārāyaṇakaṇṭha and Aghoraśivācārya. Devikottai: Bhaskara Press.

Sastri, Mahadev, ed. 1985. *Taittirīya Brāhmaṇam.* With the commentary of Bhāskaramiśra. Delhi: Motilal Banarsidass.

Sastri, R. Ananthakrishna, ed. 1940. *Pāśupata Sūtra with Pañcārthabhāṣya of Kauṇḍinya.* Trivandrum: Trivandrum Sanskrit Series.

Sastri, Visvabandhu, ed. 1960–64. *Atharvaveda (Śaunaka).* With the Pada-pāṭha and Sāyaṇācārya's Commentary, 4 vols. Hoshiarpur: Visveshvaranand Vedic Research Institute.

Śatapatha Brāhmaṇa. See Weber 1964.

Sax, William S. 1995. "Who's Who in the *Paṇḍav Līlā?*" In *The Gods at Play: Līlā in South Asia.* Edited by William S. Sax, 131–55. New York: Oxford University Press.

———. 2002. *Dancing the Self: Personhood and Performance in the Pāṇḍav Līlā of Garhwal.* New York: Oxford University Press.

———. 2008. *God of Justice: Ritual Healing and Social Justice in the Central Himalayas.* New York: Oxford University Press.

Scharf, Peter M. 1996. *The Denotation of Generic Terms in Ancient Indian Philosophy: Grammar, Nyāya, and Mīmāṃsā.* Transactions of the American Philosophical Society, vol. 86, part 3. Philadelphia: American Philosophical Society.

Schimmel, Annemarie. 2004. *The Empire of the Great Mughals: History, Art, and Culture.* Translated by Corinne Atwood. Edited by Burzine K. Waghmar. With a foreword by Francis Robinson. London: Reaktion Books.

Schlingloff, Dieter. 1964. *Ein buddhistisches Yogalehrbuch.* Sanskrittexte aus den Turfanfunden, VII. Berlin: Akademie Verlag.

Schmidt, Richard. 1907. *Fakire und Fakirtum im Alten und modernen Indien: Yogalehre und Yoga-praxis nach den indischen Originalquellen.* Berlin: Hermann Barsdorf.

Schreiner, Peter. 1988. "Yoga—Lebenshilfe oder Sterbetechnik?" *Umwelt & Gesundheit* (Köln) 3/4: 12–18.

———. 1999a. "Fire—its literary perception in the *Mahābhārata.*" In *The Perception of the Elements in the Hindu Traditions: Studia Religiosa Helvetica Jahrbuch,* vol. 4/5. Edited by Maya Burger and Peter Schreiner, 113–44. Bern: Peter Lang.

———. 1999b. "What Comes First (in the *Mahābhārata*): Sāṃkhya or Yoga?" *Asiatische Studien/Etudes Asiatiques* 53: 755–77.

Schwartzberg, Joseph E., ed. 1992. *A Historical Atlas of South Asia.* Chicago: University of Chicago Press, 1978. Second impression, with additional material, New York: Oxford University Press.

Sen, Surendranath. 1949. *Indian Travels of Thevenot and Careri.* New Delhi: National Archives of India.

Sénart, Émile. 1900. "Bouddhisme et Yoga." *Revue de l'Histoire des Religions* 42: 345–64.

Servan-Schreiber, Catherine. 1999a. *Chanteurs itinérants en Inde du Nord: La tradition oral bhojpuri*. Paris: L'Harmattan.

———. 1999b. "The Printing of Bhojpuri Folklore." *South Indian Folklorist* 3, no. 1 (October): 81–105.

Settar, S., and Günther Sondheimer. 1982. *Memorial Stones: A Study of their Origin, Significance and Variety*. Heidelberg: South Asia Institute, University of Heidelberg.

Shackle, Christopher. 2000. "Crossing the Boundaries in Indo-Muslim Romance." In *Beyond Turk and Hindu: Rethinking Religious Identities in Islamicate South Asia*. Edited by David Gilmartin and Bruce Lawrence, 55–73. Gainesville: University of Florida Press.

Shah, U. P. 1984. "Lakulīśa: Śaivite Saint." In *Discourses on Śiva: Proceedings of a Symposium on the Nature of Religious Imagery*. Edited by Michael W. Meister, 92–102. Philadelphia: University of Pennsylvania Press.

Shamasastry, R. 1938. *Drapsa: The Vedic Cycle of Eclipses, a Key to unlock the treasures of the Vedas*. Mysore: Sree Panchacharya Electric Press.

Sharma, Batuka Natha, and Baladeva Upadhyaya.1980. *Śrībharatamunipraṇītaṃ Nāṭyaśāstram*, 2nd ed. Kashi Sanskrit Granthamala, 60. Varanasi: Chaukhambha Sanskrit Sansthan.

Shastri, B. N. 1992, ed. and trans. *Kālikā Purāṇa*, 2 vols. Delhi: Nag Publishers. (Orig. pub. 1972. Delhi: Chowkhambha Sanskrit Series.)

Shastri, Jagadish. 1980. *Liṅgapurāṇam*. With the commentary of Gaṇeśa Nātu. Delhi: Motilal Banarsidass.

———. 1983. *Brahmāṇḍa Purāṇam*. Delhi: Motilal Banarsidass.

Shastri, Madhusudhan Kaul, ed. 1921–35. *The Svacchandatantram*. With commentary by Kshemarājā, 6 vols. Kashmir Series of Texts and Studies, nos. 31, 38, 44, 48, 51. Bombay: Tatva Vivechaka Press.

———, ed. 1922. *Mālinivijayottara Tantram*. Kashmir Series of Texts and Studies, no. 37. Bombay: Tatva Vivechaka Press.

———, ed. 1926–39. *The Netra Tantram*. With commentary by Kshemarājā, 2 vols. Kashmir Series of Texts and Studies, nos. 46 and 61. Bombay: Tatva Vivechaka Press.

Shirreff, A. G. 1944. *Padmāvatī of Malik Muhammad Jaisi*. Bibliotheca Indica, 267. Calcutta: Royal Asiatic Society of Bengal.

Shulman, David. 1993. *The Hungry God: Hindu Tales of Filicide and Devotion*. Chicago: University of Chicago Press.

Siddhasiddhāntapaddhati of Gorakhnāth. See Mallik 1954; Michaël 2007.

Siegel, Lee. 1991. *Net of Magic: Wonders and Deceptions in India*. Chicago: University of Chicago Press.

Silk, Jonathan A. 2000. "The Yogācāra Bhiksu." In *Wisdom, Compassion, and the Search for Understanding: The Buddhist Studies Legacy of Gadjin M. Nagao*. Edited by Jonathan Silk, 265–314. Honolulu: University of Hawai'i Press.

Siṃhāsana Dvātriṃśikā. See Edgerton 1926; Jørgensen 1939; Haksar 1998.

Singer, Milton. 1972. *When a Great Tradition Modernizes: An Anthropological Approach to Indian Civilization.* Chicago: University of Chicago Press.

Singh, B. P. 1968. *Maniṣī kī lokyātrā.* Benares: Vishvavidyalaya Prakashan.

Singh, Kavirav Mohan. 1957. *Pṛthvirāj Raso,* 4 vols. Udaipur: Sahitya Sansthan, Rajasthan Visva Vidyapith.

Singh, Mahadevprasad. n.d. *Bhairavānand Yogī.* Benares: Thakurprasad and Sons.

Singh, Nag Sharan, ed. 1981. *Śivamahāpurāṇam.* Delhi: Nag Publishers.

Sinha, Jadunath. 1986. *Indian Psychology,* 3 vols. Delhi: Motilal Banarsidass.

Sinha, Nandalal, ed. and trans. 1911/1974. *The Vaiśeṣika Sûtras of Kanâda.* With the commentary of Śankara Miśra and extracts from the gloss of Jayanârâyaṇa together with notes from the commentary of Chandrakânta and an introduction by the translator. Allahabad: Indian Press. Reprint New York: AMS Press.

Śiva Purāṇa. See Singh 1981.

Sjoman, Norman E. 1996. *The Yoga Tradition of the Mysore Palace.* New Delhi: Abhinav Publications.

Skorupski, Tadeusz, ed. and trans. 1983. *Sarvadurgatipariśodhana Tantra: Elimination of All Evil Destinies.* Delhi: Motilal Banarsidass.

Smith, Frederick M. 2006. *The Self Possessed: Deity and Spirit Possession in South Asian Literature and Civilization.* New York: Columbia University Press.

———. 2007. "Narrativity and Empiricism in Classical Indian Accounts of Birth and Death: The *Mahābhārata* and the *Saṃhitās* of *Caraka* and *Suśruta.*" *Asian Medicine: Tradition and Modernity* 3, no. 1 (Special Yoga Issue): 85–102.

Sondheimer, Günther-Dietz. 1989. *Pastoral Deities in Western India.* Translated by Anne Feldhaus. New York: Oxford University Press.

Sonnerat, Pierre.1788–89. *A voyage to the East-Indies and China; performed by order of Lewis XV, between the years 1774 and 1781.* Translated from the French by Francis Magnus. Calcutta: Stuart and Cooper.

Soper, Alexander C. 1949. "Aspects of Light Symbolism in Gandharan Sculpture." *Artibus Asiae* 12, no. 3: 252–83.

———. 1950. "Aspects of Light Symbolism in Gandharan Sculpture (Continuation)." *Artibus Asiae* 13, nos. 1–2: 63–85.

Śrī Gorakhnāth Caritr. 1981. See Gautam 1981.

Śrī Mastnāth Carit. See Sankarnath Yogisvar 1969.

Stanley, Henry E. J., trans. 1866. *A Description of the Coasts of East Africa and Malabar in the Beginning of the Sixteenth Century, by Duarte Barbosa, a Portuguese.* London: Hakluyt Society.

Stein, Sir Aurel. 1907/1975. *Ancient Khotan: Detailed Report of Archaeological Explorations in Chinese Turkestan.* Oxford: Clarendon Press. Reprint New York: Hacker Art Books.

Strickmann, Michel. 1996. *Mantras et mandarins: Le bouddhisme tantrique en Chine.* Paris: Gallimard.

Strong, John S. 1983. *The Legend of King Aśoka: A Study and Translation of the* Aśokāvadāna. Princeton: Princeton University Press.

———. 2001. *The Buddha: A Short Biography*. Oxford: Oneworld Publications.
———. 2002. *The Experience of Buddhism: Sources and Interpretations*, 2nd ed. Belmont, CA: Wadsworth.
Sukthankar, Visnu S., et al. 1933–60. *Mahābhārata*, 21 vols. Poona: Bhandarkar Oriental Research Institute.
Sullivan, Bruce. 2006. "The Ideology of Self-Willed Death in the Epic *Mahābhārata*." *Journal of Vaishnava Studies* 14, no. 2 (Spring): 61–80.
Suru, N. G. 1960. *Karpūra-Mañjarī by Kavirāja Rājaśekhara*. Bombay: N. G. Suru.
Suśruta Saṃhitā. See Ghanekar 1980.
Svacchanda Tantra. See Shastri 1921–35.
Śvetāśvatara Upaniṣad. See Limaye and Vadekar 1958; Olivelle 1996; Roebuck 2003.
Taittirīya Brāhmaṇa. See Sastri 1985.
Taittirīya Upaniṣad. See Limaye and Vadekar 1958; Olivelle 1996; Roebuck 2003.
Talib, Gurbachan Singh, and Bhai Jodh Singh, trans. 1987. *Sri Guru Granth Sahib*, vol. 3. Patiala: Publication Bureau, Punjab University.
Tantrāloka of Abhinavagupta. See Dwivedi and Rastogi 1987; Gnoli 1999.
Tantrasadbhāva. http://muktalib5.org/DL_CATALOG/DL_CATALOG_USER_INTERFACE/dl_user_interface_create_utf8_text.php?hk_file_url=..%2FTEXTS%2FETEXTS%2Ftantrasadbhava_hk.txt.
Tarkapancanana, Jayanarayana, ed. 1868. *Śaṅkaravijayaḥ Ānandagiriviracitaḥ*. Bibliotheca Indica nos. 46, 137, and 138. Calcutta: Baptist Mission Press.
Tarkaratna, Pancanana, ed. 1983. *Muniśrīmadvyāsapraṇītaṃ Vāyupurāṇam*. Anandasrama Sanskrit Series, no. 49. Poona: Anandasrama.
Tawney, C. H., trans. 1982. *The Prabandhacintamani, or, Wishing-stone of Narratives Composed by Merutunga*. Delhi: Indian Book Gallery. (Orig. pub. 1901. Calcutta: Asiatic Society of Bengal.)
Temple, Richard Carnac. 1998. *The Legends of the Punjab*, 3 vols. New Delhi: Nirmal Publishers. (Orig. pub. 1884–1986. London: Turner and Company.)
Thackston, W. M. 1996. *The* Baburnama: *Memoirs of Babur, Prince and Emperor*. Washington, D.C.: Freer Gallery of Art.
Timilsina, Sthaneshwar. 2008. "Linguistics and Cosmic Powers: The Concept of Śakti in the Philosophies of Bhartṛhari and Abhinavagupta." Unpublished paper.
Tod, Col. James. 1957–72. *Annals and Antiquities of Rajast'han*, 2 vols. With a preface by Douglas Sladen. London: Routledge & Kegan Paul. (Orig. pub. 1829–32. London: H. Milford.)
Toffin, Gérard. 1993. *Le palais et le temple: La fonction royale dans la vallée du Népal*. Paris: CNRS Editions.
———. 1996. "A Wild Goddess Cult in Nepal: The Navadurgā of Theco Village (Kathmandu Valley)." In *Wild Goddesses in India and Nepal*. Edited by Axel Michaels, Cornelia Vogelsanger, and Annette Wilke, 216–51. Bern: Peter Lang.

Tookaram, Rajaram. 1901. *A Compendium of the Raja Yoga Philosophy, Comprising the Principal Treatises of Shrimat Chankaracharya and Other Renowned Authors.* Bombay: Tatva-Vivecaka Press.

Trikamji Acharya, Jadavji. 1992. *Caraka Saṃhitā by Agniveśa.* Revised by Charaka and Dṛdhabala, with the commentary of Cakrapāṇidatta. Chaukhamba Ayurvijnan Granthamala, 34. Benares: Chaukhamba Surabharati Prakashan. (Orig. pub. 1941. Bombay: Venkatesvar Steam Press.)

Trungpa, Chögyam, et al., trans. 1982. *Sgra-bsgyur mar-pa lo-tsā'i rnam-thar mthong-ba don-yod* [The Life of Marpa the Translator. Seeing Accomplishes All by Gtsan-smyon Heruka]. Boulder: Prajñā Press.

Tucci, Giuseppe, ed. 1971. *Minor Buddhist Texts,* part 3. Rome: Istituto Italiano per Il Medio ed Estremo Oriente.

Uberoi, Mohan Singh. 1937. *Gorakhnath and Mediaeval Hindu Mysticism.* With forewords by Sir Francis Younghusband and Dr. Betty Heimann. Lahore: Mercantile Press.

Uhle, Heinrich. 1869. "Eine Sanskritische Parallele zu einer Erzählung in Galanos' Uebersetzung des Pañcatantra." *Zeitschrift der Deutschen morgenländischen Gesellschaft* 23: 443–52.

———, ed. 1881. *Die Vetâlapañcaviṅçatikâ in den Recensionen des Çivadâsa und eines Ungenannten.* Leipzig: Deutschen Morgenländischen Gesellschaft. (Reprint 1966. Nedeln, Lichtenstein: Kraus Reprint.)

Unbescheid, Günter. 1980. *Kānphaṭā: Untersuchungen zu Kult, Mythologie und Geschichte śivaitischer Tantriker in Nepal.* Wiesbaden: Franz Steiner Verlag.

Ungemach, Anton, ed. and trans. 1992. *Nilakantha, Sankara-mandara-saurabha 4.20–5.2.7.* Stuttgart: Franz Steiner.

Uttarabhāvanākrama of Kamalaśīla. See Tucci 1971.

Vaidya, Parasuram Lakshman, ed. 1969–71. *The Harivaṃśa Being the Khila or Supplement to the Mahābhārata,* 2 vols. Poona: Bhandarkar Oriental Research Institute.

Vaiśeṣika Sūtra of Kaṇāda. See Gough 1975; Sinha 1911/1974.

Van Buitenen, J. A. B. 1962. *The Maitrāyaṇīya Upaniṣad: A Critical Essay.* The Hague: Mouton & Co.

———. 1981. *The Bhagavadgītā in the Mahābhārata: A Bilingual Edition.* Chicago: University of Chicago Press.

Van den Hoek, et al., eds. 1992. *Ritual, State, and History in South Asia.* Leiden: Brill.

Van der Plas, Dirk, ed. 1987. *Effigies Dei: Essays on the History of Religions.* Leiden: Brill.

Van der Veer, Peter. 2001. *Imperial Encounters: Religion and Modernity in India and Britain.* Princeton: Princeton University Press.

Van Woerkens, Martine. 2002. *The Strangled Traveler: Colonial Imaginings and the Thugs of India.* Translated from the French by Catherine Tihanyi. Chicago: University of Chicago Press.

Varadacharya., S, ed. 1969. *Nyāyamañjarī of Jayantabhaṭṭa with ṭippaṇi—Nyāyasaurabha by the editor*, 2 vols. K. Oriental Research Institute Series, nos. 116 and 139. Mysore: Oriental Research Institute.

Varenne, Jean. 1976. *Yoga and the Hindu Tradition*. Translated from the French by Derek Coltman. Chicago: University of Chicago Press.

Vasudeva, Somadeva. 2000. "The Yoga of the Mālinīvijayottaratantra." Ph.D. Dissertation, Wolfson College, Oxford University.

Vaudeville, Charlotte. 1962. "La conception de l'amour divin chez Muhammad Jāyasī: *virah* et *'ishq*." *Journal Asiatique* 250, no. 3: 351–67.

Vāyu Purāṇa. See Tarkaratna 1983.

Verpoorten, Jean-Marie. 2005. "La verbalité et la perception selon la Mīmāṃsā et le Nyāya." In *Catégories de langue et categories de pensée en Inde et en Occident*. Edited by François Chenet, 91–124. Paris: L'Harmattan.

Vetālapañcaviṃśati. See Uhle 1881; Penzer 1924–28; Emeneau 1934; Sastri 1970; Riccardi 1971.

Vidal, Denis, Gilles Tarabout, and Éric Meyer, eds. 1994. *Violences et Non-violences en Inde* (*Puruṣārtha* 16) Paris: Éditions de l'École des Hautes Études en Sciences Sociales.

Vidyabhusana, Satis Chandra. 1910. *Nyāyasāraḥ: A Rare Brāhmaṇic Work on Medieval Logic by Ācārya Bhāsarvajña*. With the commentary of Jayasimha Suri. Calcutta: Asiatic Society.

Virupaksananda, Swami. 1995. *Sāṃkhya Kārika of Īśvara Kṛṣṇa*. With the commentary of Vācaspatmiśra. Madras: Sri Ramakrishna Math.

Viṣṇu Purāṇa. See Wilson 1980.

Visuddhimagga of Buddhaghoṣa. See Nanamoli (Bhikku) 1991.

Vivekananda, Swami. 1946. *The Complete Works of Swami Vivekananda*, vol. 1. Almora: Advaita Ashram. (Orig. pub. 1896. Calcutta: Advaita Ashram.)

Von Schroeder, Leopold, ed. 1881–86. *Maitrāyaṇī Saṃhitā*. Leipzig: F. A. Brockhaus.

Vyomavatī of Vyomaśiva. See Sastri 1983–84.

Wallace, Vesna. 2001. *The Inner Kālacakra: A Buddhist Tantric View of the Individual*. New York: Oxford University Press.

Wangyal, Geshe (Lama), trans. 1982. *The Prince Who Became a Cuckoo: A Tale of Liberation by the Lama Lo-drö of Drepung*. New York: Theatre Arts Books.

Watkins, Calvert. 1985. *The American Heritage Dictionary of Indo-European Roots*, rev. ed. Boston: Houghton Mifflin Company.

Watson, William. 1983. "Iran and China." In *The Seleucid, Parthian, and Sasanian Periods*, vol. 3 (1) of *The Cambridge History of Iran*. Edited by Ehsan Yarshater, 537–58. Cambridge: Cambridge University Press.

Weber, Albrecht, ed. 1964. *The Çatapatha Brāhmaṇa in the Mādhyandina-Çākhā*, 2nd ed. With extracts from the commentaries of Sāyaṇa, Harisvāmin, and Dvivedagaṅga. London-Berlin, 1855. Benares: Chowkhamba Sanskrit Series Office.

Weinberger-Thomas, Catherine. 1999. *Ashes of Immortality: Widow-Burning in India*. Translated by Jeffrey Mehlmann and David Gordon White. Chicago: University of Chicago Press.

Werner, Karel. 1975. "Religious Practice and Yoga in the Time of the Vedas, Upaniṣads, and Early Buddhism." *Annals of the Bhandarkar Oriental Research Institute* 6: 179–94.

Whicher, Ian. 1998. *The Integrity of the Yoga Darśana: A Reconsideration of Classical Yoga*. Albany, NY: SUNY Press.

Whicher, Ian, and David Carpenter, eds. 2003. *Yoga: The Indian Tradition*. London: RoutledgeCurzon.

White, David Gordon. 1986. "Śunaḥśepa Unbound." *Revue de l'Histoire des Religions* 203, no. 3: 227–62.

———. 1991. *Myths of the Dog-Man*. Chicago: University of Chicago Press.

———. 1995. "The Ocean of Mercury: An Eleventh-Century Alchemical Text." In *Religions of India in Practice*. Edited by Donald S. Lopez, Jr., 281–87. Princeton, NJ: Princeton University Press.

———. 1996. *The Alchemical Body: Siddha Traditions in Medieval India*. Chicago: University of Chicago Press.

———, ed. 2000. *Tantra in Practice*. Princeton, NJ: Princeton University Press.

———. 2001. "The Exemplary Life of Mastnāth: The Encapsulation of Seven Hundred Years of Nāth Siddha Hagiography." In *Constructions hagiographiques dans le monde indien: Entre mythe et histoire*. Edited by Françoise Mallison, 139–61. Paris: Honoré Champion.

———. 2002. "Le monde dans le corps du Siddha: Microcosmologie dans les traditions médiévales indiennes." In *Images du corps dans le monde hindou*. Edited by Véronique Bouillier and Gilles Tarabout, 189–212. Paris: Éditions du CNRS.

———. 2003. *Kiss of the Yoginī: "Tantric Sex" in Its South Asian Contexts*. Chicago: University of Chicago Press.

———. 2004. "Early Understandings of Yoga in the Light of Three Aphorisms from the *Yoga Sūtras* of Patañjali." In *Du corps humain, au Carrefour de plusieurs saviors en Inde: Mélanges offerts à Arion Rosu par ses collègues et ses amis à l'occasion de son 80e anniversaire*. Edited by Eugen Ciurtin, 611–27. Paris: De Boccard.

———. 2006. "'Open' and 'Closed' Models of the Human Body in Indian Medical and Yogic Traditions." *Asian Medicine: Tradition and Modernity* 2, no 1: 1–13.

———. 2009. "'Never Have I Seen Such Yogis, Brother': Yogīs, Warriors, and Sorcerers in Ancient and Medieval India." In *Ancient to Modern: Religion, Power, and Community in India*. Edited by Ishita Banerjee-Dube and Saurabh Dube, 86–113. New York: Oxford University Press.

———. Forthcoming. "Yogic and Political Power Among the Nāth Siddhas of North India." In *Asceticism and Power in Asia*. Edited by Peter Flügel and Gustaaf Hartmann. London: Curzon Press.

Wilke, Annette. 1995. "Śaṅkara and the Taming of Wild Goddesses." In *Wild Goddesses in India and Nepal: Proceedings of an International Symposium, Berne and Zurich, November 1994*. Edited by Axel Michaels, Cornelia Vogelsanger, and Annette Wilke, 123–78. Bern: Peter Lang.

Wilson, Horace Hayman, ed. and trans. 1980. *The Visnu Purana: A system of Hindu Mythology and Tradition*. Enlarged and arranged by Nag Sharan Singh. London: John Murray, 1840. Delhi: Nag Publishers.

Woo, Jeson. 2003. "Dharmakīrti and His Commentators on Yogipratyakṣa." *Journal of Indian Philosophy* 31: 439–48.

———. 2005. "Kamalaśīla on *Yogipratyakṣa*." *Indo-Iranian Journal* 48: 111–21.

Wood, Ernest. 1959. *Yoga*. Harmondsworth: Penguin.

Wujastyk, Dominik. 1998. *The Roots of Āyurveda: Selections from Sanskrit Medical Writings*. London, New York, New Delhi: Penguin Books.

———. 2004. "Agni and Soma: A Universal Classification." *Studia Asiatica* 4: 347–69.

Wynne, Alexander. 2007. *The Origin of Buddhist Meditation*. London: Routledge.

Yājñvalkya Smṛti. See Sastri 1930.

Yamabe, Nobuyoshi. 2002. "Practice of Visualization and the *Visualization Sūtra:* An Examination of Mural Paintings at Toyok, Turfan." *Pacific World* 3rd series, no. 4: 123–52.

Yarshater, Ehsan, ed. 1983. *The Seleucid, Parthian, and Sasanian Periods*, vol. 3 (1) of *The Cambridge History of Iran*. Cambridge: Cambridge University Press.

Yiengpruksawan, Mimi Hall. 2004. "The Eyes of Michinaga in the Light of Pure Land Buddhism." In *The Presence of Light: Divine Radiance and Religious Experience*. Edited by Matthew T. Kapstein, 225–61.

Yogadarśana Upaniṣad. See Varenne 1976.

Yogananda, Paramahansa. 1992. *Autobiography of a Yogi*, 2nd Indian ed. Bombay: Jaico Publishing House. (Orig. pub. 1946. Los Angeles: Self-Realization Fellowship.)

Yogasārasaṃgraha of Vijñānabhikṣu. See Jha 1992.

Yogaśāstra of Hemacandra. See Quarnström 2002.

Yogasūtras of Patañjali. 2008. See Aranya 1981; Rukmani 1987; Angot 2008; Bryant 2009.

Yogatattva Upaniṣad. See Sastri 1968.

Yogavarttika of Vijñānabhikṣu. See Rukmani 1987.

Yogavasiṣṭha of Vālmīki. See Pansikar 1918.

Yogayājñavalkya. See Geenens 2000.

Yogindrananda, Swami. 1968. *Śrīmadācāryabhāsarvajñapraṇītasya nyāyasārasya svopajñaṃ vyākhyānaṃ Nyāyabhūṣaṇam*. Benares: Saddarshan Prakashan Pratisthanam.

Yule, Col. Henry, and A. C. Burnell. 1968. *Hobson-Jobson: A Glossary of Colloquial Anglo-Indian Words and Phrases, and of Kindred Terms, Etymological, Historical, Geographical, and Discursive*, 2nd ed. New edition edited by William Crooke. Delhi: Munshiram Manoharlal. (Orig. pub. 1886. London: John Murray.)

Zimmer, Heinrich. 1948/1993. *The King and the Corpse: Tales of the Soul's Conquest of Evil*. New York: Pantheon Books. Princeton, NJ: Princeton University Press.

Zimmermann, Francis. 1975. "Ṛtu-Sātmya: Le cycle des saisons et le principe d'appropriation." *Purusartha* 2: 87–105. English translation 1980. "Rtu-Satmya: The Seasonal Cycle and the Principle of Appropriateness." *Social Science and Medicine* 14B: 87–105.

Zumbro, W. M. (Rev.). 1913. "Religious Penances and Punishments Self-Inflicted by the Holy Men of India." *National Geographic* 24, no. 12 (December): 1257–1314.

Index

abhijñās, 111
Abhinavagupta, 116–17, 146
abhiṣeka, 147
acyuta ("infallible"; attribute and name of Viṣṇu), 95, 104, 107, 146, 170, 273
Adhikari, B. V., 23, 164, 259
Ādi Purāṇa. *See* Purāṇas
Ādityas, 62, 188. *See also* sun
Advaita Vedānta, 26, 125, 260
advance. *See* kram, derivates of
Āgamas and agamic Śaivism, 64, 84, 100, 106–8, 118, 120, 133, 146, 195, 276; *Mataṅgapārameśvarāgama*, 107, 115–17, 168, 276; *Mṛgendrāgama*, 153, 276; *Rauravāgama*, 115, 138, 146; *Uttarakāmikāgama*, 146. See also *atimārga*; Pāśupatas; Śaivasiddhānta
Aghoris, 237
Agni, 16, 61, 136
Agra, 120, 220
Ahmedabad, 210
Ā'īn-i Akbarī, 202, 262
aiśvara yoga, 40, 183, 190
aiśvaryam, 28–29, 31, 40, 74–75, 92, 105–6, 108, 111, 115, 149, 153, 181, 190, 195–96, 274
Aitareya Brāhmaṇa. See Brāhmaṇas
Akbar, 6, 24, 26, 200, 202, 205, 220, 237, 297
ākhāḍas, 221–25
akṣaya ("undecaying," "imperishable"; attribute and name of Viṣṇu), 74, 94, 102
Alberuni, Abū-Rajiḥān Muhammad ibn Ahmad, 202
alchemy, 146, 200, 202, 207, 218–220, 238
Alexander the Great, 210
Allahabad, 214, 226
'Allāmī, Abū al-Faḍl, 202
Amanaskayoga, 46, 205, 264
Amaraughaprabodha, 46
Amaruka, 27–28, 36, 48, 139
Ānandamaṭh, 244
Anandamayima, 165
ananta ("eternal"; attribute and name of Viṣṇu), 94, 104, 170
Anatolia, 52, 54
ancestors, 62, 72, 132, 172, 195–96
Aṅgiras, 150, 192, 194
Angot, Michel, 263
Aṅguttara Nikaya, 43
antaḥkaraṇa, 30, 154, 156, 160, 163, 288. *See also* consciousness
Antaka, 151
anusmṛti, 97–99, 147, 274
Aparokṣānubhūti, 46, 264
Āpastamba Dharma Sūtra, 33, 39
aphrodisiacs, 218–19, 237
apotheosis, 61–62, 65, 67–77, 83, 91–92, 94, 100–102, 108, 110, 114–17, 122, 132, 140–41, 143–45, 159. *See also* ascent; hitching up; kram, derivates of; *utkrānti*

Appa Sahib, 239
Arāḍa, 145
arcis, 122, 178
arhants, 181
Arjuna, 40–41, 69, 71, 109, 117, 178, 182–84, 186, 253–54
ārṣa perception, 124, 157, 184, 280. See also *yogi-pratyakṣa*
Artemis of Ephesos, 52
Arthaśāstra, 22, 26, 134, 199, 226
ārūpyadhātus, 111, 277
āsanas, 37, 56, 58, 79, 247; as thrones or seats, 48, 51, 54, 56–59, 79, 126–27; *padmāsana*, 54, 58, 79; *siṃhāsana*, 79; *vajrāsana*, 79. *See also* cross-legged posture
ascent, 83–114, 139–40, 154, 169–71, 231. *See also* kram, derivates of; *utkrānti*; visionary ascent
ascetics and asceticism, 6, 11–12, 14–16, 19–21, 23, 25, 29, 31–37, 48, 55, 59, 69, 72, 76–78, 81, 99, 102, 105–7, 110, 114, 118, 139, 144, 149, 170, 190, 197, 199, 201, 203–205, 207, 220–224, 226, 230, 233–34, 236–37, 240–41, 243–245, 249. See also *tapas*
ashes, 2, 3, 8, 12, 33, 35, 118, 161, 164, 189, 201, 203, 205, 207, 209–11, 216, 224, 232, 234–35, 237, 250
Asita Devala, 72
Aśoka, 77, 177–78
Aśokāvadāna, 147, 177
aṣṭāṅga yoga, 56. *See also* eight-limbed yoga
Aṣṭāṅgahṛdaya, 136–137
astra. *See* mantras
astrology, 126, 193
asuras. *See* titans
Aśvaghoṣa, 55, 145, 180
Atharva Veda, 130–31, 150, 192–93
Atharvaṇapariśiṣṭa, 193
Atharvans, 150
atimārga, 105–10, 114, 276–77
ātman, 32, 39, 84–85, 105, 122, 130–31, 154, 161, 168, 172
Aurangzēb, 216, 218–19, 224, 236–37
Aurobindo, Sri, 300
avadhūta-yogi, 177
Avesta, 126, 150–51
avyaktam ("unmanifest"; attribute and name of Viṣṇu), 73–74, 88, 172
avyayam ("immutable"; attribute and name of Viṣṇu), 95, 102, 107, 130, 170, 183
Awadh, 226
Āyas Dev Nāth, 26, 219, 239
ayoga, 41
Āyurveda, 32, 81, 117, 123, 125, 136–38, 154, 164, 283–84
Azes, 51, 126

Baba Ritta, 229
Bābur, 205, 237
Bachittar Nāṭak, 241
Bactrian Greeks, 126
Badauni, 220
Bairāgīs, 215, 223, 237
Baitāl Pachīsī, 21, 238. See also *Vetālapañcaviṃśati*
balam, 27, 137, 149, 153, 160
Balarāma, 68
Balkhī, Maḥmūd bin Amīr Walī, 204
Bālnāth, 230
bāṇīs, 199
bārahmāsa songs, 13, 77–78, 229
Barbosa, Duarte, 209
bardo, 86
Basu, Pannalal, 251
Bayasaab Mātā, 10
Bayly, Christopher A., 226
beard, of yogis, 26, 204–5, 208
beggars, yogis as, 13, 15, 201, 205, 208, 212, 222, 224, 231, 235, 240–41, 243, 250
Békermadjiet. *See* Vikramāditya
Benares, 139, 165, 204, 224, 226
Bengal, 28, 159, 165, 213, 226, 240, 244, 248–52
Bernard, Theos, 300
Bernier, François, 216
Beyer, Stephen, 99
Bhagavad Gītā, 38–43, 46, 55, 68, 70, 76, 79, 88–90, 92, 96–97, 99–101, 104, 109, 118, 130, 132, 134, 141, 144, 161, 167, 171, 182–86, 189–91, 205, 253, 262
Bhagavadajjukīya, 31, 33, 36, 194
Bhagavantnāth, 228
Bhāgavata Purāṇa. *See* Purāṇas
Bhāgavatas, 40–41, 71, 99, 268
Bhairava, 4, 10, 11, 23, 33–35, 192, 197, 210, 224; Mārtāṇḍa Bhairava, 192
Bhairavānand Yogī, 1–15, 18, 23, 28, 36, 233

bhakti, 14, 40–41, 102, 109–10, 114, 212, 216, 237, 241–42; *bhakti yoga*, 40
Bhandārī, Sujān Rāi, 22, 218, 237
Bharadvāja, 68–69, 141, 145–46, 194, 268, 286
Bhārgavas, 145, 150–51, 287. *See also* Bhṛgus
Bharhut, 50–52, 54
Bhartṛhari, 21–22, 157, 228, 231, 243
Bhartṛhari Yogis, 22
Bhāskara, 153
bhikṣu(ka), *bhikkhu* (Buddhist mendicant), 20, 72, 142, 144–45, 181
Bhīm Singh, 219, 239
Bhīṣma, 68, 70–71, 94, 117, 122, 140–41, 191
Bhojpuri, 13–14
bhraṣṭayogā, 70, 118, 269, 279
Bhṛgu, 145, 149–50. *See also* Bhargavas; Bhṛgus
Bhṛgus, 145, 150–51, 194. *See also* Bhargavas
Bhūriśravas, 68–69, 71, 114, 140, 144
Biardeau, Madeleine, 104, 186
Bihar, 13–14, 243
Bikaner, 235
Bikram. *See* Vikramāditya
Birch, Jason, 264
birds, 3, 8, 10, 71–72. *See also* parrots
Black Yajurveda, 76, 89–90
Blavatsky, Madame Helena Petrova, 46, 245. *See also* Theosophists
Bloomfield, Maurice, 6, 36
Bodhi Tree, 79
bodhisattvas, 54, 57–58, 127, 147–48, 167, 177, 179; Maitreya, 54, 59, 89, 91, 265. *See also* Buddha and Buddhas
Bose, Subhas Chandra, 252
Brahmā, 33, 85, 92, 102–3, 118, 172, 177, 186, 189, 195, 218. *See also* Prajāpati, sons of
Brahma Sūtra Bhāṣya, 27, 42, 88, 151
Brahma Sūtras, 153, 180
brahmaloka, 69, 83, 86, 90, 92, 110, 113, 130, 140, 158, 186. *See also* highest path
brahman, 38, 41, 55, 69, 72, 74, 84–85, 90–95, 97, 101–5, 110, 117, 120–21, 128–32, 139, 158, 167–70, 172, 186, 189–90, 244; four layers of, 93–94. See also *kośa*
Brāhmaṇas, 61–62, 88, 123–24, 139; *Aitareya*, 16, 65; *Gopatha*, 150; *Jaiminīya*, 65, 129; *Śatapatha*, 61, 65, 120, 128, 131–32, 134; *Taittirīya*, 76, 78
brahmāṇḍa. *See* cosmic egg
brahmins and brahmanic traditions, 7, 10, 12, 14–15, 23–26, 29–30, 68, 72–73, 92, 96, 99, 106, 138, 141, 144–45, 150, 161, 170, 194, 196, 201, 205, 231, 235–36
breath, 3, 27, 37, 46–48, 55, 59, 62, 64, 69, 71, 73–74, 76, 81, 86, 90, 92, 101–2, 114–20, 128–32, 142, 146, 160, 163, 203–6, 217–18, 224, 237, 245, 247
breath control, 46, 48, 55, 59, 81, 92, 101–2, 163, 203, 205, 245. See also *prāṇāyāma*
Bṛhadāraṇyaka Upaniṣad. *See* Upaniṣads
Bṛhadratha, 70, 91–92, 94, 110, 140, 143, 145, 154
Bṛhaspati, 72
Bṛhat Saṃhitā, 193
British, 14, 24, 200–201, 222–23, 226, 233, 236–41, 244, 246, 248–52
British East India Company, 24, 215, 226, 237–38, 240–41, 251
Bronkhorst, Johannes, 54, 96, 143–44, 285
Brunner, Helène, 108
Buddha and Buddhas, 33, 42–43, 45, 54–59, 79, 97–98, 112, 123, 127, 145, 147–48, 157, 166, 177–80, 212; Śākyamuni, 54; smile of the Buddha, 178. See also *bodhisattvas*; *dharmakāya*; *nirmāṇakāya*; *saṃbhogakāya*
Buddha worlds, 147
Buddhacarita, 145
Buddhaghoṣa, 97, 110
buddhi, 30, 38, 41, 64, 75, 90–91, 101, 103, 173
Buddhists and Buddhism, 10–11, 14, 20, 24, 29, 32–34, 39–40, 42–45, 47, 50, 54–55, 59, 64, 72, 76, 84, 86, 89, 97–100, 110–11, 114, 123–24, 130–31, 144–48, 157, 164, 167, 177–81, 199. *See also bodhisattvas*; Buddha and Buddhas; Mahāyāna Buddhism; Sarvāstivādins; Theravāda Buddhism; Tibetan Buddhism
Bullhe Śāh, 229
Busse, Kendall, 284

Cakrapāṇidatta, 161
cakras: subtle body centers, 118, 160 162, 171; yogi weapons, 208, 222, 225
cakravartin, 13, 178

Calcutta, 236. *See also* Fort William
Calicut, 208, 224, 297
Candragupta, 24
cannibalism, practiced by yogis, 18, 33–36, 224
cār sau bīs jogī, 81–82, 240
Caraka Saṃhitā, 136–37, 161, 175
Careri, Giovanni Francesco Gemelli, 215, 222, 232–33
casing of *brahman*. See *kośa*
categories, metaphysical, 44, 73, 88–91, 93, 100, 103–5, 124, 172–73, 200, 240, 246, 251, 253, 275–76. See also *buddhi*; ego; elements; *guṇas*; *mahān ātmā*; *puryaṣṭakam*; *tattvas*
cattle, 63–64, 72, 75–76
caves, 25, 27, 94, 98, 115, 132, 139, 147
Celts, 53–54
Central Asia, 51–52, 96–98, 147, 204
Cernunnos, 53
cessative yoga, 45, 111. *See also* numinous yoga
chains, worn by yogis, 169, 204, 209, 211, 216, 250
Chāndogya Upaniṣad. *See* Upaniṣads
channels, subtle body, 86, 90, 92, 102, 116, 118, 125, 128, 131–32, 139–40, 146, 154, 160, 162, 165, 171, 284. See also *hītas*; subtle body; *suṣumṇā*
charging. *See* kram, derivates of
charging upward. *See* kram, derivates of: *ut-kram*
charioteers, 64–65, 73, 91
chariots, 44, 59–78, 88, 91, 94, 96, 100, 109, 114–17, 120, 122, 130, 132, 135, 141, 144, 151, 268
charlatans, yogis as, 7, 49, 81, 200, 202. See also *cār sau bīs jogī*
Chatterjee, Bankim Chandra, 244
Chatterjee, Partha, 248, 250–52, 271
Chatterji, Jatindra Mohan, 150
Chaudhuri, Nirad, 233
Chaudhury, Bikram, 248
Chidambaram, 210
Chinese: account of yogis, 201–2; cave paintings, 98, 147–48; "yoga" practice, 79, 81
Chishti order, 218, 228, 230
Chittor, 230, 236
Christ, Jesus, 59, 142, 246
Christians, 59, 142, 224
Chritro Pakhyān, 7, 36, 233
citadel, subtle body, 85–86, 120, 131–32, 143, 163
citta, 41, 157, 165, 180
city of eight. See *puryaṣṭakam*
ciugi. See *jogis*
classical yoga, 37–39, 46–47, 172. See also *pātañjala yoga*
Clémentin-Ojha, Catherine, 301
Cochin, 201
coins, 12, 51, 54, 56, 59, 126, 127
Colas, Gérard, 292
confraternities. See *ākhāḍas*
consciousness, 30, 37, 45, 60, 83, 94–95, 103, 111–13, 130, 139, 142–43, 153–56, 163–64, 167, 195. See also *antaḥkaraṇa*
contemplation, 41–42, 74–75, 96–97, 102, 206, 245. *See also* meditation
corpse, 2, 9, 20, 23–24, 29–30, 32, 164, 193–94, 255
cosmic egg, 103, 108, 115, 133, 158–59, 188–89, 195
cosmology, 72, 84–115, 159, 167, 186, 195, 273–74. See also *ārūpyadhātus*; *brahmaloka*; cosmic egg; *dhruva*: Pole Star; Dhruvīśa; heaven; highest path; Īśvara: realm of; *lokāloka*; Meru, Mount; *rūpadhātus*; spheres; Tejīśa, realm of
cranial vault, 86, 114–17, 132, 135, 158, 171, 193. *See also* fontanel
cremation ground, 23, 29, 193–94
Cribb, Joe, 57
criminalization of yogis, 240–41
cross-legged posture, 49–56, 58–59, 126, 139, 164
Cūḷapanthaka, 181
cushion, royal. See *āsanas*

Daityas, 141
daivam cakṣus. *See* eye: divine
dakṣiṇā, 63
Dandan-Oilik, 57
Daṇḍapāṇi, 115
D'Anghiera, Pietro Martire, 298
Darjeeling, 248–50
darśana, 155, 160
Daśakumāracarita, 23
Dasam Granth, 7
Dasnāmis, 26, 223, 260
Dattātreya, 225, 241, 253
De la Vallée Poussin, Louis, 42–43, 45

De Michelis, Elizabeth, 243
death, 4, 8–9, 17, 20, 24, 26–31, 48, 62, 65, 67–70, 77–78, 85–86, 88, 92, 96–97, 107, 114–123, 128–29, 133, 151, 165–66, 184, 193–98, 209, 211, 219, 228–31, 249
deer, 9, 24, 26, 70
Delhi, 22, 120, 200, 203, 205, 209, 216, 228, 236
Delhi Sultanate, 200, 209, 228, 298
Della Valle, Pietro, 208, 210–11, 219, 233–34
Demaitre, Edmund, 234
Deonāth. *See* Āyas Dev Nāth
Deorāj, 228–29
dervishes, 199, 216, 221–22
Desikacar, T. K. V., 246–47, 265
Devībhāgavata Purāṇa. *See* Purāṇas
devil, yogis consort with, 211, 215, 233
devotion. See *bhakti*
*dhammayoga*s, 43–44, 111. See also *jhāyin*s
Dharamdas, 249–50
dhāraṇā, 39, 55–56, 74–75, 165, 171, 289
Dharma, 142, 172, 284
dharmakāya, 178
dharmasūtra literature, 33, 92, 262, 272. See also *Āpastamba Dharma Sūtra*
Dhaumya, 138
Dhṛtarāṣṭra, 156, 191
dhruva ("fixed"; attribute and name of Viṣṇu), 95, 104–7, 170; Pole Star, 102, 104, 106, 273, 275
Dhruvīśa, 106
dhūni, 11, 232, 236
dhyā, verbal forms in, 43–44, 96–97
dhyāna, 37, 39, 41–42, 44, 55–56, 59, 74, 96, 110, 173, 276, 289. See also *jhāna*; meditation
digambara, 20
Dīgha Nikaya, 33
Dignāga, 124
Digvijaynāth, 223
Dikpāl, Prince, 23
dīkṣā, 62, 138, 140, 146, 162. *See also* initiation
divyam cakṣus. *See* eye: divine
door of *brahman*. *See* fontanel
Draupadī, 50, 69, 120
dreams, 8, 130–31
Droṇa, 68–71, 110, 120, 122, 140, 144
drums, 10, 28, 33, 88–89, 212, 232, 240
Dumézil, Georges, 151, 287
Durgā, 15–17
dvādaśānta. *See* cranial vault

earrings, 89, 101, 229–30, 232, 241–42
Eastwick, Edward Backhouse, 238
ego, 75, 103, 112, 153, 162, 253
eight-limbed yoga, 56, 79
eidetic imaging, 97–98
elements, 94, 103, 121, 128, 154, 163, 175, 182, 290
Eliade, Mircea, 255
embodied ascent. *See* ascent; kram, derivates of
empyrean, 95, 102, 115, 133
enlightenment, 55, 86, 178–79
eon. *See* time, divisions of: *kalpa*s
epistemology. *See* valid cognitions
ether, 75, 117
European accounts of yogis, 6, 172, 200–201, 205–25, 232–34, 236–40, 244–45
evaporation, 137, 155
eye, 8, 16, 30–31, 54–55, 69, 72, 98, 101, 122–35, 140, 142–43, 146, 148, 150, 154–61, 163, 165, 168, 185, 192, 203–4, 224, 280; Buddha, 157; *dhamma*, 157; divine, 72, 130, 183; initiation through, 146; of knowledge, 161; person of the, 128; wisdom, 157; yogi, 161

fakirs, 33, 120, 199, 206, 211–13, 215, 221–23, 225, 228, 237, 240, 249–50
Falk, Harry, 133–34
fertility, yogis ensure, 136, 197, 232–33
Filliozat, Jean, 49
fire, 11, 16, 18, 20–21, 59, 61, 72, 75, 107, 116, 118, 125, 127, 129, 134–36, 146, 150, 161, 164, 172, 185, 189, 197, 224–25, 230, 235–36
Fire of Time. *See* Kālāgni
Fitch, Ralph, 209–10
Fitzgerald, James, 169, 262, 291
five fires doctrine, 136, 143
Flores, Jorge, 251
fontanel, 27, 94, 102, 118, 121, 148
food, 1–2, 15, 25, 33, 35, 55, 65, 81, 115, 128, 130, 135–36, 138, 164, 184, 195, 202, 209, 212, 245; food cycle, 135–36
Forster, E. M., 243
Fort William, 236–38, 255
420: Mohenjo-Daro clay seal number, 48–49, 54, 59–60, 79, 81; article in

420: Mohenjo-Daro clay seal number (*cont.*)
Indian Penal Code, 81–82, 249. See also *cār sau bīs jogī*
fourfold contact, 155–56. *See also* perception
France, 53–54
Fryer, John, 213, 226
Futūḥ al-salāṭīn, 228

Gaborieau, Marc, 200
Gaja-Lakṣmī, 50
gaṇas, 79
Gāṇḍavyūha Sūtra, 178
Gandhara, 51
Gāndhārī, 161
Gandhi, Mahatma, 243, 252
Gaṇeśa, 10
Ganges River, 71, 139, 214, 218
Garhwal, 14, 138, 197, 232
Geldner, Karl Friedrich, 64, 151
Gharib, Burhān al-Dīn, 218
Gheraṇḍa Saṃhitā, 245, 300
Gilchrist, John, 238
Gioghi. See *jogis*
globule practice, 163
gnomon, 133, 135, 191
gnosis, 106, 108, 109–10, 117, 124, 148, 157, 170, 196
Goa, 203
goddesses, 16–19, 35, 50, 54, 58, 110, 118, 140, 172, 228. *See also* Durgā; Gaja-Lakṣmī; Pārvatī; *satī*; Śrī
Gold, Daniel, 26
Goldman, Robert, 150
Gonda, Jan, 44
Goodall, Dominic, 278
Gopatha Brāhmaṇa. *See* Brāhmaṇas
Gopīcand, 17, 22, 228, 231
gopīs, 185–86
Gor Khattrī, 204
Gorakhnāth, 11, 14, 22, 28, 46, 175, 198–99, 223, 228, 231–32, 234, 241, 253
Gorakhnāthis. *See* Nāth Yogīs
Gorakhpur, 223
Gorakṣa Saṃhitā, 164
Gosains, 223, 226
Goudriaan, Teun, 154
Greater Magadha, 144
Greeks and Greek language, 10, 81, 126, 172, 175, 283, 296
Griffiths, Paul, 112
gross body, 103, 173
Guan Wuliangshou jing, 148
Guhyasamājatantra, 98
Gujarat, 193, 208, 210, 215, 221, 225, 231
Gumnami Baba, 252
guṇas, 103
Gundestrup Cauldron, 53
guru, 3, 11–12, 18, 22, 27–28, 94, 140, 146, 148, 153, 160, 162, 166, 180, 189, 231–32, 234, 246–47, 249
Guru Gobind Singh, 241
Guru Nānak, 205, 241
Gymnosophists, 210

Haft iqlīm, 203
hair, 26, 178, 193, 201, 203, 205, 209, 216, 218, 222, 224, 242
Hanumān, 224
Harappa, 50
Hardwar, 226
Haribhadra, 41, 179
Hariścandra, 11, 16
Harivaṃśa, 22, 104, 144, 173
Harṣacarita, 257
Hart, George W., III, 33
Hastings, Warren, 240, 252
haṭha yoga, 46–47, 55, 90, 92, 162, 166, 175, 193, 199, 205, 213, 245–46, 249–50, 264
Haṭhayogapradīpikā, 46, 90, 245, 300
heart, 11, 20, 33, 35, 84–86, 90–96, 101, 105, 107, 115, 118, 120–21, 125, 127–28, 130–33, 135–36, 139, 143, 146, 148, 154, 157–58, 162–64, 168, 171–72, 185, 224
heaven, 31, 61–63, 65, 67, 69–70, 73, 78, 94, 114, 134, 138–39, 157–58, 168, 177, 179, 184, 212, 219, 223
Heesterman, Jan, 76–78
Hemacandra, 164, 173, 175, 179
hermits, 7, 14, 25–26, 68–73, 78, 99, 102, 115, 122, 139, 141, 144–45, 148–50, 194, 199, 203, 217
hero, apotheosis of. *See* apotheosis
hero stones, 60, 65
highest path, 68–69, 71–73, 85–86, 90–92, 97, 102, 106, 110, 117, 186, 275
Himalayas, 11, 70–71, 138, 227, 232, 239, 245
Hīnayāna. *See* Theravāda Buddhism
Hindi, 4, 13, 23, 81, 223, 224
Hindustani, 6, 21–22, 231, 237–38, 251
Hīr Rāñjhā, 229

hitās, 131
hitching up, 60, 63, 65, 69–74, 76–78, 83, 94, 117. *See also* apotheosis; rig; *yogayukta*
Hopkins, E. Washburn, 74, 78
horns, carried by yogis, 205, 208–209, 212, 218, 222, 224, 229–30, 236
horses, 17, 63–64, 67, 74, 130, 145, 221, 225, 227
householders, 72, 76, 78, 134, 145, 186
Hudson, Dennis, 103
humors, 136

Ibn Baṭṭūṭa, 35, 198, 200, 202, 218–19
immortality, 17–18, 63, 86, 88, 90, 92, 129, 157, 170, 193
Inden, Ronald, 193
Indian Penal Code, 82
Indo-Iranian religion, 126–27, 151, 191
Indonesia, 211, 225
Indo-Scythians, 51, 54, 151. *See also* Azes; Maues
Indra, 17, 21, 71, 115, 139, 148–49, 179, 219, 282
Indus Valley, 48–50, 52, 54; Indus Valley seals, 50, 52, 54, 163
initiation, 47, 61–62, 106, 109, 117, 138, 140, 145–46, 148, 153, 160, 162, 165, 194, 196–97, 234–35. See also *dīkṣā*; *nirvāṇadīkṣā*
Inner Asia. *See* Central Asia
intellect. See *buddhi*
Ioghe. See *jogis*
Iranian religion, 126, 150–51, 280. See also *Avesta*; Indo-Iranian religion; Mithra; Yima
iron, implements of yogis, 203–5, 208, 211, 216, 222, 224, 230. *See also* cakras; chains
Iṣāmī, Khwaja ʿAbd al-Malik, 228, 298
Īśāna, 105
Islam, 13, 33, 199, 202, 228, 232. *See also* Muslims; Sufis
Īśvara, 105–6, 110, 130, 146, 149, 177, 181, 185, 189–90; realm of, 106–7
Īśvara Saṃhitā, 146
īśvaras, 83, 105, 151, 190, 193; *maheśvaras*, 83
Iyengar, B. K. S., 246–47

Jahāngīr, 205, 221–22, 237
Jaidebpur, 248, 251
Jaigīṣavya, 68, 72, 141, 143–44, 145
Jaiminīya (Upaniṣad) Brāhmaṇa. *See* Brāhmaṇas
Jains and Jainism, 6, 14, 29, 41–42, 44–45, 54–55, 59, 99, 114–15, 144–45, 164, 173, 179, 207, 214, 255. See also *tīrthaṃkaras*
Jaipur, 242
Jaisalmer, 219, 228
Jalandharnāth, 17, 22
Jalore, 219
Janaka, 131, 142–45, 160, 180
Jayākhya Saṃhitā, 108, 196
Jayantabhaṭṭa, 155
Jāyasī, Malik Muhammad, 14, 230–31
jhāna, 42–44, 110, 181; Four Jhānas, 55. See also *dhyāna*
jhāyins, 43, 111–12. See also *dhammayogas*
jīnas. See *tīrthaṃkaras*
jīvam. *See* lifebody
jīvanmukti, 83, 100, 197
Jodhpur, 26, 219, 238–39
jogis, 7–9, 11, 14, 18–19, 21–22, 36, 199–252, 299
Jois, K. Pattabhi, 246–47

Kabīr, 225, 241
Kadetsky, Elizabeth, 247
Kadri, 208
Kailāś, Mount, 28, 33, 139
kaivalyam, 112, 166
kaivalyapadam, 100, 112–13. See also *prakṛtilaya*
Kāla, 130, 184, 189
Kālacakra Tantra, 47, 98, 148
Kālāgni, 189
Kālāgnirudra, 189
Káli, 19
Kālikā Purāṇa. See Purāṇas
kalpa. *See* eon
Kaṇāda, 123, 155–57. See also *Vaiśeṣika Sūtra*
Kaniṣka, 59
Kānphaṭa. *See* Nāth Yogīs
Kāpālikas, 20, 34, 196, 223
Kapila, 180
Karṇa, 141
Karnataka, 60, 246
Karpūramañjarī, 12
Kashmir, 6, 20, 97, 116, 147, 155, 162–63, 182, 217–18
kasiṇa, 97

Kaṭha Upaniṣad. See Upaniṣads
Kaṭhaka Saṃhitā, 65
Kathāsaritsāgara, 20, 23, 30, 99, 199
Kathmandu, 15–16
Kaulasūtra, 146
kavi, 99, 151, 287
Kaviraj, Gopinath, 165, 180
Kāvya Uśanas, 68, 141, 148–51, 160, 190–93. *See also* Śukra
Khajuraho, 218–19
khecarī mudrā, 55, 90
Khecarī Vidyā, 60
Khotan, 57
Khulāṣat-ut-Tawārīkh, 22, 237
king of the Gioghi (Ioghe), 208, 224, 231
kings, 1–3, 6–9, 12, 16, 18, 22, 25–28, 36, 48, 59, 125, 139, 142, 144, 208, 224, 230
Kipling, Rudyard, 226
Kiraṇa Tantra, 181
Kitāb Pātañjala, 202
Kolff, Dirk, 77
kośa, 93–94, 103, 282
kram, derivates of, 60–61, 67, 71–74, 78, 115, 120–21, 135, 266; *ā-kram*, 69, 71–72, 88, 120–21, 128–29, 162–63, 170, 269; *ati-kram*, 70–72, 75, 90, 94, 120–21, 170, 269; *niṣ-kram*, 128; *pra-kram*, 61, 65; *sam-kram*, 62, 67, 70, 115, 120, 147, 289; *ut-kram*, 86, 89–92, 129. See also *utkrānti*
Krishnamacarya, 245–47
Kṛṣṇa, 38–41, 68, 70–71, 96–98, 100–101, 109, 120, 130, 132, 134, 140–41, 167, 178–79, 182–86, 189–91, 241–42, 253
Kṣāntaśīla, 20, 22, 238
kṣatriya, 15, 61, 69
kṣema, 65, 75–78, 92
Kṣemarāja, 163
kṣetrajña, 101
Kubera, 54, 149–50, 160, 191–92
Kubjikāmata, 116
Kujula Kadphises, 59, 126–27
Kumaon, 11, 14, 232
Kumar of Bhawal, 248–52
kuṇḍalinī, 81
Kuntī, 141
Kūrma Purāṇa. See Purāṇas
Kushans, 54, 56, 59, 79, 126, 151, 191; Kushano-Sassanians, 193. *See also* Kaniṣka; Kujula Kadphises; Vima Kadphises; Vima Takto
kūṭasthā, 130
Kuvalayananda, 245–46

Laila-Majnu, 13
Lakṣmaṇnāth, 243
Lākulas, 106–7, 277
Lakulīśa, 79, 193–94
lamp, self as, 125, 153, 154
land grants, 197, 200, 227
Landhaura Case, 249
laughing skeletons, 15, 18–19, 34
Laval, Pyrard de, 296–97
Leuba, James, 244
liberation, 10, 11, 13, 18, 33, 41, 71–72, 83–84, 86, 88, 92, 94, 96, 99–100, 106–8, 110, 112–13, 115, 117–18, 124, 140, 143, 145, 153, 160, 175, 195; deferred, 100, 106; immediate, 106. See also *jīvanmukti*; Masters of Yoga; *prakṛtilaya.*
lifebody, 68, 73–74, 120–22, 161–62
light and luminosity, 44, 63, 65, 67–70, 73, 84, 86, 92, 95, 98, 102, 110, 114–15, 118, 122–28, 130–35, 137, 142, 146–48, 150–55, 158–59, 165, 170, 177–78, 182–84, 186, 189, 193–94, 216–17, 254, 269, 272–73, 282, 287, 291
Liṅga Purāṇa. See Purāṇas
Little Devotee, 33–35, 191, 197
logos, incarnation of the, 142
lokāloka, 115, 278
loka-purusa, 173
lotus, 31, 50, 54, 56–59, 79, 85, 101, 107, 114–15, 136, 168, 170, 177. See also *āsanas*: *padmāsana*
Lotus Sūtra, 147

Ma'bar, 207, 218, 219
macrocosm, 63, 93, 96, 103, 115, 136, 175
Mādhava, 27, 46
Maenads, 10
magicians, yogis as, 1, 7, 15, 30, 35, 49, 102, 157, 165, 172, 211, 213, 223, 232, 237–38, 244
Mahābhārata, 16, 27, 29, 38, 40, 43, 50, 59–60, 64, 67, 70–71, 75, 78–79, 99, 102–5, 114, 117, 124, 132, 138, 140–45, 153, 156, 161, 168–71, 173, 179–83, 186, 188–91, 194–95, 251. See also *Mokṣadharma Parvan*
Mahādeva, 189, 210, 223, 225
Mahākāla, 23

mahān (*mahat*), 84–85, 88, 172–73, 175, 185
mahān ātmā, 84–85, 88, 172–73, 175, 182, 184
mahāpuruṣa, 147
Mahāvīra. See *tīrthaṃkaras*
Mahāyāna Buddhism, 64, 97, 99–100, 114, 124, 147, 167, 177
mahāyogeśvara (epithet of Kṛṣṇa), 183
mahāyogeśvareśvara (epithet of Śiva), 189
mahāyogī, 28, 59, 71, 83, 105, 141, 173, 182, 185, 190, 193
mahāyogīśvara (epithet of Śuka), 72
Maheśvara (name of Śiva), 29, 32, 104–5, 149, 189, 190–94; Śaiva laity, 160, 194
māheśvara yoga, 193
Mahmud of Cambay, 208
Mahmud of Ghazni, 202
Maitrāyaṇī Saṃhitā, 65
Maitreya. See *bodhisattvas*
Maitri Upaniṣad. *See* Upaniṣads
Majjhima Nikaya, 54–55, 111
Malabar Coast, 201, 208, 217, 296
Malamoud, Charles, 97
Malinar, Angelika, 113, 190
Mālinīvijayottara Tantra, 109–10, 116–17, 168
Mallinātha Caritra, 20
Malwa, 219
Mān Singh, 26, 219, 239
manas. *See* mind
Mangalore, 202, 208
mantras, 13, 83, 86, 94, 106, 115–17, 120, 124, 138, 146, 150, 157, 196; *chindi*, 116; HUM, 164; OṂ, 83, 86, 90, 94, 97, 120, 130; *skṛk*, 116, 279
Manu Smṛti, 99
Manucci, Niccolao, 226
Marco Polo, 201, 207–8, 217, 232
marīci, 122, 147, 154
*marman*s, 114, 116
Marpa the Translator, 10
Marriott, McKim, 166
Marshall, John (seventeenth century), 24–26, 120, 217, 220, 222, 232
Marshall, Sir John (twentieth century), 48–49, 54, 59, 79, 82
Marut, 91–92, 94, 140, 143
*marut*s, 170, 269, 272. *See also* winds
Marwar, 26, 219, 228, 239
masterful yoga. See *aiśvara yoga*
Masters of Yoga, 30, 99, 101–3, 106, 108, 110, 113, 116, 141, 143, 158, 179, 182–83, 185–86, 189, 191, 195, 242, 278
mastery. See *aiśvaryam*
Mastnāth, 234–36
Mataṅgapārameśvarāgama. *See* Āgamas and agamic Śaivism
*maṭh*s. *See* monasticism and monastic orders
Mathura, 54, 126
Matilal, B. K., 159, 194
Matsya Purāṇa. *See* Purāṇas
Matsyendranāth, 28, 223, 234
Maues, 51, 57, 59, 126
Maya, 30–31
māyā, 25, 179, 225
meditation, 13, 37, 40–45, 55–57, 59, 64, 73, 83, 96–100, 102–3, 106–12, 114–17, 131–32, 140, 147–48, 159, 162, 169, 171–75, 205, 216–17, 225, 244. See also *dhyāna*; *jhāna*
mendicant. See *bhikṣu*
mercenaries, yogis as, 77, 221, 226. *See also* warfare and yoga
merchants, 77, 199–201, 245, 248
Meru, Mount, 158
Mesopotamia, 53, 126, 193
Mewar, 224
microcosm, 63, 93, 95, 103, 115, 135–36, 175
military labor market, 77, 220–21, 225, 231. *See also* warfare and yoga
Mīmāṃsakas, 124–25
mind, 21, 25, 30, 32, 37–38, 40–41, 45–46, 55, 60, 63–64, 69–70, 73–74, 79, 85–86, 88, 90–92, 97, 101–3, 107–9, 116, 118, 120, 123–24, 128, 130–31, 139, 142, 153, 155–58, 160, 163–64, 166–68, 170, 177, 180, 188, 204, 241. See also *citta*
miracles, 49, 177, 200, 223, 234–36, 244–46, 250
Mithila, 71, 143
Mithra, 126–27
Mohenjo-Daro, 48–49, 59, 79, 81–82
mokṣa. *See* liberation
Mokṣadharma Parvan, 43, 67–68, 73, 75, 89, 100, 105, 142, 145, 149, 151, 155, 160, 167, 169, 171, 190, 262
monasticism and monastic orders, 29, 32, 181, 199–200, 205, 218, 220, 222–23, 226, 228, 230–31, 234–35, 239, 241–42. *See also* Bairāgīs; Dasnāmi; Gosains;

monasticism and monastic orders (*cont.*)
Kāpālikas; Nagas; Nānak Panthīs; Nāth Yogīs; Nirvāṇī Ākhāḍa; Pāñcarātras; Pāśupatas; Rāmānandis; Sannyasis; Udāsīs
moon, 34, 69, 89, 95, 107, 111, 115, 125, 133, 136–39, 148, 150, 163, 192–93, 195, 224; lunar astrology, 193
Mṛgendrāgama. *See* Āgamas and agamic Śaivism
Mughals, 6, 14, 22, 24, 77, 197–201, 205, 212, 216, 218, 220–26, 229, 236–37, 242, 253. *See also* Akbar; Aurangzēb; Bābur; Jahāngīr; Śāh Ālam II; Śāh Jahān
munis. *See* hermits
Mus, Paul, 135
Muslims, 6, 22, 26, 196–201, 208, 222, 224, 228–29, 238, 250, 253. *See also* Islam; Sufis
Mysore, 246

nāḍīs. *See* channels, subtle body
nāḍīsaṃdhāna, 146, 285
Nagas, 81, 223, 225, 233
Nagpur, 239
Nānak Panthīs, 237
Nārada, 186, 225
Nārāyaṇa, 102, 141, 167, 169–70, 172–73, 182, 186, 188, 191
Narharināth, 298
Naropa, Six Yogas of, 10, 164
Nāṣir-ud-dīn, 218
Nāth Yogīs, 11, 14, 17–18, 22, 26, 28, 36, 46, 81, 89, 198–200, 206, 208, 218, 222–29, 232, 234, 237, 239–40, 242, 248
Nāṭya Śāstra, 161
Navadurgā, 15–16
Near East. *See* Mesopotamia
Nei-yeh, 79
Neo-Vedānta, 45
Nepal, 12, 14–18, 20, 23, 98, 164, 217, 228, 232. *See also* Kathmandu
Netra Tantra, 121, 162–64, 188, 191, 194, 253
New Age religions, 46
Newari, 12, 22–23
nibbāna, 76, 111. See also *nirvāṇa*
nirmāṇakāya, 153, 177–80, 292
nirodha, 39, 45, 111
nirvāṇa, 43. See also *nibbāna*
nirvāṇadīkṣā, 107
Nirvāṇī Ākhāḍa, 224
Niśvāsamukha, 106, 277
Niśvāsatattvasaṃhitā, 106
Nizām al-Dīn (Nizāmuddīn), 228, 298
numinous yoga, 45, 48, 98, 111, 147, 180. *See also* cessative yoga
Nyāya. *See* Nyāya-Vaiśeṣika
Nyāya Sūtra, 123, 154, 180
Nyāyabhāṣya, 180
Nyāyabhūṣaṇam, 125, 289
Nyāyakandalī, 159–60, 163
Nyāyamañjarī, 289
Nyāya-Vaiśeṣika, 44, 60, 74, 99, 123–25, 153–55, 158–59, 164, 185, 194, 287

Oberlies, Thomas, 75
Oberoi, Harjot, 250
Oertel, Hanns, 65
Oguibénine, Boris, 63
Oman, John Campbell, 244–45
omni-presencing, 39, 45, 158, 182–85, 189. See also *vibhūti*
Oppenheimer, Robert, 254
Orissa, 24
Otto, Rudolf, 253

Padārthadharmasaṃgraha, 124, 159
padmāsana. See *āsanas*
Padmāvat, 14, 230
Padmāvatī, 230–31
Paihāri Kṛṣṇadās, 242
Pakistan, 233. *See also* Gandhara; Gor Khattrī; Peshawar; Swat Valley; Taxila
Pāñcarātras, 108, 146, 189, 195–96
pañcārthika, 105
Pañcaśikha, 144, 180
Pañcatantra, 6, 60, 257
Pāṇḍavas, 50, 69–70, 120, 138, 142, 229
Pāṇini, 41
paññā, 43, 111
Parakāyapraveśa, 165
parakāyāveśa, 120
Parākhyatantra, 115
Parāśara, 144–45
parivrāḍ, *parivrāj(aka)*, 32–33, 60, 71, 96, 194
parrots, 3, 7–9, 23, 71, 230
Pārśvanātha Caritra, 6, 7, 10, 12, 23
Parthian, 127
Pārvatī, 34–35, 118

paśu, 105
Pāśupatas, 29, 31, 35, 75, 79, 105–6, 159, 189–90, 193–94, 196, 276–77
pātañjala yoga, 41, 111, 113, 173, 206
Patañjali, 38, 42, 56, 112
Patiala, 235
perception, 42, 44–45, 68, 70, 72, 74, 99, 101, 110, 123–25, 127, 130–32, 135, 154–61, 164–66, 169, 171, 173, 194, 251, 252. *See also* fourfold contact; *prāpyakāri*; *pratyakṣa*; valid cognitions; *yogi-pratyakṣa*
Periya Purāṇam. *See* Purāṇas
Persia, 58, 126, 213
Persian language, 6–7, 13, 18–19, 22, 57, 127; Perso-Arabic, 198–99
Peshawar, 54, 204
pilgrimage, yogis and, 82, 201, 214, 216, 226–27, 243
Pinch, William, 24, 241–42
Piṅgala, 139
pīrs, 231
planetary seizers, 192
Plato, 64, 267
pneumatics, 81
Portuguese, 208, 224
possession, 26, 36, 99
postures, 29, 46–48, 50, 52, 57, 77, 79, 81, 205, 245. See also *āsanas*; cross-legged posture
potions, 26, 31, 218
Prabandhacintāmaṇi, 6, 12, 255
prādeśa, 95, 101, 133–34, 283
Prajāpati, 75, 85, 91–92, 96, 140, 151, 186, 192; sons of, 85, 91–92, 96, 118, 140, 172, 186, 195, 218, 272. *See also* Sanatkumāra; Sanatsujāta
prakṛti, 41, 103, 105, 112–13, 170, 173
prakṛtilaya, 110, 112–13, 158. See also *kaivalyapadam*
pralaya, 188
pramāṇas. *See* valid cognitions
prāṇa, 128, 160
prāṇāyāma, 55, 92; as stoppage of the breath, 55, 59, 91–92, 205, 266, 272
prāpyakāri, 125, 127, 130, 135, 159, 280
Praśastapāda, 124, 155–59, 194, 253
Praśna Upaniṣad. *See* Upaniṣads
Pratāpbhānu, 25–26
Pratapchand, 249
Pratardana, 145–46
pratibhā, 157–58
Prātihārya Sūtra, 177
pratyāhāra, 55
pratyakṣa, 123–24, 154
Pratyutpannabuddha-saṃmukhāvasthita, 97
prāya, 69, 114–15
Proferes, Theodore, 75
progressing aloft. See *utkrānti*
Pṛthivinārāyaṇ Śāh, 228
Pṛthivirāj, 242
Pṛthvirāj Raso, 60, 224
Punjab, 14, 219–20, 229, 233, 240, 249–50
Purāṇas, 16, 29, 64, 72, 88, 100, 102, 104, 109, 114, 118, 120, 133, 158, 167, 173, 182, 185, 193, 195; *Ādi*, 114; *Bhāgavata*, 71, 99–104, 108, 113, 116–17, 133–34, 143, 158–59, 185–86; *Devībhāgavata*, 161; *Kālikā*, 118; *Kūrma*, 189; *Liṅga*, 193; *Matsya*, 188; *Periya*, 33–34; *Śiva*, 118; *Vāyu*, 72, 188, 193, 195–96; *Viṣṇu*, 173
pure being, 88, 95, 103, 133, 170, 172
Pure Land Buddhism, 148
Puri, 226
purohitas, 193–94
puruṣa, 38–39, 84, 86, 88, 90–91, 93, 95–96, 101, 103–5, 112–13, 122, 127–35, 150, 167–68, 173, 182, 186, 189
puruṣeśvara (name of Śiva), 189
puruṣottama (name of Kṛṣṇa), 39, 41, 96, 100, 134, 167, 186, 188
puryaṣṭakam, 163, 290

Quarnstrọm, Olle, 264
quicksilver, 24, 217, 219

raiding cycles, 76–77, 94
rāja yoga, 45–48, 244, 264
Rajasthan, 10, 14, 26, 236, 248
Rajputs, 11, 14, 60, 77–78, 201, 224, 238–39, 242–43
Rām Carit Mānas, 25–26
Rāma, 65, 204, 212, 229, 241
Rāmakaṇṭha, 181
Rāmānandis, 240, 242
Rāmāyaṇa, 16, 25, 65, 132, 185, 251
rās līlā, 185
Rasārṇavam, 146
raśmi, 67, 69, 86, 122, 125, 129–130, 143, 267, 270, 290
Ratansen, 230
Rattannāth, 204

Raudras, 29
Rauravāgama. *See* Āgamas and agamic Śaivism
Rāvaṇa, 185, 212
Rāwal dynasty, 219, 228
Rāwals, 240
rays, 67–69, 72, 86, 89, 92, 118, 122–70, 178, 188, 190–93, 252; seven solar, 67, 130, 154, 270, 272, 280, 291, 294. See also *arcis*; *marīci*; *raśmi*; *tejas*
rebirth, 30, 33, 86, 88, 92, 94, 105–6, 111, 118, 132, 136, 143–44, 161, 178, 195
reins, 64, 67, 69, 75, 91, 122, 130, 151, 193. See also *raśmi*
release. *See* liberation
Renou, Louis, 63, 151, 255
renunciation, 17–18, 22, 27, 76–78, 90, 92, 106, 140, 199, 222, 244, 250
Ṛg Veda, 61, 64–65, 67, 84, 93, 105, 127, 131, 134–35, 148, 150–51, 154, 179
rig, 63, 65, 69–78, 86, 94–95, 101, 144–45. *See also* hitching up; *yogayukta*
Rose, H. A., 240
ṛṣis. *See* seers
Ruci, 148–49
Rudra, 59, 105, 107, 108, 110, 114, 141, 167–68, 189, 191, 195
Rudras, 72, 106, 108, 195
rūpadhātus, 111

sacrifice, 10, 15–20, 61–63, 67, 76–78, 90, 126, 138, 146, 148, 150, 181
Sadāśiva, 108
sādhakas, 99, 108, 117, 195–97
sadhus 234–35, 241, 250, 252
Śāh Ālam II, 236, 238
Śāh Jahān, 222
Śaivāgamas. *See* Āgamas and agamic Śaivism
Śaivas and Saivism, 29, 31, 35, 89, 100, 104–8, 114–15, 118, 159–60, 192–97, 207, 220, 223, 229. *See also* Āgamas and agamic Śaivism; Pāśupatas; Raudras
Śaivasiddhānta, 106–7, 109, 153
Śakas. *See* Indo-Scythians
Śākāyanya, 91–94, 140, 143, 154, 285
Śāktas, 10, 29, 100, 114, 116, 118, 196, 197
śakti, 51, 118, 162, 166
Śākyamuni. *See* Buddha and Buddhas
salvation, 11, 40, 41, 96, 100, 108, 110, 114, 162, 166, 169, 246. *See also* liberation; *mokṣa*; soteriology
Sāma Veda, 129
samādhi ("pure contemplation"), 37, 39, 41, 43–44, 56, 97, 102, 105, 112–13, 124, 139, 159, 206–7, 263, 289
samādhis. *See* tumuli, yogi burial
Samantabhadra, 179
samāpattis, 45, 111
Samar Singh of Mewar, 224
samatha, 40, 111, 180
samāveśa, 140, 146, 165
saṃbhogakāya, 148
Saṃjaya, 156, 183
Sāṃkhya, 39–41, 43–44, 68, 88, 90, 100–101, 104, 112–14, 125, 144, 169–71, 173, 180. *See also* categories, metaphysical
saṃsāra, 40, 84, 94, 100, 104, 162. *See also* rebirth
Saṃvitprakāśa, 182
saṃyama, 113, 158–59, 288
saṃyoga, 136, 156
Sanatkumāra, 85
Sanatsujāta, 118, 186
Sanderson, Alexis, 105–6, 109, 276
Śaṅkara, 26, 28–29, 36, 42, 46, 48, 88, 92, 117, 120, 132, 139, 151, 153–54, 180–81, 223. See also *Brahma Sūtra Bhāṣya*
Śaṅkaradigvijaya, 27–28
Śaṅkaramandarasaurabha, 27–28
Śaṅkaramiśra, 156
Śaṅkaravijaya, 27–29
Śāṅkhāyana Śrauta Sūtra, 16
Sannyasis, 90, 220, 223–23, 237–38, 241–42, 248–50
Śāntikalpa, 192
Sarbacker, Stuart, 45, 111
Sarvadarśanasaṃgraha, 46
Sarvāstivādins, 97, 274
Sasanians, 58, 193, 287
Śatapatha Brāhmaṇa. *See* Brāhmaṇas
satī, 2, 7, 118, 230
sattva. *See* pure being
Savitṛ, 127, 138, 150
Sāyaṇa, 132
Schlingloff, Dieter, 147
Schmidt, Richard, 245
Schreiner, Peter, 67
seats. See *āsanas*: as thrones or seats
seers, 71, 84, 96, 112, 124, 145–46, 157, 169, 280. See also *ārṣa* perception
Selby, Martha, 289

self-magnifying self. See *mahān ātmā*
self-mortification, 48, 59, 202–3, 212, 216
semen, 46, 191
Sénart, Émile, 45
Senguehassen Battisi, 6–7, 10, 12, 18, 23, 26, 36
sense objects, 90, 94, 121, 151, 154
sense organs, 90, 123, 125, 149, 154–55, 170
senses, 30, 37–38, 40, 45, 56, 64, 70, 88, 90, 102, 110, 123, 129, 142, 154–56, 170, 180, 217, 241. *See also* perception; sight; vision
serpents, 68, 73
Seven Mothers, Seven Sisters, 10–11, 67, 154
Sháh Jahān. *See* Śāh Jahān
shaikhs, 231
Shamasastry, R., 135
Shobha Ma, 165
Shulman, David, 34
siddha-darśanam, 157–58
siddhakṣetra, 175, 194
siddhas, 14, 23, 72, 99, 102, 108, 124, 157–58, 161, 188, 195, 225, 229, 231–32, 257. See also *yogasiddhas*
Siddhasiddhāntapaddhati, 175–77
siddhis, 11, 31, 43, 45, 73, 75, 108, 112, 117, 156, 159, 190, 195, 233
sight, 123, 125, 130, 154, 183, 204. *See also* perception; vision
Sikhs and Sikhism, 7, 205, 241, 250. *See also* Guru Gobind Singh; Guru Nānak; Nānak Panthīs; Udāsīs
Silk Road, 52
Silsila-i jūgiyān, 223
siṃhāsana. See *āsanas*
Siṃhāsanadvātriṃśika, 6–7, 12, 20, 22, 26, 238; *Siṅhāsan Battīsī*, 238. See also *Senguehassen Battisi*
Simsim caves, 98, 147
Singh, Mahadevprasad, 4, 6–7, 9, 11–13, 15, 18, 22–23, 26, 28, 36, 164, 243
Śiva, 23, 29, 33–35, 48–49, 59–60, 75, 79, 82, 104–6, 109–10, 117–18, 127, 139, 141, 146, 149–51, 162, 168, 179, 188–94, 197, 210, 224, 230, 233–34. *See also* Īśāna; Īśvara; Mahādeva; Maheśvara
Śiva Purāṇa. *See* Purāṇas
Sivananda, Swami, 246
six-limbed yoga, 55, 90, 98, 265
Skanda, 34, 172
skulls, 10, 20, 33, 89
Sleeman, William, 239
smile of the Buddha. *See* Buddha and Buddhas
Smith, Frederick, 36
solar disk (solar orb), 33, 60–68, 72–73, 83, 90, 92, 96, 122, 128, 129, 132, 135, 190, 192
soma, 61, 161
Sonnerat, Pierre, 232
sorcery, 150, 232, 238, 250
soteriology, 29, 40, 43, 62, 69, 83–84, 86, 89, 96, 100–102, 106–12, 167, 173; two-tiered, 100, 108, 110, 112, 114. *See also* liberation; *prakṛtilaya*; *videhamukti*
sovereignty, 31, 50, 56, 59, 91, 105, 183, 190
space, outer and inner, 45, 70, 85, 88–90, 93–94, 96, 99–102, 111, 120, 128, 130, 133, 135, 140, 156–58, 160, 175, 184
span. See *prādeśa*
speculatives. See *dhammayogas*
spells, 12, 25, 83, 102, 115–16, 120, 150, 163, 232. *See also* mantras
spheres, 95, 100, 102, 109, 115, 170
spies, yogis as, 26, 214, 220, 224, 226, 253, 259
śrāddha, 195
śramaṇas, 20, 258
Śrāvastī, 177
Śrī, 12, 50–52, 54, 58
Śrī Mastnāth Carit, 234–36
Śrīdhara, 159–60, 289
Sriparvata, 12
Śrīvaiṣṇavas, 103
sṛṣṭi, 188
steps, strides. *See* kram, derivates of; Viṣṇu steps
stoppage of the breath. See *prāṇāyāma*
Subrahmanyam, Sanjay, 251
subtle body, 27, 101, 103, 115, 132–33, 139, 143, 162. *See also* cakras; channels, subtle body; citadel, subtle body; cranial vault; fontanel; heart; *kuṇḍalinī*
subtle yoga, 131, 162, 188, 191, 194
śūdras, 23–24
Sufis, 13–14, 199–200, 218, 229–32, 250
Śuka, 68, 71–72, 96, 120, 122, 141, 143–44, 168, 284
Śukra, 150, 191, 193, 286. *See also* Kāvya Uśanas; Venus, transit of
Sulabhā, 68, 131, 141–44, 160

Sullivan , Bruce, 289
Sumatra, 211
sun, 33, 60–63, 65, 69, 71–73, 83–84, 89–96, 104, 111, 113, 115–18, 120, 122–29, 132–34, 139–42, 145, 147–48, 150–51, 153–55, 158–59, 163, 166, 170–71, 184, 188–93, 203, 212, 282; and ecosystem, 135–38, 155; as barrier, 67–68, 86, 88; as door, 86, 88, 91, 120, 140, 158–59; daughters of, 67, 154. *See also* rays: seven solar; Savitṛ; solar disk (solar orb)
Śunaḥśepa, 17
sundial, 133, 135, 191. *See also* gnomon
supernatural powers, 11, 18, 29, 31, 39, 45, 47, 72, 75, 98, 100, 112–13, 120, 150, 153, 156–57, 159, 181, 185, 190, 195–97, 200, 205, 242–43, 245. See also *abhijñās*; *aiśvaryam*; *siddhi*s
Surat, 211, 219, 225, 299
Sūrat Singh of Bikaner, 235
Sūryaśataka, 104
Suśruta Saṃhitā, 136
suṣumnā, 46–47, 90, 102, 139, 146, 291
Svacchanda Tantra, 106, 115, 197, 253, 276
svarūpa, 112, 156
Śvetāśvatara Upaniṣad. *See* Upaniṣads
Svopajñavṛtti, 164. See also *Yogaśāstra*
Swat Valley, 54, 56
symbiosis, 47

Taittirīya: *Āraṇyaka*, 150; *Brāhmaṇa*, 76, 78; *Saṃhitā*, 65; *Upaniṣad*, 76, 89, 92
Talbot, Cynthia, 266
Tantras and tantric traditions, 6, 10–11, 13, 17–18, 22–23, 29, 34–35, 42, 47, 58, 64, 84, 89, 100, 103, 105–6, 109–10, 114–16, 118, 120–21, 131, 135, 140, 145–46, 148, 151, 154–55, 160, 162, 164, 166–67, 179, 194–97, 232–33, 253
Taoists and Taoism, 79, 81
tapas, 29, 59, 102, 266, 276
tapoloka, 110, 188
taqīyya, 253
Tāranāth, 242
tarka, 56, 98
Tattvārthacintāmaṇi, 163
*tattva*s, 104, 112, 172, 186, 189
Tavernier, Jean-Baptiste, 206, 211–12, 221–22, 225, 232, 245, 296
Taxila, 51, 59
tejas, 125, 138, 146, 287
Tejīśa, realm of, 106
Tertullian, 142
Thales, 283
theism and theistic sects, Hindu, 39–40, 95, 98–104, 108, 110–11, 115, 134, 140, 147, 167–68, 191. *See also* Śaivas and Saivism; Vaiṣṇavas and Vaisnavism; visionary theism
Theosophists, 47, 245–46, 300
Theravāda Buddhism, 100, 110
Thevenot, Jean de, 214, 222, 232, 299
Thrace, 53–54
Thugs, 237, 239
thumb-sized deities, 84, 88, 90, 95, 105, 107, 133, 168. *See also* gnomon; *prādeśa*
Tibet, 10, 246–47
Tibetan Buddhism, 10, 86, 165, 247
time, divisions of: ayurvedic year, 136–38; *kalpa*s, 100, 102, 139, 158, 188–89; semesters, 94, 136–37; solstices, 94, 134–35; *yuga*s, 74, 189
*tīrthaṃkara*s, 54; *jīna*s, 54, 167, 179; Mahāvīra, 54, 212
titans, 30, 128, 31, 141, 189–90
Tod, Colonel James, 219, 239
Toffin, Gérard, 15, 23
Traditional Knowledge Digital Library, 248
transference. *See* kram, derivates of: *sam-kram*
Transoxiania, 54
tridents, 197, 224
Trivikrama, Trivikramasena. *See* Vikramāditya
Tsongkapa, Lama Jey, 164
Tughluq, Muhammad ibn, 203
Tulsidās, 25
tumuli, yogi burial, 196–97, 206, 231
Turkestan, 98, 147, 286
two-tiered soteriologies. *See* soteriology: two-tiered

udāna, 92, 118, 120
Udāsīs, 249–51
Ujjain, 6–7, 22, 243, 258
union, yoga as, 29, 38, 41–42, 46, 48, 99, 102, 105, 139, 162, 195, 245, 263
Upaniṣads, 39, 43–44, 46, 64, 68, 84–86, 89–92, 96, 105, 115, 123–24, 129–36, 139, 143, 167, 170, 190, 262; *Ārṣeya*, 286; *Bṛhadāraṇyaka*, 64, 84, 88, 125, 128–34, 136, 143–44; *Chāndogya*, 64, 84–89,

92–93, 96, 102, 120, 125, 128–36, 136, 140, 143–44, 153–54, 171; *Kaṭha*, 39, 64, 73, 76, 88–91, 93–94, 101, 105, 167, 172, 186; *Maitri*, 39, 55, 70, 89–93, 95–96, 98–107, 110, 115–16, 120, 125, 132–36, 139, 141, 143, 145, 150, 154–55, 167, 170, 186; *Praśna*, 86, 96–97; *Śvetāśvatara*, 39, 105, 168, 190, 266; *Taittirīya*, 76, 89, 92
upward advance. See *utkrānti*
uṣṇīṣa, 178
utkrānti, 74, 88, 92, 101, 114–20, 129, 140, 164. *See also* kram, derivates of; yogic suicide
Uttar Pradesh, 11, 13–14, 252
Uttarakāmikāgama. *See* Āgamas and agamic Śaivism

Vācaspatimiśra, 41, 44
Vaiśeṣika Sūtra, 123–24, 155–59
Vaiṣṇavas and Vaisnavism, 29, 88, 98–101, 103–8, 113–14, 126, 173, 182, 195, 223, 242–43. *See also* Bhāgavatas; Pāñcarātras; Śrīvaiṣṇavas
Vājasaneyī Saṃhitā, 120
vajrolī mudrā, 46
valid cognitions, 44, 71, 122–24, 280. See also *arṣa* perception; *pratyakṣa*; *yogi-pratyakṣa*
Vāmadeva, 84
vampires. See *vetālas*
Van Buitenen, J. A. B., 89, 92
Van der Veer, Peter, 243
Varthema, Ludovico di, 208, 218, 224–25, 231
Varuṇa, 16–17, 127, 136, 172
Vasiṣṭha, 139, 144, 255
Vasu Uparicara, 151
Vāsudeva, 103, 182
Vasudeva, Somadeva, 117, 279
Vaudeville, Charlotte, 14, 231
Vāyu Purāṇa. *See* Purāṇas
Vedānta, 125
Vedas and vedic traditions, 16, 33, 36, 39, 42, 44–45, 60–65, 67, 69, 72, 75–78, 96–97, 116, 124, 126–27, 130–31, 133–35, 139, 143, 146, 150–51, 157, 188, 191, 193, 243, 266, 273, 283. See also *Atharva Veda*; Black Yajurveda; *Ṛg Veda*; *Sāma Veda*; *Vājasaneyī Saṃhitā*; White Yajurveda
Vedavyāsa, 41, 44, 79, 112–13, 145, 153, 158–59, 180
Venus, transit of, 191–92, 294
Vetālapañcaviṃśati, 6–7, 20–22, 29, 196, 238, 255. See also *Baitāl Pachīsī*
vetālas, 6, 20, 196, 255
vibhūti, 39–40, 45, 112, 158–59, 182–83, 185. *See also* omni-presencing
videhamukti, 84, 100, 112–13
Vidura, 68, 141–42, 160
Vikrama Cycle, 6, 23, 27, 48, 127, 196, 242, 251
Vikramāditya, 6, 7–9, 12, 15, 17–23, 27–28, 36, 48, 127, 196, 242, 251, 255
Vima Kadphises, 59, 126
Vima Takto, 126
Vimuttimagga, 97, 110–11, 181
Vindhyas, 54, 139
vipassanā, 40, 111
Vipula, 68, 141, 148–50, 160
vision, 31, 44, 96–97, 99, 109, 125, 127, 155–60, 165, 170, 182–83, 186, 198, 216, 241, 253. *See also* perception; sight
visionary ascent, 45, 60, 63–64, 71, 73, 93, 95, 99–100, 107–9, 114–16, 140. *See also* yoga of the vedic poets
visionary theism, 99, 147, 170
Viṣṇu, 61, 72, 91, 95, 98, 101–7, 110, 127, 132–35, 141, 167, 170–73, 182, 185–93, 283. See also *acyuta*; *akṣaya*; *avyayam*; *dhruva*; Kṛṣṇa; Nārāyaṇa; Vāsudeva
Viṣṇu Purāṇa. *See* Purāṇas
Viṣṇu steps, 61, 132–35, 191, 266
visualization, 97, 99, 109, 115–16, 147–48
Visuddhananda, Swami, 165
viśvarūpa, 39, 182
Vītahavya, 139, 146, 287
Vivekananda, Swami, 45–47, 243, 247, 251, 300
viyoga, 38, 40–41, 78, 230
Vyāsa, 70, 72–73, 112, 141–42, 156, 190
Vyomavatī, 159, 161, 287
vyūhas, 103

warfare and yoga, 33, 40–41, 60–65, 67–78, 81, 83, 85, 94, 96, 99–102, 108–10, 114–17, 120–22, 132, 140–41, 144–45, 150–51, 200–201, 220–27, 229, 231, 237, 240–42, 244, 250, 254. *See also* military labor market
Weinberger-Thomas, Catherine, 118

Whicher, Ian, 112, 159
White Sands Missile Range, 254
White Yajurveda, 128
wiles of women, 1–3, 7, 12, 22, 148. *See also* Chritro Pakhyān
winds, 8, 88, 104, 118, 129, 136–37, 148, 156, 177, 217; seven winds, 72–73, 170, 269, 272, 291. *See also* rays: seven solar
Wood, Ernest, 47
world of *brahman*. See *brahmaloka*
World of Rudra, 108

yajamānas, 61–63, 67, 132
Yājñavalkya, 143–44
Yājñavalkyasmṛti, 60, 78, 99
yakṣas, 24, 28, 172, 259
Yama, 31–32, 62, 88, 151
Yamabe, Nobuyoshi, 98
yatis, 99, 102
Yayāti, 151
yāyāvaras, 65, 76
Yima, 151
Ying yai shêng lan, 201
Yinshu, 81
yoga of the vedic poets, 63–64, 85, 95–96, 100, 108, 114, 132. *See also* visionary ascent
yoga philosophy, 41, 43, 159, 245. See also *pātañjala yoga*
Yoga Sūtras, 38–47, 55–56, 68, 74, 79, 89–92, 99–100, 105, 112–13, 120, 144–45, 153, 157–59, 173, 180, 185, 190, 202, 205, 243, 245
Yoga Treatise from Qïzïl, 147, 274
Yoga Vasiṣṭha, 118, 139, 164, 255, 284
yogabalam, 27, 142, 151, 157, 190. See also *balam*
Yogabhāṣya, 41, 43–44, 99, 105, 112–13, 158, 180
yogabhraṣṭa. See *bhraṣṭayogā*
Yogabīja, 46
yogācāra, 147, 265, 286
yogadharma, 142
yogaja-dharma, 156, 159
yoga-kṣema, 65, 76–78
yogam aiśvaram. See *aiśvara yoga*
yoga-mārga, 115, 118
yoga-mūrtis, 141, 179
Yogananda, 24, 47, 246–47
yoga-paṭṭa, 79
Yogasārasaṃgraha, 47
Yogaśāstra, 164, 173, 264
yogasiddhas, 102, 149
Yogaśikhopaniṣad, 46
yogāṣṭaka, 108, 195
Yogatattva Upaniṣad, 46
Yogayājñavalkya, 264
yogayogeśvara (name of Kṛṣṇa), 179
yogayukta, 25, 33, 60–62, 65–73, 75, 77, 101–2, 268–69, 273, 278, 289
yogeśvarādhīśvara (name of Kṛṣṇa), 186
yogeśvaras. *See* Masters of Yoga
yogeśvareśvara (name of Kṛṣṇa), 186
yogi perception. See *yogi-pratyakṣa*
yogi romances, 14, 22, 28, 200, 229, 298
yogic suicide, 114–18, 140, 278. See also *utkrānti*
yogicakṣus. *See* eye: yogi
yogīndra, 31, 224
yoginīs, 10–11, 36, 49, 154, 162, 233
yogi-pratyakṣa, 44, 124, 131, 154–55, 159–60, 194, 252, 288
yoking, yoga as, 25, 32, 41–44, 47–48, 60–65, 71–76, 78, 94, 122, 151, 153, 163, 172, 181, 193. *See also* yuj, verbal forms of: *yukta*
Yudhiṣṭhira, 68, 70–71, 138, 140, 142, 160–61, 191, 284
yuj, verbal forms of, 41–42, 60, 62–64, 135; *yukta*, 40, 62–65, 97, 101, 109, 144, 156, 183, 268, 274, 289. See also *yogayukta*; yoking, yoga as

Zeus-Mithra, 126
Zimmer, Heinrich, 260
Zimmermann, Francis, 137
zombies. See *vetālas*
Zumbro, Reverend W. M., 245–46